Disappearing Act

A Mother's Journey to the Underground

by Sharon Murphy

ISBN: 1490523448
ISBN 13: 9781490523446
Library of Congress Control Number: 2013912176
CreateSpace Independent Publishing Platform
North Charleston, South Carolina

PRAISE FOR DISAPPEARING ACT ~
A MOTHER'S JOURNEY TO THE UNDERGROUND

"Sharon Murphy has written a gripping, all-too-real Memoir about her own custody battle experience and her flight "underground" as a protective mother. Murphy does not grandstand. She is both bold and humble as she confronts an abusive husband who is also an abusive father—and her husband's formidable mother, the writer Maya Angelou. Her scenes with both Angelou and with the writer's only son ring true. They are chilling, informative, dramatic. Brilliantly, Murphy managed to save her young son from paternal beatings for five full years (no small accomplishment). Angelou herself came to collect her grandson, turned him over to his father, and then disappeared into the sunset.

"Murphy has become a writer. This is a writer's book. It is also a mother's book. Murphy had strong sisters who helped her and a network of supportive women, including feminists and lesbian feminists. Murphy was also turned in by a woman. As the author of, <u>Mothers on Trial. The Battle for Children and Custody</u> (1986, 2011) and <u>Woman's Inhumanity to Woman,</u> (2002, 2009) I can assure you that Murphy exaggerates nothing.

Brava, Sharon!

Phyllis Chesler Ph.D is an Emerita Professor of Psychology and Women's Studies at City University of New York. She is a best-selling author, a legendary feminist leader, a psychotherapist and an expert courtroom witness.

"*Disappearing Act is a story of a woman's fierce bravery and tenacity, and her refusal to be destroyed in the face of experiences that might so easily have crushed her. I love the pluck and humor and above all the big heart of this woman, and her willingness to reveal not only her moments of rare courage but just as much so her failings, as she fights not only for her son but for her own survival, against extraordinary obstacles.*" **Joyce Maynard**

> **Joyce Maynard** first came to national attention with the publication of her New York Times cover story, "An Eighteen Year Old Looks Back on Life" in 1973, when she was a freshman at Yale. Since then, she has been a reporter and columnist for The New York Times. Maynard is the author of fourteen books, including her best-selling memoir, At Home in the World.

"*Sharon Murphy's memoir is a gripping, fast-paced story about a mother's decision to break the law rather than surrender her son to his abusive father. Sharon's emotional honesty and keen sense of story deliver an exciting retelling of how she fled to the underground with her child and defeated her own demons along the way.*"

> **Linda M. Scaparotti, Esq.**
> **Linda Scaparotti** is the Past President of the San Francisco Trial Lawyers Association, Member of the Board of Directors of the Human Rights Campaign, and Equality California, and Past Co-Chair of Bay Area Lawyers for Individual Freedom

PROLOGUE

Austin, Texas: June 3, 1985

THE SETTING SUN THREW A glorious streak of tangerine across the big Texas sky. A late afternoon thundershower hadn't tamed the blistering heat and the June air was still heavy. I sat at the cluttered kitchen table in my underwear, trying to cool down after my shower. The oscillating fan was whining at its highest setting in front of the open sliding glass door. Beyond the patio, purple buds peeked out from under a tangle of vines at the edge of the creek that ran beside our yard.

I'd completed two weekend sessions of the Erhard Seminars Standard Training (est) and was now taking one of the follow-up courses. The self-help program of the decade—est was the new emotional boot camp among adherents of the human potential movement. From movie stars to politicians to musicians—all were singing the praises of Werner Erhard and his vision to transform the world. My est trainer quoted the program's founder: "At all times and under all circumstances, we have the power to transform the quality of our lives." I fervently wanted est to convince me that statement was true.

I flipped open my notebook. I'd been working on a list titled *"Things that Stand Between Me and Living Full-out."* The lined pages, covered with my loopy, back-slanted handwriting, contained the reasons—maybe real, maybe imagined—for all my suffering. My list read like a roadmap into a maze of predictable consequences of allowing others to control my life. It was clear that I regarded the world as a dangerous, threatening place— a place I was ambivalent about navigating by myself. I was 35 years old and my patterns were painfully clear—but I was trying desperately to find a way toward a better way of living.

I checked the clock on the stove—5:15. My seminar began at 7 o'clock—on the dot. At Werner Erhard programs, no one was admitted to the room once the seminar began. Tardiness was considered a breach of the members' agreement with the group. So far, I'd always been on time. A few minutes later I took one last sip of my iced tea. I stood up, stretched towards the ceiling, and headed to the bedroom to finish dressing. I pulled my white sundress over my head and slipped on my leather sandals. After a quick check of my face in the bathroom mirror, I rubbed a dollop of styling gel through my hair, trying in vain to tame my dark waves.

I turned on the tap to rinse my hands and picked up my toothbrush. Through the sound of water splashing against the basin, I heard the sharp scrape of the latch on the side gate. I froze. Reflected in the mirror, the silhouette of a man slowly darkened the corner of the opaque window behind me. Another shadow followed the first, and then another, and another—four strangers were moving towards my backyard. I dropped my toothbrush and grabbed a towel, holding it against my mouth. The water roared in the sink. I turned off the tap and heard a loud knock on the front door and then the doorbell. I took a long, deep breath.

"So, this is how it's going to end," I thought. I had been waiting for these men for more than four years.

My numb, unwilling legs moved me towards the front door. I watched my hand grip the doorknob and pull the door open. Men crowded the porch. The gold Travis County Sheriff's insignia glared at me from the row of blue windbreakers. Black and white police cars lined the curb in front of the house; red, white, and blue lights blinked from atop each cruiser. A stocky, balding officer looked me up and down. With a snap of his wrist he flipped open his badge—Sergeant Waters, Austin Police Department.

"Are you Sharon Johnson?" he asked.

I struggled to keep my voice calm. "No."

The officer lowered his eyes to the sheet of paper in his hand. "Are you Anne Marie Clark?"

A ripple of fear shot through me, and I could feel a bead of sweat trickle down my spine. What would I do if he asked for my identification? I leaned against the door to steady myself.

"No," I said.

Waters exchanged a glance with the young officer next to him. Over their shoulders, I saw a group of my new neighbors gathered at the curb on the other side of the street. They were holding their children close.

"Are you Sharon Murphy?" he said.

I had not heard my real name in a long time. I felt like I'd been doused with freezing water. Not knowing what else to say, I asked, "Who?"

Waters took a breath and shook the paper in his hand towards my face. "What is *your* name?"

This was not a simple question. As I stood there in silence, I heard a voice as clear and sharp as if someone was speaking to me from offstage. *"Be the roommate."* Knowing I'd be committed to this plan once I opened my mouth, I tried to project a mystified tone. "I'm Mindy Watrous." I furrowed my brow and shook my head for emphasis. "What's going on?"

"Sharon Murphy does not have custody of the baby," Sergeant Waters said. Then he glanced at the paper again and corrected himself. "I mean ... of the *child*."

"I don't know what you're talking about," I said with a shrug. "I don't know anyone named Sharon Murphy." I thought it would be better if I appeared willing to help. "But, uh, Anne Marie Clark is my roommate."

"And Anne Marie has a son, right?" Sergeant Waters asked.

"Yes, she has a son."

At the mention of Luke, the blood in my veins turned to ice. Yet, I forced myself to maintain a nonchalant, helpful attitude. I glanced at the paper Waters held in his hand. Two black and white photographs appeared below the seal of the Sonoma County California Superior Court. I knew that seal, and I knew those photos. It was a wanted poster. Sergeant Waters seemed to be looking directly at my picture, yet he wasn't making the connection.

"Is your roommate home?" he asked.

My son and I had just moved into this house to live with my girlfriend, Mindy. Two weeks ago, the three of us had visited friends of Mindy's in Oklahoma. These facts turned themselves into an expedient lie. "No. Anne Marie and her son went to Oklahoma to visit a friend," I answered.

"Can we come in and take a look around?" the sergeant asked.

It would appear suspicious if I tried to block their entry, so I answered by taking a step backwards. The police on the porch swarmed past me. Some turned towards the living room and others walked to the back of the house. I heard the screen door in the family room slide open, and the men from the backyard joined the rest.

Fortunately, they would find no one else at home. Luke was spending the night at his friend Zack's house, and Mindy was still at work.

Sergeant Waters hung back—still focused on me. I turned away from his gaze. A young blond officer stood in the center of the living room with his fists on his hips. He surveyed the packing boxes and the new washer sitting incongruously in front of the couch. My eyes followed his gaze as he turned his attention to the photographs of Luke and me in matching frames on top of the television. I pressed my lips together against a quick intake of breath. The officer lifted the picture of seven-year-old Luke smiling proudly, his bare gums showing the first traces of adult teeth. The officer's voice seemed to reach me from the wrong direction. "Is this the child?"

My throat was so dry I could barely speak. I nodded. "Uh-huh."

He picked up the picture of me and considered it for a moment. In the photograph, I was sitting barefoot on the floor of my old apartment on West Lynn. Mindy had taken the picture when we were first dating. The camera had caught me in mid-sentence, gesturing at her with an amused expression on my face. It was one of my favorites, not only because I thought I looked pretty, but because I looked so relaxed and happy.

"Is this your roommate?" he asked.

There were pitfalls with each answer. The matching frames seemed to imply the mother-son relationship, but I went with the most obvious response. "No, that's me."

He held the frames side by side, looked at me, and then back at the photo. He returned my picture to the console. "We'll have to take this picture of the boy." He turned the wooden frame over and removed the back. As he peeled my son's photograph off the glass, I felt as if he was squeezing my heart with his narrow fingers. He set the empty frame next to my picture and continued to scan the living room, tapping Luke's picture against his leg.

I turned back to Waters and asked, "What's this all about?" I wanted to know how much more he knew.

"Your roommate's name is not Anne Marie Clark. Her real name is Sharon Murphy-Johnson. She lost custody of her son, and then she kidnapped the boy and disappeared from San Francisco. They've been trying to locate her for years." He looked me in the eye. "You didn't know anything about this?"

"Anne Marie never said a thing."

"I have a fugitive warrant for her arrest." Waters tapped the pocket of his jacket. "Usually a case like this doesn't get much attention, but this one is a priority. This kid's grandmother is some sort of celebrity. Someone tipped her off that the mother and boy were in Austin and she hired a private detective to locate them. Have you ever heard of Maya Angelou?"

"The writer? Sure!" My voice sounded high and shrill. "What does she have to do with Anne Marie and Luke?"

Waters spoke in a soft voice—as if he were confiding in me. "She's the kid's grandmother. Frankly, I never heard of Maya Angelou till a couple of days ago," he admitted. "She's here in town—has everyone down at the station hopping. I'm not much of a reader, but I guess she's pretty famous. When we find the boy, she's bringing him back to his father in California."

Someone called to Waters and he left me alone for a moment. For years, I had been afraid that one day I'd open the front door find my ex-husband standing there, his fists up and ready. Even after all this time, my heart still sped up every time I saw a white VW bus like Guy used to drive. But of course, I should have known it would be his mother who came looking for us. I tried to focus my thoughts and followed Waters to the back of the house.

Our kitchen and dining room were connected into one large L-shaped room. The outer wall was lined with floor to ceiling windows and a sliding glass door, which gave a good view of the patio and the large backyard edged in wild flowers and shrubbery. Luke and I had just hauled our things here a few days ago. I'd taken the week off from my job at the Austin Center for Battered Women to unpack and settle in. Today, I'd organized the kitchen cabinets and arranged the furniture. Earlier the family room had looked homey and inviting—now, filled with uniformed and plainclothes cops, it was anything but. Three officers stood shoulder to shoulder facing a wall of framed photographs. I braced myself against the edge of the cluttered table and surveyed the pile of mail and papers. I eased my notebook on top of the ashtray full of half-smoked joints.

One officer pointed to the gallery of frames. "Are any of these pictures of your roommate?"

Clinging to the story that I was the roommate, I said, "No. Those are all my friends."

Waters turned back to me. "How do you know Anne Marie?"

"I'm a crisis hotline volunteer at the Center for Battered Women. Anne Marie's a shelter counselor. That's where I met her and her son. I needed a roommate and they're just moving in." I jerked my chin in the direction of the boxes and the piles of newspaper in the corner of the room. "But we're not really close friends. I don't know a lot about her."

I heard drawers and closet doors open and close as the policemen continued their search in the bedrooms. My business files were stacked up in the office. Those papers could connect my name and my face. My picture albums were piled on the floor. If the officers thought to open them, they'd see that I was the mother they were looking for. I thought of everything they might find to bring my charade crashing down around me, and felt lightheaded as the breath stuck in my throat.

"Do you think your roommate will call you before she comes back home?" asked Sergeant Waters.

"I don't think so." I heard my voice wavering, but Waters didn't seem to notice. I had to get these men out of here. I was losing the battle against the panic thundering through me. I tapped my watch, trying to appear impatient and uninterested in my roommate's problems. "Hey listen, I have a class at 7 tonight and can't be late. I'm sorry all this is happening, but I don't know how I can help you."

Waters exhaled loudly, then looked me right in the eyes as he handed me his card and said, "Well, if Sharon does call, don't tell her we were here. Okay? You just call me if you hear from her."

I was shocked at his conspiratorial tone, but kept my face impassive. Did this man really believe that I would not tell a woman—even if she was only a casual acquaintance—that the police had come to the house to arrest her and take her child away? Hadn't he heard of the feminist movement? But it was his game, so I played it. "Oh sure, if she calls I'll be sure to let you know immediately." I slid his card into the outside pocket of my purse. Waters seemed satisfied.

"Write down your complete name and phone number," he said. "I'll give you a call in a couple of days to see if Sharon and her son are back home."

"Sure," I said. I tore a sheet of paper from a notepad and picked up a pen. Among the papers on the table, I noticed a snapshot of Mindy, Luke, and me at a recent picnic at Town Lake. We were all grinning into the camera with our arms around each other. The three of us always has such fun together. I put my hand over the picture and slid it under a book. All eyes were on me, but no one noticed. I wrote *Mindy Watrous* and a random phone number on the paper and handed it to Waters. Without a glance, he folded the paper and put it in his shirt pocket.

Waters surveyed the room, apparently counting heads as his men assembled around him. The leather of their gear shifted and creaked. These officers had come to arrest me and take my child away from me and give him to his father. But now they were going to leave—just walk out the door, go back to the station, and file their report. Could I really get away again?

I threw my purse over my shoulder and made a show of searching for my car keys. Through the sliding glass door, I noticed Pearl, Revis, and our other two cats staring at me from the porch. Would I ever come back here? I coughed and blinked away the threat of tears. I forced myself to walk towards the front door, feeling as if I was wading through deep water. I opened the door and stepped aside. The officers filed out onto the porch and I pulled the door shut behind me.

Waters regarded the faded green Plymouth parked in the driveway. "Is that Sharon's car?" he asked.

My mind clicked through the details. My car, an old Buick Skylark, was at the shelter. When it hadn't started a few days ago, a friend loaned me her second car until I was able to get mine fixed. If my Buick had been sitting here in the driveway, the police could easily have checked the registration and the jig would have been up right there. This ugly old clunker was a small miracle that was going to help me get away. "No. That's my car." I smiled.

"What kind of car does your roommate drive?" Waters asked.

"Oh, I can't tell one from the other. It's blue, I think." I extended my hand and Waters gave it a firm shake.

"I'll talk to you in a few days," he said with a nod and a tight smile, watching me as I moved to the driver's side of the Plymouth.

As I opened the car door, I was met by a familiar wave of melting Texas heat, but I slid behind the wheel without hesitating. A black-and-white blocked the driveway, so I rolled down the window and waited. I jammed in the lighter and reached for a cigarette. Luke's report card lay on the seat next to me. On the way to Zack's this morning, Luke had been tallying the financial reward for his final grades. Mindy had promised him $3.00 for every "Satisfactory" mark. The five red circles meant he would be expecting $15.00. My heart clenched again. What was going to happen to us? I had to get to my son.

I watched the scene behind me through the rearview mirror. The police officers were talking—standing in the middle of the street. I saw the young blond one slip Luke's picture into a manila folder. After what seemed like forever, they got into their cars, turned off the flashing lights on their cruisers, executed u-turns in precise order, and slowly drove away. When the last police car disappeared at the end of Creekline Drive, I backed out of the driveway. Ignoring my new neighbors who were still watching from their front yards, I drove in the opposite direction.

Luke Clark, Austin Texas 1982

Anne Marie Clark, Austin Texas 1982

PART ONE

CHAPTER ONE

San Francisco, California

IN THE 1970S, SAN FRANCISCO felt like the engine room of the revolution. The air crackled with the energy of the new Age of Aquarius—the time for the revelation of truth and the expansion of consciousness. Across San Francisco Bay, local rich girl Patty Hearst had been kidnapped out of her Berkeley apartment by the Symbionese Liberation Army. Not fully understanding the implications, I felt validated in my opposition to the status quo when Hearst denounced her life of materialism and privilege and became a soldier in the People's Army.

By May of 1973, the Senate was investigating a break-in at the headquarters of the Democratic National Committee at the Watergate complex in Washington, DC. When Richard Nixon's dirty tricks squad was exposed, I came to believe that the president of my own country had declared war on me and my generation. I felt personally responsible for the liberation of women. I was opposed to the Vietnam War—and every war that might follow. I was 22 years old and filled with the passion of social uprising and the new feminism. I had made it to San Francisco and thought my real life was finally beginning.

I was born in Tulsa, Oklahoma—the country's Bible Belt and ground zero for Christian fundamentalism. Shortly before my graduation from Bishop Kelley High school, 1,800 evangelicals—including Oklahoma's governor, Tulsa's mayor, and a few state representatives— gathered for the dedication ceremonies of the new Oral Roberts University. Even though Catholic families like mine were looked upon with scorn by the fundamentalists, my mother's personal philosophy was closely aligned with the core beliefs of the evangelicals: personal unworthiness, retribution (both immediate and eternal), worldly wickedness, and suffering. It was more than coincidence that Mother's favorite curse words were "Hell!" and "Damnation!"

I rejected my mother's depiction of the world as a vale of tears. Allen Ginsberg and his ilk captivated my guilt-ridden imagination. I had a fledgling loyalty to the inside-out emotional landscape Ginsberg described in *Howl,* where the profane and the insane were the ones who saw the world clearly. My heart was with the hippies, yippies, and feminist radicals in California, those brave souls who made public their revolutionary beliefs. They all spoke to me. I felt like a hostage in my conservative hometown. When the *Summer of Love* was launched in San Francisco, 1,700 miles away, I yearned to be there. However, according to my mother, good girls left home only when they got married. My four older sisters had married young and had families of their own. I had seen the results of that strategy and promised myself not to repeat their mistakes. I was not going to be someone's dutiful wife. I was one of Ginsberg's "remarkable lamb-like youths."

Even so, my mother had an iron grip on me and I was only able to manage taking baby-steps away from her; like enrolling at Oklahoma State University in Stillwater—a vast seventy miles west of Tulsa. Mother's plan was for me to live at home and go to college or better yet work and "contributing to the family." When I moved into the dorm at OSU, mother felt I had betrayed her and in retaliation, she mailed me every frightening newspaper story she could find about young girls being victimized, co-eds kidnapped from their dorms or raped by psychopaths and left for dead in the bushes outside the campus library.

I paid my own tuition and fees through financial aid, a Pell grant, and money from a work/study job candling eggs at the OSU Agriculture Department. My sisters enclosed money in their letters whenever they could afford it. Undeterred by reality (as usual), Mother closed each of our phone conversations with, "I may not be able to continue to pay for your education, Sharon. And remember you're on the hook for those school loans. Don't think I'm going to pay them off!"

I was able to keep up a pretense of bravado with my mother, but her comments hit their mark. I was drowning in worry and anxiety – about money, about making my own decisions about my education, about what lay ahead for me. I had been an anxious kid. I hadn't stopped sucking my thumb until I was ten years old, then I switched to food for comfort. Now a college student, concerns about my weight made food an impractical tranquilizer. By the time my first semester at OSU ended, the ritual of cleaning, rolling, and smoking pot replaced compulsive eating—with even better results. Marijuana became my best friend, my all-purpose sedative. My anxiety was, for once, held at bay.

I muddled through a year at Oklahoma State with only average grades. In my sophomore year I felt more confident and finally seemed to be hitting my stride. But once I was home again for the summer, working at Kenny Shoe Store during the day and fighting nightly with Mother, my California dream reignited. Two of my sisters, Marilyn and Jeanne, had gotten divorced and had moved to Southern California with their children. Jeanne wrote me a long letter and invited me to live with her in Huntington Beach.

Marilyn called me to sweeten the deal. "After you live in California for six months, college is practically free."

The decision was a no-brainer. I immediately packed my suitcases and hid them in the back of my closet. As much as I was determined to go, I burned with guilt at my decision. I was Mother's youngest daughter—and the last one living (even part-time) at home. When I left, Mother would be all alone. She would hate sitting alone at Mass on Sunday morning. I imagined her coming home after work to our small apartment with no one to talk to, making dinner and eating all alone, falling asleep on the couch with no one to tell her to go to bed. Mother didn't have friends. My sisters and I went with her to the movies sometime. During the summer, she and I would go to free outdoor concerts in the park and go out for ice cream sundaes after. Mother called that "date night." When I imagined her life all alone, I felt selfish.

My sisters knew moving out would be hard for me. One of them called me every night to bolster my courage. I'd pull the phone into the kitchen and sit on the floor in the dark trying to soak in their encouragement. Sally Ann bought my plane ticket to Orange County and told me she'd drive me to the airport. Carol said, "You are going to have to face moving out someday, unless you plan to live with Mother for the rest of your life. You know, that's her plan."

I didn't tell Mother I was going to California until two days before my flight. When I saw the defeated look on her face, I felt my determination waver. I tried to qualify my announcement by saying, "It's just for the summer. Jeanne's working and going to school and she needs help with her kids." But I could never lie to Mother very well. Like the nuns, I always believed she could read my thoughts. She knew I was leaving home for good.

It had been over a year since my mother had tried to hit me. The last time she'd raised her arm to strike, I'd grabbed her wrist and stopped her, saying, "If you ever hit me again, I swear, I am going to hit you back." She had controlled her violent impulses since then. But I recognized the look marching across her face and I braced myself. No slap came. Instead her hazel eyes went cold and she collapsed into her gold wing-back chair.

"All my children have left me!" she wailed. "I'm glad your father's dead! I wouldn't want him to see how selfish his daughters grew up to be. It would break his heart!"

When Jeanne and Marilyn picked me up at the Orange County airport, I barely recognized them. Even with no makeup, they looked tanned and youthful—a testimonial to California living. They looked so different, vibrant and alive. The last time I'd seen them, they were both pale and haggard after bitter divorces. All three of us had left a lot of unhappiness in Oklahoma.

Jeanne maneuvered her red VW along the busy freeway as she drove towards her stucco house in Huntington Beach. I dumped my boxes and bags in the back bedroom and joined my sisters in the shaded backyard. Marilyn toasted my new adventure, and I was flooded with memories and emotion.

When I was a young, my sisters were all housewives with children not much younger than me. They were each other's best friends, often together when their husbands were at work. When we were all together, I tried to assert my status as one of the *sisters*, not one of the *kids*, but to no avail. They always pushed me off the couch and out into the blazing Oklahoma heat with the other kids while the four of them laughed and talked and drank tall sweaty glasses of iced tea in front of the swamp cooler. I resented being stuck outside with my nieces and nephews—all of us plastered against the house in the narrow strip of shade created by the overhang of the shingled roof.

But now here I was—smoking cigarettes and sipping sangria with my two oldest sisters. We were laughing and talking like girlfriends. I was finally an adult—not the baby sister anymore.

When the summer was over and Jeanne's kids went back to school, I got a job as the manager of an Indian import store in Costa Mesa. I made friends in the mall and learned how to negotiate crowded parties on the beach and at smoky jazz clubs on the Coast Highway. I accumulated some disappointing sexual experiences with tanned, long-haired boys who all seemed to drive rusted vans with daisies and peace signs painted on the side. When the Beach Boys sang about California girls, I imagined they were singing about me.

One afternoon, a young woman wearing blue tinted sunglasses glided into Raj of India. Her thick, dark hair hung long and loose down her back. She was the essence of California coolness—exactly what I yearned to be. She casually asked for an application for the sales clerk job I had posted in the display window. She had retail experience, so I hired her on the spot. Mary and I became instant friends. We played Ravi Shankar and Bob Marley music and smoked joints in the tiny bathroom in the back of the stockroom. Through a barter system, a fat joint or tab of Windowpane acid could suffice as legal tender and in exchange, sandalwood incense and bedspreads walked out of the store like party favors. Before long, Raj of India was a favorite gathering place for the society of young people working in the boutiques and trendy shops in South Coast Plaza.

As my mentor for coolness, Mary encouraged me to stop wearing frosted pink lipstick and ratting my hair. She took me to a salon on Coast Highway and gave the stylist instructions for a new long shag cut. I took it one step further and threw away my pointy Maidenform bras and let my breasts bounce freely. I bought Gloria Steinem aviator glasses and made myself a wardrobe of long Indian print dresses. The Okie from Tulsa that I was trying to kill off inside of me now had cool friends and a hip new look—at least on the outside.

Marilyn bought me a subscription to *Ms*, a new woman's magazine. Mary and I devoured each article and every book review. When we weren't together at Raj of India, we were on the phone with each other, reading passages from *Sisterhood is Powerful, The Female Eunuch,* and other feminist books. We'd cry together and talk about our lives and how we wanted the freedom that feminism foretold. We discussed women's liberation endlessly—at work, at restaurants, at clubs along Coast Highway, and parties in Laurel Canyon and Laguna Beach. We worked words like *subjugation* and *misogyny* into casual conversation.

I had run a thousand miles, but my mother still had a full-time job in my head. While I chanted, "Every child—a wanted child!" at pro-choice rallies, I could see Mother tapping her long red nails and rolling her hazel eyes. "Well, lah dee dah! Look at Miss High and Mighty!" Sally Murphy had married young and struggled to raise her five daughters. Why did I think my life could or would be better than hers?

In 1971, Mary's mother, Bea, moved to northern California to take care of her sick father. After six months, Bea was homesick and lonely. She offered to help Mary and me with rent and expenses if we would come and live nearby. Eager for a new adventure, we packed up Mary's white Malibu and headed north. After a short stint in Sonoma County, Bea rented us an apartment in San Francisco on Twenty-Sixth Street near the rolling hills of Dolores Park. I got a job with a Model Cities after-school program designed to improve the academic achievement of kids in San Francisco's poorest neighborhood—Hunter's Point. Homework houses were set up throughout the community, and I was assigned to one in Geneva Towers. One day a week, I helped interview elementary students recommended for the program by their teachers. And four afternoons a week, I worked with the kids on their schoolwork. My pay was low and I had no benefits. I could never have afforded half of our rent without the subsidy Mary's mother sent us every month.

I felt as if I were living in a dream. Mary and I drank Irish coffee at the Buena Vista Café on Hyde Street, and took the Blue and Gold Ferry to Sausalito for Polish sausage and corn-on-the-cob. We'd listen to jazz in North Beach, sitting up front so we could flirt with the musicians. On Saturday mornings, we practiced the latest dance steps in our living room while we listened to Sly Stone and the Staple Singers on the radio or watched Soul Train on television. At night, Mary and I made the rounds, showing off our moves at clubs like Friar Tuck's on Union Street and at smoky after-hours bars near the strip clubs on Broadway.

Together, Mary and I generated a lot of attention from men. We prided ourselves on our clever quips and sarcastic comebacks. One night, I was shadowed around the club by a man I had danced with for a while. I was trying unsuccessfully to discourage his attentions. On our way to the car, I gave Mary the blow-by-blow. "He kept sliding his fingers down the inside of my arm, even though I kept pushing him away," I said. "He was so persistent."

"God, he thought he owned you because you danced with him." Mary said. "What a pig!"

"Then he had the nerve to say, 'Don't you want me to hold your hand?' and I said, 'It's not heavy. I'll hold it myself.'"

"Awww! That's the line from that movie we saw." Mary said.

"Yeah, I can't believe I actually got to use it!"

Mary and I ended most outings in a booth in the back of our favorite 24-hour coffee shop on Bayshore Boulevard. We sat behind our dark glasses, usually a little hung over, drinking black coffee, eating runny eggs and toast, and re-hashing our experiences of the evening until the sun came up.

One evening, I went to bed early and Mary went out dancing with friends. When she came home, she woke me with a finger in my ribs. "Sharon, wake up." She was smoking on the couch when I stumbled into the living room. "You'll never guess who I met tonight," she said.

"Gloria Steinem?" I flopped down and searched around on the cluttered coffee table for the sandalwood box where we kept our weed.

"Maya Angelou's son—Guy Johnson! We ended up sitting with him and a bunch of his friends at the coffee shop," she said.

All young feminists knew Maya Angelou. Her book *I Know Why the Caged Bird Sings*, and her poetry in *Just Give Me a Cool Drink of Water 'Fore I Diiie*, hit the bookshelves just as women like us were searching for stories of women who aspired to be something other than a wife and mother. Maya had been anointed as a modern feminist hero, someone on *our side* of the struggle. Mary and I could recite all the mythical elements of Maya's life. She started out alone with nothing, no money, and no one to help her—nothing but guts, wit, and talent. She was sarcastic and audacious, and didn't worry about being a good girl. Since *Caged Bird* ended with her unexpected pregnancy and her son's birth, it was easy to believe that we already knew something about Maya and her son, Guy.

"Wow! What's he like?" I slipped a slim joint into the jaws of the alligator clip with a tiny glow-in-the-dark Jesus dangling from a thin strip of leather. I took a puff and handed it to Mary.

"He's really tall...about 6'5. He's light-skinned, good looking. He wears these yellow aviator glasses. He's like the guru of this group that was with him—sort of bigger than life. He told some crazy stories about being a bartender in Spain and smuggling pot from Morocco inside the doors of his Land Rover. Oh, and he loves puns." Mary took a slow toke. "I remembered this one to tell you. When we ordered our food, one of his friends said something about Guy getting fat and he said, 'I get my large circumference from too much pi.'"

"Oh, bad!" I said. "I can tell—you liked him."

"Well, he liked me." She raised one thin eyebrow. "He wants to make dinner for me."

"He cooks! Gotta love those men raised by feminists," I said.

Mary twisted her long hair into a braid, pulled a chopstick from under the stack of Chinese food cartons on the table, and used it to hold her braid on top of her head. "He calls *himself* a feminist."

"A feminist man? Is that like a Jew for Jesus?" I asked.

The following week, Mary went to dinner at Guy's apartment in the Fillmore District. She didn't come home for two days. Before long, she was spending most of her time with him. One rare evening when Mary was home, the phone rang and I answered it.

"Hello. Is this Sharon?"

"Yes, this is Sharon."

"Good evening. It's Guy Johnson." His voice was deep and round, with a musical cadence. Mary said he was 27, only four years older than me, but he sounded much older. "How are you?" he asked.

"I'm fine. I'll go get Mary."

"Wait! Can we talk for a moment?" Guy asked.

"Don't you want Mary?"

"Can't we talk for a minute?" he asked again. "Why so unfriendly? Do you have some reason not to like me...?"

In fact, I had been feeling resentful of all the time Mary spent away from home, but was not about to admit that to him. "No, I have no reason to either like *or* dislike you. I've never met you."

"Okay. Well, what's the problem then? Mary's talked a lot about you, and I'm intrigued."

Mary walked into the living room, and I tilted the phone so she could listen. "You're calling for Mary, right?" I said.

"Yes, I'm calling for Mary, but that's no reason for you and me to be strangers," Guy said.

Mary rolled her eyes and held her finger to her lips. I continued as if she wasn't there. "You're dating my best friend," I said. "That's reason enough for me."

"Dating? What are we, in high school?" Guy's deep chuckle echoed through the phone. "Mary and I aren't *going steady*. What sort of parochial ideas do you have about men and women?"

I was trying hard to perfect my cool persona and his words jabbed me in a sensitive spot. "I just don't compete with other women for men," I said.

"There is no competition that I'm aware of—unless *you* feel competitive with Mary. If so, don't project your feelings on me."

"Here's Mary," I said.

"Let me give you my number in case you change your mind," Guy said.

"If I get the urge to call you, I'll get it from Mary." I handed her the phone and felt a rush of relief.

Months went by and our paths never crossed except on the telephone. There, Guy and I continued our verbal tug-of-war whenever I happened to answer the phone. Sometimes I heard him chuckle as soon as I said hello. Guy batted away all of my reasons for not getting together with him, as if my arguments about loyalty and friendship were totally without merit.

Even though I had never met Guy in person, I always felt aroused after I got off the phone with him—and guilty, anxious, and ashamed. What was I doing? He was, after all, my best friend's lover. He asked Mary what I looked like and she showed him the pictures we had taken of each other at the San Francisco

Zoo. I was secretly flattered. Mary and I had been in this situation before and we had always honored our agreement not to cross the line with a man the other was dating. I didn't plan on changing that policy now, but Guy didn't fit into any of the convenient categories Mary and I had for men. He was not easily deterred. I suspected that his persistence had little to do with me—he apparently liked the chase, and I represented nothing more than a conquest for him—another point in his win column in whatever game he was playing with me. Still, I couldn't deny that secretly I wanted to accept his repeated invitation.

One Saturday afternoon, Mary and I were having one of our marathon chats on her long black and white couch. Our conversation inevitably turned to Guy. "I'm not surprised that he wants to meet you," she said. "He makes no secret about seeing other women. I suppose I should admire his honesty. And he loves a good debate, and you're a lot better at that than I am."

"I don't know about that! But how do you *feel* about him being with other women?" I asked.

"I wish I didn't care, but I'm jealous. I can't help but think that the other women he sleeps with are smarter and more attractive than I am. He doesn't keep it a secret that there are things he'd like to change about me. He makes me feel awful sometimes. But when I try to tell him that he hurts my feelings, he says that I'm just jealous and weak; that a strong feminist wouldn't be threatened by other women. He thinks my ideas about relationships are a part of the *old sexist paradigm.*" Mary made sharp quote marks in the air with her long fingers. "It's very confusing."

"There's something suspicious about that argument coming from a man," I said.

Mary took a drag on her cigarette and looked at the ceiling, shaking her head slowly. "I know he's right. I *should* have more self-confidence, but it does seem self-serving."

I shrugged. "Well, look who he grew up with! I guess he compares everyone to his mother. Fat chance anyone will ever measure up to Maya Angelou."

Every few months, Guy hosted a Sunday open house. He'd cook for a houseful of friends, and they'd play music all day. Sometimes celebrities would show up, and Mary would provide a colorful report on each one. Carlos Santana even sat in with them one week. Guy invited me to come to the party a number of times, but I had always declined.

Early one Sunday morning, Mary woke me with coffee. I knew something was up, because she usually slept in on Sundays. I put the steaming mug on top of *The Bell Jar* on my bedside table, and made room for Mary at the foot of the bed. She looked tired.

"Guy's having an open house today and he said I can't come if I don't bring you," she said. "Thus spoke Guy Johnson!"

I sighed. The world outside my comfy bed suddenly felt dangerous and complicated. I reached for the cup of coffee and blew across its dark surface. "So don't go!" I sounded more impatient than I intended. "You and I can go out and do something else."

Mary didn't pick up on my suggestion. She stared at the ceiling and said, "Listen, let's just go and see what happens. I don't really care anymore if you sleep with him."

"What?" I asked, totally awake now.

"I don't know..." Mary shrugged. "I care about him, but I don't think I could be *with* him long-term. He's too difficult—he's exhausting. And the idea of meeting his mother scares me to death—like Guy to the tenth power!" Mary looked at me. "I bet when you meet him, you'll want to sleep with him," she said. "I know he'll want to sleep with you."

I felt a guilty tingle of excitement. I already wanted to sleep with him and I hadn't even met him. "Please think about this. I'll go if you want me to, but I don't want a man to come between us," I said. "Promise me that Guy will never come between us."

"Deal!" she said.

We spent the next hour getting ready. I chose a short madras jacket and new bell-bottom jeans that clung to my hips perfectly. Mary wore a grey vintage blazer with high-waisted herringbone slacks and added striped suspenders. When we stepped out into the crisp San Francisco air, I felt like the second string in the battle of the sexes, going in to defend my team's good name—even though I was conflicted about what my real motives were.

On Sunday in Guy's neighborhood, worshipers parked their cars two deep along the curbs in front of the Baptist churches which seemed to be on every corner. Old black men in fedoras and shiny suits waved Mary's new orange Datsun through the narrow corridor remaining in the middle of the street. "God loves you," they assured us.

We parked a few blocks from Guy's address and struggled in our platform shoes up the hill to a mint green apartment building on the corner of Steiner and Oak. We paused to catch our breath at his door. Mary rang the bell. A young man with a fluffy cloud of dark hair stuck his head out of a top floor window, waved, and buzzed us in. As soon as we stepped into the small tiled lobby, we heard the murmur of conversation and laughter from above.

"Sorry, no elevator," Mary said.

Threadbare carpet covered the four flights of stairs up to Guy's apartment. The party spilled out onto the landing in front of his open door, and an attractive group of twenty-something men and women, some black, some white, some brown, talked and laughed and pushed bits of omelet around on their plates with crusts of sourdough bread. Mary led the way through the crowd and introduced me to her new circle of friends.

The apartment was paneled with dark wood, and the area of the floor not covered by fringed rugs was inlaid with geometric patterns of different shades of hardwood. Stone fireplaces flanked each end of the long living room, and panels of stained glass topped the far wall. Fichus trees, elephant ears, and rubber plants grew in huge pots in front of every window. Spiraling vines were tacked to the crown molding and crumpled leaves lay in fuzzy piles on the floor below. With a good cleaning, the apartment would be magnificent, but dust covered the art, books, and papers that were piled on every surface. Dishes and overflowing ashtrays peeked out from under the furniture. Had my mother seen this, she would have immediately decided that Guy was from a bad family. Mary led the way into the kitchen. Pots and pans covered with food crowded the stove and the counter tops.

"Wanna beer?" She peeked inside the fridge, looking for cold ones among the old food containers and tin foil bundles.

Live music came from the back of the apartment. After a couple of false starts punctuated by bursts of laughter, one clear voice counted off the beat and the music began in earnest. We listened to a good attempt at Stevie Wonder's *Signed, Sealed, Delivered, I'm Yours!* The volume increased with each chorus. I followed Mary through the crowd and we climbed a narrow flight of carpeted stairs towards the music. Six young men were playing percussion instruments and guitars in the large bedroom at the top of the stairs. There was no mistaking which one was Guy. He sat on a tall wooden stool, one booted foot balanced on the rung, the other keeping time. He cradled his guitar in his long arms; his thick fingers encircling the narrow neck. A tall, thin man played a bass. When the dark-skinned drummer hollered a greeting to Mary, Guy raised his eyes and looked at me over the top of the thick yellow glasses clinging to the tip of his nose. He had honey-colored skin and small, almond-shaped eyes under heavy black brows. He wore a striped dashiki and brown corduroy pants. He needed a shave and his dark brown hair poked out in clumps from under his multicolored knit cap. Still, I could see why Mary was attracted to him. I was not surprised at the rush of heat that ran through my body when our eyes met. Guy gave a slight nod and continued to sing.

Mary and I made our way across the room and sat on pillows stacked on the floor. The bright sun illuminated the heavy cloud of pot smoke above the musicians' heads. When they took a break, Guy set his guitar against the wall and swiveled in our direction. Mary's eyes moved between his face and mine.

"Glad you decided to come, Sharon," he said.

"Mary!" I said in mock surprise, "you didn't tell me this was Guy's party!"

Guy laughed and turned to greet a group of newcomers as they topped the stairs. "Welcome! Welcome!" His voice boomed above the conversation in the room.

"Let's go downstairs," Mary said.

"Are you okay?" I said.

"Yeah, I knew what was going to happen. I just need a minute to adjust."

We sat on the window seat in the living room and before long we were having an animated conversation with two young women visiting from Switzerland and a thin young man wearing purple-tinted glasses and form-fitting spandex pants. His artwork was on display in a small shop on Fillmore Street, and he had a portfolio of his latest pieces that he pushed in my direction. The first picture in the slim binder was of a chubby baby doll with a bullet for a head. The next one was a vacuum cleaner sucking a long-haired woman into the bag—her brown locks fanned out on the floor.

"I know how that feels," I said.

"You've got to come by and see the shop," he gushed.

As the day turned into evening, the party began to wind down. Guy appeared in the living room. "I'm glad you two are still here. Stick around, will ya?" he asked.

Without waiting for us to answer, he turned and went into the kitchen. I had been enjoying the party, but now my anxiety returned. I watched Guy pile fruit salad into bowls and seal them with foil. He handed covered dishes to each guest as he said goodbye. Guy was an energy field. He laughed with one person, then leaned close and spoke seriously to the next. People seemed to light up when they approached him and dim a little when they stepped away. Guy finally closed the door behind the last guest. His roommate, Mickey, the handsome, muscular drummer, disappeared into his bedroom with a young woman. Guy pulled a carved wooden box and a large pipe off the mantel piece and sat in a wing-back chair next to us. He used his elbow to clear a spot for the box on a giant lacquered spool table. He lifted the lid and flicked through an assortment of green buds, selected one, and crumbled it into the deep bowl.

"So, here we are! Smoke?" Mary and I said nothing. Guy struck a wooden match on the side of the box and took a long draw, then leaned in our direction and handed me the pipe. "So, Sharon, why don't you tell me why you finally agreed to come today?" he asked, looking into my eyes. "I'm curious."

I was caught off guard by the direct question and postponed answering by drawing smoke through the thick stem. My heart pounded. When I handed Mary the pipe, she didn't meet my eyes. She took a small toke on the pipe and handed it back to Guy. The silence became awkward and I reached for my wine glass.

"So are we going to be honest here or not? Tell me so I know how it's going to go," Guy demanded.

Mary looked at me and nodded in Guy's direction. "This is how he is. I told you," she said.

When I smoked pot, I was always more free with words, less anxious, but now I felt confused. I didn't know if I liked or disliked the challenge in Guy's tone. I could feel Mary's discomfort and what had been a fantasy up to that point, seemed too real all of a sudden. Was Guy being mean or just teasing? To cover, I raised my finger and cleared my throat as if preparing for a pronouncement. No one laughed. I took a deep breath. My pride wouldn't let me show how deeply uncomfortable I was.

I plunged ahead. "Well, Guy, I came to meet you because Mary told me that if you and I were...well, if we were attracted to each other when we met, that she, uh...was okay if—if something happened between us." I stole a quick glance at Mary, but she was watching Guy.

A flicker of surprise replaced Guy's confident grin for a moment. "So, it was really Mary's decision. You weren't being honest all those times you told me that you weren't interested in meeting me."

He and I considered each other carefully. "Correct," I said. "I considered my friend's feelings in my decision. Have you ever tried anything like that?"

"*Touché!*" Guy laughed and crumbled a fresh bud into the bowl of his pipe. "Mary, you're very quiet," he observed.

"You're going to do whatever you want to do, Guy. I know that," Mary said.

"And I make no apologies," Guy retorted. "But the real question is do *you* have the courage to do what *you* want to do?"

"Don't hassle her, Guy," I said.

"Is it hassling her to insist that she quit hiding behind her facade of weakness and passivity? She's a lot more powerful than she lets on." Guy's look was disdainful, and his words insulted and a complimented Mary at the same time.

"I am not hiding, Guy!" Mary blurted out. "If you want to sleep with Sharon, that's all right with me. There! Is that honest enough for you?" Mary folded her arms across her chest.

"Well, yes. I'm glad you can finally accept sexual attraction for what it is." Guy's broad face brightened into a smile. The shift in his expression was disconcerting. Every hint of hostility had vanished. He started recapping the party, repeating funny stories and filling in details of relationship dramas that had played out over the afternoon. I relaxed when I saw Mary become animated, laughing at Guy's characterizations of his friends and adding anecdotes of her own.

"I knew you'd be attracted to Sharon," Mary said.

They both turned to me and smiled. By the end of the evening, I had agreed to return for dinner with Guy the following week.

Mary stayed with Guy that night and I drove home alone in her car. My mind was spinning. Guy was handsome and sexy, but his boldness both thrilled and horrified me. I couldn't pretend that I wasn't attracted to him, but I still was conflicted over the situation with Mary. I'd never met anyone like Guy. Was this what a *feminist man* was like? I tried to imagine what a relationship would be like with Guy. There'd be no lies or pretending, that was certain—no subordinate female games. Maybe Guy was the kind of man I needed.

As I stood in front of Guy's apartment door the following Saturday night, I was weak with nervous energy. This was a whole different scenario from sharing the stage with Mary. Guy opened the door when I knocked. He looked freshly showered and shaved and I caught a whiff of peppermint. His thick black hair was patted into a wide Afro. He had on the same yellow aviator glasses he'd worn when I first met him. His denim work shirt was tucked into brown corduroy pants and the cuffs were turned back, revealing long, caramel-colored forearms.

"I'm on the phone." He gestured towards the living room with his chin, and then disappeared upstairs.

Fried chicken was piled on a platter in the center of the coffee table, flanked by bread and bowls of greens and potato salad. I went to sit on the high-backed couch, grateful for a moment alone. I had been preoccupied all week anticipating this night. I was excited and Guy's cool reception was a little embarrassing. I took long, slow breaths to calm down, but a flush of nervousness overtook me. I heard the mumble of conversation and laughter from upstairs so I pulled out my compact. My dark hazel eyes were my best feature and tonight I had outlined them with grey liner and doubled the usual amount of mascara. I ran my fingers through my hair to fluff up the top and smooth it behind my ears. I picked up a piece of French bread and nibbled on the crust.

After a few minutes, I heard Guy's feet on the stairs. I brushed the bread crumbs off my lap and tried to appear nonchalant. He sat next to me on the couch. I liked the feeling of his strong body next to mine. "My mom," he said as he put the phone in its cradle. "Seems like she's got a new man in her life."

This casual reference to Maya Angelou brought her out of the world of fame and celebrity and into the everyday world of chats on the phone and new love affairs. I thought of how different my life would have been if I'd been raised by someone like Maya Angelou—so alive and vibrant! No wonder Guy was daunting. "It must be the season," I said.

Guy acknowledged my comment with a brief smile. His face softened, and he held my eye with a look that was both intimate and relaxed. I smiled at him, feeling very young and naïve, the very opposite of what I wanted to project. "Yes, about that..." he said. "We should probably talk about any issue you might have with this arrangement." Guy handed me a plate and we passed bowls back and forth. I pushed back into the frayed cushions.

"What do you mean?" I said.

"I wonder if you might find my relationship with Mary challenging. From what she says, you're used to being pursued by men."

I took a bite of potato salad and felt a sharp twinge of betrayal. What else had Mary told him about me? We ate in silence for a few minutes. No one had said it aloud, but I had assumed that Guy and Mary would stop seeing each other if he and I got together. Was this the *old paradigm* that Guy talked about?

Was monogamy more baggage I needed to get rid of to be with him—this *feminist* man?

"Well, how do you see this working?" I said. "Mary and I live together. Don't you think things might get a little awkward?"

Guy pointed a forkful of greens in my direction. "I don't want any relationships based on denial. I care about Mary and intend to continue spending time with her. You care about her, I'm sure you understand."

I felt insulted by the comparison. "She's my best friend. I love Mary! The two relationships are totally different."

Guy pushed the basket of bread out of the way with his plate, pulled a thin joint from behind his ear and placed it between his teeth. He took a red lighter out of the pocket of his denim shirt, flicked it with his thumb, and inhaled short staccato puffs. After a long moment, he exhaled and handed me the joint. His eyes narrowed and a challenging look reappeared. "Are you implying that you are more capable of emotion than I am?"

Our period of affable banter was apparently over. Suddenly I didn't know what was going on. I was thrown by the rapid fire shift in Guy's mood—one moment so intimate, the next so cool and antagonistic. I took a drag from the joint and waited for the weed's calming effect, but this pot was strong. My thoughts began to fold in on themselves. "No, of course not! It's obvious you're capable of powerful emotion. But I've known Mary a long time."

The evening was not going as I had imagined. I felt out of my depth. I slid my plate onto the table and looked into Guy's deep brown eyes. I moved in his direction. "Guy, are we going to argue on our first night together?" He leaned back and pulled me on top of him. His hands felt huge on my back. When he rolled me against the back of the couch, I was engulfed by him, anchored in place.

Guy and his roommate Mickey were the two permanent residents of the Steiner Street apartment. Charlie, the tall bass player I met at the party, periodically stayed in Guy's spare bedroom, sometimes for weeks at a time. The three men were all well over six feet tall and everything in the apartment was customized to their dimensions. The beds were long and the couches were extra sturdy. When I stayed overnight, I had to balance on the edge of the tub to get the shampoo that was kept on a shelf installed far out of my reach. I used a chair to reach the towels in the bathroom cabinet. Theirs was the only kitchen I'd ever been in where the top shelves of the cupboards were in regular use.

Guy's best friend Norman lived only a few blocks away. At 5'7, Norman was the only average size man in Guy's circle. To make the rent on his large, two-story flat on Henry Street, Norman rented rooms to a host of housemates. When two people moved out, Norman invited Mary and me to join the household. After a token discussion, we said goodbye to our tidy apartment and moved into the ramshackle Henry Street house and ever deeper into Guy's world.

I was falling in love with Guy. I had never met anyone like him. He gobbled up life like a starving man. We ran on the Polo Field track in Golden Gate Park, and he always left me a hundred yards behind. We made love for hours, and then Guy would hop out of bed ready for the next experience. One evening when I was cooking dinner at his apartment, I turned from the stove to watch him. He was leaning over his giant chessboard playing both the white and the black pieces. He considered his next move while he strummed his guitar, kept one eye on the football game on television with the volume turned down, and talked to Norman on the phone anchored against his shoulder. When he saw me watching him, he winked and a spark of electricity shot through my chest.

Mary and I continued our overlapping relationships with Guy, and we spent a lot of time traveling together as a tribe with Guy's friends and an ever-changing contingent of housemates and lovers. We'd scour the *Bay Guardian* and show up en masse at bars advertising free happy hour buffets. We spent lazy Sunday afternoons playing music and singing on blankets in Golden Gate Park. We went to the movies together and had impromptu parties at Guy's apartment or at the Henry Street house. We ate pans of pizza and sipped beer for hours at long tables in cheap restaurants, conducting energetic confabs about our group dynamics, sexual politics, and the division of labor, money, and communal resources, while we envisioned a utopian future. We liked to bring strangers into the conversation, soliciting opinions from them and inviting them to join our party. We thought we were fascinating.

My mother always told me I was smart, but she cautioned that no man wants to be with a woman who's smarter than he is. She always advised keeping my intellect under cover. But I never worried about that with Guy. He was brilliant—certainly smarter that I was. Once he was coaching me at chess and told me that the word *checkmate* comes from the Persian phrase *shah mat*, which means, *the king is dead*. It seemed he could offer some tidbit of information on just about any subject.

After we saw *The Exorcist*, the conversation about how religion uses the concept of the devil to control the faithful lasted longer than the movie. Guy and I would lie in bed and read, with my book propped against the leg he slung across my stomach. Afterwards, we'd spend hours talking about what we'd read. He pushed me to have an opinion and to express it forcefully. He took me seriously in a way no one ever did before, and I wanted desperately to satisfy his expectations.

Guy was never affectionate with either Mary or me when we were all together. In fact, no one observing the group would ever suspect that any of us were lovers. With another man, I might have complained about being ignored when our friends were around, but in this instance, I was glad of it. It helped me cope with an arrangement that broke many of the principles I accepted growing up. Even though I tried, I was never completely comfortable with our unorthodox arrangement, but I didn't have the courage to try to renegotiate the relationship. I had agreed to it, and any show of jealousy would have unmasked me—and shown that I was not *evolved* enough to be in such an avant-garde relationship. Then where would I be? I'd lose Mary and Guy.

I avoided creating any mental picture of Guy and Mary together. I tried to convince myself that it was only my Catholic hang-ups that stood in the way of my being sexually liberated. I was sharing two people I loved with each other. Mary and Guy both loved me. We all belonged to each other. What could be wrong with that? It was an intellectual mind trip at best. But still, I felt like an emotional contortionist most of the time. Sometimes, late at night, when Mary and Guy were together, I burned with jealousy even as I berated myself for my romantic and outdated values. I occasionally went out with other men to avoid becoming too attached to Guy. (And to the same end, Mary occasionally shared Norman's bed.) But Mary and I had to finally admit that we were both in love with Guy. We were at an impasse. I had been with sweeter men. I had been with more sensitive men. But I'd never been with anyone more intoxicating and exciting than Guy Johnson.

One afternoon, Guy and I lay in a tangle of sheets after making love. He ran his hand absentmindedly up and down my thigh. Then his face turned serious. "Sharon, I want to feel a firm, tight thigh when I put my hand on your leg. You know that Mary's figure is her only real advantage over you. I'll pay you $50 if you lose 25 pounds."

I felt a stab of shame. This was the first time Guy had voiced any comparison between Mary and me. I jumped out of bed and started putting my clothes on.

"What's wrong? I am just verbalizing the obvious," Guy said.

Guy worked out with weights, jogged, and seemed to be able to eat whatever he wanted without gaining weight. And Mary was naturally thin with boy-like hips. The pleats of her trousers always lay in razor sharp lines down her flat stomach. I was the opposite. I had big breasts and round hips—my figure was more suited to peasant blouses and full skirts. Even so, I swallowed my embarrassment and accepted Guy's wager.

From childhood, my mother drilled into me the importance of a woman's looks and figure. How many times did I hear her say "You may not have money or advantages in life, but you can always bank on being attractive. Your looks are worth a million bucks!" My mother also assumed that I was on a perpetual diet. She'd walk up behind me, look me up and down, and pat me on the bottom. "You're getting there," she'd say. Losing weight was a constant preoccupation in the Murphy household, and I always felt fat, no matter what the scale read. It would be years before I felt that my body was fine the way it was.

To please Guy, I began my weight-loss regime the same way the Murphy daughters always did. I smoked more cigarettes. I cut down the size of my portions. I ate a lot of grapefruit, bought boxes of rice cakes, and avoided chocolate and desserts. Four weeks into it, I'd only lost a few pounds.

One morning when I reached for a piece of toast, Guy raised an eyebrow. "I'm disappointed in you, Sharon," he said. "You haven't made much progress on that bet, have you?"

I flushed, hot with embarrassment. "I can't seem to get below 145," I said. "Do you really think I look that fat?"

"It's more a question of discipline than how you look. It makes me question your ability to accomplish what you set out to do," Guy said, shaking his head.

I was wounded by his criticism and look of disgust. I wanted to remind him that when he challenged me to lose weight, it was *expressly* because of the way my figure compared to Mary's— that firm, tight thigh he so longed for was Mary's. His offer to pay me to lose weight didn't have anything to do with discipline or accomplishment when he first proposed it. I felt tricked.

"Forget it, Guy! If you think I'm fat, I can't do anything about that." I sounded more self-assured than I felt. I withdrew from the wager but continued my lifelong effort to lose weight. It was imperative that Guy be attracted to me.

Almost everyone else in our crowd worked at some marginal job or collected food stamps, unemployment, Medi-Cal, or some other form of government assistance. Mary's mother still sent her a check every month and Mary didn't feel the need to work. Somehow she still managed to dress in style, having an uncanny ability to assemble great outfits from the racks of Goodwill. The pot we smoked was always top quality, so we economized in other ways. I set up my sewing machine and altered Mary's Goodwill finds and helped everyone else keep their clothes from falling apart with well-placed embroidered patches and false hems. We bought all our food at the dented-can outlet and we smoked whatever generic brand of cigarettes we found in the chicken wire basket at the front of the store. *Lark* was the community brand for a long time. When times were the leanest, we even took our chances with the dented cans *without* the labels, since they were even cheaper than those that were merely dented. Norman could make an amazing dish with tofu and ginger root for ten people for under $5.

When the Hunter's Point Model Cities project lost its city funding and the entire staff was laid off, I made the rounds of dress shops and restaurants looking for a job. After greatly exaggerating my Tulsa Howard Johnson's waitressing experience, I began working as a cocktail waitress at the Bratskeller restaurant in Ghirardelli Square. One day Norman came up with a way for us to earn money while continuing to avoid the horrifying prospect of getting "straight" nine to five jobs. He had struck up a conversation with a young man demonstrating kites he sold at his shop in The Cannery near Fisherman's Wharf. After teaching Norman to maneuver the fighting kites, the owner gave him a tour of *Come Fly a Kite.* In the warehouse behind the shop, a row of college kids operated clattering machines, winding kite string onto colorful lacquered spools. The din in the warehouse gave Norman an idea. Norman suggested that he and "his partners" could spool the kite string off-site, and the remaining *Come Fly a Kite* staff would have a quieter and more productive place to work. The young man immediately saw the benefit of Norman's plan, and that night, Norman and Guy drew up a proposal and we became entrepreneurs.

We lugged the equipment from the shop's warehouse to the Henry Street house. We improved on the original design so that one person could operate two machines at once, which doubled our productivity. The guys bolted the small spooling machines to planks mounted on sawhorses and attached the contraption to the floor on the landing outside my bedroom. Every two weeks we picked up the order, crates of string and colorful lacquered spools, and signed up for work shifts. Guy insisted on completing his commitment early in the morning before he went to work in the file room at Langley Porter Psychiatric Institute. The clattering of the spooling machines outside my bedroom door at six in the morning was my cue to bring coffee and the first joint of the day. Receiving our check for our first completed order was a joyous occasion, and we spent our initial profits on a self-congratulatory bash.

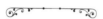

Traveling vagabonds could often be found wrapped in sleeping bags on the floor of Guy's apartment and the Henry Street house. I got to know a nomadic tribe of young men and women generally dressed in tie-dye shirts and canvas pants covered with bulging pockets. They carried tattered backpacks filled with maps and marijuana on their tanned backs, and they told animated stories about adventures on the road—a trip to Spain or backpacking up the volcanoes in Guatemala. What fascinated me the most was that they always found some way to make enough money for the next bus ticket to their next adventure. A Canadian with long blonde dreadlocks bragged that he hadn't had to work for a year because he'd made so much money picking coffee in Hawaii. I envied their travels, their freedom, and their certain conviction that somehow things would work out fine. That kind of confidence and trust in the future was foreign to me.

The only thing I was confident about was what I *didn't* want—a boring job, a house full of kids, and a mailbox full of bills—the tepid ordinariness of the life of the *Silent Majority*. I heartily joined in the rhetoric about collective living, shared resources, and egalitarian values. I did believe in it all. But underneath, I still suffered from a deep sense of anxiety, drilled into me as the daughter of a Depression-era mother. Growing up my mother had clung to me and I had absorbed her terror of the world, her fear of ending up in "the poor house" or even more shameful—on the dole. I was 24 years old and still merely surviving. What was my grand plan? Where was my sense of adventure? My future still seemed like a yawning void to me. Running away from Oklahoma, the Catholic Church, and Sally Murphy hadn't been the fix that I had hoped for.

Even so, I assured myself, no one could mistake me for the inexperienced kid from Oklahoma anymore. When I could merge my identity with the crowd I ran with, I felt solid—powerful even—surrounded by friends. But when I was alone in a room, the space felt empty. I would lie in bed at night, my heart pounding, my thoughts racing in frantic circles. I depended more and more on pot to manage the anxiety that was never truly gone.

Letters demanding repayment of my college loans sent me into a sweaty panic. Night after night, I promised myself,

"Tomorrow, I'll sign up for a writing class." "Tomorrow, I'll try to get a better job." But every morning, I woke up overwhelmed and I couldn't get to that morning joint fast enough. Round and round I'd go—another day with Guy, another potluck party, another trip to the beach, another shift as a cocktail waitress, and then another night anguishing over what I should do with my life.

In November of 1973, Guy's mother invited Guy her house for dinner, and the invitation was also extended to Mary, Norman, Charlie, Mickey, and the girlfriends of the moment. Guy asked me to come with them. Maya was getting married again in December and this party was to introduce her fiancé, Paul, to Guy's friends. Mary had met Maya a few times by now, but this would be the first time I would meet Maya Angelou. Mary and I caravanned behind Guy and the others across the Bay Bridge and up the 580 freeway into Berkeley.

"I'm trying not to think of Guy's mother as 'Maya Angelou the famous writer'," I said. "That seems so elitist—plus it makes me too nervous. I'm trying to think of her as just Guy's mother. That makes me nervous enough!"

Mary laughed. "I got so tongue-tied the first time I met her, I couldn't think of a thing to say. My mind went blank and there was this buzzing in my ears. I know she thinks I'm an idiot."

"Do you think she gets tired of people treating her like royalty? When does she ever get time to relax and be an ordinary person?" I wondered aloud.

"I get the impression that she likes being treated like royalty. Plus there's a big paycheck for being a superstar." Mary said.

"You're not making me feel any better," I said.

"I'm trying to prepare you. She's not the person you expect her to be," warned Mary.

We parked in tandem along the driveway that dipped down off Colusa Avenue and wound along the sloping yard filled with grey-green clumps of wild grass and lavender pennyroyal. My heart was pounding as I walked towards the house.

Maya pushed open the screen door of the small tan bungalow. Her features were thick and her deep maroon lipstick looked dramatic against her dark skin. She wore large brass earrings and her hair was wrapped in a blue and gold head tie. She was more commanding and vibrant than she was beautiful. I was familiar with photographs of Maya, but no picture had ever captured the energy of her presence and the intensity of her gaze. She looked from face to face and smiled broadly—her top lip pressed tightly against her teeth. She appeared delighted that we were there.

Her fiancé, Paul, looked diminutive standing in the doorway next to her. He was a slim man with a barrel chest, and was a few inches shorter than her. Maya's broad shoulders and long, expressive arms dwarfed him. Paul had pale skin and his light brown hair was long enough to brush against his collar. I heard a hint of a British accent as he and Guy greeted each other. Paul was a builder and contractor by trade, but had also been a journalist and writer. He had written the book, *Let's Hear It for the Long-Legged Women*, about his romance and brief marriage to Germaine Greer, the feminist activist and author of *The Female Eunuch*. His book ends with Paul's new love affair with Maya, his second long-legged woman.

Everyone crowded together on the porch. Maya and Guy locked each other's forearms as she turned her cheek in a ritualized greeting. Guy kissed his mother on the cheek and stepped back and turned to me. "Mom, this is Sharon."

"Sharon! Welcome, my dear!" My name sounded unfamiliar coming out of her mouth. I was at a loss for words, but Maya didn't wait for me to respond. Her powerful voice rose from deep within her chest and enveloped us all like a welcoming hug. "Come! Come! Come in. Charlie!! Norman! Welcome. It's so wonderful to see all your beee-utiful faces. I've prepared a fabulous meal for you all."

Maya led us into the house. We followed her through the living room, decorated with African masks and carvings and deep, inviting couches and chairs in tan and pink. Pictures of Maya with James Baldwin, Cicely Tyson, Coretta Scott King, and other famous people were displayed on shelves and clustered on table tops. Plaques and awards lined the walls. We arrived in the dining room, and Mary and I sat down next to each other at the long table already set for dinner. Paul and Guy poured wine into tall, thin-stemmed glasses and Maya glided between the kitchen and the dining room with serving dishes while we ate bread and cheese laid out on a wide wooden platter. Charlie was telling a story about his band's latest gig when Maya brought out the last dish and took a seat next to me at the head of the table. All conversation stopped.

"Oh, Guy, I must tell you a story," she said. Maya described a reception that was held in her honor at the University of Alabama. "...so, we're all standing around the piano in the living room and this old white man turns to me and asks me to sing. In a flash, I went from the guest of honor to the entertainment! So, I put down my drink and I sing. After they applaud, I turned to this gentleman and say, 'Now, sir, it's your turn to entertain me.'" Maya threw back her head and laughed a full-throated laugh which ended with a girlish squeal. She clasped her hands together in delight.

Paul picked up the story. "I knew what was coming, of course, and before they could collect themselves, I picked up Maya's mink and draped it over her shoulders. I offered her my arm and we walked out while they all stood there with their mouths hanging open." Paul poured more wine for everyone and looked at Maya with conspiratorial affection.

"It was deee-licious," Maya said. Then she turned to me. "So Sharon, tell me about yourself."

I thought of telling her that I wanted to be a writer, but in this crowd, that seemed presumptuous. "I'm from Tulsa, Oklahoma," I began, not knowing where to go from there.

"Tulsa, Oklahoma! Oh...," Maya turned to the rest of the table. "You know about *The Night that Tulsa Died*, don't you? There were terrible race riots in Tulsa in 1921." She turned back to me with her eyebrows raised in a questioning look, deep furrows lining her forehead. Everyone looked at me.

I felt the same sense of bewilderment I often felt with Guy—challenged and suddenly unsure of my surroundings. "So this is where he learned that," I thought. I reached for the approach that I felt the most comfortable with—sarcasm. "Oh, the riots were over by the time I was born," I said. Then ice ran through my veins. What was I doing making a joke about a race riot to Maya Angelou?

She burst into an explosive laugh and I could breathe again. She looked over at Guy, and said, "You didn't tell me that Sharon was such a wit, Guy."

Her dinner was simple but elegantly presented. She served sourdough bread with a colorful mixed salad topped with rose petals, and fresh pasta with homemade tomato sauce and bits of

Italian sausage. Next to each plate was a small dish of olive oil with an island of balsamic vinegar in the center. I watched Guy take a piece of bread from the basket and dip it in the mixture. I followed his lead.

Each dish was accompanied by a descriptive monologue as if Maya had personally discovered the intricacies of Italian cooking. "...and I rub a clove of fresh garlic in the sides of the salad bowl before adding my ingredients..."

"Maya, would you please pass the parmesan?" I said.

Maya's back straightened, and she seemed to grow larger in front of my eyes. Turning to me with a face of stone, she said, "You are not my peer, Sharon. You may refer to me as Miss Angelou or Mom. Those are your only two options." More silence. More stares. Guy frowned and Mary sent me a sympathetic look.

"Oh, I'm sorry." I sputtered and choked down the lump in my throat. When I found my voice again I said, "I'd be pleased to call you Mom. Thank you." There was a collective sigh around the table.

"We all call you Mom! Right?" Mickey said. Everyone chimed in reassuringly.

I tried to regain my equilibrium by directing the conversation to the resignation of Nixon's Vice President, Spiro Agnew. The month before, Agnew had resigned and then pled no contest to criminal charges of tax evasion and money laundering. "We were so fixated on Nixon being a crook! Who knew there were two in the White House?" I said. Guy picked up the story and detailed the qualifications of the new VP-to be, Gerald Ford.

After the meal was over, we cleared the table, loaded the dishwasher, and reassembled in the living room. Maya stood in the center of the room and looked dramatically from face to face. Everyone took a seat. Paul handed Maya a tumbler of scotch and she took a drink. She closed her eyes and tilted her head back with a rapturous look on her face. Then she began to sing—slowly like a rumble in the distance. *Over my head, I hear music in the air.*

Remembering her story from earlier and not wanting her to feel like the entertainment in her own house, I joined in. Guy smiled at me from the doorway. Maya took a step in my direction and put out her hand. I took it and moved to stand next to her. We completed the refrain with great volume and drama. *Over my head, I hear music in the air. Over my head, I hear music in the air. There must be a god somewhere.*

I tried to address Maya as "Mom" during the evening, but the word felt too awkward and false. I could also hear Sally Murphy objecting to the very idea of granting anyone else her privileged title. I vowed to avoid ever calling Maya anything if I could maneuver around it.

A few days after the dinner party, Guy called. "You made quite a hit with my mom," he said.

"Even after my indiscretion?" My cheeks warmed at the memory.

"Oh, don't feel too bad. Mom looks for opportunities to put people in their place. It's like a sport with her. She doesn't blame you. You can't help the way you were raised."

I felt defensive. "Where does she think I was raised? A cabin in the Ozarks?"

"You were raised in white America. That's the same no matter what city you're from," Guy said. "She liked you a lot. She liked your sense of humor. She went so far as to say I should stop seeing Mary and just be with you."

"Oh, really?" I wondered what Maya saw in me—a woman from white America—that made me acceptable for her son. "Why is that?"

"Oh, she's afraid I'll never settle down."

"She knows you pretty well, huh?"

Guy and his friends were providing the music for Maya's wedding and he asked me to sing with them. We dubbed ourselves *The Berkeley Irregulars* and began practicing the Dobie Grey song, *Drift Away*. While Maya and Paul stood in their backyard and exchanged vows in front of Cecil Williams from Glide Memorial Methodist Church in San Francisco, I sang for the group of people who were becoming my new family. *Oh, give me the beat, boys, and free my soul, I wanna get lost in your rock and roll and drift away.*

Maya's fans were inspired by her description of being a young, single mother and by the heartfelt way she wrote about confronting her struggles. Hers were familiar experiences, common to many women. When I went with Guy to hear Maya speak, the people in the audience—mostly young women—responded as if they were listening to a spiritual leader, not a writer. Coming to prominence when the second wave of feminism was at its crest and women craved strong female role models, the fervor surrounding Maya transcended the understandable appreciation of a moving story and a talented writer. It verged on adulation of Maya herself.

At an appearance at Mills College in Oakland, a woman in the audience tried to ask a question and was so overcome just by speaking to Maya that she broke down and couldn't continue. Maya wrote about being an ordinary woman and her admirers made her a saint. I asked Maya how she felt when that sort of thing happened. "It's important not to believe your own propaganda," she said.

To pay the bills, Guy worked as a part-time records clerk at Langley Porter, but his heart's desire was to be a writer. The characters in his short stories were complex and interesting. They could be strong and courageous but still struggle with self-doubt and fear, emotions Guy criticized in other people and never acknowledged in his everyday life. I suspected that his characters were a reflection of how he felt in the deepest part of himself, the part of him that he kept hidden, but I thought I knew that vulnerable side.

The only time Guy showed any self-doubt was when he talked about being a success as a writer. His desire appeared hamstrung by the undeniable fact of his mother's worldwide fame and success. "I know I'll be accused of trying to capitalize on her reputation," Guy said. "I don't want to be seen as just 'Maya Angelou's son.' But no matter how good a writer I am, I'll always be in her shadow."

Maya's literary career had provided Guy with incredible experiences, opportunities to travel, and intimacy with accomplished, interesting people. But being the son of a world famous figure had consequences beyond Guy's fear of literary comparison. His mother thought he was not living up to his potential and didn't suppress her criticism. She disapproved of how Guy was living his life and his low-level clerical job. The pressure she exerted on him was commensurate with the level of accomplishment she expected from him. I thought the root cause was that her being Guy's mother lay at the heart of her famous books. Her credibility and standing as a beloved icon, to some·extent, rested on the type of man Guy turned out to be and what he made of his life. I started to believe that the pressure to live up to this birthright weighed heavily on Guy and sometimes I felt that he resented his mother for this. For good or ill, Guy's choices were inextricably linked with his mother's reputation and success. He wasn't really free to chart his own course in life.

One evening when I was at home alone, Guy called in a panic. "Sharon, there is something wrong with Mary. You've got to come over right now. She's doubled over in pain." I jumped out of bed and drove the eight blocks to Guy's house. When I climbed the steps into Guy's bedroom, he was pacing back and forth in front of the fireplace and running both hands through his hair. Mary was writhing on the bed, pale and drenched in sweat. I rushed to her and cradled her in my arms.

"Mary, where does it hurt?" I asked.

"At first...at first...I thought it was cramps, but now it's stabbing...sharp stabbing pain...on my left side," she said between moans.

I turned to Guy, "Why did you call me, Guy? Why didn't you call an ambulance?"

"I didn't know what to do," he said.

"Go get your car! We're taking her to the hospital."

Guy pulled on his pants and shoes and pounded down the stairs. I helped Mary into her robe. She leaned against me, and we made our way down the stairs and out to the street where

Guy was double-parked with the door opened. I held her steady in the back seat as we sped down the quiet San Francisco streets. When we reached San Francisco General, the emergency room staff put Mary on a gurney and whisked her into an exam room.

At the admissions desk, I filled out forms and peeled off a stamp from Mary's Medi-Cal card. Guy slipped his arm around my shoulder. "Thank you, Sharon," he whispered. There was such a tender tone in his voice that I looked up at him. He didn't look away or try to hide the tears in his eyes. "I...I didn't know what was happening. The pain came on so fast." He was so nakedly distraught that I became overcome with emotion myself. I put my arms around his waist and held him. "You really came through," he said. "You're a true friend—a really good person."

I called Mary's mother and Norman to tell them what had happened. Then I sat down to wait in one of the grey plastic chairs. I watched Guy pace around the waiting room. We were both afraid for Mary, but Guy had seemed overwhelmed by the situation. He had even let me take the lead. Maybe he was beginning to trust me. Maybe he saw that he didn't have to be so guarded and defensive with me.

By the time the doctor returned, Norman, Mickey, and two of our roommates had arrived. The young doctor looked from face to face, not knowing which of us to address. "We're her family," I said.

"O.K., well then," he started. "Mary has an ectopic pregnancy. We're going to remove it surgically by making a small incision in her lower abdomen and inserting a laparoscope to remove the fertilized egg. Hopefully we can repair the incision without any permanent scarring."

I followed the doctor into the exam room to see Mary before she went into surgery. When I returned, Guy and Norman were huddled together in the corner of the waiting room. "Mary wants to see you two," I said. Guy slung his arm around Norman's shoulder, and they walked together towards the exam room.

Her surgery went well, but the doctor couldn't predict Mary's chances for a future successful pregnancy. After a few days in the hospital, I drove Mary to Sebastopol to recuperate with her mother. With Mary gone, the house felt empty. Guy and Norman were spending more time together and I was lonely. I tried to do some soul searching and had to admit—if only to myself—that I had remained in our three-way relationship because I secretly nurtured the fantasy that Guy would eventually choose me. Maya's endorsement had been like a talisman that I clung to when my jealousy got the better of me. But Guy's continuing relationship with Mary was a burning ember in the pit of my stomach. Now this. It might have been Norman's baby, but it might also have been Guy's. All my old frustrations came back full force.

I came home from work one night and saw a message from Guy tacked to the corkboard in the hallway. "Call me," it instructed. I ignored it. I got into bed with my journal and a joint, determined to separate my fantasy from what was really going on. By the time I finished writing, I knew I had to end my relationship with Guy. I couldn't pretend that I would ever get what I wanted from him. If I bowed out and he and Mary stayed together—so be it. Guy might laugh at me—he probably would—but I wanted to feel as if *I* was the most important person to my lover. Maybe I was unsophisticated and unenlightened. Maybe it was a romantic fantasy to want to feel special with the person you loved. Maybe I was a fool. Had it ever felt like that with anyone? My father had been able to make me feel treasured and special, but that had been a long time ago.

My father, Thomas Joseph Murphy, was tall—over six feet—slim with dark wavy hair that he combed straight back from his high forehead. "Tom Murphy was the catch of College Point when he was young," my mother often said.

When I was five years old, after my morning kindergarten session, I'd walk the three blocks to Mrs. Stewart's house. I liked sitting in the hustle bustle of Mrs. Stewart's living room hair salon with all the neighbor ladies getting their hair done. I tried to stay out of the way so Mrs. Stewart wouldn't tell me to go outside and play with her kids. They were older than me and I thought they were stupid and mean. I generally preferred adults to children anyway. On most days, my sisters Carol and Sally Ann came to get me after their high school classes let out. But Thursday was a special day. On Thursdays, Daddy only worked a half a day at the country club and he'd come to get me and we'd spend the afternoon together.

In my earliest memories, every Thursday Daddy would whistle for me from the corner, and I'd slam out of the screen door, jump down Mrs. Stewart's porch steps and race up the street to him. Daddy would be clutching an unfiltered Chesterfield between tobacco-stained fingers. When he saw me, he'd flick his cigarette into the street using his thumb and middle finger. I'd reach up and Daddy would catch me under the arms and swing me up and around.

Our afternoons together were always the same. We took the bus downtown to go gallivanting. Daddy and I would window shop outside the big department stores in downtown Tulsa, and he'd point out what he was going to buy me when his ship came in. He always had calls to make at the AT&T phone center, which was lined with wooden phone booths. Sometimes I'd squeeze into a booth with him and sit on his lap, but more often I'd slide around on the cool metal seats in the lobby and watch the distorted images of cars and people passing on the busy street through the wall of opaque glass bricks.

Mother believed that eating out was a waste of hard-earned money, but when Daddy and I went gallivanting, we ate lunch at The Brown Derby restaurant. We'd sit in the same high-backed booth and the same waitress waited on us every week. She knew us by name. I always ordered a cheeseburger and a glass of milk and Daddy let me press the button to call the waitress when we were finished. After lunch we'd walk around and watch the people downtown—businessmen in suits and ladies wearing high heels with dark seams up the back of their legs. I'd stare up at the tall buildings—so tall they seemed to sway back and forth with their top floors almost invisible in the clouds. Sometimes, I'd pretend to be blind and stumble around with my arms outstretched in front of me. Sometimes I only spoke a complicated foreign language and would gesture wildly. I liked to make Daddy laugh.

When my kindergarten year was almost over, my father began having headaches. He told me it was because his teeth were bad. I'd lie in bed sucking my thumb and strain to hear what my parents were talking about. "Dentists are expensive, Sally," my father said.

"You can't put it off any longer, Tom. These headaches are getting worse."

Daddy looked scared after his first appointment. I heard him tell Mother that he needed to get false teeth. The worried sound in his voice wrapped a chill around my five-year-old heart. He was going back in early June to get all of his top teeth pulled out, I heard him say.

Marilyn drove Daddy to his appointment in June. "Your father won't be in any condition to drive." Mother had said.

I skated back and forth on our screened-in porch, waiting for Daddy to come home after his appointment. When the phone rang, I pulled off my skates and ran into the house. Mother hung up and stood with her hand on the receiver. "Daddy fainted in the dentist's office," she said.

I was arranging aspirin and a glass of water for Daddy on the bedside table when the telephone rang again. Daddy had gone to work instead of coming home. He'd collapsed and no one could wake him up. His boss was driving him to the hospital. "That stubborn mule. I told him to come home to rest."

That night, Daddy didn't come home. There was an unusual amount of activity in the house for the next few days. The phone that hardly ever rang, rang again and again. Marilyn and Jeanne came over with their husbands, and Bob and John sat together with their heads down smoking on the front porch. They talked in low tones. Carol and Sally Ann usually played music when Mother was gone, but the little brown radio remained silent. I didn't know where Mother was. I sat under the dining room table in a forest of legs playing with my Tinker Toys. I wanted to stay out of the way, but close enough to hear when Daddy was coming home.

The next day was Saturday. Carol got me dressed and walked me across the street to the Tedeschi's house. Their teenage daughter was going to babysit me. I watched through the front window as my family walked out of the house wearing their church clothes. I passed the long morning coloring a picture of

Mickey Mouse and napping on the living room rug, ignoring the cartoons on the television. Daddy wasn't with them when my family came home.

Summer days in Oklahoma are long and it was still light outside when Sally Ann put me to bed. "Say your prayers, Sharon."

"Now I lay me down to sleep. I pray the Lord, my soul to keep. If I should die before I wake, I pray the Lord, my soul to take." I made the sign of the cross. "Amen."

I woke up alone in the room I shared with Sally Ann and Carol. They must have gone to bed in our room and gotten up again without waking me. I heard unfamiliar voices in the living room and crawled down from my high bed. Carol intercepted me and guided me into the bathroom to wash my face. She slipped my plaid dress over my head and held me tight between her knees as she brushed my long hair and pulled the top back in a yellow barrette.

"Go get your T-strap shoes," she said. I remembered seeing their red toes sticking out from under the couch, and I followed her into the living room to get them

On Sunday morning before church, Daddy usually shaved at the kitchen sink with a dish towel tucked into the neck of his undershirt and a mirror propped up on the window sill. I'd stand on a kitchen chair next to him and pretend to shave with a butter knife, my face full of lather that he whipped up with a brush in his heavy shaving cup with the ship on it.

"I should never have had five daughters! I haven't seen the inside of the bathroom for years." Daddy and I always laughed when he said that. By the time everyone was ready, he would be standing on the front porch smoking, waiting impatiently for us. But today, Daddy wasn't at the sink and he wasn't on the porch. He seemed to be nowhere at all.

Father Ross, the young priest from Christ the King, was sitting on the couch in his jet black suit, his white clerical collar digging into his closely shaved neck. My sisters were all standing around the living room and I could see Mother through her bedroom door. She was lying face down on her bed—her shoulders shaking. I felt a pain in my throat—I had never seen my mother crying.

Father Ross smiled when he saw me standing in my socks at the end of the couch. He put his big hand gently on my arm and pulled me close. "Good morning, Sharon."

"I have to get my shoes," I said and pulled away. "They're under the couch."

My sister Jeanne sat down next to the young priest. "I have something to tell you, Sharon," she said.

The sound of her voice was too loud and I ignored her. I stayed crouched on all fours—focused on the search for my shoes. "Oh, there they are," I said. I sat up and slowly slipped my left foot into my shoe, carefully maneuvering the narrow strap into the buckle and pushing the slim gold finger into the tiny hole. I wiped the toe with a wetted finger and neatly arranged the cuff of my thin, white socks. Everyone's eyes pressed down on me as I carefully repeated the process with my right shoe.

When I was finished, Father Ross gently lifted me into his lap and Jeanne brought her face close to mine. "Sharon, Daddy's gone. He's gone to heaven," she said slowly. I stared into her face. "He's gone to heaven to build you that swing set you've been wanting." Carol and Sally Ann stood together and watched me out of the corner of their eyes. "Daddy's in heaven with God," Jeanne said. I felt drowsy and my eyelids were heavy.

I leaned back against Father Ross' chest. I could feel his heart bumping against my back. I waited for Jeanne to say more and the silence hung thick between us. When her hazel eyes filled with tears, I nodded even though I didn't understand. The tension in the room snapped like a dry twig. My sisters busied themselves getting their purses and putting on a final coat of lipstick. Father Ross scooted me onto the couch next to him and stood up.

Sharon, Tulsa, Oklahoma 1955

I usually ran after my sisters' attention, but I willed myself into invisibility. Mother walked out of the bedroom, looking beautiful like she always did before church—every auburn hair in place, nails polished, lips ruby red. If she had been crying, all evidence of it had vanished. She didn't look at me. She just walked out of the house.

Daddy never did come home. He wasn't there to take me gallivanting or let me sit on his lap and pretend to drive his new car. We never shaved together at the kitchen sink. I worked it out on my own that he had died. If he left me to go to heaven with God, then I didn't know why people kept telling me that God loved me. But then I would forget, and every morning I would have to remember all over again. Hoping to spare myself that awful shock every morning, I whispered to myself when I went to bed, "Daddy is dead. Daddy is dead." It seemed too easy for a person to die—all Daddy did was go to the dentist. I became afraid to go to sleep at night. It felt too much like slipping away to somewhere else, it must be like dying. In bed at night, I sucked my thumb and twirled my hair around my index finger and I held my eyes open as wide as I could, but I always fell asleep. In the morning, I'd wake in a panic and check to make sure my sisters were still there.

By the time I was nine years old, they weren't and I was alone with my mother. From the day I was born, I had been in the care of my sisters. But now they were all married and had their own children to love. I had been my father's special pal and even though I tried to savor that special feeling, it faded over time. Mother had been a dim background figure—always there but never close at hand. My world had revolved around my sisters and my father. Now I tried to stay out of the way and not be demanding. One thing I knew was that it was a bad idea to upset my mother.

Mary had been recuperating after her surgery with her mother in Sebastopol for almost a month. One afternoon, Guy showed up unannounced. I was reading on the sunny deck in the back of the Henry Street house. I'd been avoiding Guy because I didn't want to confront the fact that I wanted to end our affair. I heard him talking to my roommate as he walked down the hall. He stepped onto the deck through the double doors and took the chair next to mine. When he smiled and laid his hand on my arm, I felt the familiar melting sensation.

"Don't think I haven't noticed that you've been dodging my calls," he said accusingly.

"I've had a lot on my mind," I said.

He nodded and looked away. "Sharon, I've been doing a lot of thinking too—since this thing with Mary."

I was suddenly angry. "What *thing*? The almost dying *thing* or the pregnancy *thing*?" I moved my arm away. "I'm sure this has been so hard on you." I didn't know exactly why I was so angry—or who I was angry with.

"That's not fair, Sharon. Of course, I was concerned for Mary. But this scared me. What if it had been a normal pregnancy? What would I have done if Mary was pregnant with my baby?"

"Well, she may not be able to get pregnant after this, so you might not have to worry about that ever again. Isn't that convenient for you?" Guy put his head in his hands and I suddenly felt guilty for being cruel.

"That's not what I mean. I'm sorry that Mary went through this. But Norman and I were looking at our reaction that night at the hospital. It was inordinately important to both of us to know who the father was. If we were equally committed to one another—a true community—that wouldn't have been our first concern. We would have both felt equally responsible."

"What are you saying, Guy? I'm tired of talking about Utopia."

"It's just that ..." he sat up straight. "Sharon, I've always wanted to have children someday and this made me realize that I want it to be with you. I want you and me to be together—no one else—only the two of us."

I was stunned. I thought I would never hear him say those words. "Are you sure, Guy?"

"Yes, I'm sure!" He smiled and his eyes twinkled at me over the top of his yellow glasses.

I was suddenly in high spirits—all my anxiety magically evaporated. "Guy, if you promise to be monogamous, I'm going to hold you to it," I said.

"Have I ever broken a promise to you?" he asked.
"You've never made me any promises."

When Mary came back home, she accepted the end of her relationship with Guy with equanimity and a certain measure of relief. We had somehow managed to keep our promise to each other, and our friendship stayed intact. I moved into Guy's Steiner Street apartment and Mickey stayed on as our roommate. In many ways, my life still looked the same; the same group of friends laughing and talking in the living room, the same parties, outings, the same utopian discussions, and political analysis. But every night, I was the woman in bed next to Guy. In my fantasy, I imagined that becoming a "real" couple might ease some of the tension that often flared up between us. My awareness of the very real issues in my relationship with Guy was swept away in the excitement of finally being the one he chose.

Since I was now living in the Steiner Street apartment, I set about cleaning every corner. I dug out years of ash from the fireplace, scrubbed the soot from the bricks, and shined the giant brass sword that hung over the mantel. I beat the dust and smoke out of the couch cushions, shined the plants' giant leaves with milk, and filled the planters with fresh soil. The apartment became the cozy, sparkling home it was meant to be. We hosted an open house to celebrate our newly committed relationship. Paul and Maya arrived wearing matching denim jackets lined with mink. Once the apartment was filled with the smell of Guy's gumbo and the laughter of our friends, Maya motioned for me to sit next to her on the couch. "Sharon, the apartment looks wonderful, like a real home. Maybe I'll visit more often now," she said.

"I found a couple of Guy's friends trapped under a pile of books in the back bedroom when I was cleaning. Guy thought they had moved out of town," I said.

Maya laughed and Paul looked over and we both waved at him. Maya took a sip of her wine. "I'm happy that you and my son are together. I think you two make a wonderful couple. When I was the age Guy is now, my career was already on the rise, but my son hasn't found his niche yet. Maybe now he's on the right track."

"Thank you, Mom. I appreciate that," I said. "I think we'll be good for each other."

"I'll tell you something, Sharon, I've always referred to Guy's lady friends as *Trixie*—my way of letting him know my opinion of their character and suitability for someone like him."

"I noticed how subtle you can be," I said.

"You are bad, you know that?" she said with a laugh and a shake of her head.

"So you won't be calling me *Trixie* behind my back?" I asked.

Maya laughed. "Sharon, you're priceless."

CHAPTER TWO

IN 1945, A FEW DAYS before a storm dropped a record 26 inches of snow on New York City, my family was evicted from their tenement apartment. Mother and Daddy and my four sisters were put out onto the frozen city streets. Chronically unemployed but ever the dreamer, my father decided the family's misfortune was merely proof that his big opportunity must lie elsewhere. Many men of that era fled the East Coast for the promise of California, but Daddy transplanted the family to Tulsa, Oklahoma, where I was born in August of 1949.

Tom and Sally Murphy married for love—or so the story went. They had both grown up in brutal poverty and my father painted a picture of a better life for his new bride. But he never would deliver on that promise. He cobbled together a living by working as a short-order cook, a laborer with the Santa Fe Railroad, and later as a much loved bartender at Southern Hills Country Club in Tulsa. He was only 44 years old when he collapsed of a heart attack at the dentist's office and died later that same day. Mother was left alone with three of their five daughters still living at home. I think she quit believing in love when he died.

My mother was never a woman to wallow in self-pity. Unlike Sicilian widows of previous eras, after Daddy died, Mother developed a sense of pride in a new identity. She was a "career girl." Banking on her own attractiveness and sense of style, began working at Seidenback's Department Store assisting the wives of Tulsa's upper crust design their fashionable outfits. Mother was ahead of her time in some ways. She never felt men were the betters of women. But she had a fatalistic acceptance of the status quo and some of her lessons on survival were firmly rooted in the past. For example, though she believed that the drudgery of being a "common housewife" was a waste of a woman's life, but she still encouraged me to capitalize on my looks to attract a wealthy husband. She used her customers as her example. On Sunday morning after Mass, she would review the *Tulsa Tribune's* society page and describe her interactions with the women who appeared wearing ensembles she had chosen for them for the symphony or the ballet or political event.

"These women are made of money and they're not half as smart or half as attractive as you are, Sharon," she'd point out. It was one of Mother's many confusing messages couched in a seeming compliment.

Every night, I watched my mother come home from her sales job exhausted from standing on her feet all day in high-heeled shoes and catering to the rich and pampered. Most nights, she fell asleep on the couch behind *The Tribune*, the paper crackling in small fits and starts as she dropped off. As if I needed more proof of poverty's effect on women, my beloved sisters were living the life of the housewives that Mother had warned against. My beautiful sisters were losing the luster of their youth married to men who had transformed from eager, promising suitors

56

to sullen husbands. "You're my last hope," mother would say. If I married well, I could redeem her disappointing life.

When I was in high school and I looked at my future through my mother's eyes, I felt as if I was on the last car of a train that was careening over a cliff. I felt trapped in my role as the youngest Murphy daughter, tasked with finding a husband whose only purpose was to provide for me. My mother and my sisters had married men of another generation, pre-feminist men. But now I believed that my life was on a different path. As uncertain as my future looked at times, I was in a passionate relationship with in a modern man, a feminist man. Guy and I had a relationship based on equality, mutual empowerment, and respect—the kind of relationship that my mother could never understand.

In the spring of 1974, Jeanne and Marilyn made plans for a short vacation to San Francisco. Their lives had also changed radically since their escape from Oklahoma. Jeanne was studying for her master's degree at San Diego State and Marilyn was at the California State University at Irvine working on her dissertation for a PhD in comparative literature with an emphasis on women. I would meet Marilyn's new husband for the first time. I was looking forward to impressing my sisters with my life with Guy, even though intense anxiety was erupting as their visit approached. Guy shook his head as he watched me shine the leaves on the philodendron with a soft rag soaked with milk. "What are you so worried about, Sharon? This is our life, not theirs. You're acting like a child."

"But this is my family, Guy! I care about what they think."

I anguished over every detail of their visit. I made mental notes of topics of conversation. I riffled through my cookbooks for the right food to prepare. I made a list of San Francisco sites to show them. I considered taking a drive up to the wine country, or inviting friends over to meet them. I paced in front of my closet, trying to decide what to wear. I briefly considered arranging a dinner with Maya and Paul, but immediately discarded that plan. Having them meet Guy was going to be nerve-wracking enough. I knew how he could seem at times. I was terrified that they might not see him as I did.

During our frequent phone conversations, Marilyn had been unconvinced when I represented Guy as a feminist man. "You realize, Sharon, that any man who refers to himself as a feminist is co-opting the very real struggle of women for empowerment. Do you think Jack would dare to call himself a feminist man?"

I usually made a vain attempt not to lose any ground. "Marilyn, you're talking about white men. Black men have a different power dynamic in society."

Guy and I drove to the airport on Friday afternoon and he gave a short beep on the horn when I pointed out my sisters shivering at the curb in the evening wind. Marilyn had on a tan windbreaker and Jeanne was clutching a white knitted shawl around her shoulders. Marilyn's new husband, Jack, was a psychiatrist. He was balding with a scraggly goatee and thick, horn-rimmed glasses. He stood with his arms around Marilyn and Jeanne, his plaid muffler flapping behind him in the wind. Jack and Guy shook hands and I grabbed my sisters in a three-way hug. Of the five Murphy daughters, the three of us looked the most alike. Each of us had hazel eyes, dark curly hair, and the family overbite. Jack flipped the lens cap off his camera. "I've got to get a picture of the three beautiful Murphy girls," he said.

When we arrived home, Guy gave a tour of the apartment. He led the way up the narrow stairs to our bedroom and out onto the tar and gravel roof. "Over there is the Western Addition," he said. "All these neighborhoods were the victim of urban renewal in the late 1960s – what the black community referred to it as '*Negro removal.*'" Jeanne, Jack, and Marilyn nodded and smiled. "Thousands of black homeowners sold their houses to the city, and then moved to black neighborhoods across the bay in Oakland and Richmond. This area used to be called the Harlem of the West Coast until it was gutted and black businesses and clubs along Fillmore Street were forced to close."

As Guy talked and gestured with his long arms, I tingled all over with pride. He was handsome and eloquent—he sounded as if he were reciting from a prepared text. The San Francisco skyline glittered behind him as the evening fog slowly tumbled in from the Pacific Ocean. It was as if the city itself was trying to help me impress my sisters.

"Brrrr, I'm freezing." Jeanne pulled her shawl close around her shoulders.

"Let's go in." Guy held the door as everyone filed past him.

I reached up and stroked his cheek. "I love you," I said. He smiled down at me.

After everybody took a seat in the living room, Guy bartended and I arranged tortilla chips on a platter around a bowl of dip that I'd made from a recipe in the Tassajara cookbook. I set the platter and a tray of sliced fruit on the large spool table. Looking around the room, I felt a rush of well-being—everyone seemed comfortable, smiles on every face. I sat down and picked up my wine.

"So, everyone all set?" Guy looked around the room. "Sharon and I want to welcome you to our home. Cheers!" We tapped glasses and everyone took a sip of their drink, murmuring appreciation. Guy continued to stand next to my chair and rested his hand on my shoulder. All eyes turned to him. "You are all so important to Sharon, but before the weekend begins, there are a few things I need her to say to you. She's been very worried about your visit and very apprehensive about your judgments. So, I'm going to go upstairs to give her a few minutes to clear the air." Guy took his drink and walked out of the room. Our smiles hung on our faces like streamers on the morning after New Year's Eve.

"What's this about, Sharon?" Marilyn asked. "Sharon?"

Jack stood up. "What a bastard!" he said. "Who does he think he is ambushing you like that?" He turned his back and looked out the window.

"Why would you feel nervous to see *us*?" Jeanne's voice was thin and tight. "Sharon, what's going on here?" She pulled a tissue out of the sleeve of her blouse and dabbed her eyes.

I dropped my chin and stared at my hands in my lap. "I was just nervous about you guys coming. That's all it was. And Guy was upset. He wants me to feel more ... well, more confident about myself. He can't stand this whole 'baby sister' thing that I get into. It's not about you. It's me." The blood pounded in my ears. I looked away from the hurt and surprise on my sisters' faces.

Marilyn stood up. "Let's go! Can you take us to our hotel, or are you allowed to drive the car?"

Guy came downstairs and stood by the door. He seemed oblivious to the tension radiating off of us as we filed out. "Did you have a good talk?" he asked. I shut the door without answering.

In the car, everyone found something to inspect outside the window. "I'm sorry," I said. "Guy's very direct, and I know it might make him seem insensitive. He just likes to bring things out in the open. I wanted you to like him and our life and, well, everything. Guy doesn't want me to be so affected by what other people think—he wants me to be as confident as he is."

"Confident?" Marilyn laughed. "Is that what he calls it? He's a bully, Sharon!"

I felt as if I were drowning. "He can seem that way, but he's really not," I said.

"You just keep thinking that if you want to." Marilyn turned to Jeanne for agreement, but Jeanne was focused on a group of young women in colorful African kaftans and head wraps sauntering up Steiner Street like a rainbow float. I started the car and headed towards their hotel on Union Square.

"I don't want to see Guy again this weekend," Marilyn said after a few minutes of awkward silence. "If you want to have dinner with us or join us tomorrow, fine, but come without him."

I pulled up to the curb outside of their hotel. "I'll meet you in the morning and we can spend the day together," I said. "Guy wasn't planning on coming with me tomorrow anyway."

"Oh, that's good! I'd hate to inconvenience him," Marilyn said.

I swallowed hard and blinked back tears. I didn't know what might pour out if I allowed myself to cry. We climbed out of the car onto Post Street in front of the Kensington Hotel. Sharp clanging filled the air as a cable car crested the hill on Powell Street. My sisters walked arm–in–arm towards the hotel and I opened the trunk of Guy's black Buick and helped Jack pull out their bags. He put his arm around my shoulder. "That's not how a man treats someone he loves, Sharon," he said. He hugged me before joining the others.

When I got back to the apartment, Guy was in front of the television, working his way through the snacks my family had left untouched. The sesame tahini dip was half gone and the fruit tray was covered with cantaloupe rinds and orange peels. "Do you want a glass of wine?" he asked.

I stared at him, my purse still on my shoulder. "Guy, how could you put me in such an awful position?"

He laughed and shook his head. "Why can't you tell them the truth, Sharon? Your life is none of their business!"

"That's not the point, Guy! I confided in you."

"That's just an excuse to be dishonest, Sharon. Freak out before they come and act all smiles and kisses when they get here." He turned back to the television. "I saw the Murphy's baby sister today on full display. What a performance!" Guy grabbed my hand and pulled me down on the couch next to him. "Don't worry about it," he said with a laugh. "They're only here for the weekend."

By the time I tumbled into bed that night, the glass of wine I drank and the joints I smoked had dulled the shock and embarrassment of the afternoon. I spooned Guy from behind and rested my face against his strong back. "There's nothing wrong with feeling nervous about what your family thinks. Don't you care about what your mother thinks of you?" I asked.

Guy rolled over and looked into my face. "Sharon, when I look at you I see the strong, confident woman that you have the potential to be. You're kind and beautiful—if you would only believe in yourself." Guy slipped his hand beneath me and slid his fingers down my back. He pulled me towards him, brushed my hair away from my face, and kissed me.

The next day I played tour guide for my family and everyone avoided any mention of Guy. Jack treated us to dinner in Sausalito, and we drank wine and watched the San Francisco skyline grow faint and slowly fade behind a curtain of evening fog. By the time I dropped them off at their hotel and said goodbye, I felt warm and loved and glad they had come.

When Guy and I were getting along, I felt as if no two people were ever more perfect for each other. Saturday morning doing our laundry at the Washateria near Golden Gate Park could end up being the hilarious high point of the week. A random conversation with strangers at breakfast on Cole Street might be the start of a daylong adventure with new friends. We were both raconteurs and could command the attention of any group. When we were with our friends and they reacted to a funny story or a joke I was telling, I loved to see the approving look on Guy's face as he watched me. Once at a party, a man hopped down off the kitchen counter to make room for Guy to mix a drink. When he landed, his head barely reached the center of Guy's chest. The little man tilted back his head and opened his mouth to speak, but Guy put his hand up to silence him. "If you don't ask me if I play basketball, I won't ask you if you're a jockey." The room erupted but no one laughed harder than I did. I was Guy's best audience.

My relationship with Guy became the very ground upon which I stood. But when Guy turned into my adversary, as he often did without the slightest warning, my iron-clad belief that our relationship was the stuff of destiny prevented me from clearly evaluating our problems. All couples have bad times, I reasoned. Nothing was more important than keeping our life on an even keel.

One Saturday morning, we stayed in bed making love till almost noon. When the phone rang, Guy flipped a couple of pillows behind his head and launched into a loud conversation with his friend Snooky, a sax player who had toured with Janis Joplin and the Kozmic Blues Band. I got up and went downstairs to make breakfast. Guy walked into the kitchen while I was grinding coffee beans. "We're going over to Snooky's tonight to play whist," he announced.

"Guy, I'm no good at cards, especially whist," I heard myself whining and tried to amend my tone. "Why don't you ask Norman to go with you?"

"Playing whist is just a matter of concentration. How do you ever expect to learn?" Guy said off-handedly.

"Then let's have some games with our friends, so I can practice. Snooky doesn't even like me and he always makes me nervous."

"You always want to take the easy way out, don't you?"

That evening, Guy and I stepped into the smoky haze that filled Snooky's living room. The apartment was crowded with acoustic and electric bass guitars, and amplifiers resting in nests of cords. Posters of Malcolm X, Louis Farrakhan, and Che Guevara decorated the walls. Snooky handed Guy a joint as big as a cigar, clapped him on the shoulder, and led him into the apartment as if he had walked in by himself. Smokey Robinson sang from the tape player; *Don't let my glad expression give you-u the wrong impression. Really I'm sad. I'm sadder than sad.*

A dark-skinned man in a white embroidered skullcap hunched over a small table in the middle of the room. He deftly shuffled a deck of cards and nodded to Guy.

"Ready to lose, man?" Guy said.

"Lose?" Snooky huffed. "The last time I lost at cards, my man, I slammed my dick in the car door nine times." He paused for effect. "... and the scars are gone. That's how long it's been since I lost at cards." Guy laughed and they shook hands, grasping palms, fingers, tapping fists, and finishing with a shoulder-to-shoulder hug and manly back-thumping.

We took our seats at the card table, and Guy handed me a joint. He watched until I smoked it and my slim shreds of focus melted away. Snooky dealt the first hand. The look on Guy's face announced every wrong move I made, each miscalculation. After being soundly beaten, we made it a short night.

Once in the car, Guy turned on me. "Were you *trying* to embarrass me?"

"I didn't want to go in the first place, Guy! You've played cards all your life. The only card game my family ever played was canasta—oh, and slap-a-jack. Maybe I should have suggested a few hands of that!"

This wasn't the speech I had rehearsed while I was suffering at the card table and trying to maintain a calm face. I wanted to ask Guy why he would put me in a position to be so uncomfortable and embarrassed. I would never do that to him. What lesson was that supposed to teach me?

Guy cut around the car ahead of us and sped up Lincoln Avenue. "When are you going to overcome the deficiencies of your past, Sharon? You blame everything on your upbringing."

I felt ripped in half, angry at him, but also angry at myself for my lack of skill and self-confidence. I looked out at the dark streets of San Francisco to avoid the furious look on his face. "When I feel more self-assured," I thought, "I'll know how to handle these arguments—being bad-tempered only keeps Guy from respecting me." My tortured logic didn't address the real issue, but it was convincing enough to allow me to push my resentment into a silent corner of my mind.

I started going with Guy to visit his grandmother, Vivian Baxter, at her well-appointed townhouse in Stockton, 85 miles east of San Francisco. We usually went on the weekends when Maya and Paul would also be there. Vivian was a tiny, tough woman who demanded and got deference from everyone—including Maya. I hadn't seen that before. Vivian wore her slightly graying hair in soft waves around her broad face. When we were out in public, she was always impeccably dressed, favoring tailored suits and silk blouses with tasteful gold and diamond accessories. At gatherings at her house, I watched her playing cards and telling stories while she drank glass after glass of scotch. I could see a hint of the younger woman she had been—the woman who presided over gambling houses on the wild side of St. Louis.

I never really talked "to" Guy's grandmother. She talked and I listened. (I learned my lesson and called her "Grandmother" right from the start.) There was never enough of a break in her rolling monologues to work in a polite, "Excuse me," so I didn't even dare go to the bathroom until she got up from the table to stir a pot on the stove or mix herself another drink. When Guy and I stayed overnight with her, she gave us her king-size bed and she slept in the guest room. Before bedtime, she'd slip a well-manicured hand under her pillow to retrieve the pearl-handled revolver she kept there—to protect her from what, I couldn't guess. She carried an even smaller pistol in her purse. Lady, as only her friends called her, scared me to death.

Both Maya and Vivian were past residents of San Francisco, and the escalating tension and street violence in the city was a frequent topic of conversation during our visits to Stockton. The country was reeling from the political crisis surrounding Watergate and the recession hit San Francisco hard. Gas prices climbed. People could only buy gas on assigned days based on the last number of your license plate. Unemployment numbers rose and inflation reached double-digits. As the economy worsened, racial tension rose in the Fillmore District and our integrated neighborhood became dangerous. Neighbors talked about break-ins and vandalism.

Maya began urging Guy and me to leave San Francisco and move to Stockton. Stockton was a conservative, agricultural city in San Joaquin County and every time we visited Vivian, I was happy to return to San Francisco with its creative disorder, streets ringing with different languages, food with unpronounceable names, and neighborhoods populated by people from all over the world. I had grown up in a place like Stockton and fled at the first opportunity. Vivian's boyfriend was president of the local longshoreman's union at the Port of Stockton. Uncle Knowledge, as we called him, assured Guy that he could get him a job with the union with great pay and benefits. Guy could work three or four long days and then be off for as many days in a row.

"You'd be able to concentrate on your writing," Maya said. "San Francisco isn't where you want to be when you start your family." Vivian agreed and the pressure increased. With every tumbler of scotch, the space in the conversation for our response shrunk until Guy and I sat quietly and listened to Vivian and Maya envision our future.

The second volume of Maya's autobiography had been published earlier that year and *Gather Together in My Name* was a huge success, just as *I Know Why the Caged Bird Sings* had been. She was honored with new awards and honorary degrees from universities. She appeared on *The Richard Pryor Show* and other guest spots on television, she spoke at colleges and cultural events all over the country. Her friend, Alex Haley, asked her to play the role of Nyo Boto, Kunta Kinte's grandmother in the movie adaptation of his bestselling book, *Roots*. Maya was becoming one of the most sought-after women in America, in such demand that she and Paul were away from home much of the time.

Vivian complained that Maya was gone too much and that her visits were too infrequent. I began to wonder about Maya's reasons for pressuring us to move to Stockton. Were we being offered up as her proxy? Why else would she push for such a move? But I was uncomfortable thinking that she would be that manipulative and the likelihood that we would actually move to Stockton was so remote that I didn't mention what seemed like a paranoid suspicion to Guy. The talk of moving to Stockton seemed to recede into the background for a time.

Then one Friday evening, I came home from shopping and leaned my grocery bags against the wall next to the front door of our apartment building. As I worked my key into the lock, two teenage boys walked over from the playground across the street and stood on either side of me.

"Can we help you with those bags?" the taller boy said.

I turned to my left to look up at him, but before I could respond I felt a tug on my other side. When I looked around, his pal was running full speed up the hill towards Oak Street. And then the other boy ran in the opposite direction down Steiner. I dug my hand into my purse. My rent money was in my wallet and my wallet was gone.

Guy turned from the stove and grabbed my shoulders when I told him what happened. "Did they touch you? Are you all right?" He was solicitous all evening, but by the next morning, he was furious. He took a small pistol out of its hiding place in the back of his closet. He laid it on a folded hand towel and secured the gun to the towel with Saran Wrap. I watched from our front window, like a damsel in her tower, as Guy strolled down the hill holding the bundle against his right leg. The teenagers in our neighborhood hung out and played basketball at the asphalt-covered playground on the corner of Page Street and Steiner. Guy stepped through the opening in the chain-link fence. A group of boys ambled over when he called to them—his 6'5" frame dwarfing their lanky teenage bodies. Three girls slouched against the fence watching them.

Guy pointed towards our front door and the group of kids listened attentively, but they took a quick step backward when he pulled the package away from his leg and they saw the gun. They shook their heads and held up their hands in gestures of peaceful ignorance. By the time Guy returned to the apartment, he had decided that we would take Uncle Knowledge up on his offer—we were moving to Stockton.

After getting robbed right on our doorstep, I was in a weak position to argue against the move. I couldn't refuse without a good reason. The more Guy occupied the center of my life, the more wrapped up in his thoughts and feelings I became and the less distinct my own feelings were to me. I couldn't tell him I didn't want to live so close to his grandmother. Loving San Francisco and hating the idea of living in Stockton were objections only supported by emotions—insufficient grounds for Guy. I was trapped in an argument inside of my own head. Before long, I had convinced myself that if the move and a new work schedule would help Guy focus on his writing, which was his dream for his future, it would be worth the sacrifice.

The following weekend Paul and Maya met us in Stockton to help with house hunting. Guy pulled his new VW bus into Vivian's driveway to change the oil while Maya and I read through the classifieds. I found a good prospect and made an appointment for that afternoon to check it out. Guy didn't want to go, so Paul went with me. A wiry old man with a paintbrush in his hand met us at the door of a neat two-bedroom frame house on a wide, tree-lined street. He told us to look around and returned to his work touching up the trim around the fire-place in the living room. Paul and I both liked the house. It was well cared for, had lots of room and was freshly painted. I asked Mr. Turner for an application. "My wife handles all the rentals. She'll be back in about an hour," he said.

Paul and I returned an hour later with Guy. We climbed out of Paul's car as a pale, grey-haired woman approached the house carrying an armful of mops and brooms. Mrs. Turner took a step in our direction and raised a hand to shield her eyes from the afternoon sun. I had spoken to her on the phone so I introduced myself and turned to Paul and Guy.

"This is Guy and his stepfather, Paul." Mrs. Turner squinted at us. Her watery blue eyes darted from one face to the next and back again. She stood transfixed, gaping up into Guy's brown face. I could almost hear the voice in her head scream-ing, "BLACK MAN!" I tried to ignore the rudeness of her stare, thinking that any minute she would come to her senses. But she dug a hole and jumped right in.

"My husband and I lived in this house for many years," she said. "We know all the neighbors. They're good people. I wouldn't want to upset any of them," she said, gesturing up and down the quiet street.

"And how would you be upsetting them?" Guy asked.

"Well, you know...this is a nice neighborhood," she stammered.

Guy looked down on Mrs. Turner with an innocent smile. "Yes, I'd love to live in a nice neighborhood like this," he said.

In a bizarre non-sequitur, she asked, "Well, who would do the yard work?" She looked over at her husband, who was on the porch wiping his paint brush with a cloth.

Guy's eyes narrowed to slits. "The same person who would be paying the rent," he said.

"Well, uh...you're a beautiful man. I hope I'm not embarrassing you," she said with a shake of her head.

"I hope you're not embarrassing yourself," Guy said. Paul and I looked at one another and began laughing. The three of us left Mrs. Turner with her chin impaled on the tips of her brooms and her mouth hanging open.

We found another house to rent and the plans for the move went into high gear. We quit our jobs, gave notice on our apartment, and began to pack. As moving day approached, Uncle Knowledge's union had their bi-annual election and he unexpectedly lost his union post and with it the influence to get Guy the job he had promised. When Maya called to tell us the news, I had a fleeting hope that we had gotten a reprieve.

"It's too late to change the plan now, Sharon. Mom's going to pay for our moving expenses. She's sending us a check to tide us over till we can find jobs," he said.

"Guy, the idea behind moving was so that you would have a schedule so you can write. What's the point, now? Do you really want to live in that redneck town?"

"You think any town is different from Stockton? Believe me, Sharon, they're all the same."

I wanted to argue with him. I wanted to fight to keep us in San Francisco with our friends and the life we both loved, but Guy had a look on his face that warned me off. I saw his characteristic certitude, but underneath it, he looked angry—or was he afraid? "Guy, what would happen if we told you mother that we didn't want to move now?" I asked.

His expression changed and I could almost see his mind sort through a menu of responses. Then his face settled into a look of amused smugness. "Sharon, you would never survive the shit storm of drama that would result. We agreed to do this—and this is what we're going to do."

Once we settled into our house in Stockton, I began working as a nursing assistant at San Joaquin County Hospital, a decrepit old public hospital, with long, poorly lit corridors lined with shrouded humps of outdated equipment. When I completed my training in medical terminology and procedures and passed my probationary period, I got insurance benefits, a raise and the security of a full-time day shift. I knew the difference between systolic and diastolic and the charge nurses came to trust me with patients. It was hard, physical work and nursing assistants were only a half-step above the custodial staff in the hospital's militaristic pecking order. But even though I wasn't saving the world, I felt as if I was providing a valuable service.

In San Francisco, you could round a corner and be surprised by a celebration of the Hindu New Year's Festival of Lights or a crowd of kids on the sidewalk break-dancing to music blasting from a boom box. In Stockton, happy hour was hosted at sports bars and the only live music anywhere was country western. In San Francisco, our friends stopped by unannounced whenever they were in the neighborhood. In Stockton, there was never a surprise knock at the door, or an impromptu invitation for dinner or a movie. Guy and I lived in a safe, middle-class neighborhood in a tidy white house with a green wrap-around porch and two cars in the driveway. After two months in Stockton, I felt as if the spice was draining out of our life. I had relished the image of Guy and I as hip bohemians and didn't recognize the picture of us as a settled, suburban couple.

We explored what there was to see in Stockton and around the Delta Waterway while we refined our emerging master plan. I would get pregnant and go back to school after the baby was born. Guy thought it wouldn't take much effort to work his way up through the ranks of city administration. Then when I graduated, I'd get a job—probably teaching—and Guy would concentrate on his writing. Then we'd have more children—maybe three in all. When Guy was able to support us with his writing, I would quit working and pursue my own artistic interests, take piano or singing lessons, or try my own hand at writing—maybe go back to school and get an MFA.

It was hard to believe that Guy didn't miss our friends and our life in San Francisco the way I did, but he seemed content with the change in surroundings. He was working as a grant writer with the city of Stockton, and he even began to like his bureaucratic job, which I had considered only as a means to an end. In the evening, he talked more about the political wrangling in his office than the politics of the country. After dinner, he would retreat into the second bedroom that was serving as his office. If he was writing anything, I didn't know about it.

I loved Guy, but I knew not to look to him for comfort or reassurance. I got those things from Mary, other friends, or from my sisters. But now our budget was tight and long distance phone calls were expensive. With only Guy to talk to, I felt isolated and lonely, the deficits in our relationship were harder to ignore. Luckily, I liked our new house. The kitchen was my favorite room. It had tall, bright-white cabinets and high counters with white ceramic tile edged with dark green trim. I got off work at 3 o'clock every afternoon, so I was usually cooking dinner by the time Guy strolled in. He'd throw down his briefcase, sit at the kitchen table, and open his wooden inlaid box where he kept his weed. He'd crumble a bud into the bowl of his heavy pipe. The evening sunset would be shining through the high bank of windows above the sink and the kitchen would turn a pale shade of pink. Every night, Guy would say, "This is my favorite time of day."

One weekend in June of 1974, Mary and Norman drove up for a visit and when we sat down for dinner, Norman announced, "Mary and I are going to have a baby."

"Hey, brother-man, congratulations!" Guy reached across the table, grabbed Norman's hand, and squeezed Mary's shoulder. "So, are you two a couple now?" Guy asked.

"No, we don't work as a couple, but we are committed to each other. We're going to raise the child as partners and friends," Norman said.

Mary added, "Everyone at Henry Street is on board to help."

Mary and Norman were full of plans and ideas. They seemed happy and comfortable with each other. I felt a twinge of envy when I saw the easy trust they had in each other. I was still trying to earn Guy's trust. Mary and I took a drive after dinner so we could talk privately. I pulled into our neighborhood park and turned off the engine. We watched the crimson summer sunset fade into a grey evening sky.

"This isn't the feminist dream we fantasized about, is it?" Mary said.

I laughed ruefully. "Well, I live in Hicksville and you're an unwed mother." I said. "Maybe we're just not very creative."

"But are you happy, Sharon? I worry about you here without anyone else around but Guy."

I was uncomfortable with her directness. If anyone knew how difficult Guy could be it was Mary. "I'm a little lonely," I said. "But we're working towards something—that takes some sacrifice at first. We won't always live in Stockton." I had avoided answering the question but Mary let it pass.

When Mary was five months pregnant, the reality of a baby on the way finally sunk in and the supportive spirit among the housemates at Henry Street began to evaporate. Mary was bitterly disappointed and moved once again to her mother's house in Sebastopol. Of course, Norman stayed in San Francisco. They were still committed to co-parenting, but like most single parents, they were going to be mostly alone in the endeavor.

When their daughter was born in January of 1975, Guy decided it was time for us to have a baby.

On a warm Saturday in May, I lay with my head on Guy's shoulder, stroking his flat stomach after making love. The walls of our bedroom gave off a cool blue glow as the afternoon light filtered through our sheer white curtains. I was usually preoccupied with deciphering what Guy was thinking at moments like this. Any focus on myself was an exercise in self-flagellation, but in a rare moment of peacefulness my awareness shifted gently inward. I sensed an almost audible click—like a channel opening inside of me. I felt absolutely certain that I was pregnant. A spark of joy ignited inside of me. I didn't wake Guy to tell him and I allowed myself to float on a delicious sensation of well-being. After a few self-satisfied minutes, I dozed off.

The following week, Guy waited in the van during my doctor's appointment. When I ran out into the parking lot with a smile on my face, Guy pumped both hands in the air. I had struggled many times to quit smoking cigarettes, but when I found out I was pregnant, the craving vanished entirely. I stopped drinking alcohol and smoking pot, too. But I also instantly began having morning sickness and gaining weight. I rose early to get vomiting out of the way so I could be at the hospital for my 7 a.m. shift. When I checked vital signs, the rhythm of patient's heartbeat could set off waves of nausea. I passed the meal trays twice a day, and the odors wrapped around me and spun me like a top. The halls of the hospital rolled under my feet like the deck of a ship on a stormy sea.

Just as the morning sickness subsided and I was feeling strong and full of energy again, the nursing supervisor transferred me to the Physical Medicine Department. I helped patients in and out of their beds and wheelchairs, transported them to their physical therapy appointments, and lifted them on and off equipment. My legs were swollen and my back ached and I could barely keep my eyes open by the time I drove home every afternoon. When Guy got home, I was usually sound asleep on the couch—still in my nurse's uniform.

I struggled with the new assignment for another month. "Guy, I don't think I can keep doing this job," I said over dinner one evening. "Maybe it's time for me to quit."

"You're being self-indulgent, Sharon." Guy said. "Don't get sucked into those conventional assumptions about how pregnancy affects women. You're not disabled. You'd never hear a black woman complaining like this."

"I'm not saying I'm disabled, Guy, but I shouldn't be doing all this lifting. It's not safe." I said.

"You and Mary—the original cult of weakness! She ran up to Sebastopol to have her mother take care of her the minute she found out she was pregnant. Now the baby is almost nine months old and she's still up there."

I had never known how to defend myself against Guy's criticism. I was usually judging myself as harshly as he was. But I had 15 nieces and nephews and a lifetime of experience with pregnancy, babies, and children. Not to mention my years baby-sitting for spending money. I didn't know how to play whist, or how to hold forth on any number of subjects. I might never be rich or famous, but I knew about pregnancy and childbirth. Although I had ample opportunity to learn the lesson, for the first time in our relationship, I realized that Guy was being cruel. It scared me and pushed my confidence in our relationship a little off its foundation.

One afternoon when I got home from work, I answered the phone and heard Vivian's voice. "Hello, grandmother. How're you doing?" I said.

"I'm well, thank you. How are you feeling, dear?"

I replied without thinking, "I'm having a hard time. I'm feeling really depressed and lonely." There was only silence on her end of the line.

"Sharon, what are you complaining about?" Vivian's voice could have cut glass. "We are born alone and we die alone."

I panicked—my cheeks stung as if she had slapped me. "You're right," I said. "I guess I was just having a little pity party!"

"I have to go," Vivian said. "Tell Guy to call me."

I lay down on the bed and curled around my bulging stomach. Tears pooled under my cheek. Was it a sign of weakness to want some consolation? Isn't that what family was supposed to give you? But I couldn't really imagine Vivian or Maya ever offering Guy any comfort or sweetness when he was a little boy. And he didn't have anyone else—no father or siblings—to give him love. No wonder he didn't know how to be nurturing or tender—he had a childhood filled with sharp angles. I felt a sense of foreboding. If Guy wasn't raised with any compassion and kindness, what kind of a father was he going to be?

CHAPTER THREE

MAYA BOUGHT A RANCH-STYLE HOUSE in the affluent town of Sonoma, 40 miles north of San Francisco. She and Paul were on the road when the sale was finalized and Maya asked Guy to supervise the move and get the new house settled. We drove to Berkeley early on moving day to meet the movers. After they loaded the truck, we led them across the Richmond Bridge and north up Highway 101 towards Sonoma. Guy followed Maya's directions up Arnold Drive and turned right into a small cluster of homes on Country Club Drive across from the well-manicured Sonoma County golf course.

The secluded, single-story home was bright white, with turquoise shutters and trim. It sat alone at the end of the lane, set apart from the other homes by a tall hedge. Guy punched the code into the realtor's box and opened the front door. The airy living room had a high, beamed ceiling and a wide white brick fireplace was built into the far wall. The main room led into a combination kitchen/dining room. Honey-colored wood cabinets hung over a long kitchen counter with a built-in six-burner stove and two deep stainless steel sinks. The room looked out on a patio and swimming pool ringed with cabañas, a thatch-covered bar, and a cooking grill. In the kitchen, the movers arranged the leather barstools next to a long butcher-block island with a wrought iron pot rack hanging from the ceiling. Guy helped assemble the long, rough-hewn table, and set the table and ten ladder-back chairs in front of the plate-glass window. In the distance, the gentle Sonoma County hills rose above the grey, slatted fence that enclosed the back of the house. A footbridge across a narrow creek led to a guest cottage that was surrounded by clumps of pampas grass as tall as its shingled roof.

When the movers left, Guy and I were alone in the jungle of boxes. He pulled the bubble wrap off his mother's stereo, attached the chords, and set the components on the bookcase in the living room. He sat on his heels and opened a box labeled *Music*. "Hey, Mom's got Miles' new album! Listen to this track. It's Miles' tribute to Duke Ellington." I sat on the ledge in front of the brick fireplace. A slow organ rift filled the room. Guy listened for a minute, and then he slit the tape on a box and began sorting books into stacks in the middle of the floor. He seemed to forget I was there as he disappeared into the music and the printed word, his favorite places. He paused to flip through a book and set it aside to borrow from his mother.

In unguarded moments like this, there was a look of innocent wonder on Guy's handsome face. Sometimes I imagined him looking at me with that clear expression of joy, that open smile, his eyes not clouded by judgment and criticism. I wanted so desperately for him to love me, to be happy to be with me—the way I felt about him. As it was, his feelings were a daily puzzle I struggled to solve.

"I'll set up the kitchen," I said. Guy nodded absentmindedly.

I laid down shelf paper and began to fill the cabinets and drawers with Maya's beautiful dishes and expensive utensils, napkins, and tablecloths. I lined up her cookbooks on the slate countertop and secured them in place with carved rosewood bookends of trumpeting elephants. I hung her large cooking pots on the rack and seasoned the surface of the butcher block with olive oil. After a couple of hours, the sun started to go down.

I walked through the house flipping on lights and found Guy sitting in semi-darkness arranging his mother's desk. He jumped when I switched on the overhead light.

"I can't open another box," I said.

"How about dinner?" he asked. "I'll make a run to the store."

"Deal!"

"Are you done with the kitchen?"

"It's all finished. I'm gonna rest till you come back."

When I was a child, my mother did not tolerate idleness. It was an invitation for the devil, she warned. I was trained to keep busy at all times. In college, I couldn't even study until I had cleaned my entire dorm room. I dusted bottles on the bathroom shelf while I sat on the toilet, and leaned over to wipe a drip of shaving cream off the floor with a piece of tissue or refolded the towels hanging on the rack. When I was reading or watching television, I jumped up every few minutes to slip a coaster under a cup, pick a dying leaf off a plant, or whip up a batch of cookies. Now, after only a few months of being pregnant, the immediacy of the phenomenon was elbowing its way ahead of my anxiety. My restless energy was being calmed by an unfamiliar sense of private satisfaction. I could even take a nap, soak in the tub, or sit and watch the sun go down. No matter how idle I appeared, I was still busy making a baby.

Guy returned from the store with grilled chicken and green beans and bright red peppers, and a container of potato salad. The evening was warm, and we ate dinner by the pool, stretched out on padded lounge chairs. Guy looked around and sighed. "I want us to have something like this someday."

I was always reassured when Guy envisioned the future and still pictured us together. He wouldn't see me in his future if he didn't love me, I reasoned. Our relationship might have painful moments, but days like this one, with its companionship and ease, went a long towards quieting my fears that Guy and I might not make it together.

A few weeks later, Maya and Paul came home for several appearances at local bookstores. She was going to be interviewed for *People Magazine* and called and asked us to be with her. "I want to show off my beautiful daughter!" she told me.

"I'll have to buy something to wear. I'm getting bigger and bigger and nothing fits," I said.

"A woman is at her most beautiful during pregnancy!" Maya said. "Don't let that son of mine tell you any different. And see if you can get him to wear something other than that denim work shirt."

"I'm not sure anyone has that power."

"Tell him *I* suggested it," she said.

On the day of the interview, Guy and I pushed through the back gate just as Paul was handing around drinks. I had on a loose orange sundress and even though it was a hot day, Guy wore a long-sleeved orange and blue polo shirt. His long sleeves were pushed up as far as they would go, but his face was already shiny with sweat. Maya sat on the edge of the pool with the hem of her flowing dress bunched up in her hand, her long, brown legs dangling in the water. Her hair was pulled back from her face with an African scarf and her dark skin glowed in the bright afternoon sun. The reporter shaded her eyes and glanced up briefly when Maya made the introductions. The young woman faced Maya, with her back to the two photographers, one by the diving board and the other under the thatched roof of the cabana. We needn't have worried about what we wore. The photographers held their cameras steadily in Maya's direction, clicking away like a swarm of crickets.

Once we were in place behind Maya, mother and son began to weave a practiced spell around the reporter. If tension ever existed between Guy and Maya in private, it was dispatched behind a wall of solidarity and mutual admiration. I had no public persona to step into, so I was quiet. I knew I was only there to provide background color. By now I was familiar with the veil of celebrity that fell over Guy and Maya when they were in public together. It tidied up their diction and decorum. They repeated stories and laughed on cue at each others' familiar asides. Their easy banter had been charming when I first saw them together, but now the routine sounded scripted and choreographed.

As the interview was wrapping up, the reporter turned to me. "You must be very proud to be a part of such an amazing and talented family."

Before I could respond, Maya reached over and squeezed my hand. "I could not imagine a better daughter if I had designed her myself," she put in. "And now I will have a grandchild!"

The tone of the reporter's questions had been that of an admirer and all through the interview she gave Maya every opportunity to express the grace and humor her fans expected. But when Maya received her advance copy of the magazine she was furious. Guy and I stood head to head in the kitchen with the phone between us as his mother read the article out loud. When the upcoming birth of her first grandchild was mentioned, the article referred to me as Guy's white common-law wife. "This is hardly the impression I want people to have of my family—as if we're a bunch of trailer trash," Maya said.

"Overall, it sounds like a pretty good piece, Mom," Guy said.

"I'm going to get that girl fired," she said.

Guy shrugged his shoulders and rolled his eyes. "Don't you think you're overreacting, Mom?"

"She disrespected me, Guy."

"Mom, who cares what it says in *People Magazine*?" Guy said.

"Do you know how many people read this magazine, Guy?" she said. "This will be very bad for my career." Maya hung up the phone, but she called repeatedly throughout the week, still fuming about the article and updating us on her campaign against the reporter.

Like most progressive young couples of that time, Guy and I rejected the institution of marriage, believing that the marriage laws represented government intrusion into a private and intimate relationship. As a good feminist couple, we saw state sanctioned marriage as outdated and a perpetuation of a mindset of ownership that was particularly oppressive to women. Maya knew how we felt, but our conviction did not stop her from suggesting that the best way to circumvent her imagined PR disaster was for Guy and me to get married. I was stunned.

I had been naïve about the effects of being famous. The pressure to live up to the expectations of admirers is intense. Of course, I quickly came to understand that being in the public eye could be brutal and it wasn't hard to accept that the real personality—the private person—would always be different from the celebrity personality. But I was shocked and disheartened to feel Maya's sense of her own importance eclipse the very compassion and graciousness that she was so famous for.

When I first saw this disconnection, she was pacing her living room with a drink in her hand, livid that another author, an author that she was close to, had received a prestigious award that she thought she deserved. It was an ugly scene and I felt bitterly disappointed and disillusioned. After that, the divide between her public and private persona became more of a sharp and surprising contrast to me. Still her expectation that Guy and I would get married for her convenience took the divide to a new level. Guy tried to stand firm, but his mother's will overpowered him. When he acquiesced, my objections vanished into insignificance. Opposing one of them alone was impossible. I either had to get married, or make a much more drastic decision.

I didn't call my family to tell them I was getting married. This wasn't like a real wedding after all, I thought, only pro forma. We weren't even getting rings. And how could I explain why we were getting married in the first place? My sisters wouldn't believe that Guy was suddenly overcome by a wave of romantic sentimentality. And I was still avoiding the truth—that Guy was powerless in the face of his mother's demands and that I was even more powerless against his. It was easier to exclude my family entirely.

I drifted into autopilot. I sleepwalked through my shifts at the hospital, my evenings at home, and my housework. Guy and I even made love. Then on Friday, July 25, 1975, Guy and I drove to our wedding ceremony at the office of the Justice of the Peace in Santa Rosa. Maya and Paul would be there. Norman would be there and Guy's long-time friends Steve and Carol were driving up from Berkeley to be our witnesses.

It was only early in the morning, but the day was already hot. We were both tense and argued all the way from Stockton to Santa Rosa. "What good is it having a social consciousness, Guy, if you don't stand by your beliefs?"

Guy banged the steering wheel with the heel of his hand. "This doesn't mean anything, Sharon! It's just a piece of paper."

"Yes, I understand that," I said. "Why didn't you tell that to your mother?"

Guy was already inured to this. "You don't understand what it's like having the whole world watching and judging everything you do," he said. Guy was channeling Maya's sentiments verbatim. "We're a part of something bigger than ourselves now, Sharon. You have to accept that." We drove without talking until we reached Santa Rosa.

Guy turned the van down the tree-lined road that led to the Sonoma County administration complex. He finally broke the silence. "Do you think people still have you say, '...love, honor and obey'? I think I read something about the woman having to say 'obey,' but not the man. Do you know?"

"I have no idea, Guy." My tone was clipped.

"That's so patriarchal, don't you think? If the Justice of the Peace says the vows that way, you shouldn't say 'obey.'"

I watched the flat buildings of the county complex go by and tried not to roll my eyes.

We parked the van and waited in front of the administration building for everyone to arrive. I was already uncomfortable. I had on a striped cotton sweater—the only top I had that covered my belly—and, of necessity, the zipper on my green pants was only partially closed and it was cutting into my skin. I sat down on a metal bench and watched Guy. He looked angry as he paced back and forth across the brick courtyard. Even though I was upset, my mind drifted to how handsome he looked. I had embroidered a long-stemmed red rose on the right thigh of his navy pants, and he was wearing his blue and white rugby shirt with the white collar. When Paul and Maya arrived, I had a private chuckle—Maya was wearing a long white dress.

We made our way up the elevator to the office of the Justice of the Peace and crowded into the small room. An old man in a thin-lapelled suit stood up behind his desk, and Guy and I maneuvered to a spot in the front of the gathering and introduced ourselves. When the room settled, the man gave a small smile and acknowledged us. He turned to Guy and began to speak. "Do you, Guy Bailey Johnson, take this woman, Sharon Ann Murphy, to be your lawfully wedding wife, to love and honor her as long as you both shall live?"

Guy hesitated and looked down at me. He turned back to the old man and said, "And obey...I promise to love, honor and obey," he said.

The man looked down at his notebook and back up to Guy. "You don't have to say that."

"Does Sharon have to say *obey*?" Guy asked.

"No."

"Oh, then...Yes. I mean...uh, I do." Guy said.

The JP turned to face me. "Do you ..."

"Excuse me," I interrupted. "Can I get a clarification as to whether Guy did or did not promise to obey me?" Everyone behind us snickered.

The man's wrinkled cheeks flushed. "No. I believe his vow was to love and honor."

"Too bad!" I said.

We completed the formalities and after a few signatures and handshakes, the brief ceremony was over. In an attempt to safeguard our standing as an enlightened couple, we combined our names. We were now Sharon and Guy Murphy-Johnson and our baby would be Alexis or Colin Murphy-Johnson.

Shortly after we got married, Guy and I attended a house party in San Francisco. Guy stood with his arm around my shoulder and announced the news about the baby. He looked happy and proud as we received everyone's congratulations. We weren't wearing wedding rings, so it wasn't obvious that we had gotten married and Guy didn't mention it. I knew it was ridiculous to think it mattered, but I felt slighted and hurt. Maya's and Guy's focus had been entirely on the baby—her grandson and Guy's son. My baby books cautioned the mother-to-be not to focus all her attention on the upcoming birth to the exclusion of the father. But we were moving into the converse of that typical scenario.

As the party progressed, a group gathered on the front porch with their instruments. A young man was playing *Boogie on Reggae Woman* on his guitar. I walked outside and sat down with my legs extended along the top step. I sang along, keeping time with my foot. When the song ended, Guy burst onto the porch and shoved his way through the crowd. "Let's go," he mumbled. Once we were in the car, his eyes narrowed into slits. "What was that come-on all about?" he demanded.

"What are you talking about?"

"Shaking your legs like that? Do you think I couldn't see you?"

"Are you kidding? I wasn't ..." But I had learned the hard way that when Guy withdrew behind his wall of anger, chasing him into that dark place only invited further attack. The best thing to do was to tolerate the cold banishment.

When we got home, Guy stormed into his office. I heard the scratch of a match and wasn't surprised when the aroma of weed drifted under the door. My pride kept me from apologizing for something I didn't do, and my anxiety kept me from opening the door to continue the argument by saying that he was being unreasonable. I stood frozen in the dark hallway, staring at the closed door. I lay down on the couch with my book and finally dozed off. When I woke up, the house was dark except for a dim strip of light under the office door. I tapped on the door and went in. Guy didn't turn from his desk. I walked over and leaned into his back. I wrapped my arms around his shoulders and rested my head on the soft cushion of his dark hair.

"Let's go to bed," I whispered. I ran my hand down his arm, and he let me lead him into the bedroom. We sat down next to each other on our bed. "Guy, you know I didn't mean anything by what I was doing, don't you?"

"I know," Guy looked down at his hands. "When I saw you sitting next to that guy, I felt a rush of jealousy. I couldn't shake it!" Guy was lost in thought for a moment. He turned to me and said, "Thank you. Thank you for coming in to get me. If it wasn't for you, our arguments would never end."

"I love you, Guy."

"I love you, too," he said. He turned and put his hand on the slight bulge of my stomach. It was the first time he had tried to feel the baby. "You know I love you, don't you?"

"I'd like to hear it more often, but yes, I know you love me."

Sex had always been a guaranteed way for Guy and me to reconnect after a period of distance. But once my pregnancy began to show, Guy decided that we shouldn't have sex anymore.

"It's not good for the baby," he said.

I was shocked that he could hold such a Victorian belief. "Guy, pregnant women can have sex," I said.

"I don't care what it says in those magazines you're reading! I don't think it's a good idea. And please don't walk around without clothes on." The look on his face hurt and humiliated me. To Guy, my pregnant body seemed unrelated to the highly anticipated birth of his child—as if the transformation was only an unpleasant side effect. Nevertheless, I made certain that he never saw me undressed after that. Being pregnant became my own private wonderland. I thought the physicality of my pregnancy was fascinating. My hair was thicker and my skin had never looked better. The changes in my breasts, the full feeling, and the flutters deep within me were incredible to me.

When Guy was not at home, I stripped down and examined myself in front of the full-length mirror, marveling at my protruding profile. I would lie on my back and listen to the baby's heartbeat with my stethoscope. I'd tom-tom on my stomach to feel the reaction and laugh at the undulations when the baby tumbled inside of me. My relationship with this little person was already off to an amazing beginning.

One wet evening a few months later, Guy and I pulled into the driveway of our Stockton home. He sat motionless, staring through the windshield with his hand still on the key. The porch light reflected off of a tear as it slid from behind Guy's thick glasses and down his cheek. He brushed the tear away with the back of his hand. "Guy, what happened? What's the matter?" I said. Then I held my breath.

"I have to tell you something."

"Okay."

"I slept with someone while I was in San Francisco last weekend."

I dropped my face into my hands. Guy leaned closer and put his hand on the back of my neck. "I want you to know that I felt so incredibly guilty, that I had to stop before I came."

I shoved him away. "Is that supposed to make me feel better? Why are you telling me this?"

"I wanted to be honest with you. Believe me, it will never happen again!"

He pulled me into his chest and my seatbelt cut across my huge belly. I rested my forehead against the lapel of his pea coat and Guy patted me in an awkward gesture of consolation. I pushed away. I looked into his face and watched his look of misery drain away. He gave me a dim smile.

I was witnessing the reverse of the quick shift I had grown used to when Guy dropped into his pit of anger. He had unburdened himself—the problem was over, dealt with—time for me to appreciate his honesty. I climbed carefully down from the van onto the slippery driveway, and slammed the car door in an impotent demonstration of my anger and hurt. My heavy load threw me off-balance and I steadied myself on the side of the van. Guy watched me through the glass with a blank expression. I was weighed down by sadness at this glimpse of the underpinnings of Guy's character.

I wouldn't have admitted it then, but deep inside I knew why Guy was upset. He wasn't in turmoil because he had broken his word to me or because he'd hurt me. No, he was upset because being unfaithful to his pregnant wife contradicted the noble image he had of himself. Only a lesser man would act like that. Not Guy. He needed to get that burden off his chest so he could reinstate his belief in his own good character. His guilt was cold comfort to me. He hadn't even said that he was sorry.

But Guy wasn't the only one who helped to maintain the fantasy of an enlightened character. Over the years, I've grown to accept that Maya and I were also invested in this image of Guy, each in our own way. She had her version of it—Guy as the good and loyal son, the product of all her noble sacrifices—sacrifices that were the stuff of literature. For me, the idea of Guy as an enlightened man of unimpeachable honesty and integrity validated the u-turn I'd supposedly taken from that poor Oklahoma girl destined for the altar and the suburbs. But there was mounting evidence that Guy was not the extraordinary man Maya and I needed him to be. Guy was undeniably charismatic, intelligent and articulate, but in many ways he was a weak and spiteful man who proclaimed convenient principles that may not have been rooted in his real nature. But we all had a stake in his being someone different—someone better—than the man he really was.

Now in Stockton, the people we were around most of the time were Guy's new boss and his wife, our first friends in our new home. I wasn't very interested in Daniel and Dana. I could never think of much to say when we were all together, but they made a good audience for Guy, who commanded center stage as usual. He and I got along better when other people were around, so I welcomed the nights when we all were together.

Not long after Guy's confession of infidelity, he and Daniel went out for a drink after work. The night was dreary and stormy. When Guy wasn't home by 10:30, I went to bed. By then, we'd begun living parallel lives so there was little reason to wait up for him. I wasn't smoking pot, his nighttime ritual, and there was never any sex or even physical affection. The clock read 12:15 when the snap of his lighter woke me. He was sitting on the edge of the bed in his boxer shorts, smoking a pungent bud in his pipe. The only other light in the room was a faint glow from the streetlight through our bedroom window so I could only see Guy's silhouette. I reached out and ran my hand up and down his warm back.

He lay down beside me and propped himself up on one elbow. The alcohol and pot were strong on his breath. "I think our son should play a musical instrument," he said.

For a moment I had hoped that he was going to talk about his evening. He usually told funny stories about the things that Daniel said, still awkward with his first black friend. I felt a pang of disappointment. "I'd like to have a piano in the house, but you can't decide what a child's going to be good at," I said.

"Children don't know what's best for them!" Guy scoffed.

I felt an argument coming and I adopted a lighter tone. "True, but they aren't empty vessels either. They're complete little packages when they're born. You'll see."

Guy began to worry aloud, gesturing into our darkened bedroom as if he was addressing someone standing in the shadows. "Maybe white children can go through life only doing what they like to do. Your family is a good example of wasted potential, another cult of weakness."

Guy looked down and studied my face as if he had never seen me before. His blank expression was frightening—then he brought his face closer to mine. I could feel his breath on my cheeks. "A black child has to be strong to deal with all the assholes in this world." His words slurred. He was drunker than

I had thought. His voice became a low growl. "I know what our child will face in this world—you have no idea!"

My heart was pounding and I tried to diffuse his anger. "Guy, don't worry. Our kids will have two parents to love and protect them. They will not be alone in this world." I reached up to touch his face but he shoved my hand away.

"I can see it now," he said. His voice was fierce. "You're gonna raise our child to be a weak little white boy. You won't be able to do it any other way. I know you'll project your attitude of racism towards our child."

"Guy, what are you talking about?"

His eyes flashed with hatred. "A white woman could never give a black child the upbringing he needs to survive in this world." He jabbed his finger in my face.

My cheeks began to burn and I put a protective hand on my belly. Out of the darkness a voice in me whispered, "Run." Panicked, I jumped out of bed and slipped my feet into a pair of clogs. Without a clear thought of what I was doing, I grabbed my purse and sweater off the chair and rushed out through the front door and onto the porch. When I closed the door behind me, the shock of the cold night air jolted me out of my frenzy. What was I doing? Guy would be furious that I ran away from him. I pulled my sweater around me and stood frozen in the halo of the porch light, but I couldn't make myself go back into that house.

I gripped the railing and held my belly with the other hand as I walked carefully down the wet porch steps and got into my car. I started the engine and sat idling in the driveway; the heater of my Barracuda did a poor job against the cold winter drizzle. My heart hammered in my chest and the baby began to kick. I swirled my hands over my belly and repeated, "It's okay, little baby. Everything's okay."

I know it was naïve, but before that night, I didn't believe that having a bi-racial child was an issue for Guy. Somehow, I thought we were past those considerations. Maya had broached the subject with me a few times. She wanted me to understand that parents of black children have to make a conscious effort to offset the damage that racial prejudice can have on a child's self image. Vivian, Maya and I had some great conversations about it. When Guy was young, Maya's told me that her technique was to reassure him that his ancestors, who had been stripped of their birthright and sealed in the belly of the slave ships, had paid for his place in the world with their suffering. He was the descendent of royalty and he must always think of himself as the prince that he surely was. I took her point but I also believed that a positive self image would never be a problem for our child.

Still, Guy had been enraged at the thought that I would be the mother of his child. Was he only now coming to terms with this? What if he actually believed that I had nothing to offer my own child? I had long since accepted that whites have little to say in the discussion about racism (except to other whites), but this was *my* child and I wasn't taking a backseat because I was white. Mothering is a state more primal than race.

My heartbeat was returning to normal when Guy's silhouette took shape behind the living room curtain. I expected him to open the door and look outside for me, but instead he switched off the porch light and I was engulfed in darkness. I burst into tears and flipped the car into reverse. I shot out of the driveway and drove to the end of the block, and then aimlessly through the deserted streets of Stockton. Then, in the middle of a downtown intersection, my car chugged to a stop— the gas gauge was on empty.

"Shit! Shit! Shit!" I banged on the steering wheel in frustration, crying until I was gasping for breath. When my sobs began to subside, I got out of the car. Wearing only my thin nightgown and bulky sweater, and with my enormous belly pressed against the hatchback, I pushed and shoved my Barracuda until it rested against the curb. I walked down the dark, unfamiliar street until I found a pay phone. I pulled out a handful of coins and flipped through the pages of my address book. I had pages of names of people who would have been happy to help me, but they were all far away. My family was even more distant. I didn't want to call Guy. With no other option, I dialed the phone number for Guy's boss.

After a few rings, Daniel's wife answered the phone. "Dana? I'm sorry to wake you. It's Sharon. Uh, I'm so sorry, but Guy and I had a fight and I took off in the car. Now I'm out of gas. Would you mind coming to get me, please?"

I gave her the intersection and ten minutes later, Daniel pulled alongside my Barracuda. "Do you want me to drive you home?" he asked, looking a bit chagrined.

"If you don't mind, I don't want to go home right now."

"Don't worry about it. I know what it's like." He leaned over and pushed open the passenger door.

When we arrived at their house, Dana opened the front door and I walked in—humiliated and embarrassed. Daniel disappeared down the hall, saying over his shoulder, "I'll call Guy and tell him you're okay." Dana made up a bed on the couch. I thanked her and was grateful when the house fell quiet.

I lay in the dark replaying the scenes of the last few hours and thought of other times I had run for my life—or felt like I was running for my life. I remembered countless times my mother would scream like a crazy woman and chase me through the house, arms flailing. "Come back here and let me hit you," she would yell. If I could, I escaped into my bedroom and held the door closed, while Mother banged and shoved her shoulder against it from the other side. If she got between me and an escape route, she grabbed me by the hair and shook my head, or dug her long nails into my arm. If I stood defiant when she was angry and didn't employ any protective tactics, she'd slap me across the mouth with her open hand. I remembered seeing bright stars and more than once feeling like I was blacking out. Mother didn't hold back when she was in a rage. She'd swing at me with whatever she could get her hands on—wooden spoons, rulers, or her large hand mirror. Another time, she lobbed potatoes at me when she lost her temper while she was cooking dinner. One terrible day, I blocked a blow to my face and she bit me on the tender inside of my arm. She broke the skin and the bruises remained vivid and purple for weeks. These were common scenes when I lived at home—and only stopped because I no longer lived there. I was no stranger to family violence, but I'd moved to California to get away from this, and here I was again, running because I was afraid.

But surely, I'd left that kind of violence behind me. Guy might have a temper, but he would never hit me, I told myself. I should get over that impulse to run when I felt afraid; it was just a learned response to fear. If I wanted to stop reacting in such a rash manner, I had to learn the difference between anger and the threat of violence. Now I'd made the situation worse by acting as if Guy was going to hurt me. I fell asleep feeling confident that I was taking my share of the responsibility for escalating the argument—an argument that involved some very real issues that Guy and I needed to come to terms with calmly and rationally.

The next morning, Guy was drinking coffee in the living room when Daniel and I walked into the house. I wanted to start apologizing immediately when I saw him. He gave Daniel a nod and stood up to shake his hand. Guy looked hung-over and was still in his long johns and t-shirt. He slung his arm around my shoulder, and gave me a sidelong hug.

"Hormones run riot, huh?" he laughed. I put my arm around Guy's waist and looked down at the floor. I had the best of intentions. I was going to have a serious talk with him about the things that had spilled out in anger the night before. It was critical to clear the air, but that conversation would never materialize.

Guy's position with the city of Stockton was funded for by a federal block grant. When the grant money ran out at the end of the 1975 fiscal year, the city didn't pick up the funding for Guy's position. Daniel could do nothing to help and Guy found himself unemployed once again. The baby was due on January 28, 1976.

I had already quit my job at the hospital, so we were without any income and we had no savings. Maya offered to let us stay in her guest house until the baby was born. The strain between Guy and me was unchanged—the smallest interchange could erupt into a fight. I was nervous at the prospect of having to put on a happy face for his mother, but I was very glad to leave the barrenness of Stockton and be back among the rolling, sweet-smelling hills of Sonoma County. It wasn't San Francisco, but it still was closer to home.

Guy and I stored our belongings in Maya's garage and settled into the tiny two-room cottage across the little creek from the main house. Guy enlisted some of his buddies to come up to help Paul move the wooden footbridge closer to the cottage and clear the pampas grass from along the edge of the creek. I was glad to hear Guy laughing with Norman and Mickey. We had been so isolated in Stockton, no wonder we hadn't been getting along, I thought.

I put everything out of my mind except the approaching birth and when my focus was on the baby, I was totally happy. I set up my sewing machine in the small kitchen of the guest house and made baby blankets and drawstring sleepers. I made a skirt for Maya out of the Kente cloth she brought back from Africa, and embroidered more long stemmed roses on Guy's new navy pants. I sat on our bed surrounded by pillows and did my kegels and read about water births, creating a focal point, Lamaze breathing, and the importance of breastfeeding. I applied Mothers' Friend with a light effleurage to my ever-expanding belly to sooth the baby and prevent stretch marks. Maya made me fresh-squeezed orange juice every morning and ordered me to the cottage in the afternoon for naps. I helped her with meals and we sang together and we sat around the table together watching the sunset colors of the Sonoma County sky. The atmosphere was peaceful and comfortable and free of the tension I had anticipated. Guy and I walked in the field next to the house in the evenings. A truce was seemingly in place.

Maya put out the word about the upcoming birth and cards enclosing checks and packages containing extravagant baby gifts began arriving almost daily from people around the world. I felt as if I was stealing another woman's gifts. Sometimes even Guy didn't know the person whose name appeared on the card. Sel, Maya's secretary, mailed my thank you notes and letters to my sisters. She arranged my mail on the kitchen counter next to my prenatal vitamins, made my doctor's appointments, and confirmed my arrangements with the birthing center at the Sonoma Community Hospital.

Maya decided to throw a party in honor of the upcoming birth. On the day of the party, she got up early to prepare a ham encrusted with sugar and pineapple, creamy potato salad, and pans of fluffy corn bread. Paul soaked ribs in a dark marinade and made trips into town for last minute necessities. It was a mild January day, sunny enough for guests to be out by the pool. Guy set up the outside bar with mixers and bottles of scotch and bourbon and carafes for red and white wine. He ran cables from the stereo and hung speakers next to the pool. I sat on a high stool ironing the table cloths for Maya's long dining table. Delicious aromas, music, and laughter filled every corner of the house by mid-afternoon.

Mary drove down from Sebastopol for the party. She and I had exchanged brief notes and funny cards and she sent me pictures of her baby from time to time, but I hadn't seen them in months. Mary's daughter was a petite little girl. She had Norman's almond shaped eyes and straight black hair. She was so small, she looked too young to be walking, but she was almost a year old and toddled around with confidence. Mary and I sat by the pool to catch up. Bea and Norman had offered to pay for her to move back to her hometown of Banning, in Southern California, and Mary had accepted. She had even enrolled in college there. This was the first time I heard about this plan and I was sad to realize how much our friendship had changed. In the past, Mary and I would have talked about every nuance of the plan as it developed. I was used to knowing everything about her, what she ate for lunch, what book she was reading, and how she felt about every detail of her life. I felt a painful void where our deep bond had been.

Among the very familiar faces at the party, Vivian and Uncle Knowledge, Norman, Mickey, Charlie, and a few of the roommates from Henry Street, there were a greater number of people who I only recognized from the media, their book jackets, or album covers. Even though Cecil Williams from Glide Methodist Church in San Francisco was a celebrity in his own right, I could talk with him and his wife, Jan. My community work, especially my job with Model Cities, gave us something in common. I thought I was getting more comfortable being around Maya's friends until James Baldwin waltzed through the front door with his handsome young boyfriend. Maya introduced us and my inner Okie popped right out as I got as tongue-tied as a star-struck teenager.

Once the party was in full swing, the event naturally divided into two groups—the fabulously famous and the not famous at all. Maya and her cohorts stood talking and laughing on one side of the living room and our friends hung out in the kitchen and slipped outside every few minutes to share a joint. As the party wound down, Vivian and Maya and I stood together in the center of the living room.

"Thank you for all your work, Mom. The party was wonderful," I gave Maya a brief cheek-to-cheek hug.

"The first of many parties I'll throw for my grand," she said. "The Grand" was how she had begun to refer to the baby.

"I wish I felt more at ease around your friends. They're so amazing and accomplished! I can't find anything to say. I almost swallowed my tongue when I met James Baldwin."

"Listen, Sharon," Maya put her hand on my arm and brought me closer. "Some people travel to the far corners of the world searching for the grace that you have naturally. You may not have traveled far, but you've developed insight from the life you've led. Success only gives people the opportunity to learn—it's not a guarantee."

"But I've noticed that grace doesn't pay as well as success does!" I said.

Maya smiled and threw up her hands. "Speak the truth, baby girl!"

Early one afternoon, I was writing a letter to my sisters at Maya's dining table. Guy sat across from me, reading the newspaper and sipping a glass of wine. I was still not drinking alcohol and sucked on one of the frozen orange juice bars that I had been craving.

"Surprise!" Maya walked towards me with a stack of brightly wrapped packages. Guy reached for the bottle on the sideboard, poured his mother a glass of scotch, and returned to the sports section. Maya piled boxes on the table and took a seat next to me. "I felt like giving you some baby gifts early," she said.

"Yippee!" I said. "It's been hours and hours since anyone gave me a present."

Maya laughed and handed me a small box. It was a heavy silver child's cup. "See, there's a place here where I'll have the baby's name engraved."

"It's beautiful. Look, Guy," I said.

One box contained a brightly painted clown lamp and the largest package was a striped diaper bag brimming over with tiny t-shirts and sleepers, receiving blankets, and bath sets. I was gratified to see that Maya had followed my suggestion and that the baby clothes were all yellow. (Yellow had been designated, for some unknown reason, as a gender-neutral color by the panel of political correctness.) I emptied the bag of all the tiny gifts and Maya slid her hand inside the bag. "There are slots on the inside for bottles," she said.

"Oh, I'm going to breastfeed, remember."

"I know that. But you'll need bottles for water and juice." A sharp edge crept into her tone.

Guy's eyes darted up from the newspaper and quickly returned to the page.

"No water, no juice. Breast milk is all the baby needs for at least six months," I asserted.

Maya's smiling face melted into a stony glare. Her wide-set eyes narrowed in that familiar way that Guy had. "Well, what sort of hippie nonsense is that?" she said. "You'll be dehydrating my grandchild."

My face flushed with embarrassment. Seconds before, I had been comfortable and happy, and then in a flash, as it so often happened with Guy, Maya shifted from my friend to my adversary. There was no small difference of opinion or mild reaction with either of them. We both looked over at Guy. He glanced up and his eyes darted from his mother to me and back again, then he lowered his head behind the paper.

Maya picked up her drink and turned to leave the room. "Well, it's your baby," she tossed over her shoulder.

"Guy?" I whispered.

"What?" He sounded like a petulant child.

"Why didn't you back me up?"

"Why do you have to argue with her?" Guy shook his head. "She's the authority on motherhood. Ask anyone." He gestured to the stack of fan mail piled up at the end of the table, letters from women all over the world asking for her advice.

"Oh, it's easy for those women. They don't have to live in the real world with her!" I said.

Maya received a letter from the Woman's Club of Sonoma requesting permission to host a baby shower for me. She showed me the letter and smiled. "They finally found an acceptable ploy to entice me to one of their gatherings," she said. "I suppose this one is unavoidable. Oh well, we can get all dressed up. You're bound to make a haul." The decision made, Maya told Sel to call and accept the invitation on my behalf.

"But I don't have anything to wear to a dressy party," I said.

"I'll take you shopping!"

Shopping and dressing up was the last thing I wanted to do. My due date was one week away and my belly was enormous. I couldn't get in or out of chairs without help. I was uncomfortable and breathless all day and all night, and in every position. My mother had sent me a long brown shapeless dress that had become my uniform. If I raised my arms to shoulder level, the dress resembled a dreary, square tablecloth with white lace along the edges. However, at this stage in the pregnancy, with one of Guy's big t-shirts underneath, it was a perfect maternity outfit. Regardless of my resistance, Maya took me shopping in Sonoma the next day. Once inside the cramped maternity boutique on the Square, the walls began to close in on me. I couldn't breathe and I felt faint. I escaped to the park across the street while Maya made the final selection.

On the day of the shower, I took two pairs of Queen-sized panty hose and cut them in half up the crotch, leaving the elastic waistbands intact. I hooked my toe into the waistband and wiggled my way into each separate leg—first one side, and then the other. I was sweating and lightheaded by the time the stockings were arranged. The two waistbands were stretched taut under my breasts and the center seams cut into the outer perimeter of my belly. I worked my swollen feet into my dress shoes and pulled the blue maternity dress over my head. I considered myself in the mirror. The dress had a white collar and lacy bows down the front. I resembled an enormous Shirley Temple doll.

When we arrived at our hostess's home, the well-groomed members of the Woman's Club gushed and Maya cooed. I've always felt frumpy around women like this, but Maya had been astute in her observation that giving me a shower was just an excuse to win her attendance. When I introduced myself to the ladies of Sonoma, they offered me limp handshakes while they kept their heavily lined eyes on Maya. I didn't mind the role of handmaiden to the queen; it felt appropriate under the circumstances. But one woman crossed the line. She patted my stomach without even looking at my face and said to her friend, "Ahhh, the grandchild!" I felt like a human incubator and moved away from the crowd.

The sideboard in the pastel living room was piled high with professionally wrapped gifts under a mobile of fat cherubs in pink and blue togas. I lowered myself into a champagne-colored wingback chair next to a table filled with platters of hors d'oeuvres. I nibbled on finger sandwiches and Madeleines and concentrated on keeping my knees together until it was time to go home.

In the weeks before the baby was born, Maya was finishing her new book. She spent most of her time in a room in a small hotel in Sonoma with a stack of yellow pads and a bottle of scotch. When *Singin' and Swingin' and Gettin' Merry Like Christmas* was mailed off to Random House, we all gathered in the hotel lounge to celebrate. Maya invited her friend, Jessica Mitford, and Jessica's husband, Bob Treuhaft, to join us. We ate a beautiful dinner and then sang with the white-haired gentleman at the piano bar. Even with a heavy load elbowing my lungs, I made Paul cry with my rendition of *Danny Boy*. Maya and I ended the evening with my favorite song from *Funny Girl* ... *Oh, my man, I love him so, he'll never know. All my life is just despair, but I don't care when he takes me in his arms, the world is bright, all right ...*

My due date arrived and passed but the baby was content to stay put. On the last weekend in January, Vivian and Uncle Knowledge drove up from Stockton to celebrate the completion of Maya's new book. Carol and Steve drove up from Berkeley for the afternoon. Vivian baked Chianti chicken for lunch and Maya made one of her famous salads.

Steve and Guy bent over their guitars on Maya's couch. Steve was slim with a pale redhead's complexion. He wore his copper hair in a long braid down his back. Steve was a professional musician and Guy respected his incredible breadth of musical knowledge. Guy's respect allowed him to graciously accept Steve's musical advice. He was a stark contrast to Guy's 6'5" frame, dark hair, and brown skin.

Carol was narrow and thin with a prim, prissy manner. She often twisted her long, ash brown hair into a tight bun on top of her head and covered it with an old-fashioned snood. Carol worked as a nurse in the newborn nursery at Alta Bates Hospital in Berkeley. Carol longed to have children, but after ten years of trying, she was struggling to accept that they might never have a baby of their own. Over the months of my pregnancy, Carol developed a proprietary interest in our baby and firmly announced that our kids would refer to them as Aunt Carol and Uncle Steve.

After lunch, the four of us took a drive to visit the shops and wineries in Yountville, a tourist town 20 miles away, over steep, switch-back roads through the hills of Napa Valley. By the time we pulled up to the first winery, I was sweating and nauseous. Carol led me to the ladies' room and while I steadied myself against the sink, she held a wet paper towel to my forehead. When I didn't feel any better after an hour, Carol insisted that we leave. "I think she's in labor," she told Guy.

It was 7 p.m. by the time we got home. I crawled into bed and my contractions began in earnest. Reluctantly, Carol and Steve went home and Maya and Paul were put on baby alert. Guy kept the hospital appraised by phone. I dozed between contractions while Guy finally read the pamphlets that I had been putting in front of him for months. In the wee hours of the morning, I was ready to go to the hospital. In those few hours Guy had become an expert on natural childbirth.

As a Christmas present, my mother had given me yet another in a lifelong collection of indestructible polyester robes. My current model was red with shiny rose appliqués. I looked like a giant tomato, but the familiarity of the style was comforting and I wanted to wear it to the hospital. I zipped up my robe over a big t-shirt and Guy helped me slip my feet into a pair of white socks and soft, fuzzy slippers. I leaned against him as he led me across the wooden footbridge. He settled me in the van with the heater running and ran into the main house to let Maya and Paul know that it was time to go to the hospital. I waited and waited for him to return.

Contractions came and went—nothing too bad yet. I knew I had a long way to go. Finally, Guy walked slowly out of the house. He climbed into the driver's seat and shut off the engine. "They're coming with us. Mom wants us to wait until they get dressed."

"Wait! Are you kidding me?"

"They're flying out for a book signing tomorrow morning and she wants to be ready to get on the plane."

"They know where the hospital is," I said. "Why do we have to wait?"

Guy sighed and fingered the keys in the ignition. After a few minutes, Maya and Paul came out of the house and hurried to the car carrying their luggage. Maya was wrapped in her full-length fur coat. The lights from the house glinted off her diamond bracelet as she gave me a cheery wave. I waved back without enthusiasm. They followed us along Highway 12 to the hospital and paused behind us every time Guy pulled onto the shoulder of the road so I could vomit out of the side of the van.

We parked side-by-side in the deserted parking lot. Guy rushed into the hospital and returned with an attendant and a wheelchair. The young orderly eased me out of the car and into the chair. Maya and Paul walked on either side of me and Guy led the way as our entourage headed for the entrance, Paul in his perfectly tailored suit, Maya in her fur coat and diamonds, and me in my bright red robe and fuzzy slippers.

"I'm sorry to be so under-dressed for the occasion," I said between cleansing breaths.

Maya patted my shoulder. "People treat you better when you're well-dressed," she said.

"Maybe you could let me wear that diamond bracelet then," I said.

"You're such a smart ass, Sharon," Maya laughed.

Once inside, the orderly pushed me into the elevator and we rode up to Labor and Delivery together. A single nurse wheeled me to a private labor room, while three nurses showed Paul and Maya to the family waiting area across the hall. As the door closed between us, I heard someone say, "Can I get you some coffee, Miss Angelou?"

The nurse helped me into bed and Guy commandeered an extra bedside table and set up the floating candle I brought to use as my focal point. He unpacked his blue pen and the *New York Times* crossword puzzle book, pulled a chair close to the bed, and began to rapidly fill in the small squares.

Labor was a new sensation, but I tolerated the pain and managed the contractions for the next couple of hours. I surrendered to the process as it overtook me—what choice did I have? I was even able to doze off between the sharp, gripping sensations.

At first, I thought that the hospital had an amazingly high nurse-to-patient ratio. Maybe there were so many nurses because I was in a private room, I thought. A steady stream of orderlies and nurses came in to check my vital signs, refill my water and ice, and replace my sweat-soaked sheets. Then one nurse leaned over my bed to whisper, "Is that really Maya Angelou out there?" Then I realized that I was only the co-star at my own delivery. Several hours into labor, Maya and Paul came in to say their good-byes and head off to the airport. After they left, the level of attention I received dramatically declined.

As a gift, Maya had paid for the delivery at the newly remodeled Birthing Center including both a private labor room and a private room on the maternity ward. What Maya didn't know was that as soon as Guy lost his job, I had waddled into the Welfare office in Stockton and applied for Medi-Cal. Once we were at Maya's house, I had kept an eye out for the Medi-Cal cards to arrive, so I could snatch them out of the mailbox before Maya's secretary collected the mail. As soon as morning came and the business office opened, Guy disappeared from my bedside. He was going to try to exchange a Medi-Cal sticker for a cash refund. If he could arrange it, the cash would give some relief to our pitiful financial situation. When Guy returned, he gave me a wink which told me that his trip had been a success.

By the time the nursing shift changed, my contractions stopped entirely. My nurse injected pitocin into the IV to help them along. After a few minutes, the drug kicked in and the contractions slammed into me. As the hours crept by, the intensity of the labor pains shocked me and I started getting scared. This did not feel right. Something was wrong. I thought of the little baby in the center of this hurricane of pain and grew even more frightened.

Guy stayed by my side, eyes wide, and sweat poured down his face. His hand was hot and clammy when he placed it on my arm. "Breathe slower, calm yourself by breathing slower." Guy gave a demonstration of how my breathing should be. "You're doing it wrong, Sharon."

By noon, I was done with this. "Guy, you have to get out of here before I kill you!" The nurses encouraged him to go take a break. He walked out to join a group of our friends who had arrived to share the day with us.

A dark-haired nurse appeared at my side. "Hello, Sharon, my name is Helen." Her hand was cool and dry on my arm. She looked into my eyes and smiled with a heavenly glow. "It's okay. You're doing great! This is a rough labor and I know you're tired. We could give you an epidural if you want."

"No! I want a natural birth," I cried.

"Okay, a natural birth is better for your baby. You're doing a very brave thing for your little one," she said. There was a calm tone of authority and reassurance in Helen's voice.

When Guy returned, I was sitting in a padded chair, gripping my IV pole, while Helen changed my sheets. "What day is it?" I asked

"Monday, February second." Then Guy laughed. "Hey, it's Groundhog Day!"

"... and Marilyn is supposed to show up today," I said.

Guy's smile faded at the prospect of seeing my sister again. "She'd better keep her opinions to herself," he said.

Marilyn had recently attended a weeklong feminist conference in Connecticut where she had fallen head-over-heels in love with a woman. When she got home from Sagaris, she came out to Jack and asked for a divorce. In an amazingly speedy transition, Marilyn embarked on a new life as a radical lesbian feminist. Our visit had been planned for the week after my due date so Marilyn could see the baby and I could meet her new lover, Lynn. Naively, I had assumed that the baby would come on time and that I would feel well enough for a visit. Now Marilyn and Lynn were going to show up right in the middle of the birth.

Early in the afternoon, Marilyn pushed open the heavy door to my room and gave me a big smile. "Well, this isn't the visit we planned, is it?" She looked around the room for Guy.

"The coast is clear! He's taking a break," I said.

"Good timing!" She kissed me on the lips and smoothed the hair away from my face. A small woman with cocoa-colored skin and a bushy halo of dark hair came through the door. She wore a pair of khaki pants and a white shirt with a blue tailored jacket. "Sharon, this is Lynn." Marilyn clamped her thumbnail between her front teeth and gave a quick upward jerk of her eyebrows. "She's my blazer-dyke!"

"Oh, Marilyn, stop embarrassing me." Lynn stepped towards the bed and put a gentle hand on my shoulder. "It's good to meet you, Sharon. I hope I'm not intruding."

Before I could answer, a contraction took my focus. "I'll get the nurse," Marilyn said and she and Lynn rushed for the door. "I'll be right out here if you need me."

Guy returned some time later and sat in the chair against the wall with his head in his hands. My labor had stalled again and the doctor put the baby on a heart monitor. When my water finally broke, it shot out over the end of the bed as the urge to push overwhlmed me. I pushed for almost four hours with little progress. The monitor showed that the baby was in distress.

"This baby is too big to pass through the pelvis on his own," the doctor said. "We have three options. We could do a Cesarean, or use forceps or suction to pull the baby out."

"You're not serious!" I said. "Who would choose forceps or suction?"

"Some women don't want surgery under any circumstance," the doctor said.

I looked up at Guy and he gripped my hand. "For once in my life, my hips are too small." I panted through another urge to push and then turned to the doctor. "I want a C-section. Let's get this over with."

Guy leaned over and put his head on my chest and I stroked his hair. Then Helen shooed everyone out of the room. "Now you can have drugs," she whispered.

A new crew of orderlies and nurses transferred me to a gurney, strapped me down, and wheeled me onto a small elevator and up to the surgical floor. When the doors opened, they whisked me into the cold steel operating room and up onto the table like a rag doll. I began to shiver. The anesthesiologist put his hands on either side of my hot face and covered my nose and mouth with a mask.

"Count backwards from ten," he said, and the world went black.

When I opened my eyes, I was in a quiet, dimly lit room. I was laying on a narrow gurney, surrounded by muslin curtains that hung on thin chains from the ceiling. I raised my arm and grazed the soft fabric with my fingertips. Suddenly, Guy and Marilyn appeared in the opening. They stood on either side of the gurney, looking down at me with goofy smiles on their faces. I looked from one to the other. They looked drunk and the smell of alcohol filled the small cubicle. They obviously had made some kind of peace while I had been away.

"We have a little football head," Guy said laughing. He grinned at Marilyn.

"Congratulations! He's beautiful." Marilyn said. "Well, now that you're awake, Lynn and I are going to our hotel. We'll see you in the morning." She giggled and left.

Guy had three hours more experience at being a parent than me, so he filled me in on the APGAR score and all the other pertinent stats for our little boy—ten pounds and one ounce, twenty-two inches long, born at 6:23 p.m. His head was two inches bigger than average, and the doctor had detected a slight heart murmur, but he expected that to resolve on its own. Other than being slightly jaundiced, our little boy was perfect.

The nurses arrived to take me to my room. They wheeled me down the hall and past the pediatric ICU where Colin Ashanti Murphy-Johnson was sleeping after his first big adventure. Visible through the large window of the nursery was a row of clear bassinets, filled with tiny bodies tucked tightly under pink and blue blankets. I spotted Colin immediately. He looked like a giant blue mountain rising out of the low foothills.

I had always wanted a freckle-faced, redheaded kid, but I had let go of that idea when Guy and I decided to have a child. But when the nurse wheeled Colin's bassinet into my room, I saw a topknot of copper-colored hair and a sprinkling of pale brown freckles across the tip of his nose. The four hours of pushing had given Colin's head the football-shape that Guy thought was so amusing. "The doctor said his head will round out in a month or so," he said.

I looked down into Colin's honey colored face, my own little Aquarian, bringing a new era to my life. I waited. Then I felt a moment of terror. I didn't feel the way I was supposed to. I wasn't overcome with love, heart-swelling joy, and buoyant happiness. Then Colin looked up at me from his nest of blankets and stretched one little arm towards my face. We locked eyes for the first time. I felt a rush of kinship and familiarity. "Oh, there you are!" I thought. It was like seeing the face of a good friend after a long absence.

The nurse put Colin into a bassinet next to my bed and gave me a refreshing sponge bath and a clean gown. Guy sat down in a chair in the corner, and almost immediately began to nod off. "Guy, why don't you go home and get some sleep?"

"Maybe I will. I'm beat!" Guy leaned over the crib and cradled Colin's head with one large hand. "Thank you, Sharon. Thank you for this," he said.

CHAPTER FOUR

FOR TWO DAYS AFTER THE birth, my hospital room overflowed with giant bouquets of flowers in elaborate arrangements sent by people I didn't know. A cut crystal vase with three-dozen coral roses crowded out a vase of long-stemmed purple irises on my bedside table. The windowsill was jammed with dahlias, orchids, and lilies. The nurses brought in extra tables to accommodate all the flowers. Once, Guy stood up from the edge of my bed and laughed when two nurses walked in carrying a wooden tripod displaying a huge ring of white daisies with bright goldenrod centers and a banner draped across the front proclaiming, *Congratulations!* "Mom must have told the world," he said.

"Did she tell people I had a baby or that I won the Kentucky Derby? Look at the size of that thing!"

After lunch one day, the nurse wheeled in Colin's bassinet and Maya and Paul walked in behind her. "Here's my grand!" Maya exclaimed. She was again wearing her tawny fur coat and Paul was in a suit. They both looked tired from the busy book tour and Maya had dark circles under her eyes.

Guy picked up Colin, who was tightly wrapped in his blue blanket, and handed him to Maya. Paul took a step backwards almost disappearing amid the wall of flowers. He looked uncomfortable with the intimacy of the occasion. Guy pulled up a chair so Maya could sit, but she remained standing as she regarded her grandson for the first time. She put her hand behind Colin's head and raised him up to eye level. She stared at him with tears brimming in her eyes and seemed at a loss for words. Maya looked over at Guy and they held each other's gaze in a moment filled with unexpressed but palpable emotion.

"He has the Johnson head, don't you think?" she said, her husky voice unsteady. "...nice and round." I heard an intake of breath and I felt as though she wanted to say something else, but she handed the baby back to Guy and sat down with a sigh.

Guy cradled the baby in his crossed arms and swayed from side to side. I said nothing, feeling outside of whatever was passing between them. Guy made several attempts at conversation, but each start went nowhere. After a few uncomfortable minutes, Maya and Paul made their exit.

Colin and I stayed in the hospital until I could stand up straight during my shuffling strolls down the corridor and until every hint of jaundice faded from Colin's skin. Unless the nurses took him for a treatment under the fluorescent lights or kept him in the nursery while I napped, Colin was in my arms or next to my bed in his plastic bassinet.

Every day, Guy came to the hospital in the late afternoon, and usually stayed through the early evening. He'd crowd into the narrow bed next to me, and hold the baby on his chest. Like all new parents, staring at Colin's every expression was our only preoccupation. One evening, Guy decided to change Colin's diaper himself rather than calling the nurse. "How hard could it be?" he reasoned. But his big hands and thick fingers were not up to the challenge. He finally admitted defeat when he had tar-like meconium up to his elbows. I laughed until my incision burned at the unfamiliar look of helplessness on his face.

In the mornings and evenings I was alone with Colin in my garden-like room. It was a time outside of time for me—like a deep meditation. Every hope I ever had of being better or smarter or braver—every shooting-star wish I ever made felt as if it had been granted. I was charged with the protection, care, and encouragement of this new creation. He was the essence of possibilities. I had said the word *love* many times in my life, but to feel that spark of connection to the very existence of another person gave me a new sense of myself. Being Colin's mother felt like a blessing, the truest of miracles.

In contrast, when the day came to be discharged, the ride home from the hospital was like a psychic assault. The traffic was too loud, and the world was too chaotic and dangerous for Colin's fragile new life. Guy's driving was always aggressive, but when he floored the VW to beat another car onto the freeway on-ramp, I grabbed the handle on the dashboard and gasped.

Suddenly Guy remembered our new little passenger and he backed off the gas. I didn't feel safe again until I stepped across the threshold of Maya's guest house.

I was surprised and touched when I saw that Guy had dug out my Indian print tapestry from the boxes in the garage. He had tacked it up on the wall over our bed to make the guesthouse look more like home. I put Colin in his new yellow crib and covered him with the colorful quilt I'd made for him.

I was relieved to be out of the hospital, but was still exhausted and in pain from the C section, so instead of being in a celebratory mood, I climbed back into bed. Our new routine was gentle and calm, and one day rolled quietly into the next. I curled around Colin to sleep, and every few hours Guy would stack pillows next to me so I could nurse in our unique backward arrangement which prevented the baby from shoving his foot into the midline incision that ran from my belly button to my pubic bone. I propped Colin up on the pillows and held him under my arm football style, his head resting in my hand and his legs tucked behind my back. When Colin dropped off to sleep, I got up and shuffled around the cottage for a little exercise.

Colin was a strong, hardy baby and even though he was a newborn, he could push himself up with his strong little arms and raise his big, round head to take a look around. He appeared to have inherited his parents' love of a good conversation—he'd look for whoever was speaking. If someone walked in while he was nursing, he'd turn his head to inspect the newcomer, stretching my nipple as far as he could while still remaining anchored to my breast. I had to slip a finger into his mouth to break the suction for relief. Colin had a look on his face that seemed to say, "Just wait till I'm able to get around here on my own!"

Our life took on a bizarre split-screen appearance. Quiet, slow days with an uneventful schedule and then, in the evening, we'd bring the baby across the footbridge to visit with Maya and Paul. Many times, the living room would be filled with friends – usually other celebrities – a performer making an appearance in the Bay Area, perhaps a member of the world's literati. After a few obligatory minutes admiring the baby, the party would return to matching each other story for story and enjoying a long dinner and bottles of expensive wine. The conversation might be about their new homes, their far-flung trips, or a new Hollywood project. Maya would report on the soaring sales of her book or an upcoming television appearance, and Paul would describe plans for his contracting business or his latest real estate idea. Then after being witness to such lofty conversations, Guy and I would make our way back to the cottage to hash out our next move.

We were now in the second phase of our master plan. Once Guy got a job, he would be the only wage earner while I went back to college to finish my degree. Maya was giving us the money to get settled somewhere, but after the Stockton debacle, she made no suggestions as to what we should do. Still, the pressure was on Guy to find a job—fast. His job would determine where we lived and where I went to school.

When the baby was six weeks old, Guy was offered a job with the city of San Jose working on the plan for a paramedic program for the city's fire department. Neither of us was familiar with San Jose and we didn't know anyone there, but we strapped Colin in his car seat and set out to find a place to live. We moved into a cute white frame house with a deep backyard surrounded by trees—perfect for baby sunbaths. In the very back of the yard, a stone footpath led through a maze of waist-high irises—gold, purple, bronze, and champagne—each with a little fuzzy tongue crawling like a caterpillar out of its silky throat.

I unpacked boxes, and trimmed and repotted our plants after their banishment to Maya's garage. In the sunny San Jose spring, each plant quickly perked up and sprouted new growth. I bought a rocking chair sturdy enough for Guy to sit in while he held the baby. I filled our albums with baby pictures and recorded every moment of Colin's mastery of the skills essential to roll over. I decorated the house with freshly cut flowers and guiltily luxuriated in my new life as a housewife and mother.

I located the farmer's market with the freshest produce, the butcher shop that had been in business for 40 years, and the grocery store owned by a real family, not a multinational conglomerate. My weekly shopping took the whole day, but Colin was an easy baby and he slept happily in his car seat as we made our rounds. I stopped at city parks for nursing breaks, and to teach Colin to imitate bird songs and to know the difference between a rough stick and a smooth stone. I felt as if I had privacy for the first time in months and it was like a long, delicious exhale.

At 6'5, Guy always had a difficult time finding clothes to fit him. The thirteen button, navy pants remained his favorite and I embroidered a long-stemmed rose on every new pair. But he needed other clothes for his new job. I enrolled in a tailoring class in the evening and made the breakfast nook into my sewing room. Colin bounced in his jumper hanging in the doorway while I crawled around on the kitchen floor pinning pattern pieces to yards of fabric. I made Guy a pair of grey wool dress slacks with double-welt pockets, a plaid jacket with a chain weight inside the hem, and sleeves customized the way he suggested with turned-back cuffs, not buttons. I bought little tags that said, "Handmade by Sharon" and stitched them inside each piece.

The time before and after Colin's birth was a graceful reprieve from the turmoil and stress that plagued our relationship. I hoped that Guy and I could make a fresh start, but as soon as we turned our attention to our next step together as a family, Guy's condescending attitude resurfaced. The house was well-stocked with baby books, but Guy didn't think he needed to educate himself. Even though Colin was growing and thriving and the house was cheerful and comfortable, Guy was a nervous wreck. He began having trouble sleeping and more than once jumped out of bed, certain that Colin wasn't breathing. He'd jiggle the baby till he started to cry. If I took a bath with Colin, Guy was afraid I would let him drown. If I sat outside with him, he worried that the sun would burn Colin's eyes. He checked the number of diapers in the pail to make sure he wasn't dehydrated. (His mother scared him about this because Colin's only sustenance was breast milk.) He'd lift Colin out of my arms and put him back in his crib, asserting that I held him too much. When he overheard me telling Colin he was beautiful, Guy said, "He's handsome, not beautiful. Right, my son?"

When we went for Colin's checkups, Guy peppered the pediatrician with questions. Each time the doctor reassured him that my methods for caring for the baby were customary and sufficient, and that Colin was as strong and healthy as he appeared. Even the doctors couldn't reassure Guy that nothing was wrong with Colin.

One morning, I sat on the couch in my nightgown trying to nurse the baby. He was fussy and his head felt hot. By the time Guy was ready to leave for work, it was clear that Colin was sick. Guy sat down next to me and cupped Colin's head with his hand. "Let's take him to the emergency room. I'll take the day off."

"He just has a cold, Guy," I said. "Would you go to the store and get some infant Robitussin?"

"How can you be so casual about this?" He paced back and forth across the living room and reached for the phone. "I'm calling the doctor."

A tingle of irritation ran up my spine. "Guy, the doctor will tell you to give him infant Robitussin. If he gets worse, I'll call the doctor. I promise!"

Guy finally went to the drugstore, and then reluctantly left for work. But even with the medicine, Colin's nose remained stuffed up. He was miserable and cranky. I rocked him with his head elevated and patted his back to break up the congestion. I closed the kitchen doors and boiled big pots of water on the stove. I pulled my rocking chair into the steamy kitchen and tried to nurse him. He settled for a minute, but with his mouth clamped on my breast, he couldn't breathe and he'd start crying again. I put his daybed on a table next to the stove and propped him up on pillows to breathe in the steam. I told him stories using his stuffed animals as characters. He'd smile and sneeze ribbons of snot out of his nose. When he dozed off for a moment, he'd wake up coughing again. I stroked his face with a wet towel and sang to him. *Ha, ha, ha, you and me, little brown baby how I love thee. Ha, ha, ha, you and me...*

I was dismantling the steam chamber when Guy arrived home from work. All day I had been focused on helping Colin ride out his cold, but as soon as I heard Guy's footsteps in the living room, I saw the scene through his eyes. I was still in my nightgown and my hair was a frizzy mess. The walls ran with moisture, and the remnants of my many attempts to comfort Colin lay scattered on the floor.

Guy pushed open the kitchen door and looked around. He scowled and shook his head. "You didn't take him to the doctor, did you?"

Colin had finally fallen asleep and Guy's voice woke him and he began to cry. I lifted him out of his day bed next to the stove and turned towards his bedroom.

"What are you doing?" Guy asked.

"We're going to take a bath."

Guy pointed an accusing finger at me. "Sharon, this is the type of negligence that probably caused him to get sick in the first place! His clothes are damp and his bedroom is cooler than the kitchen. He'll get a chill and be sick all over again." I ignored him and walked into Colin's bright yellow bedroom. Guy followed me. "You should have taken him to the doctor this morning like I said."

I didn't want Guy to know I was crying, so I kept my back to him. I closed the bathroom door and turned on the water in the tub to drown out his voice. Since becoming Colin's mother, Guy's approval was losing its desperate grip on me. He could still hurt me, but I was getting tired of being treated with such contempt and scorn. There was no doubt of my love for Colin. I wondered what feelings were at play in my relationship with Guy. Was our marriage based on love? The answer to the question terrified me.

I held Colin on my hip and squirted peppermint bubble bath into the stream of water. I stepped out of my nightgown and pulled off Colin's diaper and shirt and dropped them on the floor. I got into the tub, held him to my chest, and slid down into the warm suds. I held Colin's bottom with one hand, and trickled warm water down his back with the other. Tears rolled down my cheeks and into the bubbly tub. Colin pushed himself up against my chest, and looked down into my face. He giggled and gave me a toothless smile. I could see that he was feeling better.

I turned 28 in August of 1977 and Guy again was out of a job. The design for the paramedic program was finished and there were no other positions available with the city of San Jose. I suspected there was more behind Guy's terse explanation, but didn't push for more. I knew how I felt when he put me on the spot and I didn't want him to feel cornered. We still didn't have any money saved and against my advice, Guy turned to his mother for help. Not only did Maya put a check in the mail, but Paul offered to rent us a house he was renovating in an old Italian neighborhood in Santa Rosa. Guy was happy with the deal.

"Paul's still working on the house—it's not quite ready for tenants. He's stripped all the floors and hasn't finished hanging the sheetrock on the living room walls yet. But I told him I could help him finish the work while I looked for a job."

Once again, we packed our belongings, rented a U-Haul, and moved from our cute house in San Jose to Paul's shabby rental property in Santa Rosa. Not quite ready for tenants was an understatement. The house was in rough shape. When the noise of hammers and saws and workmen stomping across the roof became unbearable, I would take Colin to the park so he could practice his speed crawling. On the way, he would sit at full alert in his stroller in his white knit cap. He looked like a rotund little golfer. As I wheeled him along, Colin waved his arms and addressed every person, shrub, and fencepost. Once released, his strong arms and legs would propel him across the grass in the direction of any noisy group of kids, but a fallen branch or blade of grass could also entertain his curious spirit.

Across the street from the park was a small, family-owned Italian bakery. When seductive smells of bread blanketed the neighborhood, everyone within sniffing distance was lured away from their soap operas or afternoon chores. Neighbors cued-up for warm loaves of milk bread and other crusty treats. Allegra, the matriarch and owner, tended to the counter, while her olive-skinned sons worked the plump loaves in and out of the massive iron oven. When I told her that my grandmother had been born in Sicily, Colin and I became part of Allegra's clan. I usually found a few extra cheese rolls or sweets in the bottom of my bag.

Before buying the bakery, Allegra told me that her late husband had owned a restaurant with American business partners. He did such a good breakfast and dinner business that his partners wanted him to stay open during the noon hour to increase their profits. But every day, as he had done in the old country, her husband closed up the restaurant and came home to share a meal with Allegra and the children.

"The most important thing in life is life itself," she told me. "Time is money in America. In Italy, time is life, and *life* comes first."

In the evening, the sidewalk in front of our little, unpainted house filled with neighbors practicing the Italian ritual of the *passagiatta*, the stroll to see and be seen. Tidied after their day of work, the men walked arm in arm, and the women and children walked behind them. Even the teenage boys took their turn jostling the babies and kissing the cheeks of their friends' mothers when the families stopped to exchange news and gossip.

I liked to nurse Colin on the porch in the evening, shielded from view behind the thick wisteria vine that hung down from the edge of our roof like a lavender lace curtain. Sitting there in those perfect moments, I felt as if I had one foot in the warm gene pool of my past—babies, motherhood, and family—and one foot in a cold, uncertain future.

My sister Carol, her three teenagers, and an assortment of their friends decided to caravan from their home in Austin,

Texas, to Sonoma County to meet Colin and visit with me and my niece Susan, Marilyn's youngest, who lived nearby in Petaluma with her boyfriend David. After the visit, they would tour the Bay Area and continue their excursion up the coast. Carol assumed that they could stay with Guy and me. "The kids can sleep in the vans," Carol said. "It'll be fun!" I couldn't bring myself to tell her I didn't think Guy would allow it. By the time I mustered the courage to tell Guy that they wanted to bunk in with us, Carol and company was already on the road and unreachable.

As I expected, Guy shook his head and said, "They're not staying here."

Carol called me from Susan's house when she arrived. I was in a no-win situation, so I just choked out my justification. "I'm sorry, but Guy doesn't want so many people in the house," I said. "It's the remodeling...it isn't finished yet."

"You let Guy dictate to you about your own family?" Carol said. I could hear the hurt and anger in her voice. I tried to tell myself that Guy had a right to say whether we had guests or not, even if they were my family. But I knew it was a poor argument and I felt torn and guilty.

This new "Guy story" circulated among my sisters and solidified their collective resentment of him. They agreed that he was trying to isolate me by making it impossible for me to have a relationship with my family. They were suspicious because I'd told them that Guy complained about my long distance calls to Orange County and Texas; he'd insisted that I limit my calls because of the expense. He also resisted when I asked him if I could fly to Southern California with Colin for a visit. Although I had fears of my own about my relationship with Guy, I was conflicted when my sisters spoke against him. I was struggling for autonomy from my role as baby sister, and their strong opinions felt like an attack on my choices and on how I lived my life. I stubbornly refused to agree with their characterization, insisting always that there was another side to Guy. Now when they called me, our conversations were becoming awkward. A chilly distance was growing between us.

My application for a student loan was approved (and the new amount was added to my preexisting debt). I enrolled as a liberal arts major for the fall semester at Sonoma State College in Rohnert Park, ten miles south of Santa Rosa. Sonoma State prided itself on its progressive faculty and new-age curriculum. I signed up for a women's studies class, an early childhood development class, and a class with the extraordinary title, *On Becoming a Person*, based on the work of Carl Rogers, the humanistic psychologist. I couldn't wait for school to start.

The Sonoma State campus was ringed by the sensuous, sweet-smelling hills of Sonoma County. Tie-dye girls and long-haired boys (indistinguishable from each other) lounged on the grass outside the student union listening to young men with waving Afros slap out rhythms on beaded drums. I detected the scent of sandalwood and cannabis as I walked to my classes.

The Viet Nam war had ended in April of the previous year, but anti-war messages still screamed from flyers posted on bulletin boards, *Dropping Bombs for Peace is like Fucking for Virginity. I'm Already Against the Next War.* Rainbow posters announced rallies and demonstrations. If it wasn't for Colin at home, I would have been tempted to stay on campus day and night. I saw Caesar Chavez at a rally about the farm worker boycotts. Another time, I went to hear Phyllis Lyon and Del Martin, the lesbian feminists from San Francisco, talk about their activism for equal rights for all women.

My niece, Susan was happy to take care of Colin while I was in class. When Susan was little, she was a very prideful little thing. She never threw tantrums or whined—that would have been beneath her dignity. If Marilyn said no to her, Susan would stomp her little foot, lift her chin, and toss her long, strawberry blonde ringlets with an attitude that showed that she fully expected to get her way eventually. Now Susan was nineteen. A strong, self-possessed young woman and a natural beauty with rosy cheeks, pale gold freckles, and clear green eyes. She was a drummer and a dancer, and she wore simple clothes—long skirts, drawstring pants with Indian prayer shirts or a paisley shawl. She wore her ash blonde hair in a long braid down her back; a hint of Patchouli always trailed behind her. Susan was beginning to take Mary's place as my close friend and confidant. My alienation from my sisters was painful and I was thrilled that someone in my family was Colin's first babysitter.

Susan and Colin, Santa Rosa California 1977

I arranged my classes to accommodate breastfeeding, but Mother Nature kept Colin and me on an unforgiving schedule. If I was delayed after class or hit freeway traffic on my way home, my breasts would clench like fists. I kept a bag of face-cloths in my purse to stuff in my bra when the milk started to flow. When I pulled into the driveway, Susan would be standing in the doorway holding Colin as he wailed. My spontaneous lactating and his crying always seemed to coincide.

After the initial burst of remodeling, Paul stopped working on our house. The roof was finished, but our bedroom was still visible between the rough slats of the living room wall, and dust from the unfinished ceiling covered our books and tables in a uniform layer of white film. When I complained to Guy, he said, "If we say anything to Paul or to Mom we'll sound ungrateful. Paul could get a lot more rent from someone who wasn't family."

"What if we offer to finish it ourselves?" I said.

"No! That would look like we don't trust Paul," Guy said. "When he has the cash for the materials, he'll finish it. Until then, we're not saying anything. Understand?"

I agreed to say nothing.

One evening, Maya invited us to join them for dinner at a restaurant on the square in Sonoma. Susan was with Colin and we were enjoying a long, elaborate dinner and three bottles of wine. When Paul slipped their credit card on top of the check, Maya turned to Guy and said, "My accountant says that Paul and I have to watch our spending. I hope you're going to find a job soon." Guy reddened, but didn't respond. I was angry at the timing of this comment and I wanted to defend Guy, but I knew better than to get between them.

In three years, Guy and I had moved four times—from San Francisco to Stockton, then to Sonoma, then San Jose. Now we were starting over again in Santa Rosa and again we were in Maya's debt—and with the reduced rent, we were indebted to Paul, too. Owing family was something I couldn't get used to. I never worried about money issues between me and my sisters. If one of us was in a position to help out with a little cash, it was never mentioned again—we were all in the same leaky boat. When I saw that Guy's first solution when facing a cash crisis was always to ask his mother, I assumed that Maya was happy and willing to help him, her only child. She had the money, and she certainly knew what it was like to struggle—her books glorified her ability to prevail against adverse circumstances. However, Maya's help seemed to send Guy the message, "You will always need me."

Still, he seemed unable to resist involving her in our problems. It was as if he was acting out his part in a private game with his mother that I didn't understand.

Guy accepted an entry-level administrative job with the Sonoma County Personnel Department in Santa Rosa. He would be drafting job descriptions, reviewing applications, and coordinating interviews with candidates for jobs in county administration. The job sounded incredibly boring to me, but there was room for advancement and Guy would be earning more than he ever had before. Even so, with only one paycheck and my student loans, money was tight, but I was fine with that. I wanted us to do it on our own, and I never again wanted to see the expression on Guy's face when he asked his mother for money.

Colin was now eating solid food. To economize, I blended steamed fruits and vegetables, and froze meal-size portions in ice cube trays. I packed Guy a lunch to take to work every day and used cloth diapers instead of expensive disposable ones— they littered landfills anyway. I cut Guy's hair for him, and my own as well and I made Colin a wardrobe of overalls with snaps along the inside seam. The uniform pants from my nurse's aide job were made of indestructible polyester, and I wore them every day with a few simple tops that I made for myself.

One Saturday afternoon, I left Colin with Guy while I ran errands and did the grocery shopping. I also picked up a book on reserve at the campus library, and then hurried home. It was time to nurse the baby and my breasts were starting to hurt. When I walked into the house, Guy was sitting at the dining room table strumming a brand new Fender guitar. I felt as if he had slapped me across the face. He hadn't even mentioned that he was thinking of getting a new guitar. He saw the shock on my face and looked at me with a warning—as if to say, "You better not say anything!"

What *could* I say? He was the one working—not me.

I had expected to see Maya more often now that we lived only 40 minutes from Sonoma, but it turned out that we hardly ever saw her. She was busier than ever, her career flying at a rocket's pace. She would call from the road and talk to Guy about the details of her itinerary, the latest gossip about whoever she had visited, and how her events were going, but she never asked about me or the baby. When they were on the phone together, no one else existed. But when she was home, Guy felt obliged to bring the baby for a visit. I didn't mind. It was not a long drive, but even if we showed up early, Maya assumed that we would become a part of whatever she had planned for the day—a late dinner, entertaining friends, or a night out. I was busy with my classes, and Guy was bringing work home from the office and trying to get into a writing routine. We seldom had a whole day free; plus there was tension between us and an all day visit often got awkward. If we were at home, we would comfortably retreat into our separate activities.

One Saturday, after spending the morning with Maya and Paul, we planned to make a quick exit before her lunch guests arrived. When she noticed Guy gathering up the baby's things,

Maya sniped, "You always have time to spare when you're here asking for my money!" I watched as Guy's back stiffened. Then he finished shoving Colin's blanket in the diaper bag and stormed out of the house. I said good-bye to Maya and Paul and followed Guy out. After that, Guy and Maya had a mutual standoff for a few weeks before we saw her again—the incident ignored.

One evening I was surprised when Maya called to say she would be stopping by after a reading at Santa Rosa Community College. Guy was out with some new friends from work, and Colin was crooning to himself in his crib. I quickly straightened up the living room, but didn't have time to change my clothes before she tapped on the front door. The small living room seemed to shrink when Maya stepped across the threshold. She was dressed in a blue African print skirt and shawl, and large brass disks dangled from her ears. Her head was wrapped in an elaborately twisted gold cloth, which made her look even taller than her normal 6 feet. I kissed her on the cheek and poured her a glass of wine.

Maya sat down on the couch and without any preliminaries went straight to the point. "You know, Sharon, you haven't lost the weight you gained during your pregnancy." She tilted her head as if she had asked me a question.

Immediately I felt self-conscious and embarrassed. "I'm almost back to the weight I was before," I said apologetically.

Maya looked at me with a steady gaze. "Sharon, you have to keep up your appearance if you don't want Guy to stray."

I thought about the woman Guy slept with when I was pregnant. Did Maya know something? What was she saying? "A little extra weight is no excuse to have an affair!" I tried to sound more convinced than I felt.

She laughed dismissively. "I'm talking about the *real* world, Sharon. You know how men are." I made a vague gesture of agreement. "Well, I wanted to stop by to give my grand a kiss." Maya downed her wine and stood by the door looking at me expectantly. I got Colin out of his crib and put him in his grandmother's arms. "Oh, he is so beautiful. He looks like me, don't you think?" Colin made a grab for an earring and she handed him back to me. "Good night, Sharon. Remember what I said."

After she left, I put Colin back in his crib and sat on the couch with my face in my hands. I looked down at my drool-stained shirt and faded jeans. Guy would probably agree with me that his mother was out of line, but I didn't want to tell him that my weight had been the subject of the conversation. I didn't want to give him an opening to have something else critical to say. I promised myself to lose the extra pounds—breastfeeding was supposed to help—and tried to push her comments out of my mind.

When Guy got home from work the next day, he told me that his mother had phoned his office to say she wanted to buy us a washer and dryer.

"Are they a gift or do we have to leave the machines in the house when we move? It is Paul's house, after all," I said. I felt a rush of resentment, and then felt guilty for not being grateful.

Guy gave me an impatient look. "She didn't say and I didn't ask."

"We don't have to take them just because she offered. We can live without a washer and dryer. They'll only drive up the electric bill anyway. And Guy, you always feel bad when your mother helps us!" I said. "When are you going to ever say no to her?"

"If I say we don't want them, she'll want to know why."

"Tell her she's given us enough. She can't argue with that!" I reasoned.

"You call her and tell her. I don't want to get into it with her."

"Okay. I'll call her. But you have to back me up if she insists." I was almost looking forward to refusing her offer. I wanted to regain some of the pride I'd lost the night before.

When I got Maya on the phone, she cut me off. "Sears is delivering the washer and dryer at the end of the week," she said abruptly. "Make sure you're there to let them in."

Guy was standing next to me, listening. He shrugged and walked away.

"Okay," I said. "I'll make sure I'm home. Thanks, Mom."

I expended an enormous amount of energy managing the momentum of the days with Guy. I edited what I said to avoid an argument. I scanned the house before he came home to anticipate what he might take issue with. When we talked, I emphasized things that showed me in a positive light, and tried to avoid contradicting him. The early days of our relationship were a lost dream—I began to think that a good day was a day without a hot burning pain in my chest. No matter what I did, I would eventually violate one of Guy's basic tenets, some fundamental principle previously unmentioned. After an argument, my habit was to go off by myself and smoke a joint, ruminating in that futile, circular manner that pot encourages. I always found a way to tuck my hurt feelings into some distant corner of my heart. But I was not as blind as I had been. Watching Colin quietly witnessing Guy berate me gave me a troubling new perspective. I didn't know how to make the relationship better, easier, more loving. I just hoped that something—any-thing—would cause Guy to have a change of heart.

One day I suggested that we see a therapist. I was shocked when Guy agreed. I asked around at school and one of my pro-fessors referred me to a therapist and teacher at the Ananda Institute for Humanistic Psychology at Sonoma State—a train-ing center for Gestalt therapists. When I called to make an ap-pointment, Carl suggested that I bring the baby when we came to see him. I started feeling hopeful that with the help of a neutral third party, Guy and I could reconnect.

On the hour of our appointment, we pulled into a long drive-way that ran next to an open field and past a two-story farm-house. Three white goats poked their bearded faces through the unpainted wooden fence. We got out of the van in front of a squat, tar-and-gravel roofed building. The door swung open and Carl waved and greeted us by name. He was short and mus-cular with a warm, calm manner about him.

"What a beautiful baby!" Colin gave him one of his win-ning, toothless smiles, and Carl scooped him out of my arms and swung him up in the air. He tucked Colin expertly against his left hip and Colin anchored himself on the neck of his green t-shirt. Carl stepped back and motioned for us to enter.

Guy ducked through the low doorway. It was a cold day, but his forehead was beaded with sweat. His eyes were mere slits behind his thick lenses and his lips were pressed tightly together. After a quick look around the room, Guy said, "Thank you for seeing us. We have been ..."

Carl cut him off. "Let's get settled before we begin. Would you like some tea?"

Guy puffed up slightly at being interrupted. "No, thanks," he said.

"I'll take a cup of tea...any kind." I said. I sat down on the end of the couch and Carl handed me the baby.

A fire burned in the potbellied stove and the room smelled of pine incense and wood smoke. Overstuffed couches were arranged in a wide circle, and fat printed pillows lay in haphazard piles on the sisal rug. Guy inspected the posters on the bulletin board—a trust walk, an upcoming camping trip, new Gestalt therapy groups. He glanced over his shoulder at me with a blank expression. I worried about what he was thinking. I looked around trying to see the room as it would appear to him. He moved across the room to examine the framed picture of a smiling Dalai Lama in his gold and crimson robe and a poster of Fritz Perls, the creator of Gestalt therapy. My heart began to pound. Carl was a part of Sonoma State and everything in this room felt like being on campus, my place, a place where I felt safe and accepted. Guy was invading my private realm and I didn't like it.

Carl made tea at a table filled with cups and colorful cartons. He handed me a steaming cup and took a seat under the window on the other side of the stove. Carl held his cup with both hands and inhaled deeply. He looked from me to Colin and then over at Guy. Guy continued to prowl the perimeter of the room. Guy looked over and Carl motioned to a large rattan chair across from where I was sitting. Guy ignored the invitation. Carl's expression remained neutral, but I got the mental picture of two male cats circling one another.

Carl turned to me. "So, Sharon. Tell me what you hope to accomplish here today." Guy stopped pacing and looked at me. My mind went blank.

"Uh...well..." I stammered. I jumped when Guy cut in.

"That's the problem, right there." Guy pointed at me, but addressed himself to Carl in an eruption of words. "Sharon is a beautiful, kind, intelligent woman. But all her talents are locked up inside—frozen, wasted!"

"Sharon, how do you feel about what Guy said?" Carl said.

"Well, I think that he's right to some degree," I said.

Carl held up his hand to stop Guy from speaking and kept his eyes on me. "But how do you *feel* about what he said?" he emphasized. "Not what you *think* about it, how did it *feel* when he said that?"

My chest burned and my throat clamped shut. "What?" I could feel my cheeks redden.

Guy looked down and shook his head. "I don't know what's wrong with her."

Carl turned his attention to Guy and said, "Guy, what do you think is going on between you and Sharon?" he said. Guy warmed to the invitation. He paced back and forth across the center of the room, pumping his arms, palms upturned as he enumerated my shortcomings. I was lazy. I was unorganized. I was not living up to expectations. Carl stopped him. "You seem very frustrated, Guy."

"Sharon expects me to be strong for both of us. But I need her to pull her own weight. She is too weak and indecisive. I can't seem to make her pull herself together," Guy said.

Guy sounded so reasonable. He didn't swear or yell—his voice was low and steady. Still I wondered who he was talking about. Where was this strong, decisive man I was supposed to be married to? I wanted to laugh and cry at the same time. I sat facing the fire with my arms around Colin, feeling as if my head was being crushed in a vice. Carl watched me while Guy paced and continued his rant. I sensed that he wanted me to say something, but I didn't know how to defend myself.

"Guy, these are all mental abstractions—discipline, indecisiveness, power. Can you tell me more concretely what you are feeling?"

Guy gave him a dismissive look. "How would you feel if she was the mother of your child?"

When the session was over, I was stunned that a whole hour had elapsed. I had only mannaged to choke out how Guy's criticism hurt and discouraged me. His position remained that if I did better, he wouldn't have anything to criticise.

"We'll have to stop here." Carl picked up an appointment book on a side table. "I'd like to see you each individually the next time."

"We'll call you about that." Guy pulled out his checkbook. "How much do we owe you?"

I knew we wouldn't be back.

On Saturday morning after our therapy session, Guy rolled over and put his arms around me instead of jumping up to make coffee. I was starved for any sign that the tension between us was lifting, and when he moved closer, I smiled into his dark eyes. "Let me go put in my diaphragm." I tried to move away, but he kept his hand on my hip. He leaned closer and kissed me. I protested. "Guy, I need to put in my diaphragm."

It was as if I hadn't spoken. He rolled me onto my back and started to move on top of me. I could feel his erection against my leg. I was afraid to break the fragile mood, and we had a wordless struggle. He pushed himself inside of me and came quickly. When I shoved him off of me, he rolled over and closed his eyes.

I rushed into the bathroom. I stripped off my nightgown and turned on the shower. I pulled out an old red douche bag from under the sink and got into the tub. Filling the bag over and over, I was hoping to prevent something that could tear apart the loose fabric that barely held our life together.

After four weeks, I hadn't gotten my period. But I was nursing—my cycle was probably still irregular, I reasoned. I couldn't be pregnant—Colin was only eight months old. I vacillated between hysteria and believing that today would be the day when I would feel those familiar cramps. When I got tired of debating with myself, I went to the Student Health Center and took a pregnancy test. I didn't mention it to Guy, still willing myself to believe that this was a false alarm. But when I went back for my results, the test was positive—I was pregnant again.

I drove home in a daze. Susan was with Colin, but I didn't tell her. If I said the words aloud, it would become a reality. After Susan left, I sat in my rocking chair nursing Colin and trying to sort out my feelings. I was finally back in school. I had a baby that was still in diapers. I had a husband who sometimes looked at me as if he didn't know who I was. I felt none of the joy I felt when I found out I was pregnant with Colin—only dread and fear. I couldn't predict how Guy would react, but I decided I could not have another baby.

I settled Colin in his playpen when I heard Guy's van in the driveway. As soon as he stepped through the front door I blurted out the truth. "Guy, I'm pregnant."

His handsome face broke into a broad smile. I was so accustomed to his look of disapproval and stress that I was shocked for a moment. He dropped his leather shoulder bag and walked towards me with his arms extended. "That's wonderful, Sharon!" He held me against his chest and stroked my hair. It had been so long since he held me tenderly that I didn't want to move. I forced myself to step back.

"Guy, you can't seriously believe we should have another baby?" I said.

"What do you mean? Of course I want another baby. I'm an only child and I wouldn't wish that on anyone."

I couldn't believe we could see the situation so differently. But I wasn't going to be backed into a choice that I knew I would regret. "We didn't plan this. This happened that morning when we didn't use any protection. This is not the time to have another baby, Guy. We have no money. We're barely speaking to each other," I said. "And I want to finish my degree!"

Guy's smile drained away. "What are you suggesting?"

I walked over to the coffee table and picked up a long roach from the green glass ashtray. I lit the joint and took a hit. I hadn't smoked pot during my first pregnancy and Guy took this as my answer.

"Oh, I see," he said.

When I was anxious, my mind was a raucous chorus of yelling and screaming, but when I was stoned, I usually felt calmer. I sat on the couch and waited for the effects of the marijuana. I took another hit and slowly exhaled towards the ceiling. I held out the joint to him. "I want to have an abortion," I said.

Guy paced back and forth in front of the couch. His thick fingers creaked eerily, as he clenched his fists and pumped his arms towards the floor. "That is the most selfish thing I've ever heard you say." He looked like a caged animal. "Don't be such a coward, Sharon. We can make this work. We'll have two kids—two little redheads." He paused and gave a disgusted laugh. "You're ruining our plans. I knew you'd let me down," he said.

"I'm not saying that we'll never have another child. Just not now! Think about it. I'll be nursing one baby and pregnant with another—then another C-section. I won't be able to stay in school."

"Don't you think that other women find a way to deal with it? When did you become so delicate? How could you even think about this? What about our family?" Guy dropped onto the couch and held his head in his hands.

He looked so distressed and angry that my resolve began to crumble. I couldn't imagine having an abortion if he was against it. In the silence, the strength of Guy's argument over-whelmed my misgivings in what was becoming a well practiced routine for me. Maybe things would work out. I got back in school this time, I could do it again. "Well...if you think we can do it..." I said.

"It is a question of confidence and discipline—pulling to-gether." He took the cold roach out of my fingers and rolled a fresh one for himself. We spent the evening discussing how we would manage with two children so close in age. We hadn't talked like this in a long time. I was seduced by the smile on his face and ignored the thought growing in the back of my mind that giving Guy children might be the only way I could make him happy—and the only function I really had in his life.

When I came home from class the next day, I told Susan I was pregnant. Without Guy there to influence me, all my original doubts reignited. If Guy and I had been a solid couple, united by love and determination, I would have felt differently. I might have believed that we could face this together, as he suggested. But no matter how much I wanted us to be that couple, that was not who we were, maybe we had never been that couple. The more Susan and I talked, the more frantic I became.

"You shouldn't have another baby just because you're afraid of Guy," she said. "You can have an abortion whether he agrees or not."

"I know that in theory, but it's a lot harder in reality." I felt ashamed of myself for this admission.

"If you want me to, I'll stay with you when you tell him," Susan offered.

While we waited for Guy to come home, I made some calls and arranged to have the abortion at a clinic in San Francisco. Marilyn agreed to put a check in the mail to pay for it.

As soon as Guy walked into the living room, I told him. "Guy, I can't do it—I won't do it. I'm sorry, but I'm going to have an abortion." I braced myself for his reaction.

His eyes went cold. "You needed someone else here when you told me this, huh?"

He stepped around me and addressed himself to Susan. "I didn't think you were part of Sharon's cult of weakness, but I guess I was wrong."

He turned around and slammed out of the house. For the rest of the week, Guy and I were more distant than ever. I was determined not to change my mind, so I resisted the impulse to try to make peace.

On Saturday morning, I took the Valium that was prescribed for me. I didn't feel anxious just removed from what was happening. Guy agreed to drive me to my appointment and we dropped Colin off with Susan in Petaluma. We rode in silence down Highway 101 towards San Francisco. I gave him the address when we turned off Lombard Street onto Van Ness Avenue. "There's a parking place over there, Guy," I said. I pointed to the Medical Center building on the corner, but Guy made a u-turn and kept the car idling against the curb.

Looking straight ahead, he said, "This is your decision, Sharon, you can take care of it by yourself."

A hot lump rose in my throat and my eyes filled with tears. I climbed out of the van and Guy pulled into the heavy traffic. I was stunned and disoriented, dumped on the sidewalk like yesterday's garbage. When a wave of nausea reminded me why I was there, I retreated to a small corner of my mind and let my body carry me through the door of the medical center. I rode the elevator to the 11th floor and pushed open the door with *Women's Clinic* stenciled in gold on the plain wood surface.

No one looked up when the door tripped a sharp bell tone. The small waiting room was like any other doctor's office. Couples sat huddled together. A glass panel slid open and a young woman handed me a clipboard with forms to fill out. I was glad to have something concrete to focus on. I answered the questions...last period...general health...previous pregnancies.

"Do you have a driver to take you home after the procedure?" Tears poured down my cheeks. I didn't know if Guy was coming back for me, but I marked, "Yes." If he wasn't there after the procedure, I'd have to call someone else.

After watching a short film, I returned to the waiting room. Then a nurse called my name and I followed her into a mint green examination room. I changed into a gown and lay in the familiar stirrups on the narrow table. The two nurses in the room were talking to me, but I was on autopilot and their voices were indistinct murmurs.

The room was cold and a nurse draped a warm blanket over me. On the ceiling, I saw a large poster of a wide meadow, filled with golden poppies and wildflowers. Snowcapped mountains rose in the background against a clear turquoise sky. I knew how to remove myself and I breathed in the smell of the snapdragons and lupines. The wind whistling through the billowing grass drowned out the wet slurping noise of the medical device humming somewhere beyond the jagged mountain. After a few minutes it was over. A nurse helped me off the table and took me to a darkened room to rest.

Sometime later, a young woman woke me. "Your husband called. He'll be here in a few minutes to pick you up." She handed me a wet cloth. I sat up, dangled my legs over the side of the bed, and waited for my head to clear. I thought about what I had done. I checked my conscience for guilt or shame, but found only relief, not regret.

I was afraid to face Guy and hesitated before pushing through the door to the waiting room. He wasn't there. Two different couples sat in the waiting room filling out forms. I took the elevator down to the street and leaned against the building, shivering in the blustery November wind. After a few minutes, Guy pulled up to the curb. He didn't look at me when I got in the van. I felt lightheaded so I put my head between my knees.

Guy drove for a few minutes. When I felt the van stop, I sat up and looked around. We were near the Great Highway in front of a familiar apartment building. "So this is why Guy agreed to drive me to San Francisco," I thought.

Our friends, Tim and Karen, had called to invite us to their one-year anniversary party. I told Karen we couldn't make it, but hadn't told her why. Guy yanked on the parking brake and opened the door. I heard music coming from the upstairs apartment. It was a cut from *Songs in the Key of Life*, Stevie Wonder's new album. I had planned on buying it for Guy for Christmas. *Love's in need of love today. Don't de-lay. Send yours in right away. Hate's goin' round breaking many hearts. Stop it please, before it's gone too far.*

"What are you doing, Guy?"

"I never want to talk about this ever again." He slammed the car door and walked towards the building. I climbed down from the van and stood next to him as he rang the bell. He pushed open the gate when it buzzed.

We reached the front door at the top of the stairs. Karen gave Guy a big hug of welcome "Thanks for coming!" she said. Voices rose to greet Guy when he walked into the living room. I was just inside the front door when I felt a sharp cramp. I dissolved into hot, desperate tears. "Sharon, what's wrong?" Karen put her arm around me and led me into the bedroom.

When I told her what was going on, she turned and watched Guy through the bedroom door. He was laughing and shaking hands with the other guests in the living room. She brought me a glass of water and sat on the side of the bed until I calmed down. "I have to go talk to Guy."

After a few minutes, Guy appeared at the bedroom door. Karen and Tim were standing behind him. "I didn't realize you were feeling so bad. Come on, I'll take you home," he said.

1977 was approaching. I had many things to be grateful for. This had been the year of Colin's birth and my long awaited return to college. The whole country was in a more optimistic mood. Democrat Jimmy Carter was heading to the White House after the nationwide trauma of the Nixon years, Watergate, and

Nixon's resignation. The new president promised to appoint a record number of women and people of color to government positions. On the other hand, Guy and I were more distant than ever. He refused to discuss the abortion, and I had to come to terms with it by myself. We went through the motions of the holidays and I was relieved when the year was finally over.

On Wednesday, January 19, Guy walked through the front door after work. Colin clung to the side of his playpen, swaying on wobbly legs. He began to bounce when he saw his dad. Guy's face brightened. When he didn't look my way, I went back into the kitchen to finish dinner. He sat on the couch, bouncing Colin on his knees and making a hollow, knocking sound with his tongue that always made the baby laugh.

"How's my little man?" Colin gurgled the events of his day while Guy listened intently.

After we finished dinner, Colin pushed a piece of apricot around on the tray of his high chair, studying the physics of fingers and fruit. Guy ran a long wire in and out of the stem of his heavy pipe while I cleared the table. He opened his carved wooden box, crumbled a green bud between his fingers, and filled the bowl. After tapping it gingerly, he tickled it with the flame from a long wooden match. He took a few draws from the pipe, stood up, and stretched his long arms wide, letting out a loud groan.

"Guy, would you give Colin his bath tonight? I have to finish my Child Development paper."

"Why didn't you finish your paper before now?" he said.

I sighed. Why was everything always so difficult? I thought. "I was going to finish it this afternoon, but had to vacuum and move all our plants up off the floor." I gestured towards the living room. Our plants with the trailing vines were now all up on

147

tables or hidden behind chairs. "Your son has discovered that he likes the taste of potting soil."

Guy looked around the living room and shook his head. "Sharon, why did you wait to the last minute to finish your paper in the first place? Your family's low expectations of you are so apparent in your lack of any real discipline."

"Guy, why are you so unhappy?"

"Happiness has nothing to do with it."

He paced back and forth from the dining room to the large lacquered spool in the living room. "I want our life to stabilize and move forward, but you're always holding us back." His lips were pursed, and he clenched and unclenched his fists, making a tight creaking sound. Here we go again, I thought. We'd had this same argument a hundred times.

"Guy, what are you talking about? I'm going to college and taking care of Colin. What more do you want me to do?"

"I suppose you want me to say, 'Good job?'"

"There's nothing wrong with a little encouragement." I stacked the dinner dishes in the sink and squirted dish soap into the stream of hot water.

"Sharon, people like us should not be patting ourselves on the back for doing what is expected. Doing a good job is nothing to be proud of for an intelligent person. We should strive for excellence—always excellence. You're happy to do the minimum."

Guy lifted Colin out of his high chair and wiped his sticky face with a napkin. He pulled out a chair and laid the baby on his belly across his knees and patted him on the back. "I've been thinking about our schedule. Our days are too haphazard and disorganized. The baby doesn't have a set bedtime. Sometimes dinner is on the table when I get home, sometimes it's not. Look, there's laundry all over the couch." He leaned over and pulled a yellow tablet out of his briefcase. He glanced at it to refresh his memory and laid it on the table. "I've worked out this schedule for us. I have the evening hours broken down into 30-minute increments. If we stick to this schedule, I'll have time with the baby when I get home and time to write in the evening. You'll get your school work done without having to stay up all night before an assignment is due. But you have to have dinner on the table at 6 o'clock every night for the plan to work."

I took in a deep sigh. Colin was healthy and happy. I loved being back in college and I was making good grades. I felt proud of these things. Was this a substandard level of achievement? I looked at my reflection in the window above the sink. My face was pale, and I had dark circles under my eyes. I was only 28, but I felt defeated, trapped in a game with uncertain rules. No matter what I did, I walked around in a perpetual state of confusion.

"So, do we have an agreement? Will you have dinner on the table at 6 o'clock every night?" Guy asked.

I shut off the tap and leaned back against the counter. "No," I said flatly. "That is not a schedule for *us*—that is *your* schedule for *me*. If you're not writing, it's not my fault." Tears poured down my cheeks.

"You're pathetic," Guy said. "I really worry about you."

"Why are you doing this to me?" I screamed. I picked up a small Tupperware container of raisins and threw it at Guy. It bounced off of his chest and popped open. Raisins rained down on the baby and skittered across the floor. Guy began to stand and I stepped towards him and lifted Colin out of his hands.

My face flushed hot when I saw the look on Guy's face. I turned to run. He reached out and shoved me in the back. I lost my footing and fell forward. My face hit the floor, and I cradled the baby under me. Splinters from the unfinished floorboards jabbed into my elbows and sharp needles of pain shot up through my arms. I felt Guy squat down behind me, his hand on the floor next to my face. Colin was screaming. I started to rise, but Guy slammed his fist into my back between my shoulder blades. My forehead bounced off the floor. Pain slashed down my spine like a razor. I tried to crawl away down the hallway, but my body wouldn't respond. Guy punched me again—lower this time as if he were trying to break me in half.

"Please, Guy. Please stop!" I looked back over my shoulder and saw Guy pull back his fist and land a blow on the side of my head. I gasped. My ears filled with a dull roar. Then the room went quiet. I felt Guy get up and I could see the toes of his wing-tip shoes out of the corner of my eye.

"I'm going to get the police," he said. "I'm going to have you committed." I heard him grab his car keys. "You're hysterical."

The house shook when he slammed the door. As my head cleared, I heard a loud noise in the room. It was me—crying, howling, and panting like a dog. My body was quivering. I pushed myself up and sat back on my heels. Colin was hot and red in the face, but didn't seem hurt. I rocked him and we cried together cheek to cheek.

I tried to get up, but my body felt like stone. I rocked back and forth for a few minutes. When Colin began to settle down, I laid him on the floor and slowly pulled myself upright on the edge of the spool table. Colin rolled over and sat up, whimpering and looking at me with puffy eyes. I stretched and tested my arms and legs. My vision was blurry and my whole body felt twisted.

I could hear myself mumbling, talking to the air. "What am I going to do? What am I going to do? What am I going to do?" I was crying and listening to myself cry at the same time as if I had been split into two people. And then I thought of Guy coming back with the police. I could imagine the story he would tell them. He wouldn't have a hard time convincing them that I was hysterical. I imagined him pulling Colin out of my arms as I was led away by the cops. I had to get out of there—a shot of adrenaline sent me into action.

I grabbed the phone and called my friend, Kathy. Her husband Tom was an old friend of Guy's, but Kathy and I were friends, too. I thought she would help me.

The phone rang and rang and then she answered. "Kathy?" I cried into the phone.

"Sharon? What's the matter?"

"Guy and I had a fight...he beat me up. Can Colin and I come over?"

Kathy put her hand over the receiver and I heard a muffled conversation in the background. The seconds ticked by and after a minute, she was back. "Okay, come on over."

I ran into the kitchen and grabbed a box of garbage bags. I dug through the laundry on the couch, threw Guy's clothes on the floor, and stuffed clothes for Colin and me into the plastic bag. Colin followed me with his big brown eyes. I stripped his crib and tied blankets and diapers into a bundle. I filled my satchel with my school books, and even though I hurt from head to toe, I ran back and forth, up and down the porch steps until everything was loaded into my car. Then I tucked Colin in his car seat, and drove away.

CHAPTER FIVE

I DROVE NORTH UP HIGHWAY 101 to Healdsburg. I tried to focus on the road, but the image of Guy's face and his clenched fist kept flashing in front of my eyes. The tattered fantasy of my life shredded a little more with every replay.

Colin was sound asleep in his car seat, and the freeway lights caught the soft curve of his cheek. A crushing sense of defeat and failure weighed heavily on me. I had grown up with violence and thought I'd made a clean getaway. What kind of father had I given my son? Would Colin grow up feeling afraid of a parent like I had? What had I done? What would happen now?

I exited the freeway and turned down the narrow dirt road that cut through the vineyard of Mill Creek Winery. The road dead-ended in front of Tom and Kathy's small frame house. As soon as I stopped on the gravel driveway, the front door opened and a beam of light fell across the dark yard. I climbed carefully up the front steps with Colin on my hip. Kathy pushed open the screen door and Tom jumped up from the sagging couch.

"I'll get your stuff out of the car," he said.

"Thanks, Tom. The high chair's in the hatchback," I said.

Tom didn't meet my eyes, only gave a quick nod as he brushed past me. He had long, prematurely grey hair and was wearing his usual sharp-toed boots and faded jeans. He was lean and muscular, like an old-time cowboy. Kathy stood with her hand on the doorknob. She looked uncomfortable. She stared down at her tiny bare feet, and then out into the dark as Tom unloaded my car.

"What's going on, Kathy? Was it a mistake to come here?" I asked.

"No, but this is going to be hard for Tom. He doesn't want you to say anything bad about Guy in front of him, Okay?"

"Why did you tell me I could come here?"

"I wanted to help you. Tom cares about you too, but Guy is like a brother to him."

Tom was born in South Africa. Guy met Tom while he and Maya were living in Ghana. It was the time of apartheid— Nelson Mandela had been imprisoned on Robben Island for several years when they met. Although it was not the custom for a black man and a white South African to be friendly, Tom and Guy grew to like each other after an awkward beginning. When Tom came to the United States and settled in California, he and Guy picked up their unlikely friendship again.

Kathy was short with a small but curvaceous body, big brown eyes, and smooth ash-brown hair that framed her cherubic face. Guy teased her about being a throwback to the '50s, but I always thought he envied Tom. Kathy catered to him. She brought him his food, topped off his wine, and emptied his ashtray. But she was not really the submissive type. She was assertive and opinionated, and I could always feel the heat of sexual energy between her and Tom.

If this was the end for Guy and me, I thought, our friends would be divvied up along with our furniture and cassettes.

Tom would choose Guy, and I'd lose Kathy. I wished I'd thought about that before I came.

Kathy took the dead weight of Colin's sleeping body out of my arms and used her foot to push open the door to a bedroom. She flipped a switch on the wall and a soft yellow light filled the room. She carried Colin to the pullout couch in the corner, yanked back the sheets and blankets with one hand, and laid him down gently. A small desk from Kathy's childhood bedroom was next to the bed, and floor-to-ceiling bookshelves were filled with books, magazines, and family pictures. This room was very familiar to me. Guy and I slept in here a number of times when it got too late or we'd had too many glasses of wine to drive home. Tom came in and dropped my bundles and bags in the corner, then returned to the living room without speaking. Kathy put her hand on my arm. "Don't mind him. I'll get you a glass of wine." She closed the bedroom door behind her. I dropped heavily onto the bed next to Colin. He stirred and settled back into sleep.

I felt as if I had broken through the water's surface after a deep dive. Hot pain hammered in the back of my head, and my neck was stiff. I worked my jaw up and down and heard a popping noise in my right ear. My back was bunched up in knots, and my body listed to one side. I shrugged out of my coat and pain from my neck shot down both arms. I was disoriented. I wanted to go home. I wanted this night never to have happened.

Early the next morning, too early for Guy to be at work, I called his office and left a message telling him where we were. My thoughts were muddled and all I could manage that day was to swallow the leftover pain pills Kathy gave me and move an ice pack from my head to my neck to my back. I set up a corner in the bedroom with Colin's yellow Tonka truck and his red and blue plastic ball with star-and-moon-shaped holes filled with star-and-moon-shaped pieces. But Colin was never happy in a confined area, and his toys lay untouched. Instead, he became obsessed with seeing how high he could climb up the built-in bookshelves. I finally took him outside where he was always happiest. I spent the day watching him tumble around the yard chasing Tom's jet black puppy, Bokkie.

What did all this mean? What should I do? What did I want? Colin was my one point of clarity in all the turmoil. Being Colin's mother was the only root of my identity that hadn't been ripped from the ground. But Guy had been my emotional benchmark for so long that my own thoughts and feelings felt tentative and hazy. I was tormented with contradictory emotions. My mind would drift towards Guy, and I would wonder what he was feeling. Was he shocked that he hit me? Was he sorry? Did he think our life together was over? When I let myself wander in that direction, I felt a powerful yearning to gather up my shredded dreams and stitch them back together.

Then I'd remember Guy's fist as it slammed into my back and I'd see the look of fury on his face. I remembered the sound of Colin screaming. I didn't want my child to be in the middle of that ugliness and violence. I never wanted to see that frightened look on my child's face ever again. With that thought, my own wobbly sense of self-esteem rose up in righteous indignation. I would not allow anyone to treat me or my son that way—not even Guy.

On Friday, I made collect calls to each of my sisters, starting with the oldest as I always did. "I'm so sorry, Sharon," Marilyn said. "But I'm not the least bit surprised." Marilyn was in a new relationship and put me on speakerphone so her partner could hear me.

"Did you make a police report?" Irene asked. They were frustrated with me when I said I didn't even think about it.

When I talked to Jeanne, she said, "Guy's always been a bully, don't blame yourself for this. He's just like Mother."

I reached Sally Ann at the nurses' station on Nine West. "What a bastard!" she said. "I hope you called a lawyer!"

When I told Carol about the beating, she said, "I'm surprised he waited this long."

My total immersion in life with Guy had displaced the closeness I felt with my sisters. Now as I talked to each of them, I realized how much I had missed them. It was a relief not to shade my conversation with happy stories to prove to them how perfect my life was. Wasn't the truth supposed to set you free? I felt a renewed sense of outrage with each retelling of the details of the fight. But afterwards, a wave of guilt and shame washed over me. I felt as if I had betrayed Guy, betrayed something private.

I was alone with Colin during the next few days while Tom and Kathy were at work. In the evening, the three of us drank wine and played with Colin as if this were any other visit. Tom smoked in silence, with his boots propped on the coffee table. I didn't mention Guy, although I thought of little else. Instead, I talked about my classes and Kathy talked about her job at the winery—she was being groomed for a career in wine sales. I helped her cook dinner and we watched television together—*The Rockford Files* and *All in the Family*. Guy's absence was the only awkward reminder that anything was out of the ordinary.

Early on Saturday morning, three days after I had fled from our home, Tom and Kathy were sleeping-in on their day off. I brought Colin out to the porch to nurse him. I sat in a creaking wicker chair and wrapped a faded yellow quilt around us, cocoon style. The bare grapevines beyond the small yard were still in their winter dormancy. They were trimmed and tied and stood in rows like troops at attention. As the morning fog rose up from the vineyard and evaporated, the Sonoma County hills appeared, craggy and low in the distance.

Colin worked his finger into the corner of my mouth, his signal that he was coming out of his nursing trance. Now that he wasn't an infant anymore, the sound of a bird or some sudden creak or snap could get his attention while he was nursing. I was watching him become a part of the world beyond our private realm.

Inside the house, the phone rang. I heard footsteps and then Kathy's voice reached me from the kitchen. "Hello, Guy," she said. Colin jumped as if he had felt my heart begin to hammer under his cheek. Kathy's voice trailed off. I imagined the long phone cord stretched around the paint-chipped doorjamb as she went into her room and climbed back in bed with Tom.

Colin wiggled off my lap and plopped down on the wooden porch. He rolled onto his hands and knees and crawled towards the steps. He stopped at the edge of the porch and pushed himself up to standing, then bounced up and down and flapped his arms like a pilot checking to be sure that all of his equipment was in good working order.

Kathy's face took shape behind the screen. "Guy's coming over in a while."

"He didn't ask to talk to me?"

"No. He just said he was coming over. Tom and I are gonna take off when he gets here."

I scooped up Colin. "I'll get dressed."

By noon, everyone was showered and dressed, and the breakfast dishes were washed and put away. Kathy and I sat next to each other on the porch step. Tom was on his back under his truck, wrestling with the oil filter. Colin toddled around the yard in his moccasins and purple corduroy overalls, chanting, "Dog, dog, dog, dog, dog." His bright red hair gleamed in the sunlight. Bokkie slowed down long enough for Colin to bury his fists in the soft folds of his neck. I was dashing out to stop him from putting his open mouth over the dog's nose when Guy's white VW emerged through the rows of vines.

He parked in the grass on the far side of the driveway. Tom rolled out from under the truck and he and Guy stood talking for a moment. Guy walked around the van, leaned in the side door, and pulled out a large pink package of disposable diapers and a bag of groceries with a bunch of bananas sticking out of the top.

He glanced over at me with no change of expression. A chill ran through me. I carried Colin into the house and sat down on the couch. Kathy followed me inside and grabbed her keys off the coffee table. "Are you okay?" she asked.

"He obviously didn't come to apologize and beg me to come home."

"Have you ever known Guy to apologize for anything?"

Tom held the screen door for Guy and then followed him into the living room. "Greetings!" Guy boomed with a jovial tone. "I'll put these things in the kitchen."

I didn't speak. Colin squirmed off my lap and made an unsteady beeline towards his father.

"Hey, my son, how ya doing?" Guy slid the bags onto the kitchen counter and stooped to pick Colin up. He tickled him under the chin with one thick finger and made a string of hollow, knocking noises with his tongue.

"We're gonna take off, bro." Tom extended his hand to Guy as he came out of the kitchen.

"No need." Guy grasped Tom's hand and gave him a shoulder to shoulder hug.

"We have errands to do," Kathy said.

Guy carried Colin to the porch and watched as Tom and Kathy drove away. I stayed on the couch. Guy came back inside and put Colin in his high chair, and then sat down at the dining table next to him.

"I'm going out to see Mom and Paul this afternoon." Guy was speaking to me, but he kept his face turned towards the baby. "I thought I'd take Col with me. It's been a while since they've seen him." Guy rubbed his hand over Colin's curly head.

I was alarmed at the prospect of Guy driving away with Colin. "When will you bring him back?"

Guy turned to me with a small smile on his face, but his eyes were narrow and cold. "Oh, it won't be late. My friend Greg is looking for a roommate—he has a house in Cotati. I'm going over to look at it this evening. I'll bring the baby back before I go, by 7 at the latest." He watched for my reaction, and then turned to Colin. "Wanna go see Grandma? Huh? Huh?" Colin gave him a toothless, drooling grin, and banged his hands on the tray in assent.

"What?" I felt like an actor who finds herself in the wrong scene of a play. "You're looking at a house! What about us?"

"What do you mean 'us'? I assumed that you and Colin were living here." Guy waved his hand around the living room. His face was a study in indifference. All my stupid fantasies zipped through my mind—Guy with tears in his eyes, remorsefully hanging his head in shame.

I felt like a fool. "You're the one who packed up and left, Sharon. Don't blame this on me."

I jumped off the couch. "What was I supposed to do, Guy?" I startled Colin, and he began to cry. I walked over and lifted him out of his chair.

"Where's Colin's bag?" he asked, looking around the room. I pointed to the bedroom and sat back down on the couch with Colin snuggled tightly to my chest. I rocked back and forth and tried not to cry. Colin looked into my face and I kissed him on the forehead. I went into the kitchen to get him a couple of bottles of apple juice for his afternoon with Guy.

Back in the living room, Guy lifted Colin out of my arms. "Is your car unlocked? I need the car seat."

"It's open," I said. Guy slung Colin up onto his hip and positioned the striped diaper bag his mother had given me on the other arm. I followed them out onto the porch. "Guy?"

"What?"

"I need some cash."

"I brought you groceries and diapers," he said.

"I need money for gas."

"Well, then I guess you should get a job. That's where I get my cash."

I stood on the porch and watched him drive away. He would probably tell his mother that I walked out on him for no reason, "too weak to go the distance," he would probably say. Would she believe him? It hurt me to think that she probably would.

Once again, Maya would write a check and Guy would pack up his books and clothes in cardboard boxes. He'd lose a few leaves off his giant plants, register his new address with the post office, and take no notice that I was gone. Guy had given shape to my life for four years. Now he was neatly erasing me and taking that life with him. I was nothing to him now—if I had ever mattered at all.

The minutes crawled by while Colin was with Guy. Would Guy bring him back? If not, what would I do? Could I win a fight for Colin—a fight against Guy *and* his mother?

I would never have believed that Guy would hit me, so I obviously didn't know what he was capable of. And his nonchalance, as if nothing had happened—that was almost more frightening. It made me a little crazy to imagine how he could tuck his violence away and ignore it. I became frantic with worry as the afternoon dragged on.

When Kathy got home, she sat with me on the porch. We smoked a joint and tried to find a neutral subject to talk about. I heard Guy's van clattering towards the house at 6 and I rushed down from the porch. Colin reached for me when I opened the car door and I finally relaxed.

I was spooning cream of wheat into Colin's mouth when Guy called on Monday morning full of news, his voice bright and cheerful. He was moving from our house in Santa Rosa to share his friend's house on Lakewood Avenue in Cotati. "Paul's decided to sell this place," he said. "If you want to come by this week to get your stuff, call and let me know. Otherwise, I'll pack everything up and you can get it later. My new place has a big garage. I'll keep your things in there."

Colin's first birthday was coming, and Guy was hosting a birthday party for him. "I'll be moving the week of his birthday, so I'll have his party on February 12th. You're invited, of course."

I was still rubbing arnica on the yellowing bruises on my neck and shoulders and Guy was planning a birthday party for our son in his new house. My voice was thin, "Guy, don't you care at all about us?" I asked.

"Sharon, I spent four years trying to help you. But you're as substandard and weak as when I first met you. I'm done. It's a relief, really. But I worry about your influence on my son."

"*What?*"

"Look at you, sleeping in someone's spare room, no job. You've got nothing!"

"Except now I have a child."

"Yes, and Colin needs a mother. I hope you can rise to the occasion." The phone went dead.

I slammed down the phone. I hadn't left the house since Wednesday night, five days earlier. I hadn't gone to class or called my instructors to explain. The only bright spot had been the care package I received from my sisters—a new blouse, bubble bath, a copy of *Fear of Flying* by Erica Jong, and the newest novel by Marion Zimmer Bradley, *The Forbidden Tower*. Sally Ann sent a check for $200. I could see her chewing on the end of a pencil and scrutinizing her budget to skim a little here and there to send me that money.

"Wanna go out?" I asked Colin, who responded by pointing one chubby finger towards the door.

I dressed Colin in his Oshkosh overalls and put his white sailor hat on his head. I took off the long brown dress I had worn all week, the same one that had been my pregnancy uniform. I brushed my hair and put on mascara, an act that always made me feel a little better. I slipped into my jeans and my new white blouse. My jeans were a bit loose, which made me happy. I packed the car and drove into town.

I cashed Sally Ann's check and filled the tank of my Barracuda. I drove south toward Sonoma State. Turning onto the highway, the familiar scene felt disorienting, as if it had been an eternity since I had been out among people. Guy's words stabbed at me again and again. "It's a relief..." "It's a relief..." "You're substandard..." "...substandard."

Colin was slumped over, sound asleep in his car seat. "It's you and me now, buddy."

I checked Colin into the drop-in children's center and slowly walked across campus. In this world, I was more than Guy Johnson's disappointing wife. It had been my refuge. I reluctantly withdrew from my classes and combed through the job announcements posted on the bulletin board at the Student Services Center. I decided to stop in to see the counselor who helped me arrange the abortion. I tapped on her office door and Romanda looked up from her desk. "I was worried about you, Sharon," she said. "How are you?" She came over and hugged me.

My bravado evaporated and I dissolved into tears. I poured out everything that had happened in the last few days, details I hadn't told anyone else. "Of course, I'm only telling you my side of the story," I added.

"You have a right to your side of the story. Let Guy get his own counselor."

"Guy and I went to see a therapist once, when Colin was about six months old," I answered tentatively. "But we never went back after that first time."

"Now you know who you should call," Romanda said. "If this therapist saw you two together, he knows a lot about your situation."

When I returned to Healdsburg, I called Carl and told him what had happened. I asked to make an appointment. "I have to admit, Sharon, I may not be the best therapist for you right now. I don't think I could be very objective. I felt very protective towards you and Colin after meeting Guy." He paused. "It's not very professional to admit, but I thought your husband was one of the biggest assholes I've met in a long time."

I couldn't believe that I was laughing. "I think that's a great place to start." I began having private sessions once a week and I made plans to join a Gestalt group as soon as I could afford it.

I kept using the Sonoma State student services to look for work and I saw a flyer announcing that Tony Apoloni, one of my professors, was administering a grant to fund group homes for developmentally delayed adults. The Sonoma County Organization for the Retarded, or SCOR, was hiring staff to teach the residents independent living skills. The goal of the project was to help residents learn to live in the community with the lowest possible level of supervision. I found Tony in his office and told him I was interested in a job with SCOR. "You'd be terrific, Sharon. I'll call the office and recommend you myself."

I went for my interview at the SCOR administrative office on Cleveland Avenue a few days later. I struck up a conversation with another candidate waiting in the lobby. We exchanged brief biographies. (And I realized for the first time that I was now a member of the tribe of divorced mothers—something I never expected to be.) She invited Colin and me over for lunch the next day. Sandy lived with her three-year-old daughter in a subsidized housing project in Santa Rosa. She tole me that there was an apartment available at Valley Oak Park and she offered to introduce me to the manager.

After only a few minutes of the interview, I realized that Tony's recommendation was all I had needed—the job was mine. When I left, I was the newest counselor at Burton House, the SCOR group homes in Cotati. My life had turned in a new direction in one short afternoon.

On the night before his birthday party, Colin slept at Guy's new house, a three-bedroom tract home in a subdivision of identical putty-colored houses in Cotati. I didn't want to go to the party, but my attendance would be a face-saving exercise. I ironed my jeans and a long-sleeved blouse. I polished my boots and applied my makeup carefully.

I arrived an hour after the party began. When I walked through the open front door, I didn't recognize the people sitting around the living room, but I recognized their names when I introduced myself. Many of them were Guy's coworkers. I was relieved that Maya and Paul weren't there. I wasn't ready to see them yet. Guy waved at me casually as if I had just been out at the grocery store.

Carol had taken my place as hostess. "Welcome!" she said. She handed me a glass of wine as if I were a casual acquaintance. Mickey came up and greeted me. He gave me a big hug, lifting me off my feet the way he usually did, but then he walked away without saying anything more. Norman nodded from the dining room table next to Colin. Steve sat at the table, demonstrating a strange instrument that was shaped like a raindrop. He drew a violin bow across the slender brass rods soldered around the hollow base filled with water and an eerie, melodic sound filled the room. Colin sat next to Steve, transfixed by the music. He was wearing a new outfit, a pale blue plaid shirt and navy blue corduroys, and had a shiny gold birthday boy crown on his head.

I sat down on the sofa—the one that Guy and I had reupholstered in green velvet brocade—and took a sip of wine. Guy carried out a store-bought sheet cake with a wax number one balanced in the center of the faces of the Sesame Street characters. He had resumed his role as the life of the party. Carol snapped pictures and everyone sang. I tried to maintain my composure, but I didn't belong here anymore. I slipped unnoticed out the front door.

One Friday evening a few weeks later, I brought Colin to Guy's house for the weekend. He was sound asleep when Guy opened the door. He lifted Colin out of my arms and handed me a joint. "Stay a bit," he said. He walked out of the room to put Colin in bed. Guy had shown no interest in discussing our break-up. He acted as if the end of our marriage was of no consequence to him. I waited on the couch thinking this might be the night when we would finally talk about what happened and where we went from here.

Guy was laughing to himself when he sat down next to me. "Have you heard Col ask for juice? He says, 'bottle-a-juice.' It's so great the way he says it. He has this look on his face, like he knows he's being funny. 'Bottle-a-juice.'" Guy laughed and shook his head. "What a kid!" We finished the joint while we exchanged stories about Colin. We were still laughing when Guy slid his arm around me and pulled me towards him.

To help keep me grounded in reality and ward off my imaginative fantasies of how I could mend the breach between us, I held the image of Guy's face and clenched fist in the forefront of my thought. But those few moments casually talking as if it were the most normal thing in the world was enough for my persistent misapprehension that Guy and I were still two people in love to resurface. Every other thought slipped away and I was enveloped in the private, delicious dream of him and me together, undaunted by anything. Guy moved in before I could recover my defenses. After frantic and unsatisfying sex, I lay twisted next to him on the couch while he snored.

Suddenly, I had a moment of clarity about the treacherous dynamic I had with Guy. For so long, I had wanted his love and approval more than anything. Guy was smart enough to know that this gave him all the leverage. We were in a power struggle more than a relationship. For his part, love was not something to give freely—it was something for me to earn. Maybe at some level Guy did love me. As I watched him sleep, all the happy times we had together laughing and talking rose up as confusing memories. Did I believe I was loveable just the way I was? It certainly felt natural to me to try and try to make him love me. Either way, I was caught in the game of tirelessly running after his love and approval. After all we had been through, his love remained a promise for the future—my prize for measuring up. But Guy would *always* withhold his love, if that's what it was, and I would always chase it and fall short. It was a game that neither of us knew how to win.

I lay silently for a few minutes, testing the validity of my new insight and looking at Guy's handsome face. I slipped out from under him and put on my clothes. I checked on Colin sleeping in the back bedroom and left the house. I drove around the block and slowly passed Guy's house again. I drove around the block a few more times. Another layer of my deluded thinking melted away and I cried out loud into the dark, cold night, "You're out, Sharon! You're free!" I circled the block again and again, yelling out loud so I wouldn't forget. "You're out! You're out! You're free!" Finally, something settled deep inside of my chest. I blew my nose and put on the radio—loud—and pulled onto Highway 101. Bob Marley sang me up the road to Healdsburg. *Ev'rything's gonna be alright. Ev'rything's gonna be alright. No woman, no cry. No, no woman, no woman, no cry. Oh, little sister, don't she'd no tears. No woman, no cry.*

I began my new job as a counselor at Burton House in April of 1977. Our task was to implement the curriculum my professor, Tony Apaloni had designed—small sequential units of behavior that built up the larger skills necessary for independent living. For example, to fix yourself a bowl of cereal, you have to first learn where the bowls and spoons are kept, step by step to learn the whole task of making breakfast. There were six residents— three women and three men—who had all previously lived at Napa State Hospital. Of all the SCOR clients, our clients had mid-range ability. They could all communicate in some fashion, dress and feed themselves, and keep their belongings in order.

The counselors supervised the residents and helped them learn to function as independently as possible in the community—we taught them to keep house and to cook, interact, and cooperate with others. They also learned to get where they needed to go on public transportation. The counselors joked that if we could teach everyone these skills, the world would be a much more peaceful, civilized place. Little did they know that I was working on my own set of independent living skills.

I had been at Tom and Kathy's house much longer than I expected, almost three months. I'd kept in touch with Mary's mother and she invited Colin and me to stay with her in Sebastopol until my apartment at Valley Oak Park was available. She also offered to take care of Colin until I could arrange day care. Sitting in Bea's kitchen one morning, I stared at the phone, trying to work up the courage to call Guy and broach the subject of sharing the cost for day care. Bea handed me a cup of coffee. "This is why women hire divorce lawyers, Sharon," Bea said.

Taking her advice, I hired an attorney and gave him a small retainer. He assured me that it was standard for the husband to pay the wife's attorney's fees if she wasn't working at the time of the divorce. Since Guy's salary was $1,400 a month, my attorney estimated that he would be ordered to pay $250 in child support and make some contribution to childcare.

My job at SCOR paid $500 a month, and my subsidized rent at Valley Oak Park would be $195 including utilities. I was getting food stamps and Medi-Cal for myself, since my new job didn't offer any benefits for the first six months. Colin would be covered on Guy's insurance. If I didn't have to pay any of our credit card debt, my car was paid for so if it didn't break down, and I was very careful, I might be able to make it.

My things were still stored in Guy's garage and we agreed on a day and time for me to pick them up. Guy lifted the double garage door when I pulled into his driveway. I began unloading a stack of flattened boxes from the back of my Barracuda. He looked disheveled and unshaven, in a tattered thermal shirt, corduroy pants, and a pair of old hiking boots. He hated going to the barber and I had always cut his hair. Now his hair was long and uncombed.

"I haven't finished unpacking my things yet," he said with a shrug, gesturing to a mountain of boxes and bags stacked along the garage wall. My rocking chair was piled high and I saw the sleeve of one of my sweaters hanging out of a tear in the bottom of a green garbage bag. "You'll have to dig out your stuff." He lifted Colin out of the car seat and brought him into the house.

I began sorting out the bags and opening boxes and organizing things into stacks. I worked until my car was filled with clothes and picture albums, toys, and cleaning products. I found the set of dishes that Jeanne sent me, but I couldn't find any sheets or towels. I assumed that Guy had probably unpacked those things first. I knocked on the door that led from the garage into the kitchen. I heard no answer and stuck my head in the house.

"Hello? Guy?" I walked through the kitchen and into the living room. I heard Colin in the back bedroom and Guy's voice talking on the phone. "Guy?"

"Back here—in my office," he called out.

I walked down the carpeted hall and into the back bedroom. Guy was sitting at a desk piled high with books and papers. I laughed to myself at how quickly he had reverted to his sloppy bachelor ways. Colin lay on a narrow bed drinking apple juice from a bottle. He hummed to himself and kicked his chubby legs in the air. The head of the bed was piled with Guy's winter coats—the bed and the desk took up most of the space in the small room.

Guy hung up the phone and reached for his lighter. "This is going to be where Colin sleeps when he comes." He pulled a joint from behind his ear and lit it. "Are you finished?"

"My car is full, but I'm going to have to take this load and come back."

"I don't want you to let this drag on, Sharon. I want your stuff out of here."

My heart began to hammer against my chest at the tone I heard in his voice. "I'll just make one more trip today, okay?"

Guy's clothes and shoes spilled out of boxes piled on the floor of the closet and the mirrored sliding doors stood open. Sheets and towels were crammed into the deep shelves in the back of the closet. I turned my back to Guy and pulled my favorite blue towel from the jumble on the shelf, holding the rest of the pile with my other hand to keep everything from falling on the floor. "Oh, I was looking for these," I said.

Guy's chair slammed into the wall and he was on me in an instant. "You didn't have any goddamn towels when you came into this relationship!" he yelled. He grabbed my shoulders and shoved me sideways onto the floor. I tried to get up, but he stomped me in the side with his boot. His face was wild. He loomed over me and I covered my face with my arms.

"You are nothing! You hear me—nothing! You have nothing and you are nothing." He kicked me again and I raised my foot to shove him away but I caught only air. He grabbed my leg and twisted it. A hot pain exploded in my hip.

"No! Guy, please, stop."

"You will come crawling back to me on your hands and knees," he said. His voice was a growl from deep in his throat. I kicked out again and my foot connected with his thigh. I shoved as hard as I could. He stumbled backward into the bed, panting. Colin was screaming. His face was bright red and wet with tears, his eyes pinched shut and his mouth opened wide. Guy looked down at him, as if he had just noticed that he was there.

I jumped off the floor, grabbed Colin, and stumbled out the front door, my legs barely supporting me. I slid behind the steering wheel with Colin clinging to me. I backed out of the driveway and sped away from the house. I turned at East Cotati Avenue, pulled onto the shoulder of the highway and stopped the car. Colin was sobbing, his arms locked around my neck. I rocked and sang to calm both of us. *Ha, Ha, Ha, you and me, little brown baby how I love thee. Ha, Ha, Ha, you and me, little brown baby how I love thee. Ha, Ha, Ha, you and me...* Colin's shuddering breaths slowed and I heard him singing softly, *"Ha, Ha, Ha,"* and his little body started to relax. The traffic whipped past me towards Old Redwood Highway. As Colin dropped off to sleep, I started to cry, but not because of the pain in my hip and ribs, but in impotent fury. I was supposed to protect Colin, but how could I protect him when the most dangerous person in his life was his own father?

Burton House was only five minutes away and it was the first place I thought to go. Jo, my manager, was there when I arrived. She and I had become close and she knew my history with Guy.

"You have to go to the police!" she said. "You didn't make a report the first time and now Guy thinks he can get away with this shit."

I knew she was right. After taking a handful of aspirin, I left Colin asleep in the staff room and drove to the Cotati police station. I told the officer at the front desk that I wanted to file a police report. He shoved some forms at me and disappeared into a back room. I sat down at a table in the corner. I was shivering and in pain. Everything felt wrong about sitting there in a cold police station telling men who looked at me with empty eyes about my problems with Guy. It felt as if I was exposing something private, something only between me and Guy. I sat with my head down, my face wet with tears.

A slim man in his forties called me into his office. A wooden name plate on his desk read *Detective Phillip Palmer*. I handed him the half-empty form. He glanced at the sheet and set it aside. "Why don't you just tell me what happened?" He scribbled notes on a yellow legal pad while I talked. "Towels, huh?" he said with a smile.

"Yeah, I guess he really liked those towels," I said.

We completed the report, and he took pictures of the bright red welts and purple bruises forming along my hip and side. "So, do you want us to go out and talk to him?" he asked.

The thought terrified me. "No. I think that would make things worse. I still have to get the rest of my stuff from his house. Can you just keep the report on file—in case it happens again?"

"We'll keep it on file, but if you want my advice, don't be alone with him anymore. Take someone with you when you go to his house. These guys usually don't act up when other people are around."

I took his advice and returned to Guy's house the following Saturday with Jo and two young men who were also counselors with SCOR. Jo drove the SCOR truck. I stood in front of the garage and Simon knocked on the front door. Guy stepped out onto the small porch and glared at me. He pulled his keys out of his pocket.

"I'm gonna leave for a couple of hours." Simon walked backwards down the front steps to clear his path. Guy passed me on the way to his van. "Are these your chaperones, Sharon?" he asked under his breath.

Glen, whose head only reached Guy's shoulder, took a step closer. "As a matter of fact, we are!" he said.

Guy smirked. "Try not to steal anything. And lock the door when you leave."

I removed all of my things from Guy's garage, but I didn't have enough to set up my new apartment. I scoured the Pennysaver, and made midnight raids on the Goodwill drop box. Mary's mother gave me some of the furniture she had stored in her father's garage. Jo gave me a few donated lamps and a kitchen table, some pots and pans, and a small desk that the other SCOR houses weren't using.

When I moved into my new two-bedroom apartment at Valley Oak Park, I arranged my rocking chair, my secondhand furniture, and my family pictures. I hung my gold Raj of India tapestry on the wall. Colin and I took walks around the neighborhood and snipped cuttings from plants growing close to the sidewalk in our neighbor's yards. We rooted them in cups in the kitchen window to start our own garden. He and I had everything we needed for our brand new life.

CHAPTER SIX

WHEN I WAS A CHILD, my mother was my antagonist, my critic, and my judge. I grew up feeling unworthy and anxious. To bind me to her, she filled me with stories about the dangers in life. The world became a terrifying place for me. As I got older, my fears eroded my confidence and shoved me into the backseat of my own life. I tried to adopt a façade of confidence, but I took my cues from other people and relied heavily on other's advice and absorbed their opinions—first my sisters, then Mary, and then Guy.

But now I was 28 years old and a mother. My life wasn't only about just me anymore, and Colin needed a strong mother he could depend on. I grieved that Guy wasn't the husband and father that I hoped he'd be, but he wasn't. Continuing to cling to that fantasy was unrealistic and immature—even dangerous.

Becoming Colin's mother had given me a view of myself that I'd never had before. I was determined to be a good mother for him. He deserved to be surrounded by love and acceptance, to have a good sense of himself—real confidence and security. I wanted him to have a vastly different childhood than mine had been. I was learning about authenticity and awareness in my therapy with my Gestalt group. All I could be was who I was. That had to be good enough.

But my judgment of the situation was still skewed. In an adapted version of my original fantasy, I found myself hoping that when things settled down, Guy and I would find a way to put our animosity behind us and cooperate as Colin's parents. In my new imaginings, we would be able to share ideas on discipline or the best reinforcement during potty training, and be able to exchange anecdotes and insights into Colin's emerging personality. And as in my original dream of our life together, I was alone in my perception. A different fantasy is still a fantasy

On May 20, 1977, four months after Guy punched me and I ran from the house, I made my first appearance at the Sonoma County Superior Court for our divorce proceedings. Even after all that had happened, I still found it hard to believe that my life with Guy was going to end this way, with us as petitioner, respondent, and their minor child—our lives decided through hearings and orders and declarations. I arrived at the courtroom and pushed through the heavy door to find my attorney. Rays of bright morning light poured through the high windows and swirls of dust mites rained down on the stark room below. I don't know what I expected, but I was surprised that the pew-like benches in the courtroom were filled with people, some trying to control fidgeting children. Attorneys clutching satchels and armfuls of manila files stood clumped together in the shadowy corners. It seemed disrespectful of the private nature of what was being dismantled here to have disinterested parties casually listening in.

Guy and his attorney, Tom Kenny, walked in moments before the bailiff called our case. There was much shuffling and stamping of the papers handed back and forth between the clerk, our attorneys, and the judge. Guy and I each sat at our respective attorney's table without looking at each other.

Judge Randall signed an order giving me physical custody of Colin, now fifteen months old. Guy received standard visitation, every other weekend and every Wednesday evening, six weeks in the summer, and alternating holidays. My attorney requested $250 monthly child support. Tom objected and countered with an offer of $100, referring to Guy's financial statement, which listed thousands of dollars of outstanding loans from his mother and grandmother, all payable on demand, among various other debts.

Guy offered to keep Colin on his insurance, but I would have to pay any co-payments and deductibles for Colin's health care. The judge ordered Guy to pay a one-time amount of $250 for my attorney's fees, $150 for child support, and $125 each month towards childcare costs.

I didn't believe that Guy would ever hit me again. Now that I knew what he was capable, I thought I could prevent it every happening again. Still my attorney insisted that we document the two beatings in the Court record. He filed a request for an order of protection along with the divorce papers. The beatings were not discussed in the courtroom and the reference to "incidences of violence" took on a sanitized, generic feeling when I saw it printed on the page. I couldn't process everything that was happening. These deeply emotional events felt they were taking place off-stage, somewhere far away. Guy's attorney requested that the restraining order be made mutual. Without fanfare, the Honorable Ellis R. Randall ordered us not to molest, disturb, or harass each other. I agreed to everything. This was my first legal proceeding, and I wanted to get it over with. It all seemed unrelated to my real life. Before long, I would lose my naïve belief that what went on inside the courtroom was mere formality.

I enrolled Colin in a licensed day care home in Cotati. It was close to Burton House and convenient for Guy on the days he picked him up. The first day I left Colin, my usually affable little boy stood by the door crying. "No, mommy! No. No. No." I could hear him through the door but I forced myself to get in my car and go to work. His unhappy cry stayed with me all day. But I wasn't really worried. No one was a stranger very long to Colin and I expected that he would quickly get involved with the other kids.

But when I picked him up that afternoon, he ran to me. He lifted his arms to be picked up and snuggled his head into my neck. I noticed that all the children were sitting in the same spots they had been in when I dropped him off—all in front of the television. And the day care provider was in the same spot she had been in that morning, still stirring a cup of coffee. Something wasn't right here. There was a dead feeling to the place. Colin and I didn't go back and I began to pay closer attention to my son's instincts about people.

The next day care home I found was warm and lively. When Guy became overtly flirtatious with the attractive young mother who ran it, she told me that Guy would not be allowed to come and pick up Colin, even on the days that Guy had him. I was not going to have that conversation with Guy, so I began the search for another care situation for Colin. Finally, I settled on Huckleberry House, which was operated by a schoolteacher who was taking a few years off to stay at home with her young son. Since she was a professional teacher, she was licensed to supervise two interns from Sonoma State. They had an organized curriculum and the backyard looked like a well-appointed playground. Huckleberry House was the best of both worlds—a home environment and a professional day care program.

Colin Murphy-Johnson with daycare friends, Santa Rosa,
California 1979

As shocked and distraught as I was when Guy and I first broke up, I began to enjoy being away from him and his soul killing judgments. When we did breathing exercises in group, I felt as if I had been holding my breath for years. A new sense of possibilities added a surprising dash of excitement and energy to my life. Colin was happy at his day care. I liked my job and was making friends with some of the other staff members. My apartment was cozy and I had good neighbors. I was broke, but eating oatmeal by candlelight on a cold autumn morning with my beautiful red-headed boy could not have been more fun and special. I could feel that I was on the right track.

The families that lived in the eight square blocks of Valley Oak Park Apartments were roughly arranged into neighborhoods according to the ages of the children. Colin and I were surrounded by families with children under five. Each identical, two-story townhouse had a small patio in the front and back that was enclosed by a high slatted fence. Colin, with his big personality and flaming red Afro, quickly became a popular member of the tribe of preschoolers. In the evenings, the parents along our row propped open their gates so the kids could gather at one apartment and dash off and reassemble at another. The gang only dispersed at bedtime.

For a little kid his age, Colin had a great facility with any kind of ball. When we walked through the playground at Valley Oak Park, he'd smack his soft baby soccer ball with his sneaker-clad foot and pump his strong legs to run after it. He was only two years old at the time, even though his size and coordination made him appear older. He caught the attention of the older kids and soon the eight-year-old gang began appearing at our door to see if Colin could come out and play soccer with them.

Every week I worked with my Gestalt group. They had become an essential part of my new life. Carl's friend, David Bradshaw, organized an annual camping trip in the Sierras for members of the Gestault groups. While Colin was having his first summer visit with his father, I lugged a fifty pound pack up a trail to our campsite. For six days I slept in a tent with a view of a melting snow bank. During the day, we collected river rocks and buried them in the fire pit in the center of camp till they glowed red-hot, and every night we piled them in the middle of a sweat lodge and chanted and breathed in the hot steam perfumed with sage. I learned a lesson about letting go of preconceived fear when I had to dart out of the sweat lodge and jump into the lake without hesitating to consider the wisdom of plunging into freezing cold, pitch black water.

At the end of the week, I felt closer to the people in my group than I'd ever felt to anyone before. I began to get an idea of what real intimacy felt like. I also became friends and occasionally lovers with David, the trip's organizer. He took Colin and me on other hikes and weekend camping trips to obscure places he found on his topographical maps. Colin and I called him *Sweet David*. He wrote poetry and played the guitar and our relationship was calm and peaceful. His gentle, quiet manner, slim frame, and soft blonde hair were the exact opposite of Guy—he was just what I needed.

Before long, I had to suspend my hopeful expectation that being divorced from Guy would be any better than being married to him. It took me a long time to understand what was happening, although in hindsight, there was evidence from the very beginning. Guy had spelled it out when we got together all those years ago, but I wasn't really hearing him. I was preoccupied searching for hints of his love for me. That day on the deck of the Henry Street house when Mary was recuperating from her tubal pregnancy, Guy had said it all. He wanted children and he decided he wanted to have them with me. During that emotional speech, he hadn't said that he loved me more, or felt we made a better couple than he and Mary. I was his choice to make him a father. When I became pregnant with Colin, I was fulfilling my purpose.

But now the marriage hadn't worked out. I was becoming a nuisance. I had accused him of domestic violence. I left and took his son and he had to pay me child support. I was a net loss and he set about getting rid of me. With Maya's apparently unlimited backing, the courtroom quickly became Guy's new arena. He petitioned for a change of custody. But he did not merely ask for custody, he set about trying to convince the Court that Colin's very safety was at stake if he was left in my care. He developed a new Sharon Murphy, constructing this awful mother as carefully as he would have crafted a villainess in a novel. I was an unstable woman, a danger to Colin's physical and emotional well-being. I was a person who operated on the outer fringes of society, deficient in every way. How could the Court allow a woman like me to have access to an innocent child? Guy became the model of the mainstream dad who had made an unfortunate choice of wife. I didn't recognize either one of us in the scenario Guy was inventing.

Colin had been getting ear infections since he was a year old. I could always see them coming on; he would become uncharacteristically fussy. He would pull on his ear and want me to hold him. The minute I suspected an ear infection, we'd be off to the pediatrician. At home, I had him lay his head on a rolled-up heating pad while I massaged his head and neck with warm oil and waited for the antibiotics to kick in.

After we went through this a few times, I did some research. I read an article that claimed that antibiotics may not be the right treatment for all ear infections. Too many antibiotics could even be harmful to small children. I called the ER at the Community Hospital and a few other pediatricians' offices to get their advice. I asked my sister Sally Ann, who was an R.N. I learned that not all ear infections are bacterial. They can be viral and unaffected by antibiotics. Another nurse suggested that Colin might have food allergies, which could cause fluid to back up in his ears and become a dangerous medium for infection.

My day care provider gave me the name of a holistic health center in Cotati that did a non-invasive test specifically to identify food allergies. I made an appointment and watched in amazement as the doctor put different pellets under Colin's tongue. I could see his muscles react differently to each food that his body was allergic to, including wheat, egg whites, and cow's milk.

This happened long before I fully appreciated how important it was to shield myself from Guy. When I got the results of the test, and the doctor's recommended diet, I was so proud and excited that I had found something that might end Colin's suffering that I called Guy to share my good news. I needed him to follow the diet when Colin was in his care. I described the concept of *internal energy*, fundamental to traditional Chinese medicine, and the muscle testing the doctor used to pinpoint the foods Colin should not be eating.

The next time Guy came to pick up Colin for his visit, I gave Guy a handout, a copy of the diet, and a list of stores in Santa Rosa that sold things like rice bread and goat kefir. I didn't know it then, but in addition to a grocery bag filled with non-allergic food, I had also handed Guy a big armful of ammunition to use against me in Court. Guy's next petition for a change of custody contained a litany of my alleged offenses, highlighting Colin's treatment at the Cotati Holistic Health Center. "Colin is listless and frequently sick. Ms. Murphy lets Colin sleep under an open window and her home is insufficiently heated at night. Respondent has abandoned common medical practices. She is trying to cure the child's ear infections with chants and mantras.

"Ms. Murphy allows Colin to wear soiled diapers for extended periods of time, causing him to suffer from severe rashes. A professional pediatric nurse witnessed these painful rashes on Colin."

If possible, I felt even more betrayed. Guy's friend Carol had been drafted to lend credibility to Guy's lies. The petition concluded by stating, "Inevitably, when Colin comes for visits, he is dirty, his clothes are in disrepair, and he is not adequately dressed for the weather. Ms. Murphy is unable or unwilling to provide Colin with proper care."

I didn't recognize the mother and son that Guy described. I could understand that he was angry at me, but how could he create this image of his own child? Or of his child's mother? But when I found myself asking how Guy could sign his name *under penalty of perjury* to such fiction, I had to bring myself up short. Guy would say or do anything to get what he wanted. I needed to accept that, and to learn how to defend myself and the life I'd built with Colin.

Guy didn't pay my attorney's fees as he was ordered to do. I couldn't afford to pay him either, so my attorney quit and sent me my file along with his final bill. I had no choice but to appear at the next hearing on my own behalf. I had reviewed Guy's accusations and had written responses to each charge.

But how could I prove Guy was lying? It was his word against mine again. The fact that Guy was petitioning for custody scared me. Would a judge believe him? Would a judge believe that the entire petition was filled with lies and distortions? I tried to push away the waves of panic that overtook me in the days before the hearing. After all, I had truth on my side, I told myself. Even so, it was hard to remain positive.

Guy appeared in Court wearing the suit pants that I made for him when we lived in Stockton. The subtle reminder of how slavishly in love I had been with him then unsettled me. Guy took the stand and was sworn in. He was the very picture of rectitude and restraint.

"I don't want to take Colin away from Sharon. A small child *needs* his mother. Taking custody away from Sharon is not something I *want* to do, but I am duty-bound to request a change of custody in the best interests of my child. It is the only way to be assured that my son is safe and well taken care of."

Guy's attorney led him through his list of complaints and a chill ran through me. Tom Kenny was sharp. He wore an expensive suit and shoes and had a stylish haircut. He spoke calmly and unemotionally and treated Guy with respect and deference. Watching them together, attorney and client, I saw a powerful team focused on one goal—to take my son away from me.

I was prepared to rebut Guy's exaggerated assertions one by one, but I had the sense that these details were not as important as Guy's overall strategy. This proved to be a prescient impression. This hearing was the beginning of the end.

Walking to the witness stand, the floor turned soft beneath my feet. Seated and sworn in, I did the best I could to sound confident. I described the holistic health center and the muscle testing, but in the somber courtroom, my novice's understanding of the ancient method sounded incredible—even to me. The fact that I had seen the results with my own eyes seemed like weak validation, as if I was verifying a nightly apparition.

I ran down the notes on my yellow tablet trying to debunk Guy's other claims, but the best I could do was to say they weren't true—that I took good care of my son. I asked the judge, "How could Guy claim that Colin slept under an open window? He's never been to my apartment at night." I could hear myself sounding defensive and tried to adjust my tone. I was on the verge of tears by the time I left the stand.

To my immense relief, the judge did not change custody that day. Nonetheless, Guy's fictional portrait of me had gained a foothold. The judge ordered me to submit not only Colin's medical records but my own records as well—to the Court for periodic review. The erosion of my parental rights had begun.

Guy never did pay the $250 to my attorney, and over the next few months, my attempts at self-representation proved the axiom that anyone who represents himself in Court has a fool for a client. Even though his first attempt hadn't achieved the ultimate result, every couple of months Guy recycled different renditions of the same complaints. I was neglectful, irresponsible, had a string of men who slept over at my house. I had low standards. I didn't care about Colin's education, upbringing, or health. With no attorney to watch out for me, Guy was able to lower his child support payment, change Colin's day care center and his pediatrician, and decide how often I should bring him to the doctor for an examination—all with the approval and authority of the Sonoma County Superior Court behind him. But the Court still did not change the custody order.

I had lost a lot of ground, and I needed help. I hired Richard Barnett, a young attorney who was building a private practice. He didn't have much experience, but, after trying to defend myself, I was grateful to have any attorney. Richard knew Guy's attorney, and knew that Kenny had a reputation for being relentless and ruthless in getting his clients what they wanted. He also knew there was only a slim chance that he would be fully paid for his work.

The judge on our case assigned Mike Lentz as our Conciliation Officer. Lentz would review all subsequent filings and, if he thought it was necessary, would draft orders to be submitted to the judge for approval and signature. Lentz alone determined when and if we got a hearing in front of the judge. No attorneys were allowed in these mediation sessions with Lentz. So even though I had an attorney, I was forced to face Guy alone.

Guy was handsome, confident, and well-spoken. He always made sure everyone knew he was the son of Maya Angelou, the famous and adored author who lived right here in Sonoma County. I had seen how deftly he worked that detail into casual conversations. Unluckily for me, Guy's position with county personnel also put him in close contact with the staff of the various departments involved in our case, including the Conciliation Court.

While I was waiting in the lobby of the courthouse before one meeting with Lentz, I watched Guy emerge from his office in the Personnel Department and stroll the short distance across the courtyard for our meeting. I followed him into Lentz's office and the receptionist greeted him cheerfully, "Oh, hi, Guy!" I was alone on Guy's turf. Who would ever think such a great guy would hit his wife, lie, or distort the truth? Everyone thought he was terrific—like mother like son.

Guy began dating a woman who had two young daughters. Linda also worked for Sonoma County, and before long, Guy's petitions to the Court claimed that he was "soon to be married." He could now assert that he would be able to provide a stable family environment for Colin.

"Colin has a very close relationship with my *fiancé's* two daughters, who are eight and ten."

Guy soon had Linda handle all the contact with me. Every time she called, I was reminded of all the phone calls I made to Guy's mother for him. The only advantage for me was that I didn't have to talk to Guy as often. When Guy moved into Linda's house in a subdivision on the outskirts of Santa Rosa,

Guy began referring to her as *my wife* in his petitions to the Court, even though they were not married.

One afternoon, Guy picked Colin up from Kiddie Corner Day School, and the teacher handed him a flyer. A former student at Kiddie Corner had come down with hepatitis. The little boy had been taken out of the school five weeks before he became sick. The staff consulted with a physician, and they felt confident that none of the current students were in danger, but were obligated to inform all parents. Guy was edgy when he called and read me the notice.

"I want you to make an appointment immediately for Colin to get a gamma globulin shot," he said. "Hepatitis is very serious."

I was inclined to accept the reassurance of the school that Colin had not been at the school when the sick boy was there, but I knew better than to say that to Guy. I agreed to make an appointment with Colin's pediatrician, but first I talked to my sister Sally Ann, a nurse, and then I spoke with the ER nurse at the Sonoma County hospital where Colin was born. They each expressed concern about giving Colin the gamma globulin shot after the repeated doses of penicillin he had received for his ear infections during the previous year.

I called Guy and read from the notes I made during my conversations. "My sister and two other nurses advised *against* giving Colin the shot and I talked to one who thought he *should* have it," I said.

"I don't care what you say. I'm taking him to get the shot." Guy said.

"I didn't say I was against giving him the shot. Aren't we ever going to be able to talk about anything, Guy?"

"I don't need to discuss my child's health with an unstable person whose relationship with good child rearing is so ephemeral. You'll be hearing from my attorney."

During a brief trip to Conciliation Court to discuss the issue, Guy showed Lentz the flyer and huffed, "I had to take Colin to the pediatrician *myself* because Sharon *refused* to do it." He sounded like a five-year-old tattling on his sister.

"The school didn't think there was any risk that Colin had been exposed, right?" Lentz asked, appearing impatient with Guy and keeping his eyes on the paper from Kiddie Corner.

"The school felt that none of the present students had been exposed. The sick boy left the school five weeks before he came down with hepatitis," I said.

"Guy, did Colin have the shot?" Lentz asked.

Guy stammered. "Yes...he had the shot."

"Well, I see no problem, then," Lentz handed the flyer back to Guy and made no official entry about the incident in our file.

Shortly after Colin's third birthday, he and I were having lunch with my friend Rose in Coddingtown Mall. Colin was drinking a strawberry smoothie and playing Pac-Man, with the bill of his maroon Washington Redskins cap pulled low over his dark eyes. When it was time to leave, Colin resisted. "One more game, Momma?"

"No, that's it for today." He tried to resist but I scooted him through the door. Once outside in the mall, he threw his cup on the ground in protest and a splash of pink slid across the sidewalk. I never spanked Colin, but this time, I swatted him on the bottom. He collapsed on the ground in a fit of dramatics.

Not wanting to reinforce his tantrum, Rose and I walked to a nearby bench and waited. Colin cried as if his heart would break for about a minute. When he peeked up to see where I was, Rose and I waved at him. He picked himself up off the sidewalk and straightened his cap in a disgusted manner. I covered my mouth so he wouldn't see me smiling. When Colin was indignant, he looked just like Guy. I walked over to him and gave him a hug, then the three of us walked towards the parking lot—the incident forgotten.

I was unaware that Gloria Burgess, a coworker of Guy's, was watching us.

My attorney called me a few days later and read the document that Guy's attorney had submitted to the Court. "The child dropped his drink and Ms. Murphy allowed her friend to knock the child to the ground. It was only the comments of passers-by and Colin's screams that forced Sharon to return and assist the child."

Lentz recommended that a hearing take place before the judge. Rose, the mother of five, took time off from work and came with me, willing to testify. Fortunately she didn't have to. The judge listened to my account of what happened and to my relief he turned down Guy's request for a change of custody.

I got home from Court around noon and as soon as I had poured myself a glass of iced tea, the phone rang. I was surprised to hear Richard's voice so soon. "You won't believe this," he said.

"What now?"

"Guy is demanding that you be charged with Contempt of Court and that custody be changed immediately pending an investigation."

"Why won't he leave me alone?"

"He claims that on Friday, April 6th, he dropped Colin off after having him for the afternoon and he gave you a ten-day prescription of antibiotics. But when he picked Colin up for his weekend visit on Friday, April 13th—only seven days later— you didn't give him the bottle of medicine. He claims that you willfully failed to comply with the Court order that instruct- ed you to give Colin any and all medication that Dr. Brewer prescribed."

"That's not true. That was a seven-day prescription and I gave Colin every drop. Maybe if Guy would stop feeding him ice cream, he wouldn't have any more ear infections!"

"Also, he's bringing up the hepatitis thing again. You should see this petition! In caps and underlined, it says, 'This fact which jeopardized Colin's life should be basis alone for imme- diately changing custody for his protection and well-being.'"

On Wednesday, May 2, 1979, Judge Joseph Murphy listened as our respective attorneys questioned Guy and me. Then he called a recess and we all sat staring at an empty bench while the judge went into his chambers to call Dr. Brewer. When he returned, he confirmed that Dr. Brewer supported my version of the story. The medicine Guy gave me had been a seven-day prescription—not ten, so I wouldn't have any medicine left when Guy picked Colin up again.

The doctor also confirmed that there were differing opin- ions on the merits of giving gamma globulin shots to otherwise healthy children.

Judge Murphy said, "The minute order filed after this hear- ing will read, "Sharon Murphy did *not* willfully fail to comply with the Court order regarding the administration of medicine to the child."

I finally exhaled.

"Mr. Johnson," Judge Murphy continued. "You are divorced from Ms. Murphy. You cannot control everything she does."

Guy's face reddened and he didn't respond. I was encouraged by Judge Murphy's supportive words, but this encouragement was tempered by his ordering a comprehensive review of our case by the Probation Department. They would conduct a home study, and then make a recommendation on the question of custody. Guy's complaints had moved the process to the next legal level.

I was devastated and shaking when Richard and I walked out of the courtroom. When we got far enough down the hall so Guy couldn't overhear, I said, "Even when the judge *proves* that Guy's accusations have no foundation, I still get closer to losing my son." My determined attitude melted and tears burned my eyes. I tried to blink them away, but a breathy sob escaped from my throat.

Richard led me to a marble bench along the wall and leaned in close. "Sharon, maybe the home study will put an end to all Guy's petitions for custody."

"You can't believe that! I have to get off the defensive if I'm ever going to win in Court. I don't see that ever happening! We're too busy arguing against all the ridiculous things that Guy comes up with. He'll never stop! You know that don't you?" I was sobbing and hid my face in my hands. "Where's Guy?"

"He walked out the other way." Richard put his arm around my shoulder. I noticed that the pocket of his suit was still stitched together—a new suit, right off the rack from J.C. Penney's.

In retrospect, my attorney should have been more aggressive in giving the Court a counterbalancing picture of me and my relationship with Colin. The unsavory picture that Guy painted of me was allowed to dominate the mind of the Court. No one heard how well Colin was doing and how smart and funny he was, that I took him to Golden Gate Park so he could ride his Big Wheel along the trails through the trees and examine bugs in his magnifying box, or that we went to Bodega Bay to feed the seagulls and chase the waves and buy saltwater taffy.

I would have told him that Colin likes magic tricks, the sillier the better, and that we competed almost every night to see who could build the tallest Lego tower. That I made his clothes, that we read books and laughed and had friends and a good life together. I was never given the opportunity to talk about these things.

The funding for the SCOR group homes collapsed. The directors weren't able to find state or county funding to keep the project going when the original grant money ran out. It was a tremendous shock and my fragile new life felt as if it was imploding under my feet. I made a desperate attempt to prevent the inevitable. I organized the "Save the Group Home Coalition" and the staff worked day and night to prevent the group homes from closing. I contacted politicians and activists from all over California, parents of the residents, and other organizations and facilitated a meeting at Sonoma State to find other sources of funding. If we failed, the residents we'd had become close to would be returned to state institutions or to "mom and pop" group homes in the community that were little more than babysitting services.

During these efforts, I met Toni Novak, the Director of 4-Cs, the Community Child Care Coalition. Eventually we couldn't keep the group homes open and I found myself out of work, Toni asked me to come to a meeting at her office. 4-C's had been awarded a federally funded block grant to build a day care center in the Valley Oak Park neighborhood. Before the money could be released to build the center, there had to be a community organization to serve as a board of directors and at least fifty children had to be enrolled in a free after-school recreation program. The good news was that Toni wanted me to pull together the community organization and design and manage the after-school program, but the bad news was that my salary was almost all the funding available for the first year. There was a big mandate but very few resources. I needed a job and a distraction, so I eagerly agreed. I was excited about this new challenge—even more so because Colin could be with me at work some of the time.

I knocked on every door in the complex in search of volunteers to help the kids with games and art projects and to serve on the board. I lived on the phone. I contacted businesses, churches, and community organizations. I begged and cajoled donations of money and materials for the program. I spoke at city council meetings. A local radio station gave me 100 KZST Frisbees and Colin began wearing one of the black caps with the face of an orange panther on the crown donated by the Santa Rosa High School football team. I found a use for everything anyone could give me.

I climbed around in dumpsters behind large companies and hauled piles of carpet, paper, and cardboard, and donated tubs of paint, glue, and glitter around in the back of my Barracuda. I arranged the donated materials in the cabinets in the community room at Valley Oak Park, stacking up art supplies, books, and toys. We finally received a supplemental grant and I hired Sandy, the single mother who helped me get my apartment at Valley Oak Park, and one other woman as program aides.

The Valley Oak Park recreation program was for school-age kids and since Colin was only three, he became the program's mascot—largely because of his skill with a soccer ball. One of the older kids gave him a white helmet and he wore it as his official soccer uniform. He had no fear and was a natural athlete. Colin was full of wild abandon. We organized a recycling program, a softball team, and a mini-bike club. We put on talent shows, scavenger hunts, and hosted holiday parties. Before long, the community room hummed with activity day and night.

Colin at Valley Oak Park

Colin was so healthy and hardy that it was a shock in October of 1979 when Dr. Brewer wanted to schedule an echocardiogram for him. When Colin was born, the doctor detected a heart murmur, but he had assured us that the murmur would most likely resolve itself. But almost four years later, there was still a gentle *shush, shush, shush* in the background when Dr. Brewer listened to Colin's heart. He referred me to a pediatric cardiologist at UC Medical Center in San Francisco. While I drove down Highway 101 to San Francisco, Colin fidgeted with his new transformer, a yellow Corvette that turned into a robot. He was wearing his black batting helmet. I had agreed that he could wear it only if promised to take it off when we got to the hospital. I turned down the radio and jiggled his knee to get his attention. My mother never explained anything to me when I was a child, and I didn't want to repeat that same mistake. "I want to tell you about the test the doctor is going to do today."

"Mmmm." His focus was on his toy, which didn't look like a car or a robot at the moment.

"Remember when we looked at that drop of water under the microscope at the science museum and we could see what was going on inside?"

"Mmmm."

"The doctor is going to use a machine like that microscope, only bigger, and look inside your heart."

Colin finally looked up. "Will it hurt?"

"No, it won't hurt," I said.

"Okay, no problem!"

He made the last few rotations of the metal contraption and a robot appeared. "Cool!" He held up the toy proudly.

"Good job, sweetie."

Colin and I checked in at the reception desk and followed the maroon stripe on the floor, through the labyrinth of right and left turns to the cardiology department. Colin led the way, characteristically treating this as an interesting adventure. After a short wait, he climbed up on the exam table and took off his shirt with no fuss. The technician let him hold the transducer while she attached the leads. He was examining it when she squirted the cold gel on his skin. "That tickles!" he giggled. The doctor came in and put the transducer in the center of Colin's chest.

All eyes turned to the monitor as the inside of Colin's heart came into focus. I tried to act nonchalant as I stood next to the paper-covered table, holding Colin's hand.

"That's my heart, Momma!"

"It sure is! It looks so strong." I said.

After the exam, Colin sat on the table sucking on a lollipop while the technician cleaned the gel off his skin. They chatted away like old friends.

I stepped into the hall with the doctor. "Colin has Patent Ductus Arteriosus," he said.

"You'll have to explain that to me."

"Before birth, there's a temporary blood vessel between the left pulmonary artery and the aorta. It usually closes on its own after birth, but for some reason, Colin's is only partially closed. The murmur that you hear is the small flow of blood through that open vessel. There is no apparent heart disease. This is relatively common, but if left untreated, Colin could develop serious heart problems later on. We need to close that valve."

All the blood rushed out of my head and I reached out for the wall. The doctor helped me into a chair. *"Heart surgery?"* I asked when my head cleared.

"Not really. We don't touch the heart. We go in through the back and tie off the valve next to the heart. He'll be in the hospital about ten days."

While the nurse readied the paperwork, I called Guy. He was as shocked and frightened as I had been when I called to give him an update and get the insurance information. I braced myself, but there was no ensuing flood of blame or hostility, and for the first time in a long time Guy and I had an authentic conversation about Colin. He even thanked me for calling, "Let me know as soon as the arrangements are made," he said as he hung up.

The following week, on the night before his surgery, Colin and I treated ourselves to cheeseburgers and fries at Mel's Diner and then checked into Moffitt Hospital. We decorated the lime green walls of his room with the good-luck cards our friends and family had sent, and I placed a purple and yellow balloon bouquet on his bedside table. Under the anemic light at the head of his high bed, he tore the shiny paper off his presents— new pajamas and superhero coloring books. The night nurse brought in a green vinyl recliner and a stack of bedding so I could sleep next to Colin.

In the middle of the night, I felt Colin crawl in next to me. "I'm scared, Momma," he said. He snuggled up next to me and rested his head on my shoulder.

"Me too, baby. We're gonna have to be brave."

Early the next morning, just as an orderly was wheeling Colin out of his room on a gurney, Guy arrived with Linda. Guy walked solemnly next to Colin and Linda and I followed until they pushed the gurney through the metal doors into the surgery suite. The three of us stood in the hallway, awkwardly alone together, as the doors swung shut. Guy raked his fingers through his hair and tears rolled down his cheeks. "I can't stand this," he said. "I'll be back later." He turned and hurried off, with Linda following quickly behind him.

I waited alone in the cold blue hall of the surgery department, alternately staring at the same page of my book, and then at the oval window in the swinging door of the recovery room. After more than three hours, a nurse wheeled Colin into the corner of the room. He was lying on his back, unconscious, with an IV in his forearm. He was naked except for the thick gauze and strips of white surgical tape around his chest and right shoulder.

Without thinking, I pushed open the doors and rushed towards him. The nurse moved to stop me, but then stepped away after covering Colin with a warm sheet. I lay my head next to his on the thin white pillow. "Momma's here, baby. Momma's here."

Colin was back in his room when Guy returned. He and Linda had their arms full of presents. Guy regarded me as if he was speaking to the maid. "We'd like to visit with Colin. Do you mind leaving?" he asked coldly.

"Bye-bye, baby. I'll be back later. Do you want me to bring you anything?"

"Chips?" Colin said.

I caught the bus on Parnassus and headed towards Ocean Beach. I could feel ever block as the distance between Colin and me increased—it pulled against my chest like a magnet. I forced myself to stand in the wet wind on the hard-packed sand with my hands in my pockets and watch the October sun set over the jagged teeth of the Farallon Islands. I lasted about an hour, and then I hurried back to the hospital, stopping only to buy Colin two small bags of Doritos. I bunked in the hospital for the next seven days. David and a few other friends stopped by to see Colin and keep me company. I showered in the nurses' locker room, slept in the green recliner at night, and entertained Colin and the other kids on the ward during the day. Moffitt is a teaching hospital, and I had to physically shield Colin from overeager med students who showed up in his room wanting to poke and prod and take blood samples for unknown reasons. While Colin napped, I used the pay phone in the lounge and tried to keep the Valley Oak recreation program together—following up with donors, problem solving with the staff, and checking in with Toni.

Guy only made one more evening visit to see Colin during the next week. As soon as he stepped into the room, I left and took myself out to dinner on Haight Street, a few blocks down the hill from Parnassus Avenue. Maya showed up at the hospital unannounced on the afternoon before Colin was to be discharged. I saw her the minute she stepped off the elevator at the far end of the brightly lit hallway. I was surprised at the rush of emotion that coursed through me. I'd been hurt and disappointed when she made no effort to get in touch with me after Guy and I divorced, although it would have been out of character if she had. More to the point, Guy's continued hostility and efforts to take custody of Colin had drawn a clear line of demarcation between he and I, and Maya had been relegated to Guy's side of the divide.

In the two years since I had last seen her, Maya had attained an almost god-like public stature. I could barely pick up a magazine or a newspaper that didn't feature her or her work, or announcements of her upcoming television appearances or lectures. She had accumulated a National Book Award for *Caged Bird*, a Pulitzer nomination for her poetry, and a Grammy for her spoken word albums. She had been awarded a number of honorary degrees and was now being referred to as *Dr.* Angelou. But I didn't want a relationship with the celebrity. The love and support I thought Maya initially offered me had seemed like my chance to have the *good mother* I had always wanted, and a good grandmother for Colin. Now she represented another loss in my life. As I watched her walking towards me, I had to admit that I had missed her.

Maya clutched a small bag under her elbow and looked from side to side. I waved to get her attention. She was dressed for an event, wearing a red wool pantsuit with a red silk blouse, accessorized by a gold scarf held in place by a large gold and diamond pin. Heads turned as people recognized her. Maya didn't smile until she noticed Colin in the crowd of kids being rounded up by a nurse's aide for story time. I called after him, "Look, Colin, it's your grandmother."

Colin ran up to her. He was wearing his Snoopy pajamas and an aqua scrub cap. "Hi, grandmother, look at my scar. I have a little piece of string inside me, right next to my heart." He proudly lifted up the back of his pajama top to reveal the curved pink scar near his shoulder blade.

"Oh, well isn't that something?" Maya leaned over and turned her cheek for a kiss. "Are you going to come and visit with your grandmother?"

"No, it's story time. I have to push Dominic's wheelchair. Bye!" Before Maya could protest, Colin took his place behind a dark-skinned boy with a cast on his leg. He shoved the wheelchair down the hall towards the playroom.

Maya's face fell. She looked at me as if hoping I would call him back. When I said nothing, she nodded towards me. "Walk with me."

We walked back to the elevator and she pushed the down button. I had forgotten how overpowering her six-foot frame could be and felt awkward and self-conscious standing next to her in the small elevator. I had spent the entire week at the hospital and was worn out and unkempt in my oversized sweatshirt and jeans, no makeup, and my hair tied back under a flowered scarf.

I nervously chattered about the surgery and Colin's rapid recuperation. "The doctor told me that he'd be favoring his right arm for months, but you saw him. He doesn't seem to be in any pain at all. He's doing great. They're releasing him tomorrow—two days early."

Finally we reached the garage level and exited the elevator. The autumn sun was setting over the trees of Golden Gate Park and the garage was streaked with golden light. Maya looked around for her car and I followed in silence, the heels of her low pumps echoing against the flat grey walls. When we reached her bronze Lincoln Town Car, she laid her purse on the wide trunk and pulled out a small bottle of B&B. She leaned back against the car, twisted off the cap, and handed the bottle to me. I sipped the warm liqueur and eyed Maya over the amber bottle. Never being one for preliminaries, she got right to her point. "Sharon, I have no idea what happened between you and my son, but I'm hurt that I haven't heard from you. And you've made no attempt to bring Colin to see me."

I handed her the bottle and she took a long drink. I had assumed that Guy took Colin to visit his grandmother, although Colin never mentioned Maya when he came home and I didn't question him. I thought maybe he was learning to keep the two sides of his life separate. I had apparently been wrong.

Maya stared at me with a level gaze and my cheeks got warm. "You're Guy's mother," I said. "With everything that's been going on...when I didn't hear from *you*...I assumed you were in support of...well, of what Guy's been doing."

"What do you mean? I don't even know why you two broke up! And I don't know what he's been up to. Linda's a nice person and a good mother, but she's cold. She'll never have my heart the way you do." Maya's words were emphatic—like a proclamation.

I felt as if I was hearing something I shouldn't. I didn't know what to say. I was afraid to trust her, but she seemed genuinely bewildered. We passed the bottle again in silence. "Guy's trying to take Colin away from me. He's been taking me to Court, dragging me through the mud. He's saying I'm unstable and a danger to Colin."

She looked away. "I thought something like that might be happening."

Could she really not know? She took another sip from the small bottle and I watched an internal dialogue play across her thick features. If anyone knew about struggling to raise a child, she did. I watched her, thinking how ironic this scene was. Maya's fame sprang from her poignant rendition of her early life as a poor unwed mother, confused and angry. Every one of her mistakes and bad decisions, even being a prostitute and a madam, only made her readers love her more. I felt a small surge of hope. If Maya intervened, maybe Guy would reconsider what he was doing. As if her internal conversation had reached some conclusion, she said, "I don't know what I could do, anyway."

"You could talk to your son." Maya and I looked into each other's eyes. I could see her conflict, but could tell that she wasn't going to help me. I stepped forward and wrapped my arms around her. When I released her, she looked sad and confused. "I'm going back up," I said.

During the months after Colin's surgery, I got a welcome break from any further Court action or meetings with Mike Lentz. I had a fleeting and foolish hope that Maya might be exerting some influence over the situation. But the entire case was in a holding pattern, waiting for the judge to send his request for the home study to the Marin Probation Department.

One afternoon Colin was riding in the grocery basket's child seat while I shopped. When I wheeled the cart into the frozen food section, we started one of our games. He threw his arms around me and said, "BRRRRRRR, Mommy, I'm freezing! I'm freezing!"

"I'll save you!" I wrapped my arms around him and pushed the cart quickly to the end of the chilly aisle. I rubbed his face and arms. "Are you all right? Do you think you will live?" Colin laughed and another mother smiled as she watched us. I laughed until the incident in Coddingtown Mall popped into my mind. I looked around, worried that someone Guy knew might be looking on. I enjoyed my job, and had friends and neighbors I loved, but it occurred to me that it might be a good idea to have more distance between Guy and me. Santa Rosa was not a big town, and my circle of friends in the nonprofit world had connections to funding sources in county government and to the Sonoma County Board of Supervisors—all direct avenues to Guy. It was easy for Guy or people he knew to spy on me either intentionally or accidentally. If I didn't live in Santa Rosa, I might not have to be looking over my shoulder all the time. Even before I made a firm decision to leave Santa Rosa, I started making some preliminary inquiries about jobs in San Francisco. As if it were meant to be, I was offered a job as the secretary at The Urban School, an alternative high school in the Haight-Ashbury neighborhood. Even without knowing how I would make it work, I accepted.

The next Saturday morning, I was holding Colin between my knees, cutting his hair while he ate cinnamon toast and watched cartoons on TV. The sides of his head were trimmed close, while the top and back were still long and bushy, giving him a curly red Mohawk. The phone rang and I dropped a lock of hair into a paper bag next to me and picked up the phone.

Guy's voice was a low whisper. "You're not taking my son anywhere, you bitch."

I could hear Linda in the background. "Guy, calm down."

"I hurt you the last time—I'll kill you the next time. I'm coming over there right now."

"Guy, you're not going anywhere..." Linda's voice was cut off when Guy slammed down the phone.

I was dumbfounded. If I had any doubt about my decision to put more distance between me and Guy, his finding out about my plans proved that it was more than a choice—it was now a necessity. Panic sparked me into action. I had to get out of there. "Colin, go put your shoes on." I thought of David. He lived in Point Richmond, 20 miles east of San Francisco. I picked up the phone again and dialed his number. When he answered I told him about Guy's threat. "Can Colin and I come over? Right now?"

"Aren't you going to call the police?" David asked.

"Guy knows all the Santa Rosa cops. I'd probably end up in jail if I call them."

"Okay, get over here immediately."

I left a message for my attorney, grabbed a few things, and piled Colin—hair half cut—into the car and sped away. I stayed at David's for the weekend.

On Monday morning, my attorney returned my call. "I'll draft a demand that Guy be cited for contempt for violating the restraining order. Now we need to get that police report you filed in Cotati. Bring it to the hearing, and don't forget the pictures," Richard said. He sounded excited. "This could turn this whole case around, Sharon."

The following Wednesday morning, on my way to Court, I stopped at the Cotati police department. I supplied the date of the police report and the duty sergeant disappeared into the back room. After a few minutes, he returned empty-handed. To my dismay, he hadn't found any evidence that I had ever filed a report of domestic violence—no file, no pictures, no detective notes. He didn't know Detective Palmer. It was as if I had never been interviewed and photographed.

"Are you sure you filed a report?" The officer eyes me suspiciously.

"That's not something that I would just imagine," I said. "Is there someplace else it could be? Could someone have taken it... or destroyed it? I need it for Court this morning. Getting that report is vitally important."

"Maybe your attorney had a messenger come and get it," the officer suggested.

"Could my ex-husband's attorney have requested it?"

The officer thought about that for a moment and shrugged. "I suppose."

I had no other option. I left the station without the report. I hadn't filed a police report the first time Guy hit me. Tom and

Kathy were the only witnesses to my condition that night and I certainly wasn't calling them to testify. Richard had included the details of the second beating at his house in Cotati in the request to cite Guy for contempt of the protection order. But there was no physical evidence and coming to Court without the report or the pictures to back me up about the last beating could be worse than trying to make Guy's violence an issue at all. This was the first time anyone would be questioning Guy about his threats and brutality against me. It was going to be my word against his.

Richard called Guy to the witness stand. "Mr. Johnson, have you read my client's statement?"

"Yes, I've read it."

"Did you call Ms. Murphy and make threats of violence?"

Guy glanced up at the judge as if addressing him rather than my attorney. Guy spoke slowly, his voice deep and dramatic. "I learned from an associate of mine that Sharon was planning to move *again*. When I called to ask her about it, she became hysterical and cursed at me. She said she was moving away with Colin and planned to *secrete* herself where I couldn't find them. I'm sure you can understand why I was upset, but I certainly did not *threaten* her."

Richard described the other two violent attacks and asked for Guy's response. He rolled his eyes and shook his head. "There has *never* been any violence over *towels* or at any other time. I don't know *what* Sharon expects to gain by making these *outrageous* allegations with no substantiation." Guy looked at me with eyes as cold as stone. "Her only intent is to sully my reputation."

Having no hard evidence to present, the judge dismissed my petition. In the parking lot, Richard put his hand on my shoulder. "Let me take you to lunch." When we slid into the booth at Lyon's Restaurant, he said, "Sharon, I'm so sorry."

"I knew it was a mistake to even bring this up! Unless Guy punches me right there in the courtroom, I'll never be able to convince the judge. I am fighting an uphill battle—everyone believes him! Believing that nothing ever happened is so much simpler and easier than believing the truth. The truth is messy. I'm never doing this again. I'm the only one who can protect me and Colin."

"Real evidence is the only way to show that Guy is lying," he said.

"I had evidence! Remember?" I said.

One unexpected positive outcome of the hearing was that the judge raised no objections to my move. I dismantled my life in Santa Rosa and had an emotional going away party. David invited Colin and me to stay with him in Point Richmond until I found an apartment in San Francisco, so I stored my belongings in his basement.

I started my new job at The Urban School and enrolled Colin in a pre-school nearby on the corner of Masonic and Page. We commuted together over the Richmond Bridge into San Francisco every morning. The school occupied two side-by-side Victorians in the Haight-Ashbury. My office was in the front room overlooking the street. I answered the phone, handled the mail, and managed the general front office hubbub of students and faculty. The Spanish class was planning their trip to Mexico. The theater classes were choosing the plays they would attend. I could hear my mother observing how much easier it was to be creative when you had lots of money. I thought of my recreation program struggling along with donated materials, and I had to agree. The privileged lives of The Urban School students were worlds away from the hand-to-mouth existence of the kids in the Valley Oak recreation program. But The Urban School staff worked hard to build a creative, student-centered atmosphere and I supported the non-authoritarian philosophy of the school.

After two months at David's, I rented an apartment near the Pacific Ocean on Forty-Eighth Avenue near Noriega. The third floor apartment faced the sand dunes along Ocean Beach and the high windows were permanently streaked with sand and salt. I built a brick and board bookshelf across the center of the large living room and sectioned off a bedroom for Colin by hanging my Indian print bedspreads from the ceiling behind the partition. This left a small sitting area in front of the gas fireplace for my rocking chair and a few throw pillows. This left the second bedroom free and to help stretch my budget, I rented the room to a graduating student. Once again, I arranged my furniture and hung Colin's posters on his bedroom wall trying to make the new surroundings feel like home.

Guy was scheduled to pick up Colin from my new apartment the first weekend after I moved. The visitation order said he could pick up Colin between 8 and 10 in the morning, but Guy hadn't called to tell me exactly when he would arrive. Colin was squatting on the back porch, blowing bubbles over the fence for the dog next door to chase. The drawstring bag he carried to day care was packed and sitting by the front door. I kept checking out the front window, looking for Guy's white van down Forty-Eighth Avenue. At 9:30, I heard the clatter of the VW.

"Your dad's here, Colin. Come kiss me good-bye."

Under normal circumstances, I would have gone downstairs to ask Guy to let me know what time he would pick up Colin in the future so I wouldn't have to wait for him for two hours. I could see myself being that assertive, but I was now petrified of Guy. My fear of him made every face-to-face conversation a potentially violent confrontation.

I sent Colin down to the car and closed the door behind him. I went to the front window and watched Guy lift Colin into the front seat. I turned from the window, but when I didn't hear the van pull away, I looked back. It took me a minute to figure out what I was seeing. I watched Guy pull pants, socks, and a shirt out of a small duffle bag, then take Colin's clothes off and redress him. I didn't think anything of it. I was glad that Colin would have some new clothes. But on Sunday evening when Guy pulled into my driveway, he took off the new clothes and redressed Colin in the same clothes he'd worn when left my house. He took the new clothes with him. From then on, Guy undressed and redressed Colin in the driveway when he picked him up and dropped him off. Colin had a whole wardrobe of new clothes, but he could only wear them on weekends when he was at Guy's house.

Judge Murphy set a hearing for Tuesday, June 8, 1980 to begin the comprehensive review of the question of custody. The report that Mike Lentz submitted read as if Guy had written it himself. At the hearing, Judge Murphy took Lentz's report under advisement and signed an order for the home study. Guy and I were ordered to prepare lists of our witnesses to be interviewed for the evaluation.

That evening after Colin was in bed, I sat at the dining room table considering who would be willing to make a statement on my behalf. The lights were dimmed and a candle burned in the center of the table. I made a list of the most obvious people— my sisters, Colin's teachers, Rose, Toni Novak, Carl, David, and a few others—all people who knew Colin and me together.

I flipped open my address book to get their phone numbers and addresses. *Maya Angelou* was the first entry in my address book. Would Guy even need anyone else to validate his character and the quality of his parenting, given his relationship to the holy Maya? I was overcome with despair and bitterness. Impulsively, I reached for the phone and dialed her number. When Maya answered my voice began to shake. "Hello..., it's Sharon." I surprised myself when I started to cry.

"Sharon, what's the matter?"

I took a deep breath and continued. "I called to ask if you would do something for me." Maya said nothing while I tried to steady my voice. I tried to focus on the many times she and I had talked together, the times we sang and laughed together. It was complex, but no matter what happened, we had a bond- didn't we?

"I know it's a lot to ask, but would you talk to Guy for me?"

"What's going on, Sharon?"

I hadn't given Maya the details of my struggles with Guy. I knew he wouldn't tell her what he was doing. I had only hinted at the problem when she came to see Colin at the hospital after his surgery. But now I tried to tell her everything. Before long, I was sobbing—slumped over my knees with the phone gripped against my ear.

"I know if Guy takes Colin from me, he will try to kill my relationship with him. I know it. You know how Guy can be when he's angry and hurt. He will not give up!" My conviction that this was Guy's ultimate goal had been gathering strength in the deepest part of my heart, but this was the first time I had said it aloud.

Maya was quiet for so long that I thought she'd hung up. "Hello, are you still there?" I asked.

"Sharon, I so sorry but I can't do anything that would jeopardize my relationship with my son. I'm sorry." The phone became lifeless in my hand.

I didn't know what to think. But a few days later, Guy called me. He was furious. "Don't you *ever* try to bring my mother into this!" he screamed. And again the line went dead.

I wanted to believe that Maya tried to talk to Guy—to reason with him. She must have said something, but maybe she just told him that I called her. There was no way to know—and either way, she hadn't deterred him.

I submitted my list of witnesses and Guy submitted his. Then Colin left for his six week summer visit with Guy. The days were long and empty. I had only the bleakest of expectations.

Richard tried to tell me to forget about the case for a while. "You've done everything you can for now. I'll keep tabs on the progress of the home study. Try to relax."

"My sisters want me to take a trip with them," I said.

"Go! It'll do you good to have a change of scene."

When my oldest sister Marilyn was a Catholic housewife with four small children in Tulsa, Oklahoma in the '50s, she organized the women of the St. Peter and Paul parish to help one another when there was an illness in the family, a lost job, or a drunken husband. And during the blazing Oklahoma summers, when the Jehovah's Witnesses knocked on her door, Marilyn would invite them into her living room and give them cool glasses of iced tea and pelt them with quotations from St. Thomas Aquinas and Teresa of Avila. She was a Catholic on a mission. Now Marilyn was a lesbian feminist activist and she was as enthusiastic about her new cause as she'd ever been about the Catholic Church.

Marilyn lived with Irene, her *companion-lover*, as she referred to Irene, in Irene's two-bedroom home in Studio City, 15 miles north of Los Angeles. Marilyn conducted classes and consciousness-raising for women in a studio next to their kidney-shaped pool. Marilyn and Irene and other Southern California women had also organized The Califia Community, an educational collective named after the black Amazon goddess for whom California was originally named.

Every summer, the Califia Collective sponsored weeklong camps throughout Southern California (affectionately known as *lesbian summer camp*). They envisioned Califia as a traveling feminist university, with classes on body colonization, misogyny, classism, racism, and other women's issues. After the morning workshops there were dances, softball games, talent shows, and poetry readings. My sister Jeanne had also come out as a lesbian the year before. She was one of many volunteers who helped organize the 1980 summer session of Califia.

Marilyn had been urging me to attend Califia for years. "Straight women come to Califia," she assured me, "although not all of them are straight when they go home."

"Not ever woman is a lesbian, Marilyn," I'd say.

"Not yet."

This year, Califia was to be held at a Girl Scout camp in the hills above Santa Barbara. I flew to Los Angeles and drove with

Irene, Marilyn, and Jeanne to the campsite. The summer air cooled as Irene drove and Marilyn navigated up the winding, wooded road. Then an open field surrounded by cabins came into view. A low stucco building with a wide porch filled with picnic tables and benches was at the far end of the field.

There were women of all colors, shapes, and ages hauling backpacks and camping equipment out of cars and vans. Groups of friends spotted each other and clutched together in multi-headed hugs. As women waited in the registration line, shirts started coming off, disappearing into back pockets or twisting around heads like turbans. One young woman leaned against a tree playing a recorder. There was a face painted on her bare chest, flat brown nipples became eyes, her belly-button painted red for the mouth.

"You didn't tell me this was a topless affair," I said to Marilyn, a little surprised.

Marilyn smiled. "I always envied the freedom that boys had to strip off their shirts in the summer. Now I know how it feels!"

We got out of the car just as two women, holding a banner between them, climbed to the top of ladders that were leaning against two redwood trees. The women wore jeans and heavy boots and nothing else, their bare breasts swinging freely in the dappled sunlight. They flung white cords over low-hanging branches and suspended the orange Califia Community banner over the main walkway. A cheer went up from the crowd below when the wind unfurled the banner.

By the time we unloaded the car and set up our cabin, it was time for dinner. The dining hall echoed with the voices of two hundred women, while the music of Margi Adams, one of the early feminist singer-songwriters, played in the background. *I wonder where you are, lovable lady. I wonder what you're thinking, beautiful woman. It seems like fog is settling in within your eyes, and the weight of something is pulling your shoulders down.*

Jeanne and I ate whole-wheat pasta with meat sauce and we laughed and talked with the women sitting at our table, while Marilyn and Irene circled the room like grand hostesses. After dinner, Marilyn stood behind a microphone and called everyone to order. She introduced the nine members of the Califia Collective who were sitting on the edge of a low stage in the front of the room. Then she surprised me by saying, "...and I especially want to welcome my sister Sharon to her first Califia!"

Jeanne poked me until I stood up. All heads turned and the crowd gave me an enthusiastic round of applause and I burst into tears. The welcome and goodwill was such a stark contrast to the agony happening back home that I couldn't stop the waves of tears. I sat down and Jeanne put her arms around me and I felt a tremendous sense of release and relief.

After the meeting was over, a crew of volunteers pushed the tables out of the way, and all but a few lights were turned out. Sister Sledge got everyone on their feet. *We are family. I got all my sisters with me. We are family. Get up ev'rybody and sing.* We all danced and danced, and I felt lighthearted for the first time in a long time. We went out on the porch to cool down. Jeanne sat on a bench and leaned back against one of the redwood picnic tables, mopping her face with a tissue. I climbed up on the porch railing and looked up into the vast night sky.

"I'm so glad I came," I said.

"It's good to see you having fun," Jeanne said. "I've been so worried about you."

The porch began to fill up with women and we fell silent. A tall woman caught my eye and she smiled and walked over to us. Her short hair was wet from dancing and was swept straight back from her face. Her jeans hung low off of narrow hips and her plaid shirt was unbuttoned, exposing a flat, well-toned stomach and small upturned breasts.

She leaned in and gave Jeanne a hug. "Hi, Jeanne, how are you?"

"Hi, Miranda." Jeanne said.

"Sharon, I wanted to introduce myself. I'm Randi." She smiled at me and a giddy feeling bubbled up through my chest. I shook her outstretched hand and felt myself blushing.

"Would you like to dance?" Randi slid her hand up to my elbow as I hopped off the porch railing. She rested her hand on the small of my back and guided me towards the music.

The DJ started an Alicia Bridges' tape. *Please don't talk about love tonight. Please don't talk about sweet love. Please don't talk about being true and all the trouble we've been through...*

"This is a good song for me!" I said.

"I can imagine. Marilyn told me about your custody case," Randi shook her head. "Your ex-husband sounds like a piece of work." I wasn't surprised that Randi knew about my case. The Murphy family was a template of feminist issues that Marilyn never hesitated to use in her classes. Between my life and the lives of my other sisters, she had every example she ever needed of women struggling against unfavorable conditions. Marilyn had also started writing a column, "Lesbianic Logic," for the Los Angeles feminist paper *The Lesbian News*, so now women all over California were getting acquainted with the Murphy family.

Randi swung me around and we merged into the gyrating crowd. My heart was pounding and waves of heat skittered across my skin every time her hand touched mine. When the second song ended, every cell in my body was throbbing. "I have to go," I said abruptly. I left Randi in the middle of the dance floor. Jeanne was talking with Marilyn and Irene in the corner of the room and I zigzagged through the crowd in their direction. They turned towards me with amused looks on their faces.

"I'm going to bed." I said.

"Alone?" Irene asked.

"Have you three been talking about me?" I said.

Marilyn answered. "Sharon, if you plan on sleeping with Randi, you should know that she's got a reputation for bringing out straight women."

"Well, Marilyn, someone has to do it," Irene laughed. "You're just mad because you had someone else picked out for Sharon."

"There *is* this cute school teacher from New York who's single..." Marilyn said.

"You mean Coleen?" Jeanne asked. "She's too boring for Sharon."

"Are you three finished? Can I go to bed now?" I turned away in mock exasperation and went to my cabin.

But once my sisters and our other cabin-mates had settled into sleep, I lay awake in the dark—my heart pounding and my mind racing. When Marilyn and then Jeanne began having sexual relationships with women, I envied the new excitement and energy that filled their lives. I was happy for them, but never thought this would happen to me. I was thirty years old and thought I was much more sexually liberated than they were. Surely I would have known before now if I were attracted to women. I came on this trip to relax and recharge my batteries, not to come out of the closet. Guy had invented enough issues to use against me without handing him something like this.

For the next two days, I attended workshops in the morning and listened to women's stories about their families, their relationships, and their hopes for their lives. I shared about my case, my fear of losing Colin, Guy's anger and violence, and my dread of what it might do to Colin if he lived with his father full-time. I participated in heated arguments about raising non-sexist boys and led a workshop on the gay/straight divide in the feminist movement. We brainstormed about the best political strategy for the empowerment of women. The ideas ranged from active, non-judgmental listening to other women all the way to killing all the men. Nothing seemed to be off the table for discussion.

I volunteered in the kitchen and learned how to make homemade pasta. One evening, I emceed the talent show. I was having more fun than I had expected, but no matter what I was doing, a sonar pulse deep in my belly found Randi wherever she was; and every time I looked in her direction, she would already be watching me. Randi was on the Califia board and she was usually busy, running from one job to the next, so we were only able to have a few brief, but highly charged conversations. At dinnertime on Tuesday, I was serving vegetarian stew at the buffet table when she walked up behind me. She leaned into my back, put her hands on my hips, and buried her face in my hair.

"Can we spend some time together this evening?" she whispered. I nodded, and she kissed my neck and flew out the door to finish posting the list of raffle prizes on bulletin boards around the camp.

After the evening meeting, Randi sought me out. She slipped her hand into mine and we walked down the wide porch steps and into the dark night. The heat from the day rose up from the hard-packed ground and a soft breeze floated down over the tops of the redwood trees. When we reached a bench at the edge of the field, Randi let go of my hand and sat down. She spread her arms along the back of the bench and smiled at me. I felt like a teenager on her first date.

"Are you having a good time?" she asked. I was taken off-guard by such a casual question in what was, to me, such an extraordinary circumstance. But it relaxed me and I sat down and Randi rested her fingertips on my shoulder. We sat in the dark and talked. I told her about the workshops I had attended, and we swapped impressions about the women and gossiped about the budding romances, the jealousies, and the political divides. "There's always a lot of drama at Califia," she said. "Some dramas have extended over years. They stop when Califia ends and begin again at the next session."

"What about you?" I asked. "Are you involved in any dramas?"

Randi smiled and turned towards me. "I guess you're my drama for this session. Has Marilyn warned you about me yet?"

"She told me you like bringing out straight women."

"Are you a straight woman?"

"Well, I thought so."

"What do you think that means?"

"Is that a serious question, or are you just flirting with me?" I said.

"No, I'm serious. Being attracted to a woman for the first time can be a shock. I'm attracted to you, and I think you feel the same, but I want you to feel all right if we're going to act on this."

This was exactly what I needed to talk about. I was so relieved. I didn't feel rushed into something I wasn't ready for.

Since Randi knew a lot about my situation already, it was easier to really explore how I felt. I told her about my strong attraction to Guy, my sexual relationships with other men, and I was honest about my attraction to her. "Was I fooling myself before, or am I fooling myself now?" I said.

"You can't put your feelings into tidy little boxes, Sharon. They are what they are."

"But I don't want to be one of those straight women who decide they're a lesbian because they're mad at the men they've been with."

"I don't think you can find all your answers with your intellect." She slid across the wooden bench and pulled me close to her. She lifted my chin and kissed me. All thoughts, psychological analysis, and political implications went out of my head. I surrendered to the delicious heat. A kiss was such a familiar thing, yet this one felt as if it was my first.

After a long while, she said, "Will you come back to my cabin with me?"

I hesitated. "What if I don't know what to do?" I said, feeling suddenly like a Victorian virgin.

"Do to me what you want me to do to you," she said.

She took my hand and led me to her cabin. We undressed each other slowly in the pitch blackness of her cabin. Randi lit three white candles which warmed the cold darkness of the night. I was on my back on her narrow bunk when she lay down next to me and slipped her arm under my head. She kissed me again. Randi's face was smooth and soft and her skin smelled like lavender. Her hands were the size of my hands. Her body had the feeling of my body. When she rolled over on top of me, I couldn't help but compare her graceful movements with the aggression of the men I'd been with.

Randi arched her back and gently pressed her stomach into me. I looked up at her long neck and the silhouette of her breasts. "You are so beautiful," I said.

Making love with Randi felt like the most natural thing in the world. When my thoughts began intruding, tapping me on the shoulder to remind me of what I was doing, she sensed me drift away and she'd stop, and we'd talk for a while. One hour rolled into the next and when the pale morning light began to fill the cabin, I said, "We have to get some sleep. What time is it?"

Randi squinted at the clock and groaned. "I have to go to a collective meeting at 6:30, which is 45 minutes from now. You stay here if you want. I'll come back after," she said.

"No. I think I'll go take a shower and get ready for my day." I watched Randi pull on her jeans and a clean t-shirt.

She leaned over and kissed me and then rushed out. I got dressed and walked across the quiet campsite, making bare footprints in the blanket of cold dew. I smiled to myself. I felt as if I had broken the code of a secret language. On the way to my cabin, I detoured into the bathroom. Marilyn was brushing her teeth at the sink, also getting ready for the collective meeting. I felt like a teenager sneaking in after curfew.

"Are you all right?" Marilyn said.

"Sure," I said, trying to sound *blasé*.

Marilyn gave me a level gaze. "Don't fall in love with her. You'll only get hurt." She packed up her kit bag and walked out.

Jeanne was reading in bed when I walked into the cabin. I flopped down on the end of her bunk. "*Your* sister is so exasperating," I said. "For years, she's been telling me that most women are *really* lesbians. Now I finally sleep with a woman, but she's upset because I didn't sleep with the *right* woman!"

223

"It's hard being the sister of the Amazon Queen," Jeanne said.

The news of my early morning walk from Randi's cabin flashed through the community like lightning. Randi's friends pulled me aside to give me some valuable advice. They concurred that Randi deserved the reputation Marilyn warned about. She *did* like to bring out straight women, and she had all the right qualities. She was attractive, sexy, assertive, and confident enough to try to seduce someone who was presumably straight. She wasn't a brute about it. She was sensitive and patient enough to help women sort out their feelings, but they told me that she most definitely didn't believe in monogamy.

I was less than one day into this new adventure and I hadn't even considered the relationship potential with Randi. I was still adjusting to the shock of having sex with a woman. But I could still remember the difficulty and awkwardness when Mary and I tried having overlapping relationships with Guy. Exploring a different sexual preference probably wouldn't rewire my entire attitude about relationships. When I had a chance to really think about it, I was prepared for this to be nothing more than a fling. Randi and I spent two more nights together before Califia ended on Saturday. As I prepared to go home, I knew the exhilaration I was feeling was not entirely about Randi or even about sex. I was discovering something true and lovely about myself at a time when I was being cruelly maligned and faced the direst of consequences.

Beyond the excitement of exploring life as a lesbian, Califia had also given me a keener view of my custody battle. Although losing Colin would be a tragedy for me if it happened, applying a political, feminist frame made my situation less about my own personal failings and more about a social dynamic that affected all women. Guy was using many of the negative stereotypes of women in his characterization of me as hysterical, emotionally unbalanced, and unreliable. The connection of my situation with the lives of other women was immensely comforting. My time at Califia and all the experiences and discoveries of the week had given me back a sense of ownership of myself and my life. Stepping totally outside of my daily life into this woman-centered world gave me the chance to feel better about myself, as well as allowing space for me to notice the gentle pull of my own preferences—preferences that had always been overpowered by the cultural imperative to be partnered with men.

Sharon at Califia, 1980

CHAPTER SEVEN

IT WOULD BE ANOTHER THREE weeks before Colin came home from Guy's house. My apartment felt empty without him. After work, I went into his room, handled his toys, and lay on his bed, breathing in his scent. Califia had been a free fall into a new perspective on my life. Now I was hanging suspended between two worlds. The realizations I had at Califia felt right, seeming to allow a deeper access to myself. That solid feeling made me feel strong, and I needed all the strength I could muster for the next phase of my custody battle.

Califia had provided me with instant friendships, but I needed a community closer to home. I loved to sing, so I signed up for the San Francisco Lesbian Chorus. They were preparing for a Labor Day event at the amphitheater in Golden Gate Park. Bella Abzug and other local feminist organizers would be speaking. I began going to rehearsals on Tuesday night at the Women's Building on Eighteenth Street in the Mission District. I started meeting up with chorus members and their friends at the Artemis Café on Valencia Street. I felt as if I had found the secret door into the San Francisco lesbian feminist community.

Meanwhile, the legal machine ground on. Citing Guy's close ties with the Sonoma County administration, Judge Murphy directed the order for the home study to the Mendocino County Probation Department, although the family case would remain in Sonoma County. Still, I took this as a good omen.

I started hearing from the people I'd listed as references. They'd all agreed to be interviewed by the probation department representative assigned to our case. My friends and associates had been helpless, able only to sit on the sidelines and hear Guy's version of events. Now they had a chance to set the record straight and try to amend the horrible caricature of me that Guy had presented in Family Court. Rose called when she finished her interview. "I told that woman what a creative mother you are. I described that birthday cake shaped like a rocket that you made, and Colin's Incredible Hulk Halloween costume," she said. "And I made *sure* she understood what happened that day at Coddingtown, and how Guy twisted something so innocent. That made me so angry!"

Carl agreed to be interviewed, even though he had constraints because of client confidentiality. He told the woman that he believed Guy's characterization of me was not based on facts, but rather on Guy's bitterness and desire to punish me. He said he had first-hand knowledge of Guy's disparaging attitude toward me and his controlling nature.

Even though my friends' support made me feel better, I still believed that the home study was the final hurdle before losing Colin and the first step towards being squeezed out of his life entirely. From the first Court appearance, the momentum had been careening inexorably in that direction. But my friends' confidence and encouragement did bolster my courage. Maybe Richard was right and the home study would improve my standing in the case.

However, my dim hope was abruptly extinguished. The board of The Urban School gave the director one month's notice, accusing him of mismanagement. In retaliation and in an effort to destabilize the school, he fired me and three of the teachers. When the probation officer conducting the home study called the school to verify my employment, she learned that I had been laid off. In what felt like a decidedly one sided move, she called Guy's lawyer to tell him that I was now unemployed. Tom Kenny immediately subpoenaed my Urban School work records.

Shortly after receiving the file, Guy called to say that he would not be paying his contribution to Colin's day care or child support for the six weeks that Colin had been with him. Our custody order hadn't dealt with that technicality either way. In a final blow, my roommate announced that it was too hard to work and go to college at the same time. She was moving back home. My life was once again in chaos. I was eligible for unemployment, but my economic situation would be hard until I got another job.

A woman I knew from Los Angeles had been accepted to law school at New College and was relocating to San Francisco. Kwambe was an LVN and had a job as a home health nurse. I let her park in my spot in the garage. She slept in her van at night and used my apartment during the day to make arrangements for school and to find a place to live. She didn't want to live with a child once her classes started, but when my roommate moved out, she accepted my invitation to rent my second bedroom in the interim.

Shortly after Kwambe settled in, the probation officer called. "Ms. Murphy, this is Miriam Joscelyn of the Mendocino County Probation Office. I've finished interviewing Mr. Johnson and all the references," she said. "I will need to speak with you and any roommate you have, so I can complete my report." We made an appointment for the following Saturday at noon. Colin would be at Guy's for the weekend.

Miriam Joscelyn arrived on time. She was a mousey-looking woman, with short, colorless hair parted on the side and combed back from her narrow face which was free of makeup. She wore a beige jacket, a pale yellow shirt with a buttoned-down collar, and sharply creased khaki trousers that broke crisply across the toe of her oxblood loafers. She gave me a firm handshake but no smile, and cast an appraising look around as she stepped inside.

I had scrubbed and tidied the apartment, repotted my plants, and straightened the pictures on the walls. Coffee cake and tea were arranged on the kitchen table, which was covered with a freshly ironed tablecloth. I thought everything looked homey, but I wondered how my home looked through the eyes of this stranger. I took a walk while Ms. Joscelyn spoke with Kwambe. I felt embarrassed and apologetic that Kwambe had to be inconvenienced by the complications of my life, but she assured me that she was happy to help. When I returned, Kwambe gave my shoulder a reassuring squeeze and left for the library at New College.

Ms. Joscelyn turned to a fresh page in her notebook. "Ms. Murphy, you have lived in several different locations and have had many different jobs since you and Mr. Johnson separated. Why so much trouble settling into a stable situation?" She made rapid notes while I answered. I tried to keep from rambling, but the question had the sound of an accusation and I was nervous. I could hear myself sounding defensive.

"Tell me about the psychiatric help that you've been getting."

"Psychiatric help?" I asked. "Do you mean my therapy group?"

"If that's what you call it," she said.

I didn't want to argue the point, so I explained about my Gestalt group.

She went down the litany of Guy's familiar complaints about my ability to care for Colin. There was a veiled implication that I had some responsibility for Colin's heart surgery but I let that pass. She questioned me about his ear infections, his wardrobe, my attitude about doctors, discipline, my work history, and my current financial situation.

"I'll inspect your apartment now. Where is Colin's room?"

She fingered the tapestry divider that separated Colin's room from the living room and stepped through the opening. His bunk beds, desk, and dresser were all neatly arranged. His play table was littered with pieces of an adding machine that he was disassembling. His box of tools sat next to his trucks and his stack of books. She opened the top drawer of his red and blue dresser and dug though his clothes and underwear then walked over and touched the corner of Colin's poster of an old black man giving a young boy a banjo lesson in the dim glow of lamplight. She gave the contents of the room an apprising look.

I tried to disguise the humiliation I felt as she brushed past me. She looked into my room, and then opened the door to Kwambe's sparsely furnished bedroom. "Will you get another roommate when this woman moves out?"

"Yes."

Miriam Joscelyn walked into the bathroom and pulled back the shower curtain. She lifted the lid of the toilet, and then washed her hands. She opened the hall closet on her way into the kitchen, stood on tiptoes to look at the top of the refrigerator, and then opened it and examined the food inside. She lifted the ketchup bottle off the shelf in the refrigerator door and examined the bottom.

She sat back down at the table and tapped her fingers on her tablet. "Why do you think this case has gone on so long, Ms. Murphy?" she asked.

I hesitated. Her face had given nothing away all throughout the interview. But she didn't seem the least bit sympathetic to my situation. If some enormous lie had occurred to me that would have made her approve of me, some story that would persuade her write a report that would enable me to keep my child, I would have tried it; but I didn't know any way to answer the question except with what I felt was the truth.

"Ms. Joscelyn, this case isn't about doctor's appointments, or what clothes my son wears, or where I work or live. I don't even think that Guy really believes that I'm a bad mother. But the more dramatic Guy's accusations are, the better his chances are of getting rid of me. The fact that I'm Colin's mother means *nothing* to him. He's not thinking about the best thing for Colin. He is only thinking of himself."

Now that I had started, I couldn't stop. My face and ears started to burn and I jabbed at the table with my finger as I spoke. "Guy just doesn't want me around anymore. I have become a major inconvenience to him. He beat me and I left him. Now, I've actually told people that he hit me, so I must be crazy—a lunatic, unstable! He is lying about me and I can't quite understand why no one seems to be able to see that. He wants to have his girlfriend be Colin's mother, if he can only get me out of the picture. All this is for his own *convenience*. And he's using the Courts to get what he wants."

Miriam Joscelyn stared at me without speaking. She had stopped taking notes. "Ms. Joscelyn, I'm a good mother and I take good care of my son. He needs me." I said. "Being a good, loving parent has little to do with the kind of house you live in or the job you have. I'm sure you know that. Everything else is just a story that Guy made up."

Without comment, she made a note and slipped her tablet back into her leather briefcase. "Thank you for your time, Ms. Murphy. You'll receive a copy of my report." She shook my hand. "Good luck," she said without emotion.

I closed the door behind her and leaned against it. My angry words still hung in the air. What had I done?

For a week after the interview, I thought repeatedly about my tirade. Why did I let myself get angry? But wasn't it understandable to feel under attack? I was under attack after all. Maybe I had struck a chord with that woman? I felt alternately hopeful and desperate. Richard said it could be weeks before we got the report. "Concentrate on getting a job, Sharon," he said. "You've done as much as you can do now."

The days dragged on. I put up a notice at the Women's Building for a room to rent and I spent an afternoon at UCSF Medical Center filling out applications for jobs I saw advertised in the Chronicle. Colin's preschool had an art show at the Full Moon restaurant across from Kezar Stadium, so I rounded up a group of friends for a dinner out. Colin was the honored guest. When he pointed out his painting of a smiling moon over a rocky mountain range, we gave him a round of applause. I went to my appointments at the unemployment and welfare offices and to job interviews. I bought the cheapest groceries I could. We ate a lot of beans, rice, and homemade soup. I did what I had to do, but all I wanted to do was sit by my mailbox and wait for Miriam Joscelyn's report.

Renaye Brown was returning to San Francisco after living in Hawaii and she called about my ad for a roommate. After we talked on the phone, I invited her to come and see the apartment. The clouds in the August sky were grey and low in the sky, and a light rain had begun to fall when I stepped off the bus at the corner of Forty-Eighth Avenue and Noriega. I ducked my head inside the hood of my jacket, and leaned into the salty wind that blew strong and steady over the sand dunes that hid the Pacific Ocean from view. A dark-skinned woman was walking towards me from the other end of the block, carrying a large bag over her shoulder and herding a child in a hooded sweatshirt in front of her. We both reached the gate to my building at the same time.

"Sharon? I'm Renaye." She put out her hand. "This is Michael." The thin boy looked up at me with huge dark eyes. He was smaller than Colin, but looked about the same age—four, maybe five.

"You didn't say you had a child."

"Didn't you say that you have a son?" Renaye asked.

A gust of wind blew a sheet of rain against us. "Let's go inside and talk." Renaye and Michael followed me through the gate. I opened the mailbox and pulled out the PG&E bill and a letter from Sally Ann, nothing about the home study. I lit candles on the kitchen table, and Renaye and I began talking like old friends while we sipped steaming cups of tea in the yellow light. Michael sat next to us drawing pictures. Before long, Kwambe walked in with Colin and after introductions all around, she took a cup of tea and disappeared into her bedroom. I turned on more lights as night settled in and cut up a bowl of oranges for the kids. Colin and Michael disappeared into Colin's room, and we soon heard the clatter of Legos as they spilled out on the floor.

Renaye and I exchanged biographies. She was a lifelong lesbian who had gotten pregnant during an experimental liaison with a man. But the father wasn't in the picture. She moved to a woman's community in Hawaii when Michael was a baby, but she missed the mainland. She was a drummer and had her instruments and her other possessions stashed in a storage locker in the Mission. She had cash for a few months' rent and some leads on jobs.

I told Renaye about my ongoing problems with Guy and my newly discovered interest in women. Renaye had heard of my sister Marilyn and Califia. "But if Colin goes to live with his father," I said, "I don't know...I think having Michael in the house might be too hard for me."

"I understand," Renaye said. "We'll find something else. But I feel like I've made my first friend in San Francisco!"

I looked at the duffle bag on the floor. "Where are you staying now?"

"I have a room in a hotel downtown," she said.

I couldn't stand the thought of Renaye and her son in one of the sleazy hotels in downtown San Francisco. "Why don't you and Michael stay here till you find something else? Michael can take the bottom bunk in Colin's room, and we can make a bed for you in the living room."

Renaye gave me a shy smile. "Thank you. Thank you."

Michael and Colin quickly became great pals. Colin, with his bright red hair, was tough and husky like a little bulldog. Michael, with his delicate features and sensitive nature, was more like a dark little whippet. Renaye taught the kids to play the congas and how to keep time with maracas. She was about my height and had very dark skin, large eyes that were almost black, and she shaved her well-shaped head. Whenever Renaye left the house, she wore a man's jacket and boots with a white shirt over baggy trousers and a cap or a red bandana folded into a three-inch band around her head. But when she was at home, she wore one of her many colorful sarongs. Her yin *and* yang, she said.

Our new household was warm and comfortable even if it was only temporary. Both boys loved Kwambe. She was tall and broad, with caramel-color skin and spiky dreadlocks sticking out in every direction. When she came home, Colin and Michael would wrap themselves around her strong legs and she'd drag them across the floor. "Sharon, I'm so tired—my legs feel like they're made of lead."

I was alone in the apartment when the report arrived from the Mendocino County Probation Department in early October, six weeks after Miriam Joscelyn's visit. I sat in my rocking chair staring at the envelope. My heart pounded. I tore open the envelope and scanned the preliminary paragraphs. It was a re-counting of the history of our case. I skipped to the final page, which read:

> *Day care providers and friends of the mother praise Ms. Murphy's care of her son and her relationship with Colin, and it is obvious that Ms. Murphy is dedicated to the minor. But witnesses for the father submitted signed affidavits that Colin was frequently dirty and dressed in tattered clothing inappropriate for the weather when he*

arrived at his father's house for visits. One of the witnesses, a registered nurse who works with newborns, said that the child's health and appearance reflected a general neglect on the part of Ms. Murphy.

I conclude that both of these views are probably correct. Given the history of this case, which is well known to the Conciliation Court, Ms. Murphy will do anything to irritate Mr. Johnson. Knowing the importance that Mr. Johnson places on cleanliness, Ms. Murphy purposely delivers Colin to his father in a less than clean condition in an effort to upset Mr. Johnson.

Whereas Mr. Johnson is living with a woman to whom he is engaged and has created a family unit that includes Colin, Ms. Murphy has resided in seven different locations since their separation and currently resides with a roommate, an older woman who will be living there while she gets further education.

Although Ms. Murphy has done well with her limited resources, and the credible statements from Ms. Murphy's witnesses described her as a woman whose child is a priority to her, Mr. Johnson places a greater value on social graces and amenities and their future importance to his son than the mother does at the present time. It is the opinion of the undersigned that the minor child should be placed in the sole physical custody of the father.

The light left the sky and the apartment became dark and chilly. I was cold but couldn't move. I sat rocking and weeping until I heard Kwambe's key in the door. When she turned on the light, she jumped when she saw me. I held up the papers. She didn't need to read them to know what they said.

A Court appearance was scheduled the following Tuesday for the judge's final custody ruling. My attorney assured me that the judge did not have to follow the recommendation of the probation officer and reminded me of my references.

"Your witnesses made some extremely compelling statements. The judge will take everything into consideration. Let's try to walk into Court with a couple of good job prospects."

On the morning of the hearing, I dropped Colin off at day care and once again drove the familiar highway north towards Santa Rosa. The clouds were low and heavy in the autumn sky, looking more like evening than early morning. After an hour of driving, the sky was slate grey. A misty rain was falling when I pulled into the small parking lot next to Richard's office building. I got out of my car and clapped my notebook over my head to keep my hair dry as I ran into the building. Richard stood up behind his desk when I walked in. He was a small man with light hair and brown eyes. Not much older than me, but the skin around his eyes was beginning to sag and I could see the old man he would become.

"Hi, Sharon. How're you doing?" he said. I hated hearing the tone of sympathy in his voice. "I want to go over a few things before the hearing."

I felt as if I had never been as tired in my life, my arms and legs felt as if they were encased in lead. Instead of taking the chair, I collapsed on the couch near the door. "Is there any chance at all that the judge will surprise us?" I said.

He looked down at his hand resting on the edge of his desk. His nails were bitten to the quick. "No," he said flatly. "Probably not."

I was overcome by a wave of grief so crushing that I dared not move for fear that I would shatter into bits. I couldn't even cry. "I can't go," I whispered. "I can't bear to see Guy's face. I can't do it."

Richard came and sat next to me and put his hand on top of mine. "I understand. I'll go without you. Sharon, I'm so sorry I couldn't keep this from happening."

"I've got to go get Colin," I said. I stood and rushed out of the office.

I drove back towards San Francisco in a daze—numb. There was something beyond panic and pain gathering somewhere in the distance, like a hurricane racing towards me. But I couldn't let myself be overwhelmed—not yet. Colin couldn't see that I was upset. I needed to hold myself together until after—but then what? I couldn't imagine ever being on the other side of what was coming. What could possibly come after losing Colin? What would come after my son lived in the care of an angry, violent man—a man who also wanted to hurt me in the deepest possible way? Could there even be an *after* after something like that?

I tried to wrench my thoughts in a different direction, but there was nothing else to think about, no last minute strategy, no phone calls, and no charges to answer—nothing left but the most unbearable thing of all. I sped towards Colin's school. I had to tell him today. If I hesitated for even one day, hope might slink in and chase away my despair, and despair was the only thing that anchored me in the reality of what was happening.

Rivendell School was in an old Safeway building in the Sunset District near Ocean Beach. The ads for canned peas and Wonder Bread on the large display windows had been replaced by paintings of Elrond, the king of Rivendell, the Elven outpost in Tolkien's Middle Earth. The elf princes, Glorfindle and Erestor, stood in front of the Misty Mountains and pointed the way inside the school. I parked out front and pushed through the heavy glass doors. "I need to pick up Colin early today." The secretary read my expression and rushed down the hall towards the sound of children's voices. A few minutes later, Colin came through the double doors holding his drawstring bag with one hand and struggling to put on his jacket with the other. I wanted to grab him and hold him and never let him go, but I took a deep breath and smiled.

"Momma, I was getting ready to eat my lunch. I'm starving!"

"I'll make you a hot dog when we get home. Okay?"

"Can I have chips?" Colin was always negotiating for a better deal.

"Sure. We'll stop at the store." The beauty of a simple plan stopped my mind from whirling. Go to the store. Buy chips. Be here now. Make lunch. Be here now. Be here now. Be here now.

When we got home, I pulled lunch things out of the refrigerator while Colin dumped his jacket and bag in his room and climbed up into the green ladder-back chair. I dropped two hot dogs into a saucepan filled with water and spread ketchup and mustard on the slices of rice bread I laid out on the counter. I watched Colin as he ran his red Hot Wheels Corvette along the stems of the big flowers printed on the tablecloth. A hot pain in my chest caused me to turn away. Be here now. Be here now.

I set down a bowl of Doritos and gave Colin his sandwich. I lit a tall green candle and sat across from him staring until the hollow pillar glowed from the flame deep inside. "Colin, you know that your dad wants you to live at his house more of the time and come here for weekend visits."

His eyes widened. "How did you know that?"

"Your dad told me."

Colin took a bite and spoke through a wad of meat and bread. "Do you want me to live with him?"

I struggled to keep my voice calm. All the tormented nuances of my struggle with Guy settled into this basic truth. "No, I want you to stay here with me."

"But my dad doesn't want me to, right?" Colin looked as if he had said something he shouldn't.

"Colin, we can talk about this. I didn't say anything before, but now it's time for us to talk about it. It's okay."

Colin's words burst out of him. "My dad says mean things about you. He says you're lazy, that you don't take care of me."

"Well, Colin, you know me better than your dad does, and I only care about how *you* feel about me."

Colin climbed down from his chair and came over to me. I lifted him up on my lap and wrapped my arms around him. "I don't think you're lazy," he said.

"Thank you, baby, that makes me feel good." I rocked him, and began to hum to him. Then my resolve began to weaken, and the wheels started spinning—how could I keep him, what could I do? But I forced myself to stop. I put my hands on his shoulders and turned him to face me.

"Colin, since your dad and I couldn't agree about where you should live, we had to let a judge decide. And he decided that you're going to live at your dad's house and go to school in Santa Rosa. You'll come here for weekend visits. But I'm still your mom. I always will be your mom. You and I will still see each other. Do you understand?"

Colin gave me a hug, and we looked at each other for a long moment. Then Colin said, "My dad says he's getting me a puppy."

I forced myself to speak. "Well, that'll be fun." Colin and I stared at each other. I tried to smile, but my face was stiff, and my eyes burned.

"Can we go to the park now so I can ride my Big Wheel?" Colin asked.

"Sure thing!"

There was some last minute legal posturing between Richard and Tom Kenny. Richard asked Guy to waive his last regular visit and Guy countered by asking for custody to be changed immediately considering the *"urgency of the matter."* I read each document that arrived in the mail as if it was a story about someone else's life.

Guy finally agreed to waive his last weekend visit before the transfer of custody, but in exchange I wouldn't have a visit with Colin for the entire month of November. Guy was taking Colin to Maya's house for a big Thanksgiving gathering.

For the next few weeks, I watched Colin play with Michael. I gave them bubble baths in our deep tiled tub. Colin and I walked in Golden Gate Park and we examined insects in his magnified bug box. We drew faces in the sand at Ocean Beach and stood at the water's edge and yelled as loud as we could, laughing as our voices were sucked into the roar of the crashing waves.

But after the boys were in bed, I retreated behind my bedroom door and cried. I talked with my friends or my relatives when they called, but the conversations all started to sound the same—the same anger, the same feelings of injustice and helplessness—each conversation ending the same way. "I'm so sorry, Sharon." I'd sit in my room and smoke waiting for the oblivion to stop myself from thinking and feeling and hopefully to sleep.

Guy told me not to pack any of Colin's clothes, his Big Wheel, trucks, or any of his other toys, so I had nothing to do but count the days until Colin left. On Saturday, November 1, 1980, at 10 sharp, Guy's van pulled into my driveway. Colin was wearing his Los Angeles Rams jacket. He had filled his flowered drawstring bag with most of his Legos and slung it over his shoulder, hobo style. I hugged him at the door. "I'll see you in a few weeks, baby." My voice came out in a strangled screech.

"Bye, momma, see ya later!"

I listened through the closed door to the sound of Colin hopping down the steps. To him, this was just another trip to his dad's house. All my carefully worded explanations were understandably forgotten. When I heard the metal gate clang shut behind him, my legs went weak beneath me and I melted onto the floor, the tan carpet scratchy against my cheek, and the white brick fireplace and my rocking chair flipped onto their side, as if the world had tilted on its axis. I heard nothing after the clatter of Guy's VW faded at the end of my street. Tears clouded my eyes while the weak sunlight vanished beneath the thick San Francisco fog.

Michael and Renaye felt like family to me now. I couldn't face another loss, so when Kwambe moved into her new apartment, I invited them to stay permanently. Renaye moved her instruments and satchels into the front bedroom. Michael continued to sleep in the bottom bunk; saving the top bunk for when Colin came back to visit. His sweet presence was a comfort, not the painful reminder I had feared. My friends tended to me as if I were ill, fragile as glass. I stayed home reading or lying on my bed, staring at the hazy autumn sky. I felt as if judgment on my life had been rendered just as I was beginning to move in the right direction. For so long, I had searched for a firm place to set my foot. I fashioned my identity out of fantasy and the expectations of others. I fashioned the identity of others out of my own longing and needs.

But when I became Colin's mother, the experience had enlivened something essential inside of me—something I had been unaware of before he was born. I wasn't a mistake or an invention of circumstance or personality. I was already real—I didn't need to invent something out of nothing. I had value, not *because* I was a mother, but because the experience of becoming a mother had allowed me to see a deeper truth about myself. It helped me see through my false ideas of who I was. Now that awareness was shaken and I felt erased again.

I didn't think Guy was a monster, but he didn't have to be a monster to do harm to Colin's gentle heart. Colin would only grow up once. I was afraid that he would suffer the same way I had suffered from my mother's volatile temper and the confusion that comes from loving someone you're afraid of. That's a dangerous combination of emotions. Guy was Colin's father, nothing would ever change that. And as long as Colin had both of us, there was some balance for him, some leverage. But Guy wanted to be Colin's only parent and for me to be *mother in name only*. That could never happen. I was Colin's first parent, and he needed me. This was indisputable—a fact beyond anything Guy or the Courts had any authority over. Guy might try to build a wall so high that I couldn't reach my son, but I was going to protect Colin no matter what. This I knew. But how?

After living in a dark haze for weeks, I received a letter from UC Medical Center with the date and time to report for a job interview. I forced myself to get dressed and leave the house. I went through the interview process on automatic pilot. When the woman in the Human Resources department offered me a job as a unit secretary at Moffitt Hospital, the very hospital where Colin had his surgery, I didn't feel glad. I was mildly amused by the coincidence, but I didn't feel much of anything—only a dim sense of relief. I knew this was important—a good thing—but only in the most abstract, distant way. I took the information about where and when to report for orientation, thanked the woman, and went home.

The unit secretary kept the ward organized, checked patients in and out, ordered lab work and diagnostic tests, made sure all the charts were up-to-date, and kept track of the patients' comings and goings in a wide leather-bound journal. I enjoyed the contact with the nurses and the patients. I liked the feeling that I was some small comfort to the patients and their families as they tried to cope with a crisis. The routine of working tricked me out of my depression a little. I even started going to choir practice again. But the world felt like a psychic assault, and the only place I felt even remotely comfortable was in my own apartment.

One afternoon, I stared through the filmy window of the N-Judah streetcar, on my way home from work. A scrawny woman with a brittle ponytail climbed aboard, followed by a young boy, about seven years old. She held a large purse on one shoulder; a finger of her other hand was stuck deep between the pages of a paperback book. She slid into the seat in front of me. Her little boy was trying desperately to get her attention. "Mommy. Mommy. Mommy," the boy repeated. His mother's eyes were trained on the yellowing pages of her book. "Mommy," he said again.

Without a glance in his direction, the woman smacked the boy in the face with her book and then went back to her reading. "Shut up!" she said. It was a mile from my stop, but I jumped up and rushed off the streetcar as soon as it stopped. Tears blinded me. How could *I* be the mother who had lost custody of her child?

Like all entry-level unit secretaries, I worked as an on-call float. The nursing supervisor would call at 5 o'clock in the morning, and run down the list of shifts available that day. It could be a morning, afternoon, or night shift. I could be assigned anywhere in the hospital and was required to learn all the various routines. After three months, I'd worked in almost every department of the hospital, and received good reviews from the head nurses. But even though I took every shift I could, I was still near the bottom of the list for a permanent full-time assignment and accumulated less than 40 hours most weeks. The best way to move up the list was to accept every shift that was offered, but as I had feared, the trips to the courthouse in Santa Rosa hadn't stopped. And every time I had to go to a Court appearance or to a meeting with Mike Lentz, no matter how brief, I was forced to decline a whole day of work. Ironically, my not having a full-time job was one of the issues Guy was using to prove my unfitness as a mother.

When Colin lived with me, the visitation order gave Guy a two-hour window to pick-up or drop-off Colin. I never made an issue of it, but now there was no room for flexibility. My visits began at 6 p.m. on Friday and ended at 5 p.m. on Sunday—on the dot. Even though Guy was notoriously late for everything, punctuality became a grave issue, and tardiness became an indication of my serious emotional instability. If the consequences had not been so serious, Guy's affidavits to the Courts would have been comical. But Guy's next goal was to limit my visits and he used the same strategy that had won him custody.

One Friday evening in mid-January, I had a flat tire on my way to pick up Colin. I called Guy from the service station in Petaluma. "They're changing my tire now. I should be there by 7 o'clock, maybe sooner. I'm sorry."

Guy's response was casual and relaxed. "No problem. I'm watching TV and Col's playing outside."

I arrived to pick up Colin at 7:15 and returned him at 6 o'clock on Sunday without incident. But by the next week, Tom Kenny had filed a Contempt of Court petition which asked for a change in the visitation order. The proposed schedule suggested a six-hour visit every other Saturday; all overnight visits would be eliminated. He also requested that I not be permitted to leave Santa Rosa with Colin.

A hearing with Lentz was scheduled for the following Thursday. He would determine the merits of Guy's request. If Lentz agreed, the schedule would be drafted into a proposed order and sent to the judge for a signature. There might not even be a hearing. Since the change in custody, our case had been re-assigned to Judge Sater. Richard advised that the new judge would more than likely sign whatever Lentz drafted.

No attorneys were allowed in the conciliation session with Lentz, but Richard wanted to talk before the meeting. I pushed through the swinging doors of the courthouse cafeteria, but before I could locate Richard in the crowded room, I noticed Guy and Mike Lentz sitting next to each other at a corner table. They were drinking coffee and laughing. They looked like old friends. Richard half rose out of his seat and waved. I walked over and sat down next to him.

"Do you see them over there? That can't be right. Can't you bring this up to Judge Sater?" I asked.

"Things might get worse for you if the judge thinks we are insinuating that Guy is getting preferential treatment. Sater is old-school, very rigid."

"But Guy *is* getting preferential treatment! You think Lentz is going to laugh it up with him, then go in and rule against him? And tell me how things could possibly get any worse, Richard? Please tell me that."

My heart was pounding and the room was too hot. I felt lightheaded. "Isn't something like this more serious than being late? I want you to request a new mediator."

"I don't feel comfortable asking for a change of mediator," he said in a soft whisper. "The best thing for you to do is to keep as close to the Court order as you can. You can't give Guy any reason to complain."

I was dumbfounded and felt bitterly betrayed. "Richard, haven't you figured this out yet? Guy is going to complain until he gets what he wants. You know that!" I glared at him and he looked down at his closely bitten nail.

"I know. I know," he said.

Guy and Mike Lentz stood up to leave. Guy took a few steps towards the door, and then paused and reached across a table to shake hands with a middle-aged woman in a tailored grey suit. I watched as he introduced her to Mike Lentz. She and Lentz shook hands, and then Guy shoved open the cafeteria doors and held it so Lentz could pass in front of him.

His eyes found me from the across the room, then he nodded at me and disappeared through the swinging doors.

"I know you're in an impossible situation here, Sharon. Lentz is obviously hostile towards you. But you were late. You can't argue against the facts."

"I know I was late. Everyone is late sometime! You know this is only an excuse. The consequences really outweigh the crime, don't you think."

Richard looked at his watch. "You'd better get in there. Sharon, just apologize and try to look sorry."

Guy was seated in one of the leather chairs facing Lentz's desk when I walked in. "Good morning, Sharon," he said.

Mike Lentz was a pale, overweight man with a receding hairline and a forehead like a drive-in movie screen. He seemed to be wearing the same brown suit every time I saw him.

"Good morning, Miss Murphy," he said. "Please have a seat. Guy, would you like to begin?" I focused on the parking lot visible through the window behind Lentz.

Guy pulled his yellow tablet out of his satchel. "I have listed here every time that Sharon has been late to pick up Colin. Of course, emergencies arise from time to time. I'm not inflexible, but it's Sharon's cavalier attitude and her selfish disregard for me and my wife and children which are the real issues here. Sharon arrives at my home late to *purposely* inconvenience me."

Guy handed the legal tablet to Lentz, who looked down at the handwritten list. Guy continued to speak in grave tones. The evening when I had the flat tire had changed from a night in front of the TV to an important occasion when he and Linda had to cancel their plans.

"Sharon's inability to be on time is only one example of her instability. She doesn't even have a full-time job. She is totally unreliable as a parent," Guy shook his head.

Mike Lentz made notes in the file and turned to me. "What do you have to say to this?"

"Yes, I had a flat tire last week and I was late picking up Colin. I do not deny that." My attorney's words of caution ran through my mind, but Guy's smug look infuriated me. "Mr. Lentz, that list is a fabrication. Plus, what he is saying doesn't even make sense. Either I pick up Colin late *on purpose* to irritate him, or I am so out of control that I can't be on time even when I try! What does this have to do with being a good parent, I want to know? But I suppose you're going to believe him no matter what he says!"

"Miss Murphy, your argumentativeness only makes these proceedings worse for you. It is unnecessary for you to bring up all these side issues," Lentz said. Red bloches crept across his cheeks.

His tone scared me, "I'm sorry." I pulled myself back under control. I turned to Guy and mumbled. "Guy, I'll be more punctual in the future."

The room was quiet while Lentz completed his notes. "The visitation order will not be changed at this time. But Miss Murphy, in the future if there will be any change in your schedule; you will need to give Mr. Johnson 48 hours' notice. So please, follow the Court order to the letter or we *will* institute a limited visitation schedule."

I choked down everything I felt and everything I wanted to say, and signed off on the mediation papers.

I wanted some escape from the constant, aching pain I felt. I went for a couple of short visits to see Randi in San Diego, but the energy of that affair was dwindling and conversations were filled with awkward pauses. I started seeing a woman in San Francisco who worked at a restaurant on Haight Street. Maria was Cuban-born. She was vivacious with soft brown skin and deep dark eyes. But when I was with her, I was preoccupied with Colin and my suspicion and fear that Guy would turn his violent temper towards him. Then what would I do? No one without children could know what I was going through, I thought.

I began retreating to my room more and more, smoking the Maui-Wowi that Renaye brought back from Hawaii. I'd sit alone, write in my journal, listen to music, or read. I tried, but I would never adjust to having such a limited amount of time with Colin. Maybe I could have accepted it if I believed he was safe—if I was not so afraid of Guy's anger and violence. Or if I didn't know, with near certainty, that the short time I had with Colin would soon vanish to nothing. I knew it was only a matter of time.

Not only did I miss Colin bitterly, but I was seeing changes in him that worried me. He was nervous and jumpy when he came home for the weekend. Was it the transition, or was it something more serious? Then Colin's mood and behavior got worse. He started wetting his pants again. One evening we were sitting on the couch watching television and he began pounding on his legs with his fists. Now, even when I was with Colin, I couldn't relax. My worry was becoming desperation.

When Colin came home for his fifth birthday in February, I gave him a hand-held video game, and Renaye and I took him and Michael to the petting zoo in Golden Gate Park. We brought the Big Wheel with us, and Colin and Michael rode double, up and down the hills in the park. Colin seemed relaxed and happy when we got back to the apartment. I made cheeseburgers for dinner, Colin's favorite. The boys were lying on my bed watching *The Muppet Show* after dinner and I was running Colin's bath and lining up his matchbox cars on the edge of the tub.

When the tub resembled a snowy mountain range, I called him. "Colin, your bath is ready." I heard Kermit say good-night and Colin appeared in the bathroom doorway. "Come on, baby, get in the tub." He slipped off his pants and shirt and I held his hand as he stepped into the tub.

"It's too hot." He stood with bubbles up to his knees, and danced around in the suds while I ran more cold water. When I reached down to swirl the cool water into the hot, I saw a row of parallel bruises across his bottom and the back of his thighs.

My heart seized up and I put my hand on the purple marks. "What's this on your backside?" I tried not to sound too alarmed. He flopped down in the water and didn't answer. "Colin, what is that on your bottom?" He slid under the bubbles. I didn't want to pressure him so I squirted shampoo in my hand, pulled him up to sitting, and started washing his thick hair.

After a few silent minutes, he said, "Daddy said I didn't know how to wash myself."

"What does that mean?" I asked.

He stared at me. "You know...my penis," he said under his breath. Colin grimaced and his eyes filled with tears. He slapped the bubbles with his hand, sending suds over the edge of the tub. "Daddy says I don't know how to wash my penis!" He looked down into the water and his body shook as he cried. "Daddy told me if I couldn't keep myself clean, he'd have the doctor cut off my foreskin."

I blinked back tears. I turned on the tap and filled a big plastic cup with water. "Put your head back, baby," I said softly. Colin closed his eyes and leaned back into my hand. I poured warm water through his sudsy hair. "There! You're hair is all clean now."

"But I told daddy that I *did too* know how...that *you* showed me." Now Colin sounded defiant. "And daddy got mad and hit me with his belt." His hands under the water, cupped himself protectively.

I wanted to scream, but I tried to sound calm and reassuring. "I'll talk to your dad."

Colin grabbed my arm. "No. Don't! If you say anything, he'll hit you too."

"What if I talk to him on the phone?" I said. Colin was crying again so I let it drop. "Do you want to get out of the tub?"

"No. I wanna stay in. Will you run some more hot?" Colin's breath was soft sputtering intakes of air. I stroked his head as he tried to stop himself from crying.

I sat on my bed with my head in my hands. My whole body was shaking. Calling Guy would do no good, and I couldn't call the police or go to Child Protective Services. With all the unthinkable things that people do to their children, would they even think three parallel bruises were as troubling as I did? Trying to take action against Guy would probably backfire anyway—the Court hadn't believed me when I testified that he hit me. I had no credibility in Court. Guy would make this sound like just another empty accusation. I was powerless to protect Colin—a bitter reality that I could not accept.

On Colin's next visit, when I told him that he couldn't have a second bowlful of Rice Dream, he exploded. He ran through the apartment, knocking over chairs and screaming. "Daddy says you don't take care of me. You're lazy. You're lazy!"

He flailed his arms and tried to hit me. He stood in the hall screaming. He was hysterical, out of control. Michael looked on, his mouth open in shock. Renaye picked Michael up and carried him into her room. The hallway fell into darkness and Colin continued to scream and swing his fists at me. I ran to the bathroom and grabbed a big bath towel. I flipped the towel around Colin and wrapped him up tight with his arms at his side, like a papoose. I wrestled him to the floor and straddled him. He continued to struggle, his face bright red and wet with sweat.

"I am not going to let you hurt me or yourself. I love you. I don't want you to hurt yourself." I repeated it over and over. "I'm not going to let you hurt me or yourself. I love you. I love you." After a few minutes, he burst into tears and his body went slack. I unwrapped the towel and drew him into my lap. I sat on the floor of the dark hall and rocked him while he cried. I leaned against the wall, rocking Colin until he was asleep.

Then I began to cry, feeling the agony of helplessness. I felt as if I was betraying Colin when I dropped him off at Guy's house the next day.

In early April, I was given a three-month assignment in the Labor and Delivery Department on the 19th floor of Moffitt Hospital. The regular ward clerk was out on maternity leave and there was talk that she might not come back. I hoped that this would be my chance to be hired for a full-time permanent position. Three pale blue corridors extended like spokes on a wheel from my desk at the nursing station. At the end of each hall, floor-to-ceiling windows presented a panoramic view of San Francisco. From almost every spot in the department, I could see Golden Gate Park, the peaks of the Golden Gate Bridge, and the round, smooth hills beyond that led north to Sonoma County where Colin was in Santa Rosa with Guy.

On Friday, April 10, 1981, the early spring sky was filling with wisps of clouds. My five-day Easter visit with Colin began today, our longest visit yet. I was happy, but I was also in a panic. My old Barracuda had broken down again and no one could give me a ride or loan me their car for the evening. On my lunch hour, I called Guy at his office. "I have to take the bus to pick up Colin tonight. Would you please bring him to Courthouse Square? That would save me that last leg on the bus out to your house."

"This is not my problem, Sharon." Guy said. "Why don't you pick him up in the morning?"

It made sense to do what Guy suggested and avoid the mad dash on the bus, but then I would miss a whole night with Colin. I didn't want to lose waking up on Saturday morning and have him run into my room for a morning snuggle. "Never mind, I'll be there by 6," I said.

"Well, you better not be late. Linda and I have plans this evening."

When I picked Colin up on the bus, every connection had to be seamless for me to make it by 6 o'clock. I had to take a streetcar from the hospital to downtown and then catch a Golden Gate Transit bus to Sonoma County, 60 miles north. At Courthouse Square in the center of Santa Rosa, I switched to a local bus that took me out to Guy's neighborhood in Rincon Valley on the outskirts of town. Then I had to walk the last four blocks to his house. With no glitches, it took almost three hours and my shift ended at 2:30.

The unit had been slow all day and half of the afternoon staff was released to go home. The charge nurse and a nurse midwife were the only staff covering our one remaining patient. I wheeled my desk chair towards the stack trays on the waist-high counter. I ran my hand in and out of the empty compartments to make sure that nothing was left undone. If I could leave early, I might be able to make it to Guy's house on time.

When the charge nurse backed out of the labor room, I stood up, but Doris didn't look my way. She reached for the chart hanging on the rack at the end of the desk and fished two vials of blood out of the pocket of her scrubs. She marked them with ID numbers and recorded the tests in the chart. Then she flipped the chart closed with a snap and put the vials in the tray for pick-up. She looked up and down the desk and then at me. "This desk looks sterilized," she said with a smile.

"Everything's caught up, and I called the ER. No one's been admitted for Labor and Delivery. I was hoping I could get off a little early." My words gushed out and I glanced up at the clock. It was 1:30. "I'm supposed to pick up Colin tonight and I have to take the bus to Santa Rosa."

Doris looked at her watch and I felt a fresh wave of panic. If I was late again, I'd probably have to take off work to go to Santa Rosa and get another dressing down from Lentz. Guy didn't need any more ammunition, and I didn't want to miss any days during this assignment.

"Okay. You can take off now if you want. Just call down and have them pick up that blood work."

"Thanks!" It was almost 2 o'clock when I slammed out of the double glass doors of the hospital lobby. I broke into a run when I saw the N-Judah streetcar crest the hill at the edge of the Medical Center complex. Twenty minutes later, I got off at Civic

Center and ran the two blocks to the Golden Gate Transit stop at the corner of Seventh and Market. I felt damp and sweaty under my coat and my shoulder ached from my heavy bag.

The 3 o'clock bus was late, finally appearing at nearly 3:30. I calculated the time. I wouldn't get to Santa Rosa until almost 5:30. There was no way I could make it to Guy's house by 6 o'clock. I settled into a seat, slipped out of my coat and hospital smock, and pulled my tan and rust striped sweater over my head. I didn't like remembering that this sweater was a gift from Guy on my 27th birthday, equally regrettable was that more than three years later, it was still the nicest one I had.

When I had to pick up Colin on the bus, I tried to make the long ride fun for him, as if we were going on a trip to some exciting destination. At the bottom of my bag was a Tupperware container filled with peanut butter crackers, sliced apples, and a wet cloth in a plastic bag. He was working on a magic trick which involved making a pencil rise off the table and I had his sharpened number two pencil and the instructions, some books, his favorite Matchbox cars, and a cardboard track in one of the drawstring bags I made him.

We passed over the Golden Gate Bridge. I looked out of the window, took a deep breath and tried to relax, even as I willed the bus to drive faster up Highway 101. The sky threatened to spill the contents of its heavy, gray clouds and the bus began to rock as the wind picked up. When the door opened to let off a passenger in Novato, a rush of cold air ran down the aisle. Colin and I would have a long, wet trip back to my apartment near Ocean Beach. Even if everything went smoothly, we wouldn't get off the last bus at Noriega near the Great Highway until nearly 10 o'clock and he'd probably be sound asleep.

I leaned across the aisle and tapped an elderly woman on the arm. "Excuse me. What time it is?"

The woman consulted the tiny face of her gold watch. "We're making good time. It's only a little after five," she said. "I've seen you on this bus before, haven't I?"

"Yes, I remember you. I'm picking up my son from his father's house in Santa Rose but I'm supposed to be there at 6 o'clock and I'm afraid I'm gonna be late."

"Well, don't worry, dear. I'm sure his daddy is glad to spend a little extra time with him. You're lucky his father wants to see him at all. So many fathers run off and don't want anything to do with their children once there's a divorce." The woman shook her head at the sad thought.

"I suppose so." I turned towards the window to end the conversation. Twenty minutes later, the bus pulled into Courthouse Square in downtown Santa Rosa. Through the window, I saw the local bus begin to pull away from the curb. I grabbed my bag and when the doors opened, I flew down the steps to the sidewalk. I ran, yelling and waiving my arms. The driver stopped and opened the door. "Thank you. Thank you!" I said.

The bus let me off at the edge of Guy's neighborhood. It had to be at least 6 o'clock and I still had four blocks to walk. I hoisted my jute bag onto my shoulder and walked across Sonoma Highway and into the suburban neighborhood of low slung, ranch style homes, all different versions of each other. Pastel bicycles lay here and there, their young owners casual about the security of their possessions. Most driveways held a pair of autos, either a small compact and a large van, or a BMW, or a Bronco. The streets were deserted. "Dinner time at 6 o'clock sharp," I thought ruefully.

Whenever I was in Guy's neighborhood, I thought of the Malvina Reynolds' song. *Little boxes on the hillside, and they're all made out of ticky-tacky. Little boxes made of ticky-tacky and they all look just the same.* This was the kind of neighborhood that Guy and I used to make fun of.

I walked three blocks and turned the corner onto Montclair Avenue. Guy's white VW was parked next to Linda's Audi in their double driveway. His old van looked out of place, a little too old, a little too funky, and still sporting the red and white-checkered curtains I'd made for the van in another lifetime. I walked up the driveway against a cold gust of wind. Front steps led to a small porch edged with a black wrought iron railing. Colin's small, round face peered out the narrow window along the edge of the door. He was wearing his favorite LA Rams jacket. His deep red hair was brushed. His caramel colored face was shiny and clean.

"Hi, baby," I mouthed through the glass.

Colin brightened when he saw me and reached up to turn the brass knob. But before he could manage the latch, Guy swung the door open and stepped onto the landing, closing the door behind him. He gripped a plastic bag as if he was strangling it and pulled out a rumpled pair of Colin's jeans. At the end of his last visit, Colin had wet his pants as I was getting ready to drive him back to Santa Rosa. I didn't have time to make a trip to the Laundromat, so I rinsed out his pants and his underwear, put them in a plastic bag and stuck them in with his other clothes.

Guy towered over me and I backed up as far as I could on the narrow porch. "I'd like an explanation of how you felt justified in returning this urine-sodden clothing, Sharon." I didn't answer. "Your personal habits are your own business except when they impact my son."

"You kept these wet pants for two weeks just to make an issue out of this?" I said.

Guy's eyes narrowed to slits below his heavy black eyebrows. "I don't want your sarcasm, Sharon. I want an answer. What I see here is neglect. And when I see your slovenliness impact my son, I'm going to address it."

I jammed my finger into the soggy denim. "What you see here is laundry, Guy, dirty laundry." I motioned to the matching machines visible through the opened garage door at the foot of the stairs. "For chrissakes, you have a washer and dryer right there in your garage."

"Don't make a scene. I can see there's no talking to you."

Guy opened the front door and stepped back into the house. Colin clutched his drawstring bag under his chin. He looked up at his father's face and then looked back at me through the beveled glass. A stab of alarm cut through me. Guy wasn't going to let Colin come for his visit. I could imagine how he would justify it to Mike Lentz. He would describe how hysterical and slovenly I was. Couldn't get to his house on time, couldn't even get the laundry done, doesn't even have a decent car, and has to go around on public transportation—all the traits that add up to an unfit mother. The front door bumped against the latch.

Desperately and without thinking, I reached up and stopped the door before it closed. The door reversed itself and began to swing open. I leaned into the foyer, grabbed for Colin's outstretched hand, and pulled him onto the porch. But Guy hadn't walked away. He was standing behind the door. The edge of the door caught the corner of his thick glasses as it swung open. When I saw Guy grabbing at his glasses as they tumbled down his chest, I said, "Let's go, Colin. Now!" Holding the railing with one little hand, still clutching his flowered bag with the other, Colin's short, sturdy legs pounded down the stairs. Guy reached around the door and caught me by the back of the coat. Colin looked back over his shoulder and hesitated. "Go!" I said.

"Come on, Mommy, hurry!" Colin reached the driveway below and rocked from one foot to the other, gravel crunching under his feet. "Daddy, don't!"

Before I could reach the top step, Guy yanked me backward by the shoulder of my coat. I was thrown off balance and stumbled, dropping my bag. I jerked out of his grip and steadied myself against the railing, holding on as tightly as I could. Guy reached for me again and got a better grip on the shoulder of my coat. His thick fingers dug into my shoulder and my muscles strained against him. I leaned forward, bending out over the railing at the edge of the porch.

I scanned the neighborhood, looking for someone to help me. With the exception of one small boy in front of the house across the street, the street was deserted. I screamed, hoping to catch someone's attention. "Help! Please, help me!"

The little boy ran back into his house. Guy yanked me backward by the shoulder and I heard the back of my coat tear away. He pulled me towards the opened front door and I clutched the porch railing, my arms outstretched. I thought he might kill me if he got me inside that house.

"Help! Help me!" I screamed, but I didn't see a soul. I was asking the anonymous frame houses and the cloudy sky to save me.

Guy shook me. "Shut the fuck up, Sharon!" Holding my coat with one hand, Guy punched me on the neck and the back of my head with the other. My head snapped to the left and I felt a hot pain burn across my shoulder. He yanked me towards him and my hands lost their grip. My fingertips scraped the surface of the metal railing.

Guy spun me around and slammed his fist into the side of my face. I felt an explosion of pain and saw a sharp flash of silver light. Then everything was quiet. I didn't feel the other blows. I didn't feel anything at all. For an endless silent moment, the world was quiet and calm. Then Colin's voice reached me through a hazy mist. He was calling to me. "What's Colin saying?" I wondered.

"Mommy. Mommy!" I heard the gravel of the driveway crunching under Colin's feet. He was jumping up and down at the bottom of the steps.

By the time I realized what was happening, Guy had me halfway into the house. He was dragging me by the front of my coat. I anchored myself against the doorjamb and pain shot up my arms.

At that moment, Linda appeared from behind the door. "Guy, don't. Let her go!" she commanded. "Call the police. That's what she deserves."

Guy's focus was riveted on me and he didn't react to Linda's command. He kept pulling, trying to drag me into the house. Linda ducked under Guy's outstretched arms and pushed into the space between us—her back to Guy and her hands shoving against my chest. Guy's fingers slipped from the front of my coat.

Seizing the opportunity, I quit pulling and almost lost my balance. I set my feet against the threshold and grabbed Linda by her narrow shoulders. I shoved her as hard as I could backward into Guy's chest. They stumbled into each other. I grabbed the strap of my bag and ran down the stairs, the bag bumping against each step behind me. I swept Colin up into my arms and ran down the driveway towards the street.

I bent to put Colin down on his feet and a searing pain shot through my back and neck and I nearly blacked out. I blinked and shook my head to focus. Blood poured out of my nose onto Colin's blue and gold jacket. Colin buried his face against my legs. I cupped my nose and tried to wipe away the blood with the sleeve of my shredded coat. I looked up and down the street and then back at Guy's house. Everything was quiet. Guy's front door was closed. Even the garage doors were closed. It was as if nothing had happened. I felt naked standing there bleeding on the curb. I wanted to lie down, curl up around Colin, and disappear into the earth.

A teenage girl came out of the house the little boy had retreated into earlier. She came down the stairs and I stumbled towards her, herding Colin by the shoulder. She winced when she was close enough to see my face.

"I need some help," I said.

"Come on. My mom will help you." I followed her across the neatly groomed yard. A wooden plaque at the foot of the low brick steps read *Welcome to the Campbell's' House.* I stepped into the quiet foyer. "Wait here." The girl disappeared into the back of the house.

I could feel my pulse hammering in my ears. My face throbbed and I could taste blood running down the back of my throat. I leaned against the doorjamb and pulled Colin towards me. He was breathing in shallow intakes of breath and again buried his face against my leg. I ran my hand over his curly head and we waited.

The house was totally still. After a minute, I took a step forward and looked into the formal dining room. Unlit candles in brass candle holders and four brocade place mats with pale china plates and silverware were arranged at one end of the long oak table. Still life prints hung on all visible walls and sheer curtains with valances that matched the place mats covered the windows. Everything was neat and sparkling. I was going to be a shock to the mother of this family.

A short woman with light brown hair stepped through a swinging door on the opposite side of the dining room. The teenage girl and the young boy were nowhere to be seen. Dinner aromas escaped from the kitchen through the door that settled into place behind her. Mrs. Campbell stood without speaking, wiping her hands on a yellow checkered apron. She looked back and forth from me to Colin without speaking.

"I'm sorry to barge in like this, but my ex-husband lives across the street. I came to pick up my son and we had a fight and Guy punched me. Your daughter said you would help me."

Mrs. Campbell looked as if she was paying close attention to my words, but she stood very still with her hands resting on her belly with no emotion on her face. I felt as if I was speaking a language that she didn't understand.

"Yes, my daughter is a good Samaritan. She told me some-one needed help but she didn't say what happened." Her voice was devoid of expression. She sounded as if she were reading the words from a script.

"I'm really sorry, but if I could just use your phone and may-be your bathroom for a second ... I'm so sorry to bother you." I heard myself begging.

"You have blood on your face. I'll get you something for it. Come here and sit down." She didn't ask my name or offer hers. She gestured to a high-backed chair next to the sideboard and disappeared into the kitchen. I had no other options, so I stepped forward, pushing Colin along with my leg and closed the front door carefully behind me.

I put down my bag. My shoulders were stiff and spirals of pain ran up my back when I sat down. Something felt very wrong in the back of my neck. I tried to lift Colin into my lap, but the pain wouldn't allow it. He leaned against me and laid his head on my lap. My head started to spin and blood began to flow again. I leaned my head back and held my fingers against the base of my nose.

Mrs. Campbell appeared silently and pressed a small, wet towel into my hand. She put an ice pack wrapped in a soft cloth into the other. I leaned forward and rested my face in the cool pillow, closing my eyes with relief. When I felt the bleeding stop, I asked to use the bathroom.

"It's down the hall on the left. There are more towels in the cupboard in there."

"Thank you. Come on, baby. Let's go to the bathroom." I nudged Colin up from my lap and followed Mrs. Campbell into the hallway.

When I reached the bathroom, I heard the front door open. Mrs. Campbell turned and said, "That's my husband. Let me go and tell him what's going on."

I felt safe as soon as Colin and I were alone together in the pastel bathroom. I never wanted to leave the cool darkness of that room. I washed Colin's face and hands with a warm cloth and tried to get the blood off his jacket. I shrugged out of my torn coat and cleaned up as much as I could. There was a pin in a dish on the tank of the toilet and I pinned the back of my coat together. I wiped the sink and hung the face cloths and towels neatly over the shower curtain. Colin sat on the edge of the tub and didn't take his eyes off my face. He hadn't said a word since we ran from Guy's house. I sat on the edge of the tub next to Colin and put my arms around him. We sat there, quietly breathing in and out together. "Okay, let's go," I said.

When I walked back down the hallway, the young boy and the teenage girl lay on the floor together in front of the television in the family room. Their father was obscured by the evening paper, his legs propped up on the elevated footrest of his lounge chair. The girl looked over her shoulder and gave me a weak smile.

An extension had been pulled onto the sideboard next to the chair where I had been sitting. "Here's the phone," Mrs. Campbell said.

"I'm going to call the police and then see if someone will come pick me up. What is this address and I guess I need your phone number?"

Mrs. Campbell hesitated and then wrote the information on the pad next to the phone. She directed herself to Colin. "Would you like something to drink, honey?"

Colin looked at me. "It's okay." I said to him.

"Can I watch TV?" he asked.

Mrs. Campbell stepped forward and guided Colin towards the living room. "Sure, you watch television while your mother uses the phone. I'll bring you some juice."

"Thank you," I said towards her retreating back. I dialed 911 and waited for dispatch to come on the line. I explained what had happened and read off the address and phone number. The dispatcher told me a patrolman would come and take a report. I hung up the phone and dialed my home number. Renaye answered and I dissolved into tears at the familiar sound of her voice. "Can you try to find someone to come and get me?"

"I'll try," she said. I gave her the Campbell's number and hung up. My thoughts were racing, as if someone inside my head was screaming. I leaned back against the wall and put the ice pack on my face. I closed my eyes and everything on the other side of my eyelids floated far away.

"Here come the police," Mrs. Campbell said.

When I opened my eyes, I saw her holding the curtain slightly open with an extended finger. I stood up and joined her in front of the window. A black and white cruiser was driving slowly towards the house. But before it reached the Campbell's it stopped in front of Guy's. Two uniformed officers got out of the patrol car and walked up the driveway.

I watched as Guy opened the front door and Linda joined him. I got a familiar sinking feeling as I watched Guy put his arm around her shoulder. The officers looked around as they walked up the front steps. Guy and Linda moved out of the doorway and the officers stepped inside. Guy closed the door behind them.

Mrs. Campbell looked at me and then back towards Guy's house. "I've seen your son playing outside with those two little white girls, but I've never met his father. Is that woman his wife?"

The last thing I wanted to do was stand there and gossip about Guy and Linda with this woman. "No." I answered.

The phone rang and Mrs. Campbell walked to the sideboard and answered. "It's your roommate." She extended the receiver and then returned to the window.

"Sharon? I can't find anyone to pick you up," Renaye said. "Maria will drive up there, but she doesn't get off work until 10."

"Forget it! I'll take the bus home. The police are here. I gotta go." I returned to the window and saw the officers leave Guy's house. They drove slowly to the Campbell's and sat in their cruiser, looking in the direction of the house. When they climbed out of the patrol car, Mrs. Campbell let go of the sheer curtain and adjusted the folds.

"I'll leave you alone to talk to them." She walked to the front door and opened it.

Officer Douglas Schlief and his partner stepped into the house and looked around. Their uniforms, guns, and boots were as incongruous in the pastel tones of this quiet house as I was. Mrs. Campbell nodded and walked back into the kitchen.

"Are you Sharon Murphy?" Officer Schlief asked.

"Yes."

"We're responding to a domestic disturbance called in by Guy Johnson."

"What? I was the one who called," I said, my voice high and thin. I choked down the lump in my throat.

"Mr. Johnson called and said that you attacked him," Schlief said.

The top of my head began to tingle and my legs became wobbly. I couldn't get a breath. I lowered my head for a moment and tried to keep myself from blacking out. "Did you see the size of him?" My voice came out weaker than I wanted it to sound. "Do you see my face?"

"Mr. Johnson said you broke into his house."

"Why would I break into his house? I came to pick up my son for a visit. It's approved in our custody agreement. When I got there, Guy lost his temper and punched me in the face." As if on cue, my nose started to bleed again and I held the towel against my face.

"Calm down, Miss Murphy, there is no need to get hysterical. We saw scratches on his face."

I held up my hands and turned my short, neatly trimmed nails towards Schlief. "Do these look like they could scratch someone's face? Are you looking at *my* face? This is bullshit! Are you going to take my report or not?"

"Mr. Johnson and his wife have made a report and he is intending to press charges against you. If you also make a report, we will have to arrest you because you were on his property."

The officer's words sounded as if they were intended to make sense, but I was having a hard time following the logic of what he was saying. All I heard was, *"We are not here to help you. You are on your own."* I felt invisible and something shifted inside of me. I wasn't scared anymore and I wasn't angry. My last available drop of anger and outrage had plopped into the tank and it was filled.

"Could I get your name and badge number?" I wrote down his information on the notepad next to the phone. I put the paper in my pocket and picked up our bags. I walked into the living room. "Come on, Colin. We're leaving."

Colin was sitting next to the two Campbell kids in front of the TV. The teenage girl looked around. "Bye, Colin."

"Bye." Colin got up and turned towards me.

"Where're you going?" the young woman asked.

"We're going to go catch the bus at Courthouse Square and go home."

"Do you want a ride to the bus stop?"

"That would be wonderful." I started to cry at this small act of kindness.

Colin took my hand. "Come on, Mommy."

Mr. Campbell glared at me from his lounge chair, the newspaper crumpled in his lap. He directed himself to his daughter. "You don't need to do that, dear."

"I know." The young woman got up, slipped on her shoes, and picked up her purse from the table in the foyer.

"I appreciate your help," I said to Mr. Campbell.

"Humph!" He lifted the newspaper in front of his face.

Colin eyed the police officers as we walked past them and out the front door. We followed the girl to the silver sedan. We drove in silence and as we pulled up to Courthouse Square the San Francisco bus appeared from around the corner.

"Well, that's lucky." I gave a small laugh. "I appreciate the ride."

"I'll be in trouble when I get home—but I don't care." The girl raised her chin in defiance.

"It's important to do what you think is right. And tell your mother I appreciate her help, too."

"She didn't want to help you."

"But she did."

"I guess."

"Well, good-bye."

Colin and I walked towards the Golden Gate Transit bus. He climbed up the steps ahead of me. My legs and back screamed as I pulled myself up into the stairwell. The driver looked down at Colin. "Hey, little man! Aren't you Guy Johnson's son?"

I pushed Colin into the aisle and handed the driver the second half of my round trip ticket. "No, he's my son."

PART TWO

CHAPTER EIGHT

San Francisco, California: April 10, 1981

"I SHOULD NEVER HAVE LET you go there by yourself." Renaye pounded her hand on the table. "This was bound to happen again sooner or later."

"Renaye, I'm the one who should have known better." I fingered the bridge of my nose. It was tender to the touch. "It's time for me to face what's going to happen and quit acting so shocked when Guy acts like Guy."

"What do you mean?" she asked.

"Guy's going to pound on me whenever he gets ticked off. And he'll smack Colin around and still be able to convince people that he's this great dad. He'll brainwash Colin until he's convinced him that I don't love him and that I'm a loser. They'll live in Linda's big house and Linda can be Colin's mother. And anytime I try to prevent any of this, Guy will twist the facts to shore up his story that I'm a paranoid hysteric. And his buddy Mike Lentz will make sure it's all nice and legal. Nothing I do or say can make a bit of difference. Nothing and no one will ever stop him."

I felt as if my words released a genie from a bottle—a whisper in the back of my mind said, "*Run!*" I dropped my head into my hands and felt a dull thudding behind my eyes.

"You need to go to bed," Renaye said.

"I'm going to take a shower first."

"Let me know if you need anything."

The face that I saw in the bathroom mirror was a shock. The bridge of my nose was swollen and my left eye was bloodshot. Both my eyelids and my cheek were discolored and puffy. I stripped off my clothes and turned on the shower. I let the sharp spray massage the knots on the back of my head and neck. When I turned my face into the steaming water, blood poured from my nose. I hung my head with both hands resting on the shower wall and I watched pink eddies of water disappear down the drain. The water turned cold and still I stood there. What was I supposed to do now? Again the whisper said, *"Run!"*

When I switched off the bathroom light, the apartment was quiet and dark. The small ceramic lamp next to my bed glowed softly. Renaye had left an ice pack and tight little joint in the ashtray on my bedside table. I hung my wet towel over the doorknob and slowly wrestled my nightgown over my head, my neck and shoulders were tight and sore. I threw back the covers and lay down, arranging the icepack behind my neck, and then lit the joint with a long kitchen match. My thoughts drifted away on the funnel of smoke that swirled towards the ceiling. I had Colin with me for five days. I'd know what to do by Wednesday.

Saturday morning, April 11, 1981

Colin and Michael were at the table eating Rice Krispies and coloring when I walked into the kitchen the next morning. Colin was wearing his thermal pajamas and Michael was wearing the blue and white checkered dress he had fallen in love with when he found it in the "Free-Box" in front of the co-op on Haight Street. Renaye and I couldn't come up with a forward-thinking, politically correct reason why he couldn't wear his dress if he wanted to, so we compromised and he agreed to only wear it in the house. "To keep it from getting torn," we reasoned. Colin had been learning about *boy things* and *girl things* from Guy and he quit playing dress up with Michael—his dress-up outfit had been an orange nylon nightgown that he said felt cool against his skin, but he'd never said an unkind word about his buddy's little blue dress.

Colin jumped down from his chair and ran to me. "Hi, Momma." He held his arms up and I hoisted him onto my hip, ignoring the pain. "You gotta black eye," he said.

"I'm okay," I said. Colin locked his fingers behind my neck. I winced and then peppered both of his freckled cheeks with kisses and blew raspberries on his warm neck. I held his hands and he did a back flip onto the floor. As soon as I straightened up, a trickle of blood ran out of my nose and I pulled a tissue out of my pocket and turned away so the kids wouldn't see.

Renaye stood in a beam of morning sun light from the opened back door. She poured us both a cup of coffee. "I heard you on the phone earlier. What's happening?"

"I called my sisters and left a message for my lawyer. I asked Richard to try to get me in front of the judge as soon possible. Maybe if Judge Sater sees my face, he'll see Guy a little clearer." I motioned to the back porch and Renaye followed.

"You don't sound too sure," Renaye said as she sat next to me on the top step.

"A lot of people would have to change their opinion of Guy to turn this thing around. It's just more convenient for every-one to continue to believe that I'm a crazy liar."

"Have you thought of...taking off with Colin?" Renaye said under her breath.

I was shocked to hear my secret thoughts spoken out loud. "I'm going to try to get him back the right way first," I said. "I have to at least try—just one more time. This face is evidence that I haven't had before."

I looked through the back door. Colin was pulling on Michael's arm, trying to get him to arm wrestle. He swept aside the coloring books and planted his elbow on the table. "Come on, Michael," he said. "Let's see who's stronger." Michael pulled back in horror.

"Colin, Michael doesn't want to arm wrestle," I called out. "Leave him alone."

"I know you're stronger," Michael said matter-of-factly.

"You two go get dressed," Renaye said. The boys climbed down from their chairs and headed towards the bedroom. Renaye called after them. "Bowls, please." Michael and Colin turned back, grabbed their bowls off the table, and took two steps in the direction of the sink, "...spoons, too!" The kids complied then disappeared into their room.

The phone rang and I used the railing to pull myself up to standing. Renaye reached out to help me. "I'm okay," I said, but my whole body hurt and I had a blinding headache.

"Go to the Emergency Room immediately!" Richard said when I picked up the phone. "And be sure to get a copy of the report. Then write up everything that happened and fax me your statement and the hospital report. I haven't heard back from Lentz yet."

"Talking to Lentz is a waste of time, Richard! Can't you get me in front of Judge Sater?" I protested.

"Sharon, the conciliation officer is the gatekeeper. Lentz has to make the recommendation before we can talk to a judge," he said. "And Lentz will probably want to talk to Colin this time."

Tuesday, April 14, 1981

My meeting with Mike Lentz was set for 10 a.m. on Tuesday, April 14, the day before my visit with Colin was scheduled to end. June, a new friend from the chorus, offered to drive Colin and me to Santa Rosa. June's tiny frame was toned and muscular. She'd invited me to work out with her at her gym many times, but I never took her up on the offer. She managed the Longs Drugstore on Ocean Boulevard and was the only one of my friends who wasn't constantly short of cash. June insisted on treating us to breakfast on the way to the hearing, so we left early and stopped at a restaurant in Sausalito. From our table near the window, we had a view of the turquoise water of Richardson Bay and the San Francisco skyline in the distance.

I drank my coffee and watched Colin chatting with June. He had on his best yellow knit shirt and khaki shorts. He looked so beautiful with his red hair reflecting the morning light. Colin was telling June about Max, the pit bull puppy that his dad had gotten for him. "Max is brindle, that's black *and* brown. And he has white paws—he looks like he has on socks." I felt a swell of pride. Colin was so gregarious and knew instinctively how to carry on a conversation. He enjoyed the attention and genuinely liked talking to adults. One of the few things that Guy and I had in common had been a mutual distain for people who talked to children as if they were mentally impaired.

I hated to dampen the mood at the table, but after the waiter took away the remains of our omelets, I said, "Colin, when we get to the Santa Rosa courthouse, I'm going to ask the mediator if you can come back to live with me. And after I talk to him, he'll talk to you, too."

Colin looked worried. "What's a mediator?"

"A mediator is a person who makes the decision when divorced people can't agree on something. He's like a Judge."

"What does he want me to say?"

"He will probably ask you about the fight I had with your dad."

"Will my dad get in trouble?"

"No, this isn't about getting your dad in trouble. I want you to just tell the truth," I said. "That's all you have to do."

Richard had arranged for me to speak with Lentz without Guy present, the first time the conciliation judge had agreed to this request, although we asked many times before. Then Guy's private meeting with Lentz would follow at 11:30. When the three of us stepped into the outer office of the Sonoma County Conciliation Court, the receptionist who had always been so friendly with Guy was at the front desk. Her eyes lingered on the bruises on my face, and then she looked down at her appointment book. "Go right in, Miss Murphy."

"We'll wait for you out here." June said. I paused a moment to watch as she tried to settle Colin on the floor next to the blocks and trucks arranged in a corner of the waiting room. Colin ignored the toys, climbed up into the chair, and started tapping his fists against his thighs.

I knocked on the office door and then opened it. Mike Lentz was seated behind the desk in his small, cluttered office. "Have a seat, Ms. Murphy," he said, "and tell me what this is all about?" He looked at my face without any reaction to what he saw there.

I took one of the upholstered chairs facing him. "Did you get the papers from my attorney?" I asked.

Lentz flipped open the file on the desk in front of him. "Uh, I think something may have been filed yesterday."

I saw the pleading with Richard Barnett's caption attached to the inside of the folder. Richard had asked for an *ex-parte* order temporarily changing custody pending a hearing before a Judge. Our request was based on my sworn statement that Guy had beaten Colin and left bruises on him and that Colin had witnessed Guy beating me last Friday. I concluded my statement by saying,

"Because of the beatings Colin has received, the violence he has witnessed, and the extreme emotional turmoil he is experiencing, I believe it would be physically and emotionally damaging to him to be returned to the custody of his father. Because of my fear for his welfare, I do not intend to return him when my Easter visit ends at 5 o'clock on Wednesday, April 15, 1981."

I watched the top of Lentz's head while he read my words. He lifted the top page, then the next with the tip of his pen. The third page was the report from the Moffitt Hospital Emergency Room. Lentz tapped his pen against the desk as he read Dr. Noreen Bennett's handwritten notes.

"Patient complains of general body aches and headache behind the eyes. My examination found bruising and swelling on the right shoulder, and right side of her back near the armpit and bruising as if patient was grabbed on the right arm above elbow. There is swelling on the left side of the scalp, left side of the face, and left arm. Swelling and bruising across the cheekbone and small laceration on left side of the nose. Good range of motion, no loss of consciousness. Assaulted by ex-husband last night—happened previously X2. Incident was reported to the police. No charges filed and social services not contacted."

Lentz stroked the pages flat and closed the file. "Ms. Murphy, it says here that you do not intend to return Colin to his father. Is that correct?"

I shouldn't have been surprised at where Lentz's attention landed, but still I was shaken. By my own words I had stated that I was intending to defy the Court order. I was suddenly aware that Guy would be here any minute and that Colin was sitting right on the other side of the door. I tried to choose my words carefully and mitigate the intensity of my written statement.

"I just want to ask Judge Sater if Colin can remain with me while the situation is reviewed. You know I've tried to bring up Guy's violence before, and now he's beaten Colin with his belt. What could a five-year-old child do to warrant a beating with a belt? Then Colin watched his father punching me in the face. Don't you think this should be a factor in this case? It's certainly pertinent to Guy's credibility and to the kind of father he is. Is it so hard to believe that Colin is afraid to go back to Guy's house?" I asked. "He's only a little boy."

Lentz pursed his lips and looked down at his chubby hands that were folded on top of my file. Then he leveled his gaze at me. "Ms. Murphy, just because Guy beats you does not make him a bad father."

At first I wasn't certain that I had heard him correctly. "Wh...what?" I stammered.

"I know you've tried to make this case about domestic violence, but just because Guy beats you, it doesn't mean that he is a bad father. I'd like to talk to Colin now," he said calmly.

A flame of anger surged through me so fast that I thought I would faint. I bolted to my feet and was immediately dizzy. I closed my eyes until my head cleared. Maybe what I did then was a mistake. Maybe someone else might have known a different way to respond, a better way, a less emotional way to react, but that person would have had to believe that there some way to improve the situation. As for me, I knew it was hopeless and I saw the inevitable end to all this.

"No. I'm taking my son home!"

I had only been in Lentz's office for a few minutes and June looked up with surprise when I stormed into the waiting room. "Let's go," I said. I had to get out of there before Guy showed up. I pushed open the heavy glass doors and stepped out into the bright spring sunshine. Colin and June followed behind me. My head was pounding and tears brimmed in my eyes. I looked down into my shoulder bag and dug around for my sunglasses. When I looked up, Guy was walking towards me. The three of us stopped and I instinctively put my hand on Colin's shoulder.

Guy looked June up and down, then smiled as he got closer. "Hi, Colin! How's my little man? I've missed you."

Colin leaned back into my legs. "Hi, Daddy," his voice was soft and low. Guy crouched in front of Colin with his hand on his arm.

Guy looked up at me over the top of his glasses, which had slid to the end of his nose. "I thought since you're here, Sharon, I could take Colin home with me now and save you the trip back up here tomorrow."

"I'm not playing this game with you anymore, Guy," I said.

Guy stood up and I took off my sunglasses and looked at him. He took a small step backwards. Maybe it was my black eye and the bruises on my face or maybe it was my expression, but Guy's eyes widened in look of surprise. I thought I saw a flash of fear run across his face. He stood there without speaking. June touched my back and led the way passed Guy to her car.

I told June about the meeting with Lentz. "What are you going to do?" she asked.

"I know what I *want* to do, but I'm not quite sure how to do it," I said. June said nothing and turned her attention back to the road. Colin dozed off in the back seat on the drive home. He slept a lot now, too much stress for a little boy, I thought.

I stared out the window and began a mental inventory of the pros and cons of the terrifying plan that had been gathering steam in my mind, almost without my conscious assistance. What if I just disappeared with Colin?

When we got home, June and Renaye took the kids to the zoo so I could have some time to think. At Colin's request, June put the top down on her new MG. He assembled a driving costume complete with diving goggles and a helmet. "You look like a mad astronaut," I told him as I kissed him goodbye at the door.

When I was alone in the apartment, I took off my suit and put on my sweatpants and my orange Califia sweatshirt and paced around the apartment in bare feet. I got my green jacket and my wicker sewing basket from the hall closet and carried them into Colin's room. Emotions ricocheted through my body. I sat tailor-style on the floor and began stitching the shreds of my coat back together. I could always think more clearly when my hands were occupied.

There would certainly be serious consequences from my walking out of my meeting with Lentz. I might have already lost my visitation. And if Guy had full custody and I had even less or no visitation, I'd have no way at all to protect Colin. If Guy's only parenting tool was his belt and Colin was only five, what would he be like when Colin became a willful adolescent or a mouthy teenager? I knew the answer. Guy would use his fists the way he had with me.

I came to the end of a row of stitches and re-threaded the needle. What I was considering was incredible but what were my options? Maybe I really had no options. I could return Colin as the Court had ordered me to and hope that what I feared wouldn't happen or I could act preemptively and take my son and disappear. I thought about that for a while. I had the force of the law on one side and Guy's violence and rage on the other. It felt as if the only real option I had was illegal and seemed impossible to pull off.

I tried to project as far into the future as I could imagine with both scenarios. Then a mental image of a truck barreling down on Colin sprang into my mind. If I could save my little boy, I wouldn't speculate about the terrain along the side of the road before I grabbed him and jumped. I'd grown up with a violent, dominating parent. There was no speculation about what that was like. The most important thing to me was for Colin to have a safe, nurturing home to grow up in—the kind of environment that would allow him to feel happy and loved so he could grow up to be kind, self-confident, and sensitive. Would he have that if he remained with Guy and had to fight and struggle every day of his life? How could he feel safe if I was squeezed out of his life?

So what were the risks of running away? Maybe it would harm Colin in some way. Would it feel like normal life if I was living as a fugitive? I had no way to tell. And if I got caught, Colin would go back to Guy anyway and I would probably go to jail for who knows how long. But what if we had a year or two years—both of us safe—a year or two year without Guy? Colin was so young. If we could have just a little time for him to live without all this violence and fighting, would the risk be worth the benefit?

I turned my coat inside out and ran my thumbnail along the even whip stitching on the shoulder seam—good as new. I poked the needle back into the red tomato pincushion and put the lid on my sewing box. The toe of a blue sneaker was sticking out from under Colin's bed. The side of his shoe had split open before I had the cash to buy him a new pair. The shoes still fit him so I used an upholstery needle and stitched the seam back together. When Guy accused me of dressing Colin in *tattered clothing*, I wondered at the time if he had noticed my handiwork. Even my mother, who never missed an opportunity to criticize me, would have thought I was being resourceful. I sighed and put Colin's sneaker on top of my mended coat.

I lay on my back on the floor of Colin's room and stared at the shadows moving across the ceiling. This battle with Guy tore at me at the very deepest level. I closed my eyes and remembered a speech Malcolm X gave in the last year of his life. I was certain that Malcolm X wasn't thinking about a white, working-class mother when he made his proclamation, but I thought his sentiment was germane.

"We declare our right on this earth ... to be a human being, to be respected as a human being, to be given the rights of a human being in this society, on this earth, in this day, which we intend to bring into existence by any means necessary."

With a silent thank you to Malcolm X, I decided on my course of action.

I called my attorney and told him about my meeting with Mike Lentz. Richard must have heard something unusual in my voice, because he said, "I know what you're considering, Sharon. Don't tell me if you're planning to do something illegal." I was silent and he continued. "But honestly, if Guy has his way, it may be your only way to preserve any kind of relationship with Colin. Still as your attorney, I am officially advising against ignoring the Court order."

"I understand," I said.

"Well...," Richard's voice trailed off. "Mike Lentz is supposed to send his report to the judge tomorrow. I'll call you as soon as Judge Sater makes his ruling." I made no reply and Richard said, "You know you are supposed to return Colin tomorrow at 5 o'clock."

"Yes, I know." There was an extended silence before Richard hung up.

I called Marilyn, Sally Ann, and then Jeanne. I asked them to get together and call me back. Carol was living in Texas and we decided to call her after my plan was in place. My sisters' support was immediate and unquestioning. Sally Ann was working a double shift, but Jeanne agreed to drive up to Marilyn and Irene's house in Studio City. "We'll call as soon as I get there," Jeanne said.

I sat at the dining table and began making notes. Forty-five minutes later, the phone rang. "We have you on speaker," Marilyn said. I'd been at Marilyn and Irene's house when I took my trip to Califia and I could picture them all sitting around the phone in the breakfast nook with the crimson bougainvillea peeking through the windows. They'd be drinking coffee and smoking cigarettes with worried looks on their faces.

"So what are you going to do?" Marilyn asked.

"I'm going to leave town with Colin. I'm supposed to bring him back to Guy tomorrow at 5, so I have to get out of my apartment fast," I said. "I want to come down there by the end of the week and then we can I figure out how I'm going to do this."

"Sharon, you don't have to give up your entire life just because you're a mother. No one would blame you if you decided to bring Colin back to Guy," Marilyn said. "I want you to know that."

"I know. I'm not giving up my life."

I heard Irene's deep, raspy voice in the background. "We love you, Sharon!"

Jeanne spoke up. "Sharon, if you do this don't expect Colin to thank you some day in the future. Be sure that you're doing it for your own reasons. This is a huge step."

"I'm not safe around Guy and neither is Colin. It's my responsibility to protect both of us. Those are my reasons."

"Okay. We'll make the arrangements and call you back," Marilyn said.

When June and Renaye came home with the kids an hour later, I was in the kitchen slicing yellow peppers and steam was escaping from pots on the stove. Robert Cray was tearing up his blues guitar at full volume from my cassette player. They gave me quizzical looks.

I felt better now that everyone was in the house. "We're having a dinner party," I announced.

"Cool!" Colin said. I gave him a big hug. Without any further explanation, everyone pitched in to get ready for dinner. Kwambe came in the front door waving a bottle of white wine. Maria arrived with strawberries and frozen Rice Dream for dessert, and while I cooked, she took the boys for a ride around the neighborhood on her Harley. With the kids gone, I could explain my plan to Renaye, June, and Kwambe.

"We need to be somewhere Guy doesn't know about until we leave town," I said. "June, can we stay at your place? It won't be more than a couple of days."

"Anything you need, Sharon."

"Okay, then, let's celebrate!"

We had a feast of ham and green beans with slivered almonds and wild rice with yellow peppers and currants. We topped off the meal with strawberry sundaes. It was good to see Colin laughing and relaxed. After dinner, June cleared the table and I sat on the couch with Maria. Kwambe refilled our wine and gave the kids wine glasses filled with apple juice.

"Here's to us!" I toasted. Everyone tapped glasses and drank. Then Renaye slapped out an Afro-Cuban rhythm on her drums. Michael and Colin danced and kept time with the maracas.

"Colin, do you have any new magic tricks?" Maria asked.

"Sure!" Colin pulled a bath towel out of the hall closet, then ran to his room and got his red cape with the black stars that I'd made him. I tied it around his neck. He turned to his audience. "As you can see, this looks like an ordinary bath towel," he said. I hummed suspenseful music while he gestured melodramatically. He flipped the towel so the audience could inspect it on both sides. Holding his pinkies at an exaggerated angle, he gripped the towel by the edge so that it covered him from the waist down. He slowly raised the towel in front of his face so that both of his legs were visible. Then he lowered the towel to the floor.

"Now will you all please be silent? Abracadabra!!" My humming got louder and he bent one leg up behind him so when he raised the towel again, only one leg was visible. "Voila!" he said. Everyone cheered and applauded and Colin took a deep bow from the waist.

"Let's sing our song, Colin," I suggested. He climbed up next to me on the couch and we sang, *Oh, we ain't got a barrel of mooo-ney. Maybe we're ragged and fuuu-ny. But we'll travel along, sing'n a song, side by side. Oh, we don't know what's coming to-mooo-row. Maybe it's heartache and sooo-row, but we'll travel along, sing'n a song, side by side. Through all kinds of weather— what if the sky should fall? Just as long as we're together, it doesn't matter at all.*

Later that night, Michael was asleep across Renaye's lap and June was finishing the dishes. I led Colin into the living room. I sat in the rocking chair and pulled him up into my lap. We rocked quietly for a few minutes and Colin rested his head against my chest and dangled his legs over the curved arm of the chair.

"Look how big you're getting," I said. "I remember when your feet didn't even reach the arm of this chair."

Colin twisted around to gauge where his feet were. "When will I be bigger than you?"

"Oh, we have a long way to go before that happens." We rocked quietly for a moment longer, and then I said, "Colin, it's not right for you to see all the fighting between your dad and me. I know it scares you. And I think it's wrong for your dad to hit you with a belt. Nobody should be hurt like that. So I'm going to take you away where your dad does not know where we are. It will be just the two of us—you and me—and you won't see your dad for a while. Do you understand what I'm saying?"

Colin sat up and looked at me as if he were in a trance. "We're gonna go hide from my dad?" I was surprised that he had so quickly grasped the meaning of my words.

"Yes, we're going to hide from your dad. So tonight we're going to June's apartment for a couple of days. Okay?"

"Okay, Momma."

I grabbed the overnight bag that I had packed earlier and June drove us to her peacock blue apartment building on the corner of Hancock and Church Street across from San Francisco's Dolores Park. That night Colin and I slept together in her guest room, cuddled around each other. It was the first night of our underground life.

Wednesday April 15, 1981

My face and neck were still discolored and my shoulders and back were stiff and sore, but the adrenaline and pain pills were keeping my discomfort at bay. I sat at June's kitchen table, writing notes and making one call after another. I called my apartment to check the messages on the answering machine. Guy and his attorney had each called several times warning me of the consequences if I didn't return Colin at 5 o'clock.

I listened to a message from Richard and returned his call. "Judge Sater denied our request for a hearing," he said. He sounded frustrated. "Lentz attached the ER report and your statement and Guy's statement to his report, but it's obvious that both Lentz and Sater believe Guy's version of what happened even though the scene he describes is physically impossible. I think Guy could say anything he wanted to and they'd believe him at this point. It's incredible. Is there somewhere I can fax this to you? I want you to see how Guy explains how you ended up with bruises all over your body. How could anyone believe this?"

I pulled out June's business card and gave him the fax number at her office. Before he hung up, he asked, "Are you all right?"

I fingered the spiral phone cord and sighed. "I guess in some small part of my brain, I thought it might make a difference if Lentz saw what Guy did. It's hard to believe, even though he said it right to my face. I guess that's it, then. Thank you, Richard."

"Take care of yourself, Sharon. I wish I could have done more for you and your boy."

I sat down on the couch with my arm around Colin and watched Shaggy and Scooby-Do deal with a ghost from outer space. The miniature grandfather clock on June's mantel ticked in the background, reminding me of every minute that passed. It was 1 o'clock now. Once 5 o'clock arrived everything would go into high gear and the consequences would begin to pile up.

I went to the hall phone and checked my answering machine again. There were more calls from Guy. I was surprised that he hadn't offered to drive down and pick up Colin himself—he just made threats and expected me to do as I was told.

Colin would always rather be outside on his Big Wheel or climbing a tree than inside in front of the television, but I couldn't let him go outside. He looked out the window at Dolores Park and tried to look pitiful. "Mom! The park is right there. Look, there's kids out there! I'll go to the park by myself if you don't wanna go. You can watch me cross the street."

"No, Colin. I want you to stay inside."

"I'm bored. Play with me," he whined. "You've been on the phone forever!"

At 4 o'clock, June came home and handed me the fax from Richard. Guy's statement said that when I came to pick up Colin for my Easter visit, I stormed into his house and attacked him. He did not provide any motive for this attack. His words had a tone of incredulity as he described how I tried to throw *his wife* down the front stairs.

"When I tried to guide Sharon out of the house, a scuffle ensued."

"It is my opinion that the petitioner is suffering from severe mental problems and needs psychiatric care. Sharon has become philosophically aligned with a very militant group advocating women's rights and I fear that her thinking has become distorted."

5 o'clock came and went.

Thursday April 16, 1981

Marilyn called with information on our flight to Los Angeles. "We decided you should fly out of the Oakland airport," she said. "Less chance of running into someone who knows you or Guy."

June and Maria had taken off work to be with me for my last day in San Francisco. I could hear June and Colin in the background, laughing while they played UNO in the dining room.

"I win!" Colin shouted.

"You cheat," June replied.

Maria was making lunch when I walked into the kitchen. Even though the scene was so familiar, I felt as though I was looking at it from the wrong side of the looking glass. "I'm flying to LA tonight. Will you drive us to the airport?"

She turned towards me, holding a sandwich on a plate in each hand. Her dark brown eyes clouded with concern. "Isn't this ironic? My family and I escaped from Cuba after Castro came into power, and my parents always warned me to steer clear of anything that might involve the police." Nonetheless, she agreed.

When it started getting dark, Maria drove me to my apartment to pack what I could carry. She left her Harley at her apartment and borrowed her roommate's car for the evening. I got out of the car at the corner and walked towards my apartment with the hood of my jacket pulled low over my face.

Guy had been waiting more than 24 hours for me to return Colin. I feared that he might have driven to San Francisco and would be waiting for us at my apartment. If he wasn't there, the San Francisco sheriff's department might be waiting for me. Maria circled the block. If she saw anything suspicious, she would call me from the gas station on the corner. We agreed that she would let the phone ring once and hang up, then call back again. As I got closer to my apartment I scanned the street, but saw nothing unusual. Nevertheless, I didn't turn on any lights when I got inside.

Most people think about what they'd grab if they had to escape from their home in a fire. My apartment was quiet, but I felt the same sense of urgency. The red message light on the answering machine flashed off and on like a warning signal in the dark. I rushed around gathering up the things I had on my list. I pawed through Colin's drawers, aided only by the streetlights on Forty-Eighth Avenue. Weak shafts of light cast shadows across his red and blue dresser with the yellow knobs. I was sorry to leave it behind. I pared down Colin's collection of Legos into a small drawstring sack and threw in his favorite red Hot Wheels, the good ones with the rubber tires, and stuffed the bag into his backpack. I looked with regret at Colin's poster of The Banjo Lesson.

After thirty minutes, my jute bag was jammed with my important papers and some shoes. I piled it next to the front door on top of a duffel bag with toiletries, some clothes, and a few books. I crammed Colin's underpants, socks, jeans, shirts, and pajamas into his red and blue backpack. I had to squeeze the sides together before I could zip it up.

I looked around at the furniture I had worked so hard to collect. I sat down one last time in my rocking chair, but emotion threatened to overwhelm me and I jumped back up. There wasn't time for any sentimentality. I piled all three bags outside my front door and locked the door behind me. My load was awkward and heavy, and my progress down the two flights of the cement staircase was slow. I was still sore from the beating and a pain shot down my leg as the toe of my white leather tennis shoe reached for each step. The Polaroid pictures that Renaye had taken of the bruises on my face, back, and arms were sealed in an envelope in my purse. Halfway down, my vision blurred and my head started to spin. My scalp felt like I was wearing a hat that was too tight.

I gripped the wrought iron railing to steady myself. I was still breathing through my mouth after almost a week, and I could hear myself panting. I willed my neighbors to stay in their apartments. Luckily, the Cantonese Evening News blocked out any noise I made as I passed their front doors.

When I reached the lobby, I was drenched in sweat. I leaned against the rough stucco wall to catch my breath. A cold wind blew a shower of rain through the iron gate that opened onto the street. I stepped into the dark garage on quivering legs and signaled Maria by flipping the light on and off. Almost instantly, I heard her pull the car into the driveway. The car door slammed and I felt a cold rush of wind blow across the floor as Maria lifted the heavy garage door.

"Let's go get Colin," she whispered. She didn't look me in the face as she reached for my bags.

There was a pause in the rain and the San Francisco streets looked freshly scrubbed. After a quiet fifteen minute drive out of the Sunset district and through the Castro, we were back in front of June's apartment. Maria pressed the lighted button on the brass plate next to the door. I shivered as I made my way slowly up the carpeted stairs.

When June opened the front door, Colin turned from the TV. He and Michael were wrapped around a large bowl of popcorn on the couch. "Hi, Momma! June got us a movie—*Herbie Goes Bananas*."

"Is it almost over?" I asked.

"I dunno," Colin said, and he turned back to the television.

It was almost 8 o'clock and our flight left at 10:15. I followed June and Maria into the brightly lit kitchen. Renaye was at the kitchen table, and she smiled at me shyly, staring into her teacup as if there was a message there. I sat down in a padded chair and unzipped my shoulder bag. My friends sat around me, uncharacteristically quiet. "Are you hungry?" June asked.

"No. I need to take a pain pill." My voice sounded strange to me, as if it was coming from some faraway place.

"I'll get you some water." June filled a small glass from the tap. She stroked my shoulder as she handed it to me and I popped a codeine tablet into my mouth.

"Thanks. I mean it," I said softly. "Thanks for everything." My throat was hot and dry and I took a sip of tea.

My three friends looked at me and then at each other. "We all love you," Maria said.

"I love you too. I've gotta go talk to Colin."

I walked into the living room as the movie ended. Renaye followed me and took Michael back into the kitchen. I sat next to Colin on the red velour couch and picked up the remote to switch off the set. The only light in the room was from the hallway and the orange glow from a turtle nightlight in the corner. Colin scooted closer and I put my arm around him.

"Your face isn't purple anymore, now it's all yellow and green. Does it still hurt?" Colin reached up and gingerly touched the left side of my face with his chubby fingers.

"A little, but I'm okay." I gave him a hug and kissed him on his soft cheek.

"We're going to get on a plane, and go see your Aunt Jeanne," I said trying to inject some lightness into my voice.

"We're going on a plane? When?" he asked.

"Tonight—right now!"

"Okay!"

Maria appeared in the doorway. "It's almost nine. We've gotta go."

"Ready to go, baby?"

"I'm ready," he said.

Colin put his arms around my neck and kissed me on the lips. I patted him on the back and rested my face against the soft cushion of his curly red hair.

"Okay! Let's go have an adventure!" I said.

The bustle of going to the bathroom, gathering up Colin's things, and zipping him into his sweatshirt and his Rams jacket distracted us all from the reality of what I was doing. I hugged Renaye and June at the door.

June handed me an envelope of cash. "Take care of yourself."

"Thank you," I said.

"I'm not going back to the apartment till tomorrow," Renaye said. "If anyone calls or comes over, I don't know anything about anything."

"I'll call you when I get to LA. Say good-bye, Colin."

Colin hugged Renaye and June, and he and Michael shared an awkward little boy hug. We waited in the lobby while Maria carried the bags to the car. "I don't want you to take your hood off, okay?" I tucked Colin's hair back under his hood.

"It's too tight!" Colin said, hooking a finger in the loop of the tie under his chin.

"Keep it on. Okay?"

Colin tugged at it again. "Okay, but it's too tight."

Colin sat leaning against the bags in the back seat as Maria made her way to the Bay Bridge on-ramp. The guardrails of the bridge blocked the view of the San Francisco skyline, so I focused on the slim ribbon of black water visible below the railing. It began to rain again, and Maria flipped on the windshield wipers. The blades slid across the glass, paused, and shimmied, and then continued their ineffective work.

She slid the lever on the heater but the smell of burning rubber was the only thing that came out of the vent. She grunted under her breath and shook her head. The vibration of the old car and the slapping of its bald tires against the wet pavement were the only sounds in the car.

"What am I doing?" I asked. Maria glanced my way, but said nothing.

We took 880 after the bridge and then took the exit onto Hegenberger Road. The long road leading to the Oakland Airport gleamed in front of us. Maria pulled up at the curb in front of American Airlines.

"We made good time," she said. "Wait here. I'll go get the tickets." Sally Ann had purchased the tickets by phone under the name Barbara Hughes and paid for them with her credit card. I was grateful that we could pick them up without showing any identification.

Maria returned with the tickets in her hand and I tried to shoulder the door open, but winced in pain. She opened the door and helped me out of the car. Then she flipped the seat forward. "Hey, buddy, wake up. We're here." She lifted Colin out of the back seat and set him on the sidewalk.

A skycap approached us. Maria handed him my mismatched bags and exchanged the one-way tickets for boarding passes. "Gate 9, Miss," he said and paused for a tip, but after looking at my face, he returned to the terminal.

Maria and I looked at each other. Neither of us had mentioned the fact that, among so many other things, our sweet affair was ending. "Good luck," she said. She walked quickly to the driver's side of her roommate's old car, got in without looking back, and pulled away from the curb. I watched her, frozen to the spot. I was all alone with my decision now. Colin was leaning against my legs. He almost fell over when I turned towards the terminal.

"Carry me," he said and reached his arms up to me.

"You've got to walk, Colin."

"I'm sleepy. Carry me."

"I wish I could, baby. Come on. We'll be on the plane in a minute."

At the mention of the plane, Colin perked up. We made our way into the glare of the deserted terminal and followed the signs to Gate 9. The plane was boarding and they closed the cabin door as soon as we settled into our seats. Colin tried to stay awake, but he was slumped against the window by the time we were in the air. I reached over and tucked one tiny red curl back inside his hood.

CHAPTER NINE

Los Angeles, California: April 16, 1981

I SPOTTED JEANNE AS COLIN and I shuffled down the crowded jet way. She was wearing turquoise drawstring pants and a matching hooded sweatshirt. Her short curly hair was tinted a bright shade of auburn. Jeanne smiled and waved when she saw us, and I felt my eyes welling up in relief. Colin ran up to her when crowd in front of us cleared. "Hi, Aunt Jeanne," he said.

"Hi, Colin." She gave him a hug, and then wrapped her arms around both of us. With that gesture, I felt some of my burden move onto her shoulders. The knot in my chest began to unwind and I started to cry, but Colin was watching so I held myself together. We collected our bags and walked out of the terminal into the cool Los Angeles night. "You and Colin are going to stay at Bridgette's house in Pasadena," she said.

"Ah, I get to meet the new girlfriend!" I said.

Jeanne laughed and pointed down the line of cars parked at the curb outside of baggage claim. "That's her in that maroon van," Jeanne said.

When our mother realized that three of her five daughters were lesbians, she had a one-of-a-kind reaction. She called me and said, "Marilyn couldn't wait to call me to tell me what you're up to, Sharon. She has used her influence as the eldest to turn both you and Jeanne into lesbians. I don't understand it! Some children have the decency to lie to their mothers about being gay! But Marilyn is *forcing* me to think about my three beautiful daughters burning in hell." In response, I put Mother on the mailing list for PFLAG, Parents and Friends of Lesbians and Gays, a national advocacy organization.

Bridgette jumped out to help me with my bags. Jeanne and Colin got into the back seat and I climbed into the front. Bridgette was a small, masculine-looking woman wearing tan slacks and a grey UCLA sweatshirt. She got back into the driver's seat and did a double take. "Gawd, you look like your sister," she exclaimed.

"We get that a lot," I said. "Say hello to Bridgette, Colin."

Bridgette tilted the rear view mirror to see into the back seat. "My daughter's so excited to meet you, Colin." But Colin didn't answer. He was watching a jet as it rose above the terminal. The van fell quiet, and Bridgette pulled into the line of cars heading for the freeway. Even though it was midnight, traffic was heavy on the Century Freeway. Bridgette took the connector onto the 110, and we drove north towards Pasadena. Red tail lights snaked up the hill ahead of us. Jeanne patted my shoulder from the back seat, and I held her cool hand against my hot cheek.

When I was in high school in the 1960s, Jeanne was married with small children. None of us ever saw her smile back then. She and her children were all suffering at the hands of her sadistic husband. Once, I ran through the house, sheltering her oldest in my arms as her husband chased after us to beat him. When Jeanne asked her parish priest what she should do, he listened quietly and said, "You need to go home and pray that your husband will return to the Lord. Only then will your problems be solved."

The Catholic Church loomed large in all of our lives then and Jeanne tried to heed the priest's warning about the everlasting consequences of destroying a Catholic family, but eventually she got a divorce and left the Catholic Church. She had successfully turned her life around since then, and she was on her way to a career as a therapist. It was good to see her genuine smile finally.

When Colin and I dragged ourselves through Bridgette's front door, Sally Ann gave me a quick hug and handed me a bottle of Valium, saying quietly, "I thought you might need these." Sally Ann was the middle sister, a blonde in a family of brunettes. While the rest of us were outgoing, she was serious and quiet. Tonight, there were dark circles under her big green eyes and her full lips were pressed together in a thin line of anger.

Marilyn came out of the kitchen and gathered Colin and me into her arms with hugs and kisses. Her partner Irene stood off to one side. With my arms around Marilyn, I could feel that her happy love life had translated into about twenty extra pounds. Irene was in her mid-50s and her unlined face was framed with a smooth cap of silver hair. She was wearing a red *Ladies Sewing Circle & Terrorist Society* t-shirt over dark Bermuda shorts. Irene referred to herself as an "LLL," a lifelong lesbian, and she called Jeanne, Marilyn, and me "LCLs," or lesbians-come-lately. Jeanne and I had dubbed Irene our "sister-in-love." Irene patted Colin on the shoulder and said, "I brought some great pastrami and soft rolls for sandwiches. Come on, I'll make you a snack."

We all gathered around the oak table in Bridgette's spacious kitchen. Irene passed around paper plates while Marilyn sliced a long loaf of sourdough bread. Colin knelt on a chair with his hand jammed into a jumbo bag of corn chips.

"When all else fails, eat!" Jeanne said with a wide smile.

I leaned forward with my plate and Jeanne gave me a spoonful of potato salad. "Well everything on this end is a miserable failure, so load me up," I said. The tension of the night gave the line a bigger laugh than it deserved.

After we finished our midnight snack, Sally Ann, Marilyn, and Irene went home. Bridgette picked up our bags and led Colin and me to a bedroom at the end of the carpeted hall. Crisp green and white striped drapes, held back by a sailcloth tie, framed an expanse of well-groomed lawn that was visible through the large bedroom windows. Small lanterns outlined the edge of her brick patio and illuminated the back yard. Twin beds with white sheets and moss green blankets were separated by a squat bedside table. Bridgette slid open the closet with her foot and put our bags on the floor. "Make yourself at home, Sharon. Use anything you need."

"Thank you so much, Bridgette. I can't tell you how much I appreciate your help," I said.

Bridgette closed the door behind her and Colin climbed up next to me on the bed. I felt raw from days of adrenaline and anxiety, but I was buoyed by the love and support of my sisters and the warm presence of Colin. He trusted me. What a treasure that was. I had been backed into a corner, and now I found myself free-falling through unknown terrain. I wanted to be worthy of his trust. Protecting him was the first step. "One step at a time," I told myself. "Just one step at a time."

After all the excitement of the evening, Colin was wide awake. "How about a bath before bed?" I asked. He nodded and wrestled his red t-shirt over his head. I dug out our pajamas and toothbrushes and we found the bathroom. I squirted strawberry bubble bath into the steaming water as it rushed from the tap. Colin pulled a wind-up tugboat out of the respectable collection of tub-toys hanging in a mesh bag on the wall next to the tub. I switched off the overhead light and the seashell nightlight next to the sink filled the tiled bathroom with a dim coral glow. I helped Colin into the tub and sat on the floor with my hand dangling in the warm water. We sat quietly in thoughtful, companionable silence.

Bridgette kept her daughter out of preschool to keep Colin company. Sarah, a thin, pale girl with wispy blonde hair, had a bedroom that resembled a well-stocked toy store, including a large dress-up box. Colin dug out a fetching pirate's hat with silver studs and a dramatic black feather. Unconcerned when Sarah warned him off her collection of dolls (including clothes and tiny accessories), Colin nationalized her assortment of dinosaurs and building blocks.

I agreed to act as if every stranger was a potential risk to our anonymity, so I couldn't risk being seen in the neighborhood. Bridgette's house and backyard, which fortunately was surrounded by a stand of tall trees, became our universe for the time being. It was a providential decision, because when Guy and his attorney deduced that not only was I not going to return Colin, but that I seemed to have left town with him, they rightly assumed that I would be near my sisters in Southern California. Within a week, Marilyn and Jeanne each spotted men in unmarked cars watching their homes. Sally Ann lived in the center of a condo complex and she didn't see anyone giving her front door any undue attention. Still she was cautious. When my sisters left their homes to come to see me, they detoured to the grocery store or the bank, or they drove in random directions on the freeways to make sure that they weren't being followed.

Jeanne kept Carol, in Austin, Texas, apprised, but Carol reported that she hadn't seen anyone suspicious around her house. "I still go by Carol Kemplin. Murphy isn't on anything connected to me, so they'd have a hard time finding me," Carol said.

"Even if Guy knew your last name, he'd never find you. You've moved so many times, I have trouble keeping track of you myself," Jeanne replied.

We were the Murphy sisters once again—one for all and all for one. "We" as a team made all of my decisions. We had brainstorming sessions and compiled lists of things we needed to accomplish. We tried to imagine every eventuality and predict and think through every large and small issue. I couldn't take the risk of contacting anyone myself, so all the legwork fell to my sisters. Marilyn contacted legal advocates at battered women's shelters and made discreet inquiries within the Califia community for tips on how people disappeared and how women found safe places to relocate. They talked to attorneys as if they were researching papers for college and asked about laws governing parental kidnapping and what the likely penalties were. Jail time seemed to be directly commensurate with how long the mother went undetected, but it didn't seem as if women had much luck evading capture. It was enlightening to learn that mothers rarely pressed charges against fathers who kidnapped their children—but mothers almost always ended up doing jail time. We didn't exactly know what information we were looking for, but there seemed to be a lot of it out there. Again, I realized that this was not just my own personal problem. How many mothers were there out there on the run with their children?

One evening, Sally Ann said, "You know when you open your wallet to pull out a dollar and the slots are filled with different cards: library cards, membership cards, credit cards? When you're settled, you need to get an assortment of cards like that to fill up your wallet. We don't want even the smallest thing to strike people as off about you. And you need to subscribe to some magazines, so mail comes to you in your new name."

We tackled a number of less significant but still perplexing problems. I had a temporary cap on one of my molars. I needed a dentist who would make a crown for cash without any explanation or dental records. I needed to find some way to cash my tax refund check without leaving a trail. Jeanne was worried about my stress level. She found a trustworthy therapist who came to the house to talk to me a few times a week and agreed not to keep any records. They collected money from their friends and books and clothes for Colin and me. Irene even bought me an ounce of pot.

I response to her inquiries about new identity papers, Marilyn received a call from a Califia woman whose daughter had recently committed suicide. She asked to meet me. Late one night, Marilyn and Irene picked me up and drove me to the woman's small bungalow. It was on a hillside, cradled by a thick grove of redwood trees. Incense and candles were burning in the small living room and it took a moment for my eyes to adjust to the dim light. Pictures of the woman's daughter were arranged on a low table in front of the couch. Marilyn and Irene took seats against the wall and the grieving mother took my hand and led me to the couch. With no introductory small talk, she began speaking about her daughter and her struggle with depression. "I had a dream last night. Star wants me to help you. Maybe her death won't feel like such a waste if I can help you and your little boy."

I showed her a picture of Colin and told her about his funny personality, his bright red hair, his love of magic tricks. All the while, the woman stared intently into my eyes. When I stopped talking, she got up and left the room. I looked over at Marilyn and shrugged. When the woman came back, she handed me a large white envelope containing Star's birth certificate and Social Security card.

"I'm happy to have met you, Sharon." Then she turned to Marilyn. "Will you keep me posted about how this works out?" Marilyn stepped forward and hugged her. I thanked her and we left. We hoped that a huge obstacle had been overcome, but as it turned out, Social Security death benefits had been paid as a result of Star's death. Income reported under her Social Security number would send up a red flag. We couldn't take the risk, so we had to decline her mother's gracious offer. We returned the documents and kept searching for another solution.

Easter Sunday slipped by without anyone noticing. After ten days at Bridgette's, I took a break from drafting the blueprint for my fugitive life and cooked a big Sunday dinner. Sally Ann set a bouquet of yellow roses in a heavy glass vase in the middle of the table, and Jeanne lit four tapered candles in a brass candelabra. I carried out a silver platter of roasted chicken stuffed with lemon and orange slices on a bed of wild rice, and arranged it on the table next to the white dish piled high with fat green stalks of broccoli shiny with garlic butter.

I had given Colin and Sarah their dinner earlier and they were watching a video in the living room. Yoda was saying to Luke Skywalker, "Size matters not. Look at me. Judge me by my size, do you?"

I poured everyone a glass of wine. This appeared to be like any other family dinner until I turned the mood in a more serious direction. "When I called to check in with Renaye this afternoon, two police officers had just left. What if they'd still been there when I called? Or what if Guy had been there?" The table became quiet.

"We have to use what we've learned from the detective novels we've been reading all these years," Sally Ann said.

"Let's try to tap into our Sicilian gene pool, too," said Jeanne.

"Here's to the lesbian mafia!" I raised my glass. We all toasted and took a drink.

"I have an idea," Marilyn said after a moment of thought. "Have you ever heard of Ernestine Rose?" I shook my head. "Oh, she was wonderful—an amazing public speaker. Irene, you know who she is. She was an atheist and a socialist. She was born in Poland in the early 19th century. When she came to the U.S., she worked in the anti-slavery movement and with the early suffragettes, Elizabeth Cady Stanton and Susan..."

"Marilyn, we don't have time for a seminar," Sally Ann interrupted.

"Oh...," Marilyn sputtered to a stop. "When we have to call Renaye, we can say, 'Is Ernestine Rose at home?' Then if someone's there, she can say, 'You have the wrong number.' That would be safe even if they're tapping the phone." Marilyn looked satisfied with herself.

"Ernestine would be proud," Irene said, looking at Marilyn approvingly.

Then Sally Ann spoke up. "And we have to decide what we're going to tell Mother. I don't want a call from the police to be her first clue that Sharon's missing." Our mother was a robust 72 years old and lived in a seniors' community nearby in

Huntington Beach. It was common for us to spend a portion of every gathering, even under normal circumstances, discussing our mother, who she was currently mad at for what imagined slight, who she had attacked recently, and why.

Irene said, "Next to Guy and Maya, your mother is the last person to tell that Sharon's here."

"It wouldn't be hard for them to find her, her number's listed in the phone book," Jeanne said. "Can you imagine if Guy called and asked Mother where Sharon was?"

"If Mother knew that Sharon was in Los Angeles, she'd spill the beans just so Guy wouldn't think she didn't know what was going on," Sally Ann said. "We can't tell her what's really happening, but we have to tell her something."

Silence drifted around the table. We all had a lifetime of painful memories to remind us not to expect support or understanding from our mother. I thought of a time after Sally Ann divorced her engineer husband. She moved with her four children to Huntington Beach after she sold her house in Tulsa. They were going to bunk in with Jeanne until Sally Ann got a job and bought a house. Jeanne's house would be bulging at the seams, but it would only be for a short time, and everyone was willing to make the sacrifice.

But then one afternoon, Sally Ann was riding her bike along one of the indistinguishable palm-lined streets of Jeanne's subdivision and she took a terrible fall and crushed the bones in her leg. During the long period of recuperation, Sally Ann only had the money from the sale of her house to live on. After two years and several surgeries, her entire nest egg was gone. When she was finally able to work, Sally Ann got a nursing job and moved with her children into a small apartment. She survived on a bare-bones budget after living a comfortable middle-class life with Michael. On the outside, she was the same involved, creative mother she had always been. She went to soccer games, painted Easter eggs, and made a dozen kinds of candy at Christmas. But she lived inside a grey cloud of depression. When any of us mentioned to Mother that we were worried about her, Mother would inevitably say, "That accident wouldn't have been so devastating if Sally Ann wasn't so fat. That's what she gets for letting herself go."

We sat around the table lost in our thoughts until Marilyn broke the silence. "I'll call Mother," she said. "It's easier for me to lie to her." Everyone nodded in agreement. The next day Marilyn called me. "I talked to Mother," she said. "I told her that your roommate called me to say that Guy had beaten you again and you took Colin and left town. I told Mother we didn't know where you were."

"What did she say?" I asked.

"Well, she didn't believe me for a minute. In fact, she was indignant. She said, 'Don't treat me like a child, Marilyn. You know more than you're telling me!'"

"Mother is eerily psychic," I said.

"Indeed! Oh, and she mentioned how handsome Guy was, as if that was some kind of mitigating factor," Marilyn said. "I know she is really upset and worried though. But as usual, I had to read between the lines."

"Everything is always sideways with her, like speaking in code. I wish we didn't have to lie to her," I said.

"But we do! Don't get sentimental about Mother," Marilyn said. "She'll only disappoint you and we can't afford any slip-ups now."

*The Murphy Women: Carol, Marilyn, Jeanne, Mother, Sally Ann &
Sharon, Studio City, California 1980*

Relocating anywhere in California was out of the question.
Although Maya was well known all over the world, Californians
knew her best. The further Colin and I were from the center
of Maya's reputation, the safer. We scoured the Califia mailing
list for possible contacts in other states. We were looking for
homeowners, not renters, so there would be no meddling from
a landlord. After a few dead ends, Marilyn contacted a woman
in Phoenix, Arizona who remembered meeting me at Califia in
June of 1980. She owned her house and agreed to let us stay in
her second bedroom. Marilyn warned her, "It might be months
before Sharon can pay a full share of rent." But Abby said she
was pleased to be able to help me.

I had been at Bridgette's for two months, planning and writing in my journal, playing pre-school teacher with Colin and Sarah, and keeping Bridgette's house neat. The therapist Jeanne found came twice a week. I read a stack of science fiction novels and watched hours of movies and daytime TV. At first, the protective cocoon was a comfort after years of stress, but now I had cabin fever. The ties with my old life were loosened, and I was ready to get on with my new one.

Early one morning before the sun appeared in the sky, I knelt on the carpet in front of the fireplace and held a long match to the twisted newspaper and kindling beneath a tepee of dry logs. A flame flickered and the kindling began to glow. I dug inside my jute bag and pulled out a large manila envelope and poured the contents out on the rug in front of me. I lined up my birth certificate, my marriage license, Colin's birth certificate, my divorce papers, the probation department report, the doctor's record from the emergency room, and Mike Lentz's last report. Renaye had mailed Marilyn the bench warrant for my arrest that arrived at the apartment the week I left. I read the warrant again.

The Sonoma County Superior Court had eliminated all my parental rights in addition to sentencing me to two weeks in jail for Contempt of Court for violating the custody order. The document demanded that I relinquish my son to the custody of his father and turn myself in. I laid the bench warrant at the end of the row of documents—a miserable narrative of my life to date. I read each document one more time, gathered them up like playing cards, slid them back into the manila envelope, and flattened out the metal clasp. Marilyn would keep all these documents in a safety deposit box until I needed them again.

I leaned back against the couch and watched the growing flames. I unzipped the inside pocket of my purse and pulled out the envelope of pictures Renaye had taken of my bruised face and back. I tossed them into the fire without looking at them. I pulled my Social Security card out of my wallet and examined it. It felt so flimsy and inconsequential until I flipped it into the fire and dropped my driver's license on top of it. A shock ran through me as I watched them curl and darken and burn.

Colin came into the living room carrying a tub of blue paint. His red pajama bottoms hung low under his round belly and for some reason, he'd taken off his shirt. "Momma, what'cha doing?"

"Nothing. You need something?"

"Will you put some paper up so Sarah and me can finger-paint?"

I put the envelope and my purse on top of the piano. When I stood the screen in front of the fireplace, all I could see was a steady flame enveloping the dry logs. There was no turning back now.

The night before Colin and I left town, Jeanne brought over bags of Chinese takeout for our last dinner together. She opened the bulging white cartons on the kitchen table next to a stack of plates and silverware and set a bag from a local drugstore on the kitchen counter. "You said you might want this."

She pulled out a box of Lady Clairol Dark Auburn hair color. We stared at it as if it might explode. We both glanced over at Colin who was spooning noodles, half onto his plate and half onto the table. The bright light from the swag lamp over his head illuminated his bright red hair like an autumn sunset. By the time I put Colin in bed that night, he was my beautiful brown-haired boy. He took the change of hair color right in stride.

Early the next morning, Sally Ann drove to the Los Angeles airport. She paid cash for two one-way tickets to Phoenix, once again in the name of Barbara Hughes. When she returned to Bridgette's, she circled the block, then sat at the corner for a few minutes. When she was satisfied that no one was following her or watching the house, she pulled into the driveway. Jeanne, Marilyn, and Irene crowded around Colin and me and we all piled into the car and sped off to the airport. We arrived with just enough time to hand the skycap our luggage and offer him a small tip. Our goodbyes were brief and casual.

June 5, 1981
Phoenix, Arizona

Sally Ann had given me a goodie-bag for Colin filled with granola bars, crayons, a tablet, and a book of mazes and puzzles. I tucked the bag into the seat pocket in front of him and buckled him into his window seat in front of the wing. I pointed out the window. "See if you can spot your backpack." Colin craned his neck and watched the ground crew as they tossed the luggage onto the conveyor belt that rolled into the belly of the plane.

The flight to the Phoenix Sky Harbor airport would be less than two hours, hardly enough time to absorb the enormity of the step I was taking. This wasn't an abstract plan anymore—it was the real thing. I was relieved that the early afternoon flight wasn't crowded and the seat next to me remained vacant. I was traveling with no identification and an envelope of cash. I felt as if I had a neon sign blinking above my head that said "FUGITIVE!"

My heart raced, and my throat was so dry I could barely swallow. I tried to appear relaxed for Colin's sake. "Let's see what we can see," I said. Colin and I gazed out of the window of the plane at the desert landscape below. I had been planning this escape for months, but all my planning had only brought me to this point. Where would we go from here?

When we landed and stepped through the cabin door of the plane, I was momentarily blinded by the blaze of the afternoon sun. My first Arizona breath was like a snort of hot sand. I took Colin's hand, and we walked down the metal stairs and onto the soft tarmac below. We followed the line of passengers towards the terminal, as I scanned the crowd behind the high chain link fence.

I recognized Abby as she waved her arms above her head in an awkward, jerky fashion. Her round stomach strained against the buttons of her plaid blouse. She appeared older than I remembered, maybe in her late 30s, with jet black shoulder length hair and pale, doughy skin that contrasted greatly with the heavily tanned people in the crowd around her. Abby wore heavy rubber sandals with wide straps and khaki shorts which showed her muscular calves.

This scenario had been an idea, but now everything was real, exaggerated, and bizarre. From this stranger greeting me like an old friend, to the unbearable heat, to the white hot blaze of the sun in the screaming blue sky. I leaned against the fence to clear my head.

"The heat can get to you!" Abby said as she approached me. "You'll get used to it."

This stranger was my savior, I told myself. Keep going. We collected our bags and loaded them into the trunk of Abby's silver car. By the time we were buckled in, I had collected myself. "I can't tell you how much this means to me, Abby. Thank you."

Her cheeks reddened. "I'm happy to help you, Sharon." She started the engine and headed towards the exit of the parking lot. "I need to tell you something though." She glanced at Colin in the backseat. "After I told Marilyn you could have the room, a friend of mine called and needed a place to stay. I rented him the spare bedroom. I'm sure you understand."

I stared at her in disbelief. "What about us?"

"Well, you can still stay with me, of course. I've set up a bedroom on the back porch for you two."

"Oh..." What could I say? I was at her mercy. We would have to make the best of it. I sat in silence as she drove through Phoenix, which had a generic, model city look to it. Soon, Abby turned into the driveway of her small cinderblock house in a flat subdivision of cinderblock houses only distinguishable from each other by its particular sun-bleached shade of a pastel color.

"Momma, what are those?" Colin pointed to the row of trees as tall as skyscrapers, with sparse whirlybird plumes of green at the top. They were the only foliage on the razor straight street.

"Palm trees," I said.

"They look like Dr. Seuss trees."

Abby led us through her house to the back porch, which was not so much a porch as an unfinished slab of cement with a flat shingled roof. The outside walls of the house created two enclosed sides. The open corner was supported by a single square post. A series of faded bedspreads were affixed to the edge of the roof to block the view from the house next door. A four-drawer pressboard dresser and a double bed were pushed against the wall and a pile of sheets and pillows were stacked on the corner of the stained mattress. The porch had a view of her big backyard, covered with scrubby grass and knee-high weeds bleached nearly white by the sun.

"Of course, you can use the house during the day," Abby assured me.

Colin knew I was upset. His thick eyebrows were knitted together as he looked from Abby to me and back again. I forced myself to smile down at him. "It'll be like camping!"

During the day, I cleaned Abby's filthy house, scrubbed her food-encrusted refrigerator, and rearranged her kitchen cabinets. Colin built forts and played on the living room floor in front of the air conditioner. Late in the afternoon when it was supposedly cooler, Colin and I took walks around the sparse, flat, neighborhood looking for the non-existent playground. When we didn't see any evidence of children, I said, "Arizona children must be afraid they'll burn to a crisp if they come outside."

"Let's go back. It's too hot," he said. Even Colin's buoyant personality was dampened by the heat.

It was the middle of June in the desert, 120 degrees almost every day. I used some of my cash to buy a wading pool with stiff plastic sides. We cleared the weeds and burs so the pool wouldn't spring a leak and filled it with cool water. It was too hot to be outside during the day, so Colin and I used the pool at night, while Abby and her new roommate drank beer and watched TV inside.

Even at 10 o'clock, it could be over ninety degrees. We'd play pool games that I made up—car wash or undersea explorer. Or we lounged around in the cool water and read books by the light from the porch. When it was time for bed, I'd run to the store in Abby's car to buy a block of ice to put in front of the fan that I aimed at the bed. Abby complained that running the fan all night was going to drive up her electric bill, and each morning, I saw her arm reach out from the doorway to switch off the fan. I began experiencing an uncomfortable mix of gratitude and resentment towards her.

When the initial blast of adrenaline wore off, the enormity of what I had done began to sink in. While Colin was sleeping, I sat in a lawn chair in Abby's scrubby backyard with my feet in the pool and stared into the inky sky. I felt paralyzed and overwhelmed, flattened like a penny on the railroad tracks. I thought I had been prepared for this when I made the decision to leave California, but a person can't know ahead of time how it will feel to step totally out of your life.

I had imagined a version of the life I had, minus Guy and all the heartache and problems, of course. But with nothing familiar around me to help me get my bearings, I was in a constant state of emotional vertigo.

I was no longer Sharon Murphy—I was Anne Marie Clark. The real Anne Marie Clark was my niece, Marilyn's oldest daughter. She was three years younger than me and had changed her name from Anne Marie to Lilith. She lived in a hippie community in Humboldt County, north of San Francisco. Lilith and her entire community were attempting to live off the grid; she didn't even have a driver's license. When she heard that I needed to disappear, she agreed to let me use her birth name and identification. She drove down to Pasadena and presented me with her birth certificate and Social Security card. She even gave me her astrological chart.

But I had none of these things for Colin. I thought a great deal about how attached young children are to their name. I didn't want to upset Colin anymore than I had already, but I knew it was a bad idea to continue calling him Colin. As a white woman with a red-headed black child in Arizona, we were already very noticeable. I couldn't do anything permanent about our physical appearance and Colin's natural hair color was already beginning to show through the brown rinse. If someone got a clue as to where to look, how hard would we be to spot, especially if I still called him Colin?

One morning, Colin was sitting on the floor in the living room, spooning small heaps of Cheerios into his mouth. I sat on the couch behind him and ran my hand over his head. He kept his eyes glued to *Sesame Street*. I tapped the remote to lower the sound. He turned to protest and milk dribbled out of the corner of his mouth. I picked up the napkin and wiped his face.

"So, baby, let's talk about a new name for you. What's a good boy name that goes with 'Clark'?" He put his bowl on the coffee table and glanced once again at Bert and Ernie. I took a sip of my coffee.

"How about George?" he said off-handedly, glancing over at the TV.

"How did you come up with that name?" I asked.

"I dunno. I just thought of it," he said.

"Well, you keep thinking about the name you want. We'll talk about it again later."

"Okay." Colin picked up his bowl. "Can I watch TV now?"

That afternoon, I was sitting on the couch, trying to read. Reading had always been my safe haven, but I'd been carrying around the same Marion Zimmer Bradley book for weeks. Colin was building an impressive structure with his Legos and little model cars on the floor.

"How about 'Luke?'" he said. The serious look on his face touched me.

I laid the paperback on my chest. "Luke? Like the Jedi, Luke Skywalker?" I asked.

"No!" He sounded insulted at the thought.

"Luke Clark," I tried it out. "I like it. Okay, that's it then. Anne Marie and Luke Clark!"

Luke Clark

Back in California, our disappearance was already having consequences for my friends and family. Everyone whose number appeared on my phone bill had their phone records subpoenaed. My friend Diane and some other women in San Diego were filing a formal complaint with the phone company

319

and the Sonoma County District Attorney for the invasion of their privacy. Even before we knew about the subpoenaed phone records though, my sisters and I had developed an untraceable procedure to stay in contact with each other. A friend of the family offered to pay for all of our long distance calls. Whenever I needed to talk to my sisters, I made a collect call to this intermediary. She would contact one of my sisters and they would call me at a prearranged time from her house or from a pay phone.

Renaye, my old roommate, stayed in contact with Marilyn. Guy's phone calls had finally stopped but the police still dropped by occasionally to ask about my whereabouts and to walk through the apartment. Feeling that it was safe to assume that this would continue to happen as long as a friend of mine lived there, Marilyn worked out a system to get some of my things out of the apartment. Friends would pull their cars into the street-level garage and close the door. Using the inside staircase, they were able to enter my apartment and box up what they could. They could carry the boxes down the stairs and into the garage without ever being seen from the street. Keeping the boxes low and out of sight, they were able to drive away without anything appearing different from when they arrived.

A woman in Half Moon Bay was storing the boxes in her garage. When the last load was safely stashed away, Marilyn called me. "When you get a place of your own, we'll find a way to ship this stuff to you. We couldn't move anything too big, so Renaye will have to deal with your furniture."

"She doesn't have anything of her own. Tell her she can have the rest of my stuff. She can sell it if she wants to," I said.

Understandably, Renaye didn't want to stay in the apartment. The next time I spoke to Marilyn she told me that Renaye had found another place to live and my old apartment was now empty. "Renaye thought that moving out would break her ties to the situation, but she unwittingly stepped right back into it," Marilyn said.

"What happened?" I asked.

"After Renaye was settled in her new place, she bought a used copy of *I Know Why the Caged Bird Sings* for $.25 at Modern Times book store. She had never read it and thought that now was a good time," Marilyn said.

"Oh, was she curious about the origin of the Maya Myth?" I asked.

Renaye was sitting on the Muni bus reading *Caged Bird*, and a short, dark skinned man in a heavy overcoat slid into the seat next to her. The man's eyes had a drugged glaze. At first, Renaye assumed that he was one of the many San Francisco homeless addicts. Then he pointed to the book in her hand. "That's my sister's book." Renaye laughed at first, but then she remembered my telling her about meeting Bailey, Maya's older brother. I had described *this* man all the way down to his dependency on heroin. The story had stuck in her mind, because of the vast differences between the siblings, including the fact that Maya is more than six feet tall and Bailey is extremely small in build and stature.

Renaye told Bailey that she was not just an interested fan of Maya's. She took the opportunity to repeat what she had seen Colin and I go through with Guy, his nephew. When Renaye reached her stop, Bailey asked for her number. He wanted to talk to her some more about Guy. Against her better judg ment, she gave him her number. But it wasn't Bailey who called Renaye later that night. She was shocked when she heard Maya's distinctive voice on the line. Maya asked Renaye to help her reunite with Colin. Renaye was at first intimidated but then repeated what she had said to Bailey.

"You had your chance to help Sharon," Renaye told Maya. "Even if I knew where they were—which I don't—I wouldn't tell you." She had not heard from Maya again.

One afternoon, I received cash and a note from Marilyn telling me that the money included a donation from a famous lesbian author. She had heard about my situation and wanted to help me. The gift and the letter from Marilyn gave me the boost I needed to get out of the house. Depression had been paralyzing me, but I tried to remember that I wasn't as alone as I felt. I had a lot of people rooting for me. When I finished reading Marilyn's newsy letter, I said to Luke, "Hey, wanna go shopping? Let's go to Toys-R-Us! Then we'll go have a burger and fries."

Luke jumped up from the floor where he had been struggling to figure out a magic trick that involved three interlocking rings. "Great! Can you find a place where I can play Frogger?"

"Sure. But first, you have to go with me to get a driver's license."

"It's a deal," he said. I had a sudden rush of a familiar feeling—my kid and I going on an outing. It was such a delicious sensation that I nearly burst into tears. When I had been stuck in my fear, I lost touch with the small, daily joys that make life sweet.

As we rode to the DMV, I said to Luke, "Now I'm going to tell these people that I never had a driver's license, so don't say anything, okay?" He shrugged in agreement. I had a back story ready that included a domineering ex-husband who didn't allow me to drive while I was married.

Luke and I stepped off the bus and the heat from the scalding pavement sizzled through the soles of my canvas shoes. We sprinted to the sidewalk. A crew of men was remodeling the minty green DMV. A palm tree with its fronds wrapped in something resembling a hair net was being lowered by a crane into a giant hole next to the cement walkway. Painters suspended on scaffolding were running rollers on long poles against the rough surface of the building.

Noticing odd things in the world around us was a game that Luke and I liked to play. "Luke, look at those painters. That side of the building is already painted, and that side is not. What do you see that's weird?"

He studied the crew of painters then looked up at me with a smile. "Both sides look exactly the same!"

"Very good!"

Once inside, my back story proved unnecessary. I went through the application process and the driving test without anyone asking why a woman in her thirties had never had a license. The clerk pointed across the crowded room, "Step over to Window C for your picture and thumb printing."

"Why do I have to give a thumb print?" I asked.

"It's required by the State of Arizona," the clerk said impatiently. She looked around my shoulder to call the next customer to the window, but I was stuck in place, uncertain of what to do next. I wanted to ask if the thumbprint would be cross-checked with other states. I had been fingerprinted at Moffitt Hospital. But I couldn't say anything—only someone with something to hide would ask a question like that, I thought. Luke looked up at me, but knew he wasn't supposed to say anything. "What if I refuse?" I asked.

The clerk gave me a curious look. "Then you won't get a driver's license."

To cover my panic, I adopted an indignant air. I made an impromptu speech about Big Brother and governmental invasion of citizens' privacy and stormed into the parking lot with Luke trailing behind me. I sat on the hot metal bench at the bus stop. Tears made shiny tracks down my hot cheeks.

"Are you okay, momma?" Luke put his hand on my shoulder.

"Sure, sweetie. That woman was a...." I let it drop and tried to change my tone. "Let's go shopping." We splurged on lunch and replenished Luke's Lego supply at the mall.

When we got back to Abby's, I started making phone calls. I could get a license in Las Cruces, New Mexico without any fingerprint, but there were a number of obstacles. I'd have to borrow a car and drive over five hours to Las Cruces and back, and I would be vulnerable on the road with no license or ID. Plus, I couldn't use a post office box so I'd have to give an address in New Mexico as a residence. All that would take too much time. Taking the bus might be safer, but I'd have to spend a lot of my cash and stay overnight. Plus, I'd be in Arizona with a New Mexico license. Every solution led to a new set of problems.

I saw no way around it. I had to have a drivers license so I had to take the risk and give my thumbprint. There was no way to be one hundred percent safe. I returned to the DMV the next day and my new license arrived in the mail ten days later. Luke had tried to make me laugh with silly faces but in the picture I looked drawn with dark circles under my eyes. Looking at an official State of Arizona driver's license with my face and the name *Anne Marie Clark* on it was like looking in a fun house mirror. I had spent a long time and hours in therapy, trying to rid myself of the sense that I was Marilyn's little girl, but according to the state of Arizona, Marilyn was now officially my mother.

It was time to start looking for a job. I ironed a sundress that looked nice enough for job hunting and left Luke alone with the admonition not to open the door no matter what. "I'll call you when I get there to check on you," I said. I walked down Van Buren Boulevard to the Camelback mall. There wasn't a wisp of a cloud in the vast, pale blue sky. Sweat dribbled down my legs into my shoes. Each step sounded like I was walking in a puddle. My hair was glued to my neck in ringlets by the time I saw a *Waitress Wanted* sign in the widow of a Shakey's Pizza Parlor.

A hostess with orange hair and black roots pulled an application from under the cash register and handed it to me. "Wait over there in that booth," she said with an exuberant smile.

I wrote my name and address on the application, which stuck to the top of the round lacquered table. I filled in common names of restaurants in Tulsa, Oklahoma and plausible addresses. A young man pushed through the swinging doors from the kitchen and slid into the booth across from me. He gave me a broad smile and reached across the table to shake my hand. He introduced himself as Brian, Day Manager.

He asked me personal questions about my life and ambitions, as if being a waitress in a restaurant that smelled like rancid oil and ammonia was a real goal. I began to recite my prepared answers, but I found it harder than expected to lie to this total stranger. "I'm not feeling well," I said. It was not a lie. "I'm going to have to come back." I peeled the application off the table and left Brian, Day Manager in the vinyl booth.

I walked aimlessly around the mall trying to calm my nerves. Everything felt bizarre, like a bad dream I couldn't wake up from. The unbearable heat jumbled my thoughts. I longed for even one moment when I felt like myself. I called Luke from a pay phone.

"Did you get a job, Momma?" he asked.

"Not yet, baby. Are you okay?"

"Sure, but hurry back, will ya? I think I figured out this trick."

"When I get home, you can show me." I hung up the phone. Home? I didn't have a home! I pulled my mind away from that particular thought and forced myself stay on task.

I noticed a blinking sign in front of a video game room that read, *The Starship Enterprise.* I could hear Journey playing behind the double doors of the arcade. *Do-on't stop...be-lieving. Hold on to the fee-ee-eeling.* There was a sign in the window: "Cashier Needed. Inquire Within." I pushed through the glass doors.

The cool darkness of the arcade provided blessed relief from the blistering heat outside. I wanted to work there just because of the air conditioning. When my eyes adjusted, I saw pinpoints of light illuminating giant replicas of space ships and rockets hovering close to the ceiling. A man with a protruding belly was lying on his back on the floor in front of an open machine. He was tinkering with the change mechanism with a foot-long screwdriver. He identified himself as the owner and I told him I wanted to apply for the cashier job. He looked me up and down and decided I was qualified. I didn't need any kind of back-story to sell tokens and keep teenagers from making out in the bathroom.

The Starship Enterprise paid cashiers $9.00 an hour and I was supplied with a pair of red jeans and two red *Enterprise Crew* t-shirts. It was a mortifying job for a grown-up, but I liked the rest of the crew, and at least Luke thought I had the coolest job in the world. Arizona provided subsidized day care for low-income working families, so Luke was safe in *Pre-K Arizona* during the day and he could come with me when I worked the night shift. Before long, he became the mascot of the game room and acquired an entourage of teenagers who followed him around making deals with him for a share of his stash of free tokens. Luke became a five-year-old power broker.

The tension between Abby and me became more heated. Our conversations were perfunctory and brief. I still resented her letting Jimmy move into the bedroom she had originally promised me and Luke. Even though I knew I was being unfair, I couldn't seem to shake the attitude. Still, now that I was working, we were able to come to an agreement for a share of the rent and I kicked in money for gas. Abby helped me drive Luke to and from day care. Luke was making friends at school and slowly a more normal life began to take shape.

One evening, Abby suggested that we go out for a drink. "You deserve a night out. My treat! We'll celebrate your new job!" This felt like an attempt on her part to improve our relationship. She saw me considering her offer and she sweetened the deal, "Jimmy said he'd watch Luke!"

"All right, let's do it!"

That evening, I put on my makeup, rolled my hair on Abby's hot rollers, and then brushed it loose and full over my shoulders. I ironed a pink cotton shirt with a cross-over bodice and a low neckline and put on my wide-legged hip-hugger jeans.

When I walked into the living room, Colin said. "You look pretty, Momma. Look! Jimmy got us a pizza."

"I guess it's a party night for everybody!" I said.

Jimmy and Abby sat side by side on the couch in front of a delivery pizza box. Jimmy was a slim young man with a feminine air about him. He sat curled up on the couch wearing a spangled cowboy shirt with the sleeves cut off and very short cut-offs. His well-shaped arms and legs were totally hairless and tanned.

"Oh, I have just the thing for that outfit," Jimmy said. He jumped off the couch and dashed into his bedroom. He came out with a light fuchsia scarf and draped it around my neck. "Perfect! Oh, I love your eye shadow," he purred.

"You look great!" Abby said. Her face lit up with a big smile. She had on a button-down shirt and pressed chinos. She had gelled her thick hair and comb lines ran straight back from her face.

"So the fluffy hair and the business suits you wear to the bank everyday is your corporate drag, huh?" I said.

Abby blushed. "Ready to go?" she said.

We pushed into the smoky darkness of *Sister Sue's*, a woman's bar in the industrial area of Phoenix, tucked away in the back of a strip mall. "Excuse me," I said. "I'm going to the bathroom." I deftly moved away from Abby's hand as she attempted to lead me towards the bar.

When I came out of the bathroom, Abby was leaning against the bar, talking with three women. Two tall beers were dripping rings onto paper napkins behind her. The group smiled as I approached and Abby made the introductions. "This is Syd 'n Melanie and Phyllis. This is Anne Marie." By the rhythm of her introductions, I knew that Syd and Melanie were a couple, and Phyllis was single.

The sound of my new name made me ill at ease. I shook their hands and slid up onto the stool next to Abby. I took a sip of beer. There was an awkward pause, and then they headed towards the empty dance floor. Alone at the bar, I fingered the slender beer glass. Every thought and every action I'd taken for months had been of the gravest consequence. This club, the music, the flirting and dancing felt frivolous. But didn't I want a normal life? What about friends, sex, maybe a relationship? I had never wanted to be one of those 1950's moms who lived solely for her children, but maybe that was part of the choice I had made. Maybe running away had precluded everything but raising my son. Maybe I should be grateful that I would get to do that and forget everything else.

My ruminating was interrupted by the sense that someone was watching me. I looked up and a woman smiled at me from the end of the bar. She had curly ginger hair, freckles, and big hazel eyes. When I smiled back at her, she came over and took the stool next to me. "You look like you're deep in thought. I'm Caroline." She put out her hand and I shook it.

"Hi, my name is Sharon." Then I broke out into a cold sweat. "I mean, uh, I'm Anne Marie." I tried to laugh off the mistake, but I was obviously shaken.

"Well, then, who's Sharon?"

"Oh, someone I was thinking about. How stupid of me," I stammered. My face was burning.

"Can I buy you another beer?"

"I have to go. Excuse me." I slid off the stool and signaled to Abby, who was still on the dance floor. I went outside and leaned against her car in the parking lot.

The redhead followed me out. "Are you all right?" she asked.

"I wasn't really in the mood to go out tonight."

"Well, when you are in the mood, you can give me a call." She handed me a napkin with her name and number. "Take care."

On my days off, Luke and I hung out at the local feminist bookstore and café. *The Desert Moon* had a kid's play area, books, cold drinks, and cheap sandwiches. Chris Williamson sang on an endless loop in the background. The women who worked there usually brought their children with them so there was always someone for Luke to play with. I read or worked crossword puzzles while I sipped lemonade and thought about my next step. It was cheap entertainment. There was a community resource center in one corner of the shop with notebooks filled with notices of support groups, social events, jobs, and house rentals. One afternoon, I saw a notice that a woman with a son about Luke's age was looking for a roommate, preferably with a child. I used the pay phone and rang the number.

"I hope you don't have a lot of furniture," she said. "The house is furnished."

"Hallelujah!" I said. "My ex-husband kept all of my furniture."

Even though she had helped me through a hard time, I was happy to end our time at Abby's house. Luke and I easily said our goodbyes to her and to our back porch bedroom before we moved our few belongings into the four bedroom house with red shingles on West Indian School Road.

The house was surrounded on all sides by an eight-foot high oleander hedge. I liked the feeling of having a protective barrier between me and the outside world. Now that I had a permanent address, my sister's friend in Half Moon Bay began sending my belongings through her company's shipping department, complete with a packing slip. Every few days a box would appear on our doorstep. I could wear my favorite gold hoop earrings again. Luke was glad to have his red magician's cape and his collection of tricks. My dishes didn't survive the trip, but they did provide a fun mosaic project for the kids. Familiar knick-knacks took their place on my dresser. Sally Ann sent two red Schwinn bikes as a house-warming present and Luke and I started riding to Encanto Park so he could play on the jungle gym and throw crusts of bread to the ducks in the lake. Even though I had been cautioned against it, I eventually told our new housemate, Cate, our secret. I told her the cast of characters and the broad strokes of the complete story. I thought if anyone was going to be trustworthy, it would be another lesbian mother.

One afternoon, a letter from Jeanne arrived. She was coming for a visit. The following Sunday, I heard her Honda in the driveway. I ran onto the porch and saw my rocking chair strapped to the top of her car. In fact, the entire car was filled with books, picture albums, toys, Luke's poster of The Banjo Lesson, and personal things I had thought I'd never see again. Jeanne jumped out of the car and threw her arms around me. She patted my back and rocked me while I cried.

That night, after Luke went to bed, Jeanne and I opened the boxes. We inspected each item, throwing out any memento which connected me to San Francisco, cutting out the title pages of my books with my old name written on them, and slicing Guy's face out of the pictures in my albums. Then we had a little bonfire in the backyard and burned the evidence. Jeanne stayed two days. When she left, I felt more alone than ever.

Usually, I've found that traumatic events in life lose their initial sting as time passes. The routine of living takes over our attention. But I was a fugitive, a mother who had kidnapped her child. Everything in my day was filtered through that lens. Even after more than six months underground, a fire truck blaring down the street in the middle of the night could send a shock of panic through me. Every police car put me on alert. I woke up with a start every morning, heart pounding, ears ringing, and sweat chilling my skin. No warm moments languishing under the soft covers after a good night sleep. But I pushed through the morning panic and ignored the thoughts of jail and my fear of losing Luke forever. I forced myself to get up and put on the water for oatmeal. I just kept moving.

And if I was ever tempted to pretend that Luke and I were just like everyone else, there were regular reminders to the contrary. I received a letter from Marilyn telling me that a new woman had begun attending Califia Community meetings. After a few months they discovered that the woman was a detective hired by Maya to infiltrate Califia. She befriended a poor single mother in the group. After the detective had gained the woman's confidence, she told her the truth. She offered to give her money for any information she could get from Marilyn about my whereabouts. The woman desperately needed money, but she stood up at a collective meeting and told everyone what had happened. The collective was outraged by the invasion of what they had considered a safe space, but still they were proud that the group's trust had not been compromised, even with the promise of cash to a mother who desperately needed it.

When I first arrived in Phoenix, I was so scared and upset that it wouldn't have mattered where I was. But I'd been in

Phoenix long enough now to know that I hated this place on its own merits. The unbearable heat, the giant Palmetto bugs, and the unnaturally organized razor straight streets—a stoplight every mile, a stop sign every half mile—it was like living on a sheet of graph paper.

Then the suffocating heat of summer changed to the warmth of winter and life in Phoenix became even worse. The Snowbirds returned in their RV's to escape the cold winter weather in other parts of the country. One of the few things I liked about Phoenix had been that it wasn't very crowded, no traffic jams or long lines at stores. But as the year drew to a close, the streets began to fill up with goliath-sized motor homes. The grocery stores were packed with grey-haired women with tight perms, wearing stretch pants and long t-shirts with pictures of bunnies and kittens with sequined ears. They were inevitably followed by pale men in straw hats wearing Bermuda shorts and sandals with black socks.

My sister, Carol, was still living in Austin, Texas. "Sharon, why don't you move if you hate Phoenix so much? Why make this harder than it has to be?" she asked. "You should come to Austin. You'd love it here." I was inclined to seriously consider this suggestion. I sent a message to my other sisters that I needed to talk to them.

"Being near a family member might not be a good idea," Marilyn reminded me.

"But Guy doesn't know where Carol is," I said. "If he knew, they would've contacted her by now."

"I like the idea of you being near someone in the family," Jeanne said from an extension.

"I think it's a good idea," Sally Ann added. "A move to Texas puts one more variable between you and San Francisco."

CHAPTER TEN

Austin, Texas: 1982

THE TRAIL BEHIND US SEEMED cold, and although it was still a
source of anxiety, the initial shock of transitioning to an underground life began to fade into a dull hum in the background
of every day. Also, I was more convinced that the inevitable
harm of being raised alone with abusive father far outweighed
whatever negative affect living with a big secret might have on
Luke. I was less worried about him; in fact, Luke seemed to be
flourishing. As for me, I was as comfortable as anyone could be
with the cold isolation of hiding in plain sight.

Once I made the decision to leave Phoenix, it was a simple
matter to put a plan together, certainly less complicated than
my preparations had been the year before. Our housemate,
Cate, asked if she and her son Michael could move to Austin
with us. She had moved there from Kalamazoo, Michigan to follow her last girlfriend and she hated Phoenix as much as I did.
She offered to share the expenses and pay half the rent once
we found jobs in Austin. I liked the idea of Luke being with a
friend during the transition to a new town, so I agreed.

But as we prepared for the move, Cate kept bringing up my
situation and asking for more details. I told her again and again
how important it was to keep what I had told her a secret, and

she always told me not to worry, but I began to regret having brought her into my confidence. I didn't think that she would compromise our safety intentionally, but I began to suspect that she might not be as dependable as I had originally believed. To amend this breach, I decided to sever my ties with her as soon as I could. In the meantime, however, Cate and Michael followed in her red Ford Escort as Luke and I drove the U-Haul toward Texas.

When we arrived in Austin, my spirits began to lift. Austin was a big city and a small college town all rolled into one. Town Lake snaked through the city center and a mirror-image of Austin's modest downtown skyline rippled on the sparkling water. The bright colors of spring were everywhere. The neighborhoods were gently nestled into the rolling hills, and the roads curved respectfully around stately old trees.

When we pulled in front of Carol's squat stone house on her tree-lined street, I rolled down the truck window and relished the misty cool evening breeze on my face. The contrast to Phoenix, which seemed at war with its desert environment, was almost a physical relief.

My sister Carol was almost ten years older than me, Murphy Sister number four. She had earned a master's degree and a teaching certificate at Oklahoma University, and she worked at a nonprofit organization that helped low-income mothers connect with social services. Carol was small like Mother, with eyes the color of dark chocolate. She had been dubbed the "Goddess of Beauty" in her Marquette High School yearbook. But now, 25 years later, she had traded in her matching pastel sweater sets and smooth pageboy hairdo for bright tie-dyed shirts, long Indian-print skirts, and she wore her wavy black hair long and wild down her back.

Carol's three children were all musicians in their early twenties. They also lived in Austin and during our first few weeks at Carol's house, we had bar-b-ques and jam sessions in her backyard. It was a wonderful family reunion.

I began waitressing at the Nighthawk Restaurant, a famous Austin steakhouse. Cate looked for work during the day and we traded off babysitting. Carol's house was across the street from the municipal golf course, and Luke and Michael created their own cottage industry, filling a tin pail with golf balls that sailed over the club's fence, and then selling the balls back to the golfers at the clubhouse. I had absconded with a bag of tokens from the Starship Game Room and they worked nicely in the quarter slots at the Laundromat. With everyone pitching in, our essentials were covered, but I needed a better job if I was going to be able to afford to rent a place without a roommate.

After a couple of months in Austin, I saw an ad in the classifieds. Brackenridge Hospital was hiring entry-level ward clerks. I left Luke drumming with his cousins in the living room and took the bus downtown. Brackenridge Hospital was a square, grey building, built in anonymous, industrial-style architecture. It could have been an insurance company or a prison. As soon as I located the employment office in the basement, I detoured into the ladies room. I was sweating and my stomach was knotted into a tight fist. Qualifying for unskilled jobs had been uncomplicated, but interviewing for a job as a ward clerk was going to be more of a challenge. And I needed this job. I sat in a toilet stall and did a quick review. I didn't want to draw a blank on the basics so I had prepared a list for myself—date of birth, social security number, previous addresses—things people usually have committed to memory. Then I washed my hands and inspected my face in the mirror.

I'd been told all my life that I was attractive, but I didn't think I looked pretty anymore. My brown hair was dull and pulled back with a plastic headband. My skin was pale and splotchy. I had big hazel eyes, long lashes, and dimples, but my eyes looked glassy, and my lips were dry and pressed together in a thin line. I blew out my lips and practiced smiling in the mirror. I had fooled myself into thinking that this time looking for a job would be easier, that I was more used to living this double life, but the face in the mirror looked terrified. Every time I presented my false identity was an opportunity to get caught.

Nearly all the orange plastic chairs in the waiting room were occupied. I took a packet off the counter and sat in the back row. The hospital application was simple enough and there was a long list of jobs available. I checked the box next to *Ward Clerk* and filled in my identifying information. I stared at the blank spaces under *Previous Experience* with bitter regret. I couldn't say I had been a unit secretary at Moffitt Hospital because Sharon Murphy had that job. I couldn't even put down my job at Starship Enterprise because I wanted to cover the trail between Phoenix and Austin. I skipped to the empty box at the bottom of the sheet. I wrote, *"I am highly organized, intelligent, and a fast learner."*

I handed in my application and sat down to wait. I stared at the reminders printed on yellow post-its on the cover of my notebook: "Breathe!" "Keep it simple." "You're okay." I took deep breaths to relax and told myself that filling out an application was an ordinary thing to do. People do this all the time. I'm just another person applying for a job. But the longer I waited, the more time I had to imagine all the things that could go wrong.

When the clerk stepped into the waiting room and called, "Anne Marie Clark," the sound of that name gave me a jolt and my heart began to hammer.

I followed her down a hall lit by grey fluorescent lights to a cubicle with a silver nameplate affixed to the wall next to the opening. Rita Gutierrez smiled and stuck out her hand when she saw me. "Miss Clark?" Her thick black hair had streaks of grey and was held back by sequined combs. She had gentle brown eyes and her voice was deep and slightly accented. When I reached out to shake her hand, the room started to spin and I broke out in a cold sweat. I grabbed for the edge of the metal desk to steady myself. "Are you alright?" she asked. "You're pale as a ghost."

I dropped heavily into the chair and thrust my head between my knees. A wave of despair washed over me and a sob erupted. Footsteps hurried away. A moment later, a cup of water was pressed into my hand and I felt a soothing wet cloth on the back of my neck. Tears spilled out of the corners of my eyes and I sat up and dabbed my face. The cloth came away smeared with mascara. Rita sat behind her desk, watching me with concern.

"I'm so sorry," I said. I looked into her deeply lined face and felt humiliated, but I didn't know what else to say, so I plowed ahead. I took a sip from the paper cup, took a breath, and choked out my fabricated story, punctuated by involuntary sobs. "I have a little boy. My husband...he left me...with nothing...no money. He didn't want me to work...I don't have any experience. But...I'm really smart and I need a job."

"He sounds like *my* rotten ex-husband. Let's see what we can do," she said resolutely. Rita looked down at my application and tapped her pencil against her front teeth.

As if my own personal genie had been released from a lamp, within a few weeks I breezed through the testing process and became the new ward clerk in the Emergency Department at Brackenridge Hospital. With Carol's help, I found a little house I could afford near the university. Cate was not pleased when I amended our agreement, but she had a new job and had no problem finding a house she could afford for herself and Michael. Sadly, Carol, ever the vagabond, decided to relocate to Vermont, and within six months, one by one, all her kids decided to try their luck in Vermont, as well. Our short family reunion was over.

Our new house was on Avenue D, a street filled with potholes, but also lined with graceful Quaking Aspen trees. The rent was only $195, probably because the doors and windows were all slightly askew, and the wind blew in through cracks in the frames. We began to call it our "little crooked house" and recite the old poem whenever we got home.

There was a crooked man, and he walked a crooked.
He found a crooked sixpence against a crooked stile.
He bought a crooked cat, who caught a crooked mouse.
And they all lived together in a little crooked house.

Our little crooked house was also in the flight path of the Bergstrom International Airport. But it had two bedrooms, a garage for our bikes, and a big backyard. Nearby was a large open field filled with old oak trees perfect for climbing, and Luke immediately started scavenging materials to build a tree house.

Our house was at the end of the street next to the University of Texas practice field. Luke would squeeze through a hole in the fence and watch from the sidelines. He was only six, but his gap-toothed grin and easy confidence around adults soon endeared him to the coaches and players. Before long, he was carrying around their bags of equipment and getting tips on catching and throwing. At night, the field's bright lights filled our house with a yellow glow. We could hear the whistles and grunts of the athletes as if they were scrimmaging in our front yard.

Nearly all our neighbors had children for Luke to play with and a dog or two running in a furry pack up and down our dead end street. He'd leap off the side of our front porch, give a loud whistle, and dogs would come running from every direction and surround him with wet noses and wagging tails. Luke dubbed himself *The King of the Dogs*.

We relied on our bikes to get around. I used a big backpack to transport our groceries or laundry. Even though I begged and threatened, Luke insisted on riding his bike across the open fields that were covered with razor sharp Texas burs, just long enough to make slow leaks in his inner tubes. His tires were regularly flat when it was time to leave in the morning. If I didn't have time to patch the inner tube before work, we had to ride double on my bike. I struggled and sweated up the Austin streets with Luke clinging to my back. To motivate me to the top of hills, Luke chanted, "I think I can. I think I can. I think I can."

It was summer again and I enrolled Luke in Sunshine Camp in Zilker Park, a free program for kids from low-income families, sponsored by the Young Men's Business League of Austin. Luke was excited to be going to his first overnight camp and I was equally excited to have three nights of privacy, my first since leaving California. As our first summer in Austin ended, I had been able to get a decent job without any references and a place to live without any credit history. Now I needed another miracle. It was time to try to get Luke into first grade without a birth certificate.

When I decided to leave San Francisco, I went to the nursing office at Moffitt Hospital and tried to get my next paycheck a few days early. Even thought I tried to communicate a sense of urgency and my face was bruised and swollen, the request was denied. I left the nursing office and hurried up to Labor and Delivery. Maybe someone there knew a way around the policy. Doris, the charge nurse, and my other friends on the staff huddled around me in the break room. The result of the beating was obvious and I hinted at my plan, but no one knew how I could get my check before the fifteenth.

As I was saying goodbye before I left the ward, one of the nurses hugged me and tucked something into my purse. "I hope this will help you," she whispered. When I got home and opened the envelope, I was shocked. She had given me a blank application for a late registration of birth and a sample birth certificate from a home birth, the form for a midwife's verification, and a blank immunization record. She had risked a lot to help me.

The immunization record had been simple enough to forge. I copied the dates from Luke's actual immunization record and filled in his new name and some fictitious doctors' names. I had no problem when I used it in Phoenix to get him into pre-school and now there was even a legitimate entry from the pediatrician at Arizona Health Plan. I pulled out the form for the birth certificate many times to study it. I went as far as to fill out the papers with what I thought were convincing facts about my home birth.

I drafted a statement from my midwife with scrawling penmanship and signed the verification. The scene was vivid. I could almost hear the flute music playing in the background. My friends and my wise old midwife (looking a bit like Sacagawea in my imagination) gathered around my labor bed to welcome my fatherless child into the world. But this was not just a literary pursuit. An application for a birth certificate had to navigate all the way through the Department of Vital Records in Sacramento without raising any red flags. I was just not familiar enough with the procedures to risk it. What if I mailed it and some follow-up documentation was required? I would have to provide contact information for myself in Austin. So far, every time I pulled out the papers, I slid them right back in the envelope and put the form away.

When I received the enrollment packet from Matthews Elementary School, I filled in the name of the Phoenix preschool Luke attended. I took the acceptance letter from Pre-K Arizona and doctored the dates to make it appear as if he had attended for a full year, then I poured Coke on the paper to disguise the alteration. I knew it wouldn't take the place of a birth certificate, but at least it gave me something with his name and age on it. We went to Matthews School on the last day of registration. I hoped the staff would be rushed and eager to get on with the school year.

Before Luke and I walked in, I sat down on the steps in front of the school and looked into his face. "We're going to go out for a hamburger after we finish here, but you have to remember our secret. Okay?"

"I remember! I remember! Why do you keep asking me?" Luke pulled away from me and rolled his eyes.

"It's important. I don't want you to forget."

The lobby of Matthews had a sharp smell of ammonia and fresh varnish. Registration tables were set up along the both sides of the long hallway. I handed the papers to the young man behind the spot marked, "A through C." The nametag pressed to his plaid shirt identified him as Mr. Watkins. He glanced at the papers and up at Luke's face. "Hi, Luke, are you ready for first grade?"

"Sure. Does this school have a soccer team?" he asked.

I interrupted before Mr. Watkins and Luke could launch into a conversation. "He just loves sports," I said. "When is the new parent orientation?"

Mr. Watkins gave me the speech he had probably given a hundred times over the last three days. "...and here's your packet. We'll send you his room assignment in the mail along with the schedule for the first day of school."

"Okay, thanks!" I turned Luke by the shoulder and took one step towards the door.

"Wait! I don't see his birth certificate," the young man said.

My stomach dropped. I took a deep breath and turned back to the table. "Oh, that's right. I forgot to tell you," I said with a laugh. "We just moved here and I can't find his birth certificate anywhere. I think I may have given the original to the people at his school in Phoenix. I've written to them and asked them to check his file and mail it to me." I shrugged my shoulders.

"We'll need it before the first day of school," said Mr. Watkins.

"Of course," I said.

I didn't go to orientation to avoid the likelihood of being asked about the birth certificate again. And even though I wanted to, I didn't walk Luke to his classroom on his first day of first grade. Luckily, he was eager to begin this new adventure and bolted up the school stairs, waving his Spiderman lunchbox as a farewell. I signed him up for a city soccer league, so no one at Matthews would be reminded of his non-existent birth certificate.

Luke looked older than six, so there was no question that he was old enough for the soccer team. I gave the coach the letter from Matthews to verify that Luke was in the first grade, and I suppose he assumed that the school had verified his age. By some small miracle of bureaucratic oversight, the birth certificate was never mentioned again, but I remained on alert. This was an unfinished piece of business that could become a problem at any moment.

One afternoon, I leaned my bike against the rack outside the school and waited for Luke. It was payday and I had decided to skip paying the electric bill this month to take Luke out for pizza and video games. He ran down the stairs, waving an embossed certificate. "Momma, I met the governor! My class got their picture taken with him."

Rather than being pleased (as any mother would be), my heart froze. Luke handed me the certificate which proclaimed that Luke Clark was a citizen in good standing of the proud State of Texas. I wondered what they would do with that picture. Would they publish it in the paper to show how pro-education Governor Bill Clements was? Would someone recognize Luke? He was a striking child, with his bright copper hair, brown skin, and big dark eyes. He was the type of kid that people noticed, not the type that blended into the background. I watched the paper for weeks but the picture never appeared.

Maintaining a false identity is like protecting a sand castle against an incoming tide. It takes constant vigilance. I was hyper-alert in every situation where someone might notice anything amiss, in all the ordinary situations where a person shows their driver's license or answers simple questions, usually without a second thought. Applying for phone service, utilities, even a library card, required a litany of identifying numbers and facts that most people don't even think about—because they have nothing to hide. Sharon Murphy's birthday is in August, but Anne Marie's driver's license gave me a birthday in March. "You don't seem like an Aries," one astute woman observed when I applied for a Blockbuster membership.

New employees were required to place a signature on file when they picked up their first paycheck from the hospital accounting department. I never appreciated how personal your signature is until I had to sign a false name. It still felt awkward signing *Anne Marie Clark*, even though I had practiced writing my new name over and over again, like a teenager with a crush. When I went in to sign the signature card, the clerk said, "You sign your name like it's not your name."

I tried to laugh off her unnerving observation. "Oh, I haven't felt like myself all day."

I knew that someday I would have to face the consequences of stealing this time to protect my son and safeguard our relationship. I had to be vigilant and take precautions, but I knew that every moment I spent preoccupied with fear and dread of what *might* happen was a waste of something precious. Luke operated in the moment and he had an innate ability to accept whatever came his way. He became my role model for appreciating what was right in front of me—a sunny afternoon, a new friend, a good belly laugh. I was giving Luke the safe, carefree childhood I thought he deserved. I didn't have money, so it was the only thing I had to give. If I could learn to fully experience the blissful ordinariness of everyday life the way he did, it would be worth any price I might have to pay.

Luke was barely five when we left San Francisco but now he was more aware of the big secret we lived with. Matthews School was near the International Student Housing of the University of Texas and his fellow students came from countries all over the world. He came home one day and told me that his teacher had asked the children to talk about where their families were from. Even though we were alone in our living room, Luke leaned in and cupped his hand around my ear. "I said I was from Arizona. No one at school knows that I'm special," he whispered. He looked me in the face and gave me a conspiratorial nod.

"You did good, baby."

Periodically, I gave Luke an opportunity to talk about our unusual situation. I didn't want him preoccupied with it, but I wanted to help him vent any feelings he was having and to re-member why I made the decision to run away and hide from his father. I wanted to have the opportunity to answer any ques-tions that would inevitably develop as he got older.

One evening after dinner, Luke was lying on the living room floor playing with our new black kitten, Pearl. "I wonder how Max is doing?" I said. Max was the pit bull puppy that Guy got not long before we left San Francisco. I never made a casual reference to our old life, and Luke's expression told me that he understood what this conversation was really about. He sat up and crossed his legs tailor-style with Pearl trapped under his tanned arms.

"How old is Max now?" he asked.

"He must be at least three. He's probably full grown."

"I think about him sometimes," Luke said. "Do you think he misses me?"

"Dogs don't remember people the way people remember dogs," I said.

Then we moved to the heart of the matter. "Do you think my dad misses me?"

"I'm sure he does," I said. "You'll see him again someday."

"Yeah, I know. Do you think my dad knows why we ran away?" Luke always asked some version of this question during our conversations about Guy.

"Yes, I'm sure he knows the reason, even if he might blame it on something else. Do you remember why we left?" I dreaded bringing up the painful memory.

"Yeah, I went to live with him, and then he hit you." Luke became quiet. He looked down at Pearl, and she scrambled out of his lap and made a beeline for her food bowl.

"I remember that day," he said. "Before you came to get me, I was helping Daddy wash the dishes, and there was this little knife in the dish drainer. He told me to be careful—it was sharp. When I was on the driveway and he was on the porch hitting you, I thought about that knife. I thought if I could go and get that knife, I could make him stop."

My heart froze. Luke had never told me that story before. "Luke, it wasn't up to you to make him stop. You were a little boy, and he's a grown man. He should know that it's wrong to hit people."

"I guess." Colin got on his knees, and looked under the coffee table with his butt in the air. He reached for Pearl, who scooted away. When he came to sit next to me on the couch, the kitten jumped up on his lap and Luke buried his nose in her black coat.

"What else do you remember?"

"He said he was going to have the end of my penis cut off if I didn't keep myself clean, and he hit me with his belt."

"I didn't want your dad to ever hit either of us again. I grew up that way and it is a terrible way for a child to have to live. That's why I thought we should leave. And that's why we need to keep our secret to ourselves." Luke nodded and leaned against me. Pearl jumped off his lap and tangled herself up in the small rug in front of the door.

The number of people looking for us would be limited if Guy was just some ordinary man. Unfortunately, he was the son of the internationally-known and respected Maya Angelou with unlimited resources available. She could muster private detectives and police departments all over the country to find us. I lay awake nights wondering if the FBI was involved, particularly if Guy and Maya suspected that we weren't in California anymore. I was already surprised we had gone undetected this long. I didn't know what they were doing to track us down, but I assumed they were doing something. For quite a while there hadn't been a hint of anything that my family or friends in the Bay Area knew of but it was wise to prepare for the worst.

I watched the newspaper and scanned bulletin boards so I'd know when Maya was scheduled to make an appearance in the area. She'd actually spoken at the University of Texas at Austin during the Black History Month celebration that February. It had been a shock to open the paper while I waited in line at Safeway and see her smiling face. *"Maya Angelou has been hailed as one of the great voices of contemporary literature and as a remarkable Renaissance woman,"* the article read.

Luke and I both played hooky the day she was on campus. Luke thought we were taking our own private holiday. We watched videos, played with our cat, and ate homemade nachos.

If Maya was in the backseat of a limo cruising on an Austin street, I wanted us safely indoors.

Anne Marie and Luke, 1983

In the spring of 1983, I read an article in the paper that The United Way had increased its funding for statewide domestic violence programs. The Austin Center for Battered Women (CBW) was using part of the money to hire another counselor for the shelter. I liked my job at the hospital, but it barely paid the bills. The shelter job paid well—$20,000 a year. Also, for me, the job would be so much more than just a paycheck. I'd be back in community service, doing the kind of work that was close to my heart.

I knew what those women were going through. If I hadn't had people to help me, I might have had to turn to a place like CBW. I sensed that if I applied for the counselor's job, I would be hired. I drafted a letter of inquiry and mailed it to the address provided in the article.

The location of the shelter was confidential so screening interviews were being held at the offices of the Texas Coalition against Domestic Violence in downtown Austin. The receptionist showed me to a conference room and I sat in one of the mismatched chairs at a heavy oval table. A tall, slim woman in her thirties came in with an armful of papers. She was tan with long dark hair, and wore a green cotton shirt tucked into pressed jeans with a leather belt decorated with Native American beadwork. She was holding a pen between her straight, white teeth. Her manner was rushed, but her movements were graceful and elegant. She settled herself at the table, folded her long fingers, and visibly relaxed.

"Thank you for coming in. I'm Judy. I'm a counselor at the shelter. Let me start by telling you a little bit about us. CBW's services include a family shelter, counseling, and legal assistance for battered women and their children. We provide hospital advocates and a 24-hour hotline. Today we are looking for candidates for the in-house counselor position to coordinate daily activities at the shelter and work one-on-one with the women to help them create an action plan for themselves and their children." Judy paused and smiled at me.

I told Judy about my background with community organizations, recreation programs, and group homes for developmentally delayed adults. I was vague about where these jobs had been, but I spoke about the substance of Sharon Murphy's life in a way I hadn't in a long time. We wandered quickly from a job interview to a personal conversation. Judy told me about her divorce and her kids.

"I wasn't a feminist before I started working at the shelter," she said. The job had changed her outlook on life.

Finally, I decided to take the risk. "I want this job and I think I'm qualified, but my situation is complicated," I said. "You won't be able to check any of my references except the hospital job I have now."

Judy's eyes narrowed. "Oh?"

I chose my words carefully. "I'm hiding from my son's father."

"Are you hiding because he was violent with you and your son?"

"Yes. And then he took custody of him."

Judy paused in thought for a moment then she asked, "Are these your real names? Anne Marie and Luke?"

"No," I said. A cold chill ran through me and I wondered if I had just made an irrevocable mistake.

Judy tapped the tip of her pen on the table. "Well, I suppose helping women like you is the reason the shelter exists."

"I was hoping you'd see it that way." Relief warmed me from the inside out. I felt more like myself in that moment than I had since I'd fled from San Francisco.

My second interview was scheduled for noon the following Monday. I borrowed a friend's car and followed Judy's directions to the outskirts of town. At the shelter, Judy and the other women on the hiring committee had just received their lunch order. They chatted and laughed, passing around bags and cans of soda.

Judy handed me a fajita and pointed to a chair in the corner of the counseling office that was filled with beat-up couches and desks. When everyone was settled with their food, their focus turned to me. They took turns posing hypothetical situations that the clients might find themselves in.

"Say we have a client who is being beaten by her husband and now her 15-year-old son is starting to hit her. Our primary purpose is to provide a safe place for women so we can't knowingly take a violent teenager into the shelter. But the woman doesn't want to leave the boy with his father. What do you think we should do?"

I took a small bite of the fajita to give myself a minute to think. Then I suggested placing the boy in a group home for violent teens rather than taking him into the shelter. I also recommended counseling for the teen and his mother by someone in a batterer's program. A reunion with his family could be his reward for good conduct at the group home. The women nodded to each other and scribbled notes on their tablets.

When the interview was over, Judy asked me to wait in the volunteer office. After a few minutes, she returned. "I want you to meet Ellen, the shelter director." I followed Judy into a small office crowded with file cabinets and a cluttered metal desk. Ellen reached over a stack of papers to shake my hand, and then Judy and I sat down facing her.

"Judy told me about your interview, and we want to offer you the counseling job," Ellen said. "But—given your circumstances—we need an agreement with you first. Our top priority has to be the shelter and the residents. As far as the rest of the staff will know, we've checked your references and you are exactly who you appear to be. Judy and I will be the only ones who know your real situation. Is that agreeable?" Her words dashed out of her mouth at a fast sprint.

"I wouldn't have gotten this far if I didn't know how to keep a secret," I said.

"Welcome to CBW, Anne Marie." Ellen stood up and shook my hand.

I needed a car to get to my new job at the shelter. With my sisters' help, I bought a 1972 Buick Skylark for $600. The car was missing large patches of its metallic silver paint, but this ugly car with its bordello red upholstery was a luxury to Luke and me. With my higher salary, Luke and I could afford to say goodbye to our crooked little house on Avenue D. I rented a two- bedroom apartment in a small complex on West Lynn, right across the street from Luke's school.

Within days of dragging the last box up the two flights of stairs, Luke spied a boy about his age. Zack lived with his mother Dianne in an apartment on the first floor. Zack introduced Luke to his friend Aubrey who lived around the corner with his parents. The boys were a trinity of extremes. Zack was eight, long and slim with fine features and feather soft blonde hair. Aubrey was ten, awkward and gangly with pale skin and confused red hair. Luke and his two new pals became an inseparable trio.

When I first ran away, I imagined that Guy might involve the authorities but that would also try to find me himself—if the situation were reversed, that's what I would have done. I flinched every time I saw a tall, olive-skinned man in the distance or heard the engine of a VW van like the one Guy drove. But once again, I had misjudged Guy. He hadn't called or even written to anyone in my family. He hadn't shown up at anyone's house to talk to my friends face to face, although the phone subpoena had provided him with the names, phone numbers, and addresses of my friends in the Bay Area and San Diego.

I'd felt betrayed when Maya remained passive during my struggle with Guy. I still resented it and resented that she was reaping immense financial reward for her glorification of women and motherhood—but when I asked her to put her inspiring words into action, she had balked. Nonetheless, I regretted that she had to suffer because of what I had done. I knew that she missed her grandson. For a time, my sister Marilyn received periodic telegrams with Maya's name printed at the bottom. The telegrams promised that she wouldn't ask any questions if only Marilyn would arrange a phone call with Luke. But I didn't trust her and my priorities didn't include compromising our security to assure Maya that her grandson was all right. After Marilyn received four such telegrams, even that contact had stopped.

Apart from the telegrams and the detective that Maya hired to infiltrate Califia, we heard nothing. If other efforts were being made, I assumed that my family or friends would be contacted and questioned and I'd hear about it. It began to dawn on me that Maya was not going to use her considerable power in the search for Luke—no TV ads, no nationwide advertisement in the newspaper. It was curious. With their resources, it seems as if it would be easy to publicize their search for me. A few national news stories showing our pictures would be all it would take. Why weren't they doing that? Maybe they didn't want to bring attention to the situation. Maybe they didn't want to give me the opportunity to explain why I felt it necessary to take such a drastic step. I began to feel more at ease. I had a job I loved and a peaceful life with no one threatening or harassing me. Luke was safe and happy and had two friends that he loved.

I was careful not to portray Guy as a monster to Luke because I assumed that when he was older, he would probably insist on resuming a relationship with his father. I could see him making contact with Guy and Maya when he was a teenager. But if they didn't find me, I could decide when to resurface. Then I would face whatever charges were brought against me. Right now though, life was good.

In all years I'd been living underground, I'd never been settled enough to enjoy the luxury of self-examination. I was too preoccupied with the basics of food, shelter, and security. But now my new friends at CBW and my work with the residents gave me a renewed sense of community, and my self-esteem was getting a giant boost. I may have only climbed up to the third level on Maslow's *Hierarchy of Needs*, but I was heading in the right direction.[1]

I started seeing a therapist, then followed the lead of some of my friends and signed up for the est training. The trainer who conducted my admissions interview said that our lives were about everything we were hiding. If my experience of life was to transform, what was hidden had to come to the light. That was truer than even he knew.

One evening, I was leading my support group at the shelter and the newest resident, Evelyn, was sharing. She was crying so hard she could barely speak. We all waited patiently. When she calmed down enough to talk, her words cracked open a locked door inside my heart.

"When Jacob and I first got together, it was the most intense feeling I'd ever had. Being with him felt like destiny. The first

---

1   A native New Yorker, Abraham Maslow first proposed his theory of human motivation in a 1943 issue of the journal Psychological Review.

time he hit me, I couldn't believe it! But after that first time, it happened again. And he started hitting the kids, too. But he could still be so wonderful at times. Even now, I think I will never love anyone that much again."

When I was in bed that night, I thought about Evelyn's words. I, too, had believed that Guy and I were perfect for each other, and accepted that the cause of our problems lay with me. From my new vantage point I could see my denial—ignoring all the clues in Guy's behavior that foreshadowed the physical violence.

Most of the men who brutalized the shelter residents were like Evelyn's husband. They had outbursts of cruelty and violence followed by periods of regret and remorse. They would apologize, cry, and beg for forgiveness. One man, who knew the shelter's secret location, would leave love notes and roses and candy at the door every time his wife was in residence. Only a small percentage were like Guy, either denying that anything happened or rationalizing that the woman deserved it—that was the deepest psychological wound. Guy never apologized or asked me to come back to him. He had just predicted that I'd come crawling back while he kicked me in the ribs.

What would I have done if he had ever shown any remorse? I felt humiliated even thinking that I might have gone back to him. What would my life have been like now if I had never left him? I tried to convince myself that I had never loved him. That the passion I felt wasn't love, it was just dependency, I told myself. I thought of what Judy often said. She said we should never regret our ability to love, that this ability was a capacity to be proud of. It was letting ourselves be mistreated that was the habit we needed to break. I lay in the dark and cried and allowed myself to feel my broken heart.

When I worked late, Luke came with me to the shelter. One evening, I noticed a new volunteer in the front office talking and laughing with him. It's hard for a mother to overlook someone so obviously taken with her child. This young woman was adorable with a great smile and big brown eyes with long, thick lashes. I found myself looking forward to seeing her every Wednesday night. While I rushed around gathering up the residents for group, I could feel her looking at me. Her gaze would linger and she would give me slow suggestive smiles. I was trying to make better choices than I had in the past so I decided to ignore her. I knew her name was Mindy from the volunteer calendar. She looked very young, maybe early twenties, and it was a bad idea to get involved with people you worked with. Even though I tried not to, I began finding things about her to like in addition to her soulful brown eyes. I appreciated the fact that she gave her free time to volunteer for the hotline. And when the staff reviewed volunteer notes, Mindy's comments were always insightful and compassionate.

When they are finally ready, battered women often leave home suddenly, as soon as an opening presents itself. Unfortunately, sometimes they are forced to leave their children behind, and it's common for the men to use the kids as leverage to coerce the women to come back home. In an ironic twist, retrieving residents' kids from uncooperative husbands had become an expertise of mine. I had a client who needed me to do just that and I'd concocted a plan.

I decided to ask Mindy if she would help me. After group, I cast my previous resistance aside and walked into the volunteer office. Luke and Mindy were bent over one of his books.

"Hi, Mom! This is Mindy," he said. "This is my mom."

"Hi! I'm Anne Marie." I shook Mindy's hand and sat down on the couch.

"Good to finally meet you. I thought you were going to ignore me forever." Mindy laughed and turned her chair until she faced me.

"That was my original plan, but I need to ask for your help," I said.

"Anything!" Mindy replied quickly.

"Do you remember Claire? I noticed in the log that you talked to her on the hotline a few times. She finally came in a couple of days ago."

Mindy's attitude became serious. "Sure, I remember her. I read in the log that she came in, but I haven't seen her yet."

"Craig punched her in the face and then went to the 7-11 for cigarettes. He took their little girl with him to make sure Claire didn't go anywhere. But when she saw Craig's truck disappear down the road, she thought this might be her last chance to get away. She followed your advice and had been setting aside a little money whenever she could. She hid it in a sock above one of the ceiling tiles. So last night she got her money, packed a bag, and called the cops and asked them to bring her here."

Mindy shook her head slowly. "Is she okay?"

"She's got a couple of black eyes and her nose is broken. I thought you might want to go with me to get her daughter. But the dad's not going to make it easy."

"Yeah, I know. He's already called three times tonight. He said if Claire doesn't come home, he's taking their daughter to Oregon."

Claire and her husband and their two-year-old daughter lived in a mobile home in Buda, south of Austin. Before we left the shelter the next afternoon, Claire described the interior of their mobile home and all the vehicles that Craig or his buddies might have parked nearby. She assured us that Craig didn't have any weapons.

Mindy and Claire and I took the shelter's rusted white Datsun and drove down Highway 35. Claire's eyes looked like over-ripe plums and there was an hourglass band-aid across the bridge of her nose. She sat in the back seat wearing large dark glasses. Her blonde hair was tucked inside the hood of an orange Texas Longhorn sweatshirt.

The mobile home park was only a short distance from the main road through Buda. We pulled off and turned the car around so it was facing the way we came. We unlocked all the doors, and left Claire lying on the backseat so Craig wouldn't see her if he happened to drive by.

It was difficult to decide on the most direct route of retreat. The narrow spaces between the trailers were crowded with barb-que grills and aluminum chairs. We paused in the shade of the canvas awning above the window at the front of Claire's trailer. The side door was open. We could hear the sizzle of oil and could smell food frying. A white truck was parked in the gravel driveway. We didn't hear any conversation from inside the trailer, only cartoons on the TV. We assumed that the little girl was alone with her father.

We returned to the car to get Claire. I pulled a wide, wicker laundry basket out of the trunk, and we walked in single file back to the trailer. I knocked on the screen door and stepped inside without waiting for an answer. Mindy and Claire walked in behind me. Claire's daughter, Dawn, was leaning against the tattered arm of the living room chair, sucking her thumb and holding a sock monkey against her cheek. When she saw her mother, her eyes widened, and she started to cry loudly. I advanced towards Craig as he turned from the stove. He was a short man with wire-rimmed glasses and bad skin. I gripped the basket in front of me, and, as Claire had predicted, the basket blocked the center of the room in the narrow mobile home.

"We're here to help Claire get some of her things," I said.

Craig looked around me and tried to address himself to his wife. "You're not taking anything, Claire!" he said. At the sound of her father's angry voice, the wails of the little girl turned to a whimper. Claire pulled the hood further down around her face and made no response.

"Is this your stuff?" Mindy said to Claire as she picked through the laundry strewn across the couch. She dropped a shirt over my shoulder into the basket.

"Who the hell are you?" Craig said.

"We're friends of Claire. She needs to get some of her clothes, and then we'll be out of here." I advanced a little further into the room. Craig shifted from side to side looking for an opening. Out of the corner of my eye, I saw Claire lift her daughter and turn towards the door.

"Okay, let's go," Mindy said.

I shoved the basket into Craig's chest and then dropped it at his feet. I turned to run. We scrambled down the wobbly metal stairs and ran behind the trailer. Claire cradled Dawn's small body against her like a quarterback heading towards the goal line. We heard Craig's boots hit the gravel as he jumped through the door. The flimsy screen door slammed behind him.

"You bitch!" Craig screamed.

We piled into the car and sped away. In the back seat, Claire held Dawn against her cheek and sobbed. "Thank you, Anne Marie! Thank you, Mindy."

After a couple of minutes, we saw Craig's white truck swerve onto the narrow country road a short distance behind us. I sped towards the on-ramp. The heavy evening traffic jammed the freeway into Austin. Making nerve-snapping lane changes, I put a few big trucks between our little Datsun and the white truck. Mindy watched out the back window. When there was enough traffic between us, I veered off at the next exit. Craig couldn't change lanes fast enough to make the exit and was carried away in the flow of heavy traffic. It was clear sailing the rest of the way to the shelter.

After that adventure, Mindy and I started spending time together, and she became my partner in other capers to retrieve the children of other residents. She was crazy about Luke and happy to have Luke and Zack and Aubrey claim her garage as their playroom when the four of us began spending weekends at her house. She didn't mind the chaos of three boys shooting spit wads at each other and never complained when her vacuum got clogged with popcorn after movie-night sleepovers. We made weekend trips to Schlitterbahn, a water park 40 miles south of Austin, spending long hot days chafing our arms and legs on old, black inner tubes and flying through the tube chute into the Congo River.

I had given up believing in happily ever after, but I had been lonely. Mindy was sweet, fun, and as easy to be with. I cared deeply for her, but was non-committal about the future. When she began to talk about combining our households, I decided to come clean. I dropped Luke off at Zack's after my shift and invited Mindy to go to Uncle Charlie's for margaritas.

When our frosty mugs were half-empty, I laid out the truth of my situation. I could see that she was quietly absorbing every detail. When I finished my story, Mindy sat back in the booth and stared at me, wide-eyed. Then she slapped both hands on the table. "I knew there was something going on with you," she said. "You never mention Luke's father—that's pretty unusual for a single mom. And you never talk about your past—it's just this blank space that you refer to in a vague way. I got the definite message that I shouldn't ask for details."

"Really?" I said alarmed. "I'm going to have to look at that. I don't want to appear secretive or make anyone too curious."

"Well, I was paying closer attention than most people," Mindy pointed out. She reached across the table for my hand.

I continued, "So I can only promise one day at a time. That's the only thing anyone can guarantee if you think about it. I know it's not very romantic, but that's all I have to offer."

She took me up on the offer, and we decided on an official move-in date of June 1, 1985. Two days later, Sergeant Waters knocked on our front door.

PART THREE

CHAPTER ELEVEN

Austin, Texas: June 3, 1985

AS SOON AS THE PROCESSION of police cars disappeared around the corner, I turned the old Plymouth towards Mindy's office. My hands shook on the steering wheel, but traffic was light and I made good time. When I pulled into the parking lot behind Davidson Staffing, the clock on the dashboard read 6:30, and I was relieved to see Mindy's car in its regular spot.

When I walked through the back door, Mindy's boss, Angela, was busy at the copier. Her crisp white blouse was pulled halfway out of her tailored blue slacks, and her long ash-blonde hair looked as if she was standing in a strong wind. Their agency was always busy on Mondays, which explained why Mindy and Angela were both still at work more than an hour after the office closed.

I gave Angela a quick hello and rushed to the front of the office. I found Mindy hunched over the phone at her desk, probably describing a morning assignment to one of her temps. I put my quivering hand on her shoulder as she hung up the phone. She jumped as if a car had backfired, then looked up at my face. "What happened?"

"They found me." Mindy stood up to put her arms around me, but I shook her off. "The police were just at the house," I whispered.

"They were there...at the house? How did you..."

"I told them I was Mindy Watrous." Mindy raised her eyebrows and nodded as I continued. "I can't risk getting stopped on the street, so you've got to go get Luke from Zack's house. And we've got to get somewhere safe right away, but we can't go back to the house."

I watched as her mind shifted into overdrive. "Okay. I'll ask Angela if we can go to her house," she said. "What should I tell her?"

"Give her the short version for now. I've been hiding from Luke's father and he found us." It was a shock hearing those words out loud, and I leaned against the edge of her desk and hugged my purse against me. I could feel my heart thudding.

Mindy gripped both of my shoulders. "We'll handle this," she said, and hurried to the back of the office.

Angela was more than Mindy's boss, she was a friend, but I couldn't predict what her reaction would be. As Mindy talked, I saw Angela's big green eyes dart in my direction over her shoulder. After a few minutes she nodded. She walked over to her desk and started gathering up her things. In less than five minutes, we stepped out of the office into the parking lot.

Angela locked the back door and we hurried to our cars. I felt as if a spotlight was trained on me from above and I scanned the parking lot, but nothing seemed out of the ordinary. I didn't think the police had taken down the license plate number of the Plymouth I was driving, but this car wouldn't stay anonymous for much longer. I fooled Sergeant Waters, who never met Sharon Murphy, but it wouldn't take them long to figure out that the woman they talked to at the house wasn't Mindy Watrous.

Angela and her family lived in West Lake Hills on the other side of town. It would be a long drive even if we took the direct route down Bee Caves Road, but Angela was going to lead me to her house through the backstreets. Mindy was behind me in her Subaru. She'd get Luke and bring him to Angela's. When I looked in my rearview mirror, Mindy gave me a wink and nodded her head as if to say, "Don't worry."

I followed Angela's tan minivan when she turned right out of the parking lot, away from the highway and into the subdivision behind the office complex. Mindy turned left towards Lamar Boulevard.

Sergeant Waters said that Maya was here in town. I couldn't imagine her waiting patiently in a molded plastic chair at the police station. It was more likely that she was in one of the big downtown hotels. I could almost feel how close she was...could see her, waiting confidently, scotch in hand, for the police to arrest me and bring Luke to her. The look on her face would be the one that the public never saw—never knew existed. And what about Guy? Was he on a plane heading to Austin? It had been a long time since I'd seen Guy, but Luke had some of Guy's big gestures, especially when he talked and pumped his arms for emphasis, palms upturned.

The photograph of Luke that the police took from the house was one of my favorites. He'd been wearing his blue vest and striped knit shirt, his 'get-away outfit,' as he called it. It sickened me to think of his smiling face pinned to a bulletin board in a police station.

Luke and Zack had spent the day at Zilker Park, swimming in the Barton Springs pool. The pool was fed by an underground spring, but the cold water never bothered Luke. He stayed in the water until his teeth were chattering and his fingers looked like raisins. If he had been with me when the police came to the house, he'd be gone now, and I'd be sitting in a jail cell. Given the circumstances, I had been lucky.

The rush hour traffic thinned and it was easier to keep Angela's van in front of me. We drove past Lions Golf Course on Lake Austin Boulevard and turned left onto the short bridge across Town Lake. The calm water reflected the last bits of light draining out of the low clouds. I felt the familiar adrenalin bringing every cell of my body to full alert. I thought of Mindy, who was probably driving too fast, sliding through red lights on her way to get Luke. I knew her, and knew she wouldn't let us leave without her. Another person's life ruined by this mess, my mess.

My mind was racing. What should I do now? Should we leave town as soon as Mindy returned with Luke? Should we just go somewhere and take a few days to decide what to do? Of course the police would be watching the house. How was I going to get back to pack anything? I couldn't afford to replace our clothes. And we couldn't stay in a motel. The authorities had both of our names now, plus I had to preserve my cash. If we drove all night, we could get to Mindy's parents' house in Bartlesville, Oklahoma, but we'd have to give Ted and Gloria a plausible reason for being there, and that might be one of the first places the police would look.

I had organized a legal advocacy program for the clients of the shelter. I testified in Court about the battered women's syndrome and conducted trainings for local attorneys willing to provide pro bono advocacy for CBW clients. I became good friends with one attorney and after Carla got to know Luke, I confided in her about my situation and asked her if she would line up attorneys for me if I was ever found. Carla was not a family or criminal attorney, but she had promised to help me. That day had arrived.

If I called Carla, I knew she'd tell me to turn myself in and take my chances. But what were my chances? I didn't know it when I first left California, but a lot of mothers consider running away with their children when the Courts disregard their accusations about abusive fathers. Since the abuse usually happens behind closed doors, it's hard to reach the Court's standard of proof in these cases. And fathers' rights are sacred— more sacred at times than the rights of children to be safe and protected.

Good mothers are responsible for shielding their children from all harmful influences right up to the point where a father's rights begin. A mother who violates the rights of the father—no matter how justified she feels she is—loses all her credibility. Guy would be seen as the victim when we stood side by side before a judge. What Court would ever believe that I took my son because I was a good mother?

I lit another cigarette as a feeling of emptiness washed over me. Here I was again, thrashing around like a cat in a sack. I rolled down the window and focused on Angela's tail lights ahead. What if I did run again? Could I do everything all over— drive to another unfamiliar city, pick up the phone book and the newspaper, and start another new life? Tell some new story to a new landlord? Find another low-paying job that didn't require references, or try my luck at another battered women's shelter?

I checked my rearview mirror. Red and white lights might flash on behind me any minute. At least then the agony of making a decision would be out of my hands. After another ten minutes of driving, Angela turned onto Redbud Trail and streetlights started popping on one by one. Her brake lights flashed and I heard a small motor kick in. A heavy chain pulled a wrought iron gate back across the road that led into her subdivision. Angela drove a block and then paused in front of a two-story brick house. She waved me around her.

I pulled onto the circular driveway and drove to the back of the house to keep the car out of sight. She met me on the patio and unlocked the back door. She led me through the kitchen and into the wood-paneled family room with a vaulted ceiling. The room was decorated with cowboy paraphernalia and an ocher couch and tan leather chairs faced a fireplace with a flagstone mantel.

"I'm so sorry this is happening." Angela said. She gave me an awkward hug and began flipping on the track lighting.

"Would you mind turning on the news?" I sat on the couch and Angela picked up the remote and pointed it at the console. A shot of our house on Creekside Drive filled the screen. A reporter stood on our porch in front of the green double doors, exactly where the police had stood only a short time ago.

"Neighbors in this quiet South Austin subdivision were surprised to learn who was living right down the street..."

"That's your house!" Angela said. "Why is this on television?"

Before I could answer, we heard Mindy, Luke, Angela's husband Dan, and their two kids at the back door. I switched off the TV and Angela and I looked towards the commotion. I had never met Dan, but had imagined him as slim and fair like Angela. Instead, he was a dark, muscular man. He set bags of groceries on the kitchen counter and her kids stuck their heads into the refrigerator. Dan glanced at me, signaled to Angela, and herded the kids out of the kitchen.

"I'm going to go talk to Dan," Angela said as she walked past me and followed Dan upstairs.

At that moment, to my immense relief, Luke burst into the family room. His blue swimming trunks peeked out from under his oversized t-shirt, which reached almost to his freckled brown knees. His caramel skin had a rosy glow from his day in the sun and the sprinkle of freckles across the bridge of his nose was darker than it had been this morning. His red Luke Skywalker cap was pulled low over his face and his copper hair poked out above his ears in tight ringlets. Luke's self assurance made him appear older than nine. He was losing his little boy belly, and his legs were getting long and muscular.

He ran over to me, wide-eyed and breathless. "Momma, Mindy made me lay on the floor of her car. What's going on? Did my dad find us?"

"Yes," I said.

I opened my arms and Luke stepped into them. I closed my eyes and nuzzled the top of his head with my cheek. He smelled of cocoa butter and sweat. Mindy sat beside me and slipped her arm around my waist. We all took a deep breath together. I rocked Luke for a moment and then pulled him next to me on the couch.

"Am I gonna see my dad?"

"I don't know what we're going to do yet. You have to wait until I decide. Can you do that?"

"Sure, but I want to see him," he said.

Even though I knew that Luke's feelings about his father would always be different from mine, I was stung by his eager tone. I thought of one of my clients at the shelter. Her husband had thrown their four-year-old daughter against the wall and fractured her pelvis. The child's hips and legs were buckled into a leather brace which hung from a frame over her hospital bed. I was keeping the little girl company while her mother was in surgery—her husband had broken the woman's arm when she tried to protect her daughter. When the husband walked into the child's room, I watched in amazement as the little girl raised her arms and gave her daddy a loving hug and smile. That day, I witnessed first-hand that a child's bond with an abusive parent defies logic.

Angela came back in and fidgeted with the amethyst ring on her finger. She glanced back and forth between Mindy and me, and then nodded towards Luke. "Can I talk to you two in the other room?"

Mindy turned the TV back on, flipped to the cartoon channel, and said off-handedly to Luke, "You stay here a minute. Okay?"

We followed Angela into the kitchen and she pushed the door closed and turned to face us. "You can't stay here."

"What?" Mindy said.

"Dan heard about this on the radio in the car. Maya Angelou? Are you kidding me? Dan thinks we could get in trouble for harboring a fugitive. That's what they're calling you! A fugitive ..."

"We only need time to decide what we're going to do. No one knows we're here." Mindy said.

"The police showed up at your house, didn't they?"

Mindy swatted at the tears escaping from the corners of her eyes, and I felt a stab of guilt. I could see that it was dawning on Mindy how powerless she was to protect me and Luke. How could I have let her get so involved in our life? I had lived though all the precipitating events that led up to this day, but this crisis had wrenched Mindy's life abruptly into frighteningly unfamiliar territory.

"I know, but Dan doesn't want you here. I'm so sorry."

Suddenly Angela's words became a warning. It would be easy for Dan to pick up the phone and call the police. I put my hand on Mindy's arm. "We can't stay if Dan doesn't want us here." I turned to Angela. "If I could just make a couple of calls..."

"There's a phone in the breakfast nook." Angela gave us a sympathetic look and went to tell Dan, who was sequestered with his kids in another part of the house.

"I'll go check on Luke," Mindy said.

The corner of Sergeant Waters' card was sticking out of the side pocket of my purse on the kitchen counter. A shiver ran through me and I tore it into small pieces and threw it in the trash. I dug out my phone book and sat down in the breakfast nook in front of the white princess phone, personalized note pad, and pen on the table. Red rooster salt and pepper shakers sat on a lacquered tray. They matched the wallpaper border in this cheery little room. How could I have let myself pretend that Mindy and Luke and I could have a normal home life like this when I knew this day might come?

Mindy came in holding two open beers and sat down across from me. She slid a cold Heineken in my direction. We looked at each other for a long moment. "Was it only this morning that you left for work and I started unpacking?" I said.

"Wonder how fast we can get all that shit back into the boxes?" Mindy asked with a weak laugh.

"Where can we go?" I asked.

Mindy snapped her fingers. "Mason!"

"Perfect." I pushed the phone in front of her and watched her punch in Mason's number. Mason also worked at Davidson Staffing. The three of us went out dancing regularly at Uncle Charlie's, our favorite gay bar, and Mason was a regular at our house on movie night. Mindy's hair fell across her high forehead as she talked. She still had on her business suit, but the hem of her pale silk blouse was hanging out from below her tan jacket. She preferred sweatpants, t-shirts, and high-top sneakers, and she usually stripped off her work clothes the minute she hit the front door.

Mindy and I favored each other in many ways. We had the same wavy dark hair and brown eyes, the same light complexion. We both had broad hips and shoulders. Sometimes people sensed an intimacy between us and guessed that we were sisters. I was twelve years older, and Mindy enjoyed teasing me about the time someone thought I was her mother.

She hung up the phone and smiled. "We can use his place. He said he'll go to his boyfriend's house."

"Great! But don't tell Angela where we're going," I cautioned.

Angela was full of apologies as we said good-bye. Once again I yanked open the heavy door of the green Plymouth. I felt as if there were eyes in the sky searching for us. Luke threw his backpack in the back seat and lay down on the front seat without being asked. I slid behind the wheel and he put his head on my leg. We followed Mindy in the direction of Mason's apartment complex on the other side of town near the Bastrop Highway.

Luke was quiet and I rested my hand on his chest as I drove. I could feel his heart beating fast. "I bet you were surprised when Mindy showed up at Zack's." I patted his chest and tried to sound normal. "What were you guys doing?"

"His mom brought us hamburgers and we were playing video games. Mindy seemed scared or something when she came in. At first I thought you were sick."

"I'm okay. We're going to Mason's apartment for a day or two. It's lucky you have all your stuff with you."

"I have my Hot Wheels and that snap-together track. Zack's mom showed me this disappearing penny trick that I've been working on."

"I was talking about your toothbrush and pajamas."

Luke and I pulled next to Mindy's Subaru in the parking lot of Mason's complex. When Mason opened his front door, his round cheeks were flushed and his big smile didn't disguise the concern in his light hazel eyes. He threw his arms around my neck. "Stay as long as you need to, honey."

I smelled spaghetti and was suddenly starving. I unpacked Luke's backpack next to the couch where Mason had laid out matching sheets and pillows for him.

"Do you wanna eat something?" I asked Luke.

"Naw." If Luke didn't want to eat, I knew he was upset.

"So how about a bath?"

Luke lined up his little cars around the edge of the deep tub and I poured some of Mason's spicy bubble bath into the stream of the warm water. I held his hand as he stepped into the bubbles and disappeared below the surface. I left him with his thoughts and returned to the kitchen.

I took a seat next to Mindy at the Formica table. Mason scooped meat sauce over golden noodles on my plate and moved a basket of garlic bread in front of me. Tina Turner was wondering what love had to do with it from the tape player in the living room.

"So, Mason, how was *your* day?" I asked. It felt good to laugh. The feeling that my head was being squeezed in a vice abated momentarily. We all turned to the food in front of us and ate in silence. I knew the first thing I said about police warrants, lawyers, or Luke's father would end the illusion that this was just another dinner in the long line of dinners we had enjoyed together. But I could feel that this life, the life that included Mason and Mindy and Luke and Anne Marie, had already started to fade like a mirage.

When we were finished, Mindy cleared the table and started working her way through the stack of dishes and pans smeared with the remains of spaghetti. Mason handed me the keys and picked up his overnight bag. "Bye, Luke," he called down the hall.

"Bye, Mason," Luke answered through the bathroom door.

I put a bowl of sliced oranges on the coffee table for Luke and locked the door behind Mason. The Tina Turner tape began again and I switched it off. Luke appeared in the doorway wrapped in a large, fluffy towel. "Mom, what's gonna happen?"

I sighed and sat on the coffee table. I picked up his pajama bottoms and held open the elastic waist and he dropped his towel, leaned on my arms and stepped into them. "Bend over and let me dry your hair."

I rubbed his head with the towel, and then pulled a bottle out of his bag, squirted coconut oil in the palm of my hand, and massaged his head. "Mmm, that smells good," I said. I pulled his pajama top over his head and smoothed the soft cotton over his stomach.

"Is my dad gonna put you in jail?"

"I don't know. But I'll be okay, even if I have to go to jail."

"Will I stay with Mindy if you go to jail?"

"No, I suppose you'll go stay with your dad."

"I can't remember what he looks like."

"You'll remember him when you see him. Don't worry."

"I love you, momma."

"I love you too, sweetie." I hugged him and led him to the couch. "Here's a snack—do you want to watch TV for a while?

"Yeah." Luke slid under the flowered comforter and picked up the remote.

I returned to the kitchen and leaned against the counter next to Mindy. I drained the last sips of my beer. "Everything in me wants to grab Luke and run out that door and drive away. I feel exactly the way I did the night I left San Francisco. There's this voice in my head that keeps saying, 'Run! Run!' I'm so scared about what will happen to him if he has to go back to Guy."

There were tears in Mindy's eyes when she turned to me. "Luke is a great kid, Anne Marie. You've done a good job with him."

"When I first ran away, I didn't know how hard it was going to be. Now I know and..." I stopped. "Mindy, I just can't do it all again." I had made my decision.

We stared at each other for a long moment. "Do you realize how lucky I've been up to now? I've had more than four years with Luke without any violence or hostility. As much as I hate the idea of that life ending, I'll never have that much luck again."

Mindy wiped her hands on the dish towel that was draped over her shoulder. "It's your decision. I'll help you no matter what you decide," she said. "We could even move to California to be near him. But for now, let's go to bed and see how things look in the morning."

Mindy went into the bathroom and I walked back into the living room. Luke was asleep, and I turned off the TV and the lamp, rearranged his arms and legs, and pulled the sheet up over him. I stood in the dark and watched him sleep. I could feel the buzz of panic in the pit of my stomach, but the rest of me felt numb.

I leaned over and put my cheek against his and felt Luke's warm breath against my face. Mindy appeared in the doorway, backlit from the light from the bedroom. She looked more comfortable in a pair of Mason's sweatpants and a big t-shirt. I kissed Luke's forehead, followed her down the hallway, and closed the bedroom door behind us.

"It's 10 o'clock. Let's check the news," I said. I hit the remote and the small TV on top of the dresser blinked to life. Mindy and I sat huddled together on the edge of the bed. After two local stories, our house appeared on the screen. My old driver's license picture was superimposed in the top corner.

"A nine year old boy, who was living in this house on Creekside Drive in south Austin, has been the object of a nationwide search since he disappeared after a bitter custody battle over four years ago. A confidential informant contacted the boy's grandmother, world-renowned author Maya Angelou, and gave her information which led police to this house. Dr. Angelou arrived in Austin this morning intending to bring her grandson back to California. But the boy's mother, Sharon Murphy, who has been living under the assumed name Anne Marie Clark, eluded police and is now at large. Authorities are asking anyone with any information on the whereabouts of this woman and her son to call the Austin Police Department at the number on your screen."

I clicked off the TV, and we sat staring at the blank screen. "I think it only seems like I could get away because we're here at

Mason's—so safe and normal. But if I tried to run, I might not even make it to the city limits." I felt like I couldn't breathe, and began to pant in short gasps.

"What do you think that meant," Mindy asked. "A confidential informant?"

I turned and looked into Mindy's face. "Did someone turn me in?" We both considered the possibility for a minute, and then Mindy put her arm around me and held me tightly.

"I don't care what they do to me, but what about Luke? He can't go back to Guy." I said. "What if Guy starts beating him again? I'd be powerless to stop him and no one else will be able to, either."

"But we might be able to get him back. Remember, you're his mom. That'll never change," Mindy said. "And whatever happens, I'll be there to help you."

I thought of everyone I knew in town seeing the news. "I guess it's time to call Carla," I said. "And Ellen and Judy need to know that we're okay. Will you go to the shelter in the morning and talk to them? The police have probably been out there, but don't tell anyone where I am. It's better if they don't have to lie." I lay back on the bed and rolled onto my side. I drew up my knees under my wrinkled sundress.

"Oh, my God! I can't believe this is happening," I said, as Mindy curled around me. "I can't believe I'm going to have to face Guy and Maya again."

Mindy stroked my hair and gave me a comforting smile. "Oooo! I get to meet a celebrity!"

CHAPTER TWELVE

WHEN I TOOK COLIN AND ran in 1981, I was only thinking about my son and my life. But without knowing it, the moment I stepped aboard that plane, I became a part of a national maelstrom. The kidnapping of 26 children in a school bus in Chowchilla, California in 1976, the disappearance of Adam Walsh in 1981, and other high-profile kidnappings around the United States trained the eyes of the nation on the issue of missing children.

One result was the establishment of the National Center for Missing and Exploited Children (NCMEC) by the United States Congress in 1984. Stories of runaway and thrown away children, stranger abductions, and parental kidnappings were collected, counted, and analyzed. The epic social changes of the 1960s and 1970s were affected by the historic rise in the national divorce rate. When the father's rights movement emerged in reaction to the feminist movement, the presumption that the mother would retain custody of her children after a divorce started becoming a thing of the past. It was as if women were being punished for challenging the patriarchal social order. By 1985, 30 states had adopted some form of joint custody legislation, unheard of up to that time.

As attitudes and legal precedents began to change, there was a sharp increase in the number of legal contests involving struggles over custody and visitation. Between 1986 and 1989, 15 percent of all divorces of couples with children entailed issues of custody and visitation, 150,000 each year.[2]

Unfortunately, the inequities women and mothers faced in the legal system were not eliminated first. In her 1986 book, *Mothers on Trial ~ The Battle for Children and Custody,* feminist activist and author Phyllis Chessler addressed this dilemma.

"The equal treatment of [legal] unequals is unjust. The paternal demand for equal custodial rights; the law that values legal paternity or male economic superiority over biological motherhood and/or maternal practice degrades and violates both mothers and children (ibid p xii)."

I was just one of thousands of mothers who flee with their children every year. In 1988, 354,100 family abductions occurred in the U.S., nearly 1,000 per day. One hundred sixty-three thousand of these cases involved the concealment of a child, transporting the child out of state, or taking a child with the intention of keeping the child permanently. (Although as a non-custodial mother, I was in the minority, as most parental kidnappings are undertaken by the non-custodial father.[3])

Of the many women I talked to at the Center for Battered Women, it was a rare few who expected the legal system to provide an equitable remedy to their situation. Even without identifying as feminists, most women instinctively understood

....

2   *National Incidence Studies of Missing, Abducted, Runaway, and Thrown Away Children, (NISMART) First Report, 1990.*

3   *National Incidence Studies of Missing, Abducted, Runaway, and Thrown Away Children, (NISMART) First Report, 1990.*

our society's cultural misogyny. Most of these women at least considered how much better their lives and the lives of their children would be if they could just run away and disappear. "But you can't just disappear," I would tell them. "You have to work and your kids have to go to school. You have to find a way to hide in plain sight." Without disclosing how I knew how impossibly difficult running away would be, I encouraged them to find another way to reorganize their lives and the lives of their children.

When I fled, I had no idea how long I would be able to successfully hide from Guy. While we were gone, almost every day I thought, "This could be the day that he finds me." I was genuinely surprised when months and then years rolled by. Of all the cases of parental kidnapping, 33 percent are resolved within the first month, 50 percent within two months, 80 percent within the first year, and 90 percent of all cases are resolved within two years.[4]

Because I was not discovered for over four years, the Sonoma County District Attorney who issued the warrant for my arrest characterized me as a person with "criminal sophistication." I'm an intelligent woman, but it wasn't my cunning or a penchant for crime that made the difference for me. I was able to hide successfully for over four years because of two major factors. One, I didn't attempt it on my own. I was helped along the way by many people—mostly women, dozens of them, beginning with my sisters who formed a network—an "underground railroad" some would say—that spirited us away. On my own, I wouldn't have made it out of California.

....

4   *National Incidence Studies of Missing, Abducted, Runaway, and Thrown Away Children, (NISMART) First Report, 1990.*

But the second factor might have been equally important. It was astounding to me, but Guy never used his mother's notoriety to try to find us. If Maya had reached out to the press with a plea for help finding her grandchild, pictures of Luke and me would have been splashed across the nightly news from California to New York until we were found. Other families of missing children use the media. That's what I would have done in their place. With national publicity, I could never have stayed hidden so long. But Guy didn't do any of the things I expected him to do. After a few fruitless attempts, he sat at home and waited for the authorities to find me.

June 4, 1985

Mindy left Mason's apartment early to go and talk to the shelter staff about what was going on. I got on the phone. My sisters didn't miss a beat when I told them I'd been found. They were preparing to get my story out to feminist and domestic violence groups in California and make a plea for donations to help pay the attorneys I needed.

By the time Mindy got through to me between my many phone calls, the word had spread and a full-scale support effort was underway. Everyone at CBW had seen the news on television and read the story in the paper. Judy was going to open a bank account for *The Sharon Murphy Legal Defense Fund* and she was drafting a fundraising letter. She already had some checks from CBW staff and volunteers.

People were writing letters to the Sonoma County District Attorney demanding that he drop the charges against me. Others offered testimonials about my character, my relationship with my son, and my work in the community. Mindy read me one letter that a volunteer dropped off at the shelter:

"Sharon Murphy is a person of integrity. If she claims that she ran away with her son because they were being physically abused, I for one choose to believe her."

But then Mindy gave me some shocking news. For years I had juggled a multitude of everyday lies. It was not difficult to imagine that some forgotten detail or misstep would lead Guy and Maya right to my doorstep. Secrecy was important, but I had confided in a few people over the years—it was hard to feel close to friends when even my name was a lie.

On my desk at the shelter, Mindy found a stack of messages from Cate, my old housemate. When Mindy called her, she found out that Cate had been Maya's 'confidential informant.' Cate had moved to Columbus, Ohio with Michael and went to hear Maya speak at the University. She approached Maya after her talk and told her where we were. She wanted to talk to me and explain her reasons for turning me in.

"I'm not talking to her! Nothing she could say would make one bit of difference," I said. "I did this to myself. I should never have trusted her."

"At least that's one question answered," Mindy said. There was silence on my end of the line, and Mindy asked, "How's Luke doing?"

"It's hard to tell. I told him we'd talk later when I knew more about what's happening. He's as cool as ever—you know how he is—takes everything in stride. He's watching TV now."

"That's because he's a great kid and he knows his mom loves him. That's why he never worries about anything. He knows you've got his back."

"I guess."

"That's a fact!" Mindy said. "Listen, I'm staying here at the shelter for a while. Later on I thought I'd go and get some of our clothes and things from the house, and I need to feed the cats."

"Oh my God! I forgot all about the cats. Please, be careful! I don't want you getting picked up. And make sure no one follows you here," I warned.

"Don't worry. I'm getting the hang of this life of crime. I'm going to park the car on the block behind our house and go in over the fence and through the backdoor."

Trusting my attorney friend was proving to be a much better decision than placing my trust in Cate. Carla jumped into action as soon as I talked to her. She lined up a criminal attorney and a family attorney in Austin, and now there was an additional criminal and family attorney in California to handle the case on that end. The attorneys would represent my interests in Family Court and work to mitigate my punishment in Criminal Court. Carla was staying involved to help me sort through everything as it was happening.

My local family attorney, Bea Ann Smith, made it clear that Luke would most likely have to leave with Maya—probably within the week. "You have no legal basis for holding onto him without custody or parental rights," she said. "We'll try to get him back as soon as we can. But right now everything depends on the direction the criminal case takes."

In California, Sam McKee, the Sonoma County District Attorney, had filed three felony charges against me: child abduction, concealment, and false imprisonment. McKee was demanding the maximum sentence—at least ten years in state prison. But that was the worst case scenario.

Bill Goodman, my criminal attorney in California, did not believe that a Sonoma County judge would give me such a lengthy prison sentence. Bill believed that a good outcome in Criminal Court depended on how persuasive we were about my reasons for the kidnapping and how successfully we demonstrated the worthiness of my character and reputation.

To distract myself from the fact that my life was spiraling out of control, I took a break from my phone call marathon to make a nice lunch for Luke and me. I heated up the leftover spaghetti and spread slices of French bread with garlic and butter and slid them under the broiler. I called Luke into the kitchen and he took a seat at the table. He began telling me the story of *The Goonies*, a movie about a gang of kids who try to follow a treasure map. I watched his dramatic expressions and exaggerated gestures. He looked so grownup now compared to the baby he'd been the night we left California. I remembered how he looked as he slept against the window of the plane with his hood tied tightly around his face.

"That sounds like the kind of thing you and Zack and Aubrey would get into," I said when he finished.

"Yeah, and I'm the leader of the gang," Luke bragged.

"Of course!" I agreed. When we finished eating lunch, I asked, "Hey, do you wanna learn a new magic trick?"

"Sure!"

I searched through Mason's drawers until I found his lunch sacks. "Okay, see how I'm holding this sack with my pointer and ring finger and pinky on the inside of the bag and my middle finger and thumb on the outside?"

Luke grabbed another bag from the drawer and wrestled it between his fingers. "Okay, now hold your middle finger back with your thumb," I instructed.

"Like this?"

"You look like you're having a seizure—lower your elbow. Okay, now watch." I reached into the empty bag with my left hand and pretended to scoop out a ball and throw it in the air. I followed it with my eyes—up to the ceiling and down. Then I flipped my middle finger against the side of the bag as if a ball had landed in the bottom of the sack.

"Cool. Do it again, Mom!"

I repeated the trick a few more times and when it looked like Luke had it, I took a Coke from the fridge and returned to the bedroom. I propped myself up on a stack of pillows on the bed, which by now was cluttered with notepads, ashtrays filled with cigarette butts, and wads of soggy Kleenex.

The afternoon sun was hiding behind heavy rain clouds, and the room was dark except for the bright beam of a small high intensity lamp. I spent the rest of the afternoon talking on the phone, asking and answering question, jotting down notes, and making lists. An onlooker would get the impression that I was facing this crisis head-on—but I was drifting. I crouched behind a wall of words trying to maintain my equilibrium. I leaned against my attorneys' professional detachment and their objective discussion of applicable penal codes and possible defense strategies. The minutia of my legal situation was much easier to think about than the direction my life was taking. I wouldn't allow myself to think about what would happen after Luke left the peaceful, supportive world I had created around both of us. Even though our time together was growing short, I avoided the living room where Luke was catching an invisible ball in a paper sack.

June 5, 1985

My first call of the day was to my attorney Bea Ann. Arrangements were being made to turn Luke over to Maya. But how? Bea Ann proposed that the transfer happen during an informal get-together. She described the alternative and it was stark: I would bring Luke with me to the hearing on the fugitive warrant. He'd see me get formally arrested, and uniformed officers would escort me away while he would be led away by a stranger from Child Services who would turn him over to Maya. Of course I preferred an informal meeting. Such an arrangement would provide Luke with a calm, peaceful atmosphere for his reunion with his grandmother, no courtrooms, and no police. He'd see his grandmother and me treating each other respectfully. Bea Ann worked out the arrangements with the Austin attorney Maya had retained.

"Maya and Guy do not want to press charges," Bea Ann told me. "She thinks they would look bad in Luke's eyes if you go to jail. Frankly, I'd be happier if she told the DA that you don't *deserve* to be incarcerated, but this is better than having them pushing for a stiff jail sentence. And their wishes *may* hold some weight with the Judge, especially considering who Maya is, but you have to remember that it's the State of California bringing the charges, not Guy and Maya. The District Attorney has his own agenda. He's been looking for you for a long time and he may want to send a message with your case. You've made his whole department look ineffective. The local police are giving you amnesty until 6 o'clock tomorrow to meet with Maya. Anne Marie, uh, can I just start calling you Sharon?"

"I suppose I should start getting used to it," I said.

"Good. Well, Sharon, the police are taking my word that after your meeting with Maya, you'll surrender at the hearing on the fugitive warrant."

"Why would I run away again if Luke is with Guy?" I asked blankly.

"To avoid going to jail," Bea Ann said.

"Oh," I said. It was hard to imagine that I would care about anything after Luke left. My vision of the future faded to black at that point. I pushed away my notebook and curled up on the bed with the phone under my cheek. "I hadn't thought about that."

"Your meeting will be at noon tomorrow at the home of Barbara Kazan, Maya's attorney," Bea Ann continued. "First, we'll talk with Maya, and then you should have someone standing by to bring Luke when you call."

I couldn't speak as I absorbed the significance of these simple instructions.

June 6, 1985

Mindy snored softly beside me but I lay awake, staring through the sheer curtain as the moon blinked from behind a bank of luminous clouds racing across the sky. How could I tell Luke that he was going back to his father today? What should I say? If he saw how desperate I felt, it might scare him; but I couldn't fake an upbeat attitude—he'd see right through that.

My mother's voice derided me. "What kind of a woman loses her own child?" I could hear her acerbic tone. "Who's the bad mother now?"

In the final analysis, my idealistic notions had made no difference. Even my most basic instincts were defective—just look at the father I gave my son, violent and arrogant. Now Guy would have Luke and I'd be in jail. Everything Mother had raised me to believe—everything I had rejected so high-handedly—had turned out to be true after all. The world was a treacherous place filled with heartbreak and loss. Would a marriage based on economics have turned out any worse than mine, which I had imagined was based on loftier ideals?

My son had never challenged my reasons for running away—he had trusted me entirely. But he was so young when we left San Francisco that our secret became just a part of life. What would he think of my actions when he got to know his father again? How would he look back on this time when he was an adult? Would Guy and Maya be able to convince him that I had kept him away from them for no reason; that I acted out of spite, or worse, because I was crazy? Could Guy poison him against me like so many custodial fathers tried to do? Now Maya and Guy would probably finish what Guy alone had tried before. They would close ranks around my son and I would be shut out entirely. My only hope was that Luke wouldn't let that happen. But maybe that was too much to expect from a child.

Maya had been a part of the fantasy of what I thought my life with Guy would be—the enlightened husband, the loving, creative mother-in-law. How blinded I had been by my own longing. I dreaded the prospect of sitting across a table from her. No matter how magnanimous and high-minded she pretended to be, I knew she hated me now, if she ever really cared for me. She was not the kind of woman to forgive someone who had crossed her.

After breakfast, Mindy retreated to the bedroom and I sat on the couch in my robe and drank a second cup of coffee. Luke came in wearing his blue swimming trunks and a striped t-shirt, a hint that he could be persuaded to go swimming at Zilker Park today. Could it be only two days ago that he and Zack spent the day at Barton Springs? He flopped down next to me and I put my arms around him and laid my cheek on the top of his head, our familiar embrace. I took a deep breath and plunged forward. "Luke, your grandmother is here in Austin. She's going to take you to your Dad," I said. I had wanted to be honest, but stopped short of saying, "take you to live with your Dad."

He sat up. "When? Today?"

"Yes, later on this afternoon. I don't know all the details. The only thing I know for sure is that you'll leave with her this afternoon."

Luke's big brown eyes searched my face, as if looking for a clue about how to react. I smiled at him, and he smiled back. "Where does my Dad live?" he asked.

"He's in California—I think he's still in Sonoma County."

Luke slid onto the floor and began running his Hot Wheels over the brim of his Luke Skywalker cap. His voice softened and he didn't look at me. "When will I see you again?"

I didn't trust myself to speak. I wanted to tell him that I was only kidding. Our life wasn't going to change. We were going to pick up Zack and Aubrey, spend the day at the pool, and then have a sleepover. But I couldn't start lying to him now.

"It might be a while," I said finally. "I'll come and visit you in California as soon as I can."

He turned around and rested his chin on his folded arms. "Are you going to go to jail, Momma?"

My stomach tightened. "Maybe...probably. But you don't need to worry about that. I have a lot of people helping me."

He dropped his gaze and began running his little car across the couch cushion and up onto my lap. "Is my Dad going to be mad at me for running away?"

I pulled him up next to me. "Baby! No, your Dad won't be mad at you. He knows running away was my idea. Once he sees you, he's going to be so happy. He won't be mad about anything."

I smoothed Luke's dark bushy eyebrows with my finger and he responded with a grin and rubbed them until they were a tangled mess again—it was a silly game we played.

"Does my Dad live with anybody?" His tone sounded a bit lighter, shaded with more curiosity than fear.

"Luke, you'll find out all these things when you get to his house. Then you can call me and tell me everything. Okay?"

"Okay," he said.

"Luke, you know I'll always be your mother, no matter what."

"I know that!" he said, rolling his big brown eyes.

"Are you okay?" I asked.

"I'm kinda scared," he said.

"Me too, honey," I said. "Everyone feels afraid when there's a big change. At first, we don't know what to expect and we imagine all sorts of things. But then we get used to the new stuff, and we're not afraid anymore. I always told you that you would see your Dad again someday. Now that day is here. Aren't you sort of excited?"

"I guess," he shrugged his shoulders and bounced my hand up and down in his palm—his big boy way of holding it.

"Just remember that no matter where you are, I'll always be with you—even when you're a grown man." I put my hand on the center of his chest. "I'm always right here. Can you feel it? Can you feel how much I love you?"

"Sure, Momma." He put his hand in the center of my chest. "And I'm always with you!"

I couldn't speak without crying. I didn't know when I'd have another moment like this so I put my arms around him and closed my eyes. I wanted to remember every sensation. Luke didn't pull away and we swayed back and forth with our arms around each other.

An hour later, I was ready to leave for my meeting with Maya. Mindy would be standing by to bring Luke when I called. It was all I could do to keep from breaking down when I hugged them both goodbye at the door of Mason's apartment. I hurriedly put on my dark glasses and walked towards the car. As if scripted for a movie, dark clouds crowded the sky.

Just before noon, I pulled up in front of the house of Maya's attorney, but I don't remember driving to the address that was underlined several times on my notepad. I felt myself come awake hopping over the puddles on the wide walkway. A thick rope of ivy climbed up the front of the brick house, partially covering the shuttered windows before the vines separated and spread out over the peaked roof. The door stood slightly ajar, so I hugged my shoulder bag to my chest and stepped inside, knocking lightly on the doorjamb.

The living room was filled with shadows, but the dining room on the far side was brightly lit by four brass wall sconces. I saw Carla standing in the corner of the room talking with two women in business suits—but my gaze was pulled elsewhere. Maya sat at the dining room table in front of a hutch filled with crystal stemware and china.

All at once, everything became very real. This was really happening. Maya was really here. She wore dark slacks and a long-sleeved light blue blouse and she had a straw newsboy cap pulled low across her brow. Even though I was wearing jeans and a cotton sweater, I was surprised that she was so casually dressed. I was also surprised to see the evident strain on her face, along with dark circles under her eyes. She had aged quite a bit since I last saw her. I read somewhere that she and Paul had divorced. I quickly calculated the years—she must be 57 now. Maya's lips were pressed together tightly. This was difficult for her, too, I thought.

Maya splayed her long fingers on the table's surface and half stood and then sat back down. "Hello, Sharon," she said. "You look well."

I tried to remember how I had looked the last time I saw Maya. My hair was shorter now and I was a bit heavier. But even though the best part was grinding to a halt, the life I created as Anne Marie had been happier and more satisfying than Sharon Murphy's life had been at the time I made the decision to run away. I straightened my shoulders and walked towards her.

"Hello, Maya." I wanted my voice to sound strong and clear, but the old prohibition against using her first name zipped absurdly through my mind. I was unsettled—the time between then and now bending and contracting. I coughed to choke back an automatic apology and turned away to regain my bearings.

Carla gave me a sympathetic smile. She covered the distance between us and slipped her arm around my waist. "Bea Ann, this is Sharon Murphy," she said. The shorter of the two attorneys smiled and came towards me.

I had spoken to Bea Ann on the phone many times in the last two days, but this was the first time I'd seen her in person. She had warm hazel eyes and a smooth cap of thick dark hair. She patted my shoulder reassuringly, seeming more like a kindergarten teacher than a lawyer.

Barbara Kazan, Maya's attorney, was almost as tall as Maya and her severe black suit accentuated her broad shoulders.

Barbara and I shook hands and I took a seat at the head of the table to Maya's left. The others remained standing and Barbara addressed us. "Now that everyone's here, we will retire to the kitchen and let you two have a private chat."

I didn't want to be left alone with Maya. I had been counting on their presence to dilute the tension. But then I noticed the expression on their faces—that familiar adoring attitude that people adopted around Maya. Carla glanced at me and hesitated, but then followed the others. The swinging door settled into place without a sound. This must have been Maya's idea, I thought.

Her deep voice broke the silence. "Sharon, while we have these few moments together, I need you to hear me." When I turned to face Maya, her smile had melted and her expression was icy. But I had met the person behind the gracious public personality before, so the cold look was not unfamiliar.

"Hear me and understand this, Sharon, if you do anything to interfere with our custody of Colin, I cannot be held responsible for what might be unleashed on you and your family."

So this is why she wanted a private chat, I thought, she wants to scare me with no witnesses. I leaned forward and looked her in the eyes. "Well, as long as we're speaking frankly, I want *you* to understand that I ran with my son because Guy was scaring and brutalizing him—a 6'5 man using his belt on his four-year-old son! I saw the bruises and Colin told me how he got them. And Guy beat me and was trying to force me out of Colin's life."

I tapped my finger on the table in front of her. "Your son beat us. Do you hear me?" But my bravado was no match for Maya's steady gaze. I started to ramble, trying to justify myself. Then I forced myself to stop. What did I want her to say anyway? Did I want her to agree with me? Tell me I did the right thing?

Maya looked at me impassively. I had no idea what she was thinking. We had been close once. Was she thinking about that as I was? Then she dropped her gaze. When she spoke again, her tone had changed. Her voice was soft and tinged with sadness. "My son is in no condition to use his hands at all now, Sharon."

She looked up at me. "You know that Guy broke his neck in a car accident when he was very young. It was before you two met, but you must remember—he had a spinal fusion in his neck."

I was startled by the abrupt segue. "Yes, of course." I thought of the long keloid scar across Guy's hip and the one that snaked up the back of his head.

"A year or so ago Guy had surgery to remove some calcification that was causing pressure on the nerves." Maya rested her fingertips on the back of her neck. "During the operation, he became paralyzed."

She moved her hand to my arm and I flinched at her touch. Her eyes brimmed with tears, and she looked at me as if we were once again intimates. "His doctors say that he might never walk again. But, you know Guy. He is not one to give up. He's struggling to walk, even though it's agony for him."

Maya shook her head at the thought. "I had rails installed all through his house to help him. But, Sharon, he's in no shape to care for a young child. Colin is going to live with me in North Carolina. I have a wonderful home in Winston-Salem and a bedroom I decorated just for him."

I slumped back in my chair—this was too much to take in. What did this mean? If Colin lived with Maya instead of Guy, at least he'd be safe. She might be overbearing, but I couldn't imagine that she'd ever hit him. She'd probably hire a nanny to take care of him anyway. I might have a better chance of getting him back if he was under the care of paid staff.

Then I thought about Guy and felt a surprising sense of regret. He was only about twenty when he broke his neck in a car accident. He was living in Africa, and was parked on the side of a road looking at a map when the driver of an oncoming truck lost control and slammed into his car. Guy had recovered slowly, but becoming paralyzed had become his worst nightmare. Then my reverie hit a snag. If Guy was really paralyzed, how could he learn to walk again? I must not have understood her, I thought.

Before I could do more to process this turn of events, the door to the kitchen swung open and the others rejoined us. The attorneys took their seats and pulled folders out of their briefcases. Carla was smiling when she brought in a coffee tray. I accepted a cup and took a small sip, breathing in the warm steam.

Carla seemed excited about something and gave me a small wink.

"Did you have enough time to talk?" Barbara asked.

Maya smiled broadly. "We had a wonderful chat."

I said nothing. I didn't know what to feel. Were we allies or were we enemies? I was still playing catch-up, but it appeared that Barbara Kazan had briefed Carla and Bea Ann while they were in the kitchen.

Everyone was talking at once and the scene felt hectic until Barbara once again took control of the conversation. "Sharon, would you mind helping Dr. Angelou become re-acquainted with Colin? I'll just run down this list of questions. All right?"

While I answered her questions, I pretended that I was just talking about my son the way I often did—bragging really. I tried to remember to say 'Colin,' but 'Luke' kept popping out.

I talked about how he loved scary movies, soccer, and magic tricks. I told them what a silly sense of humor he had—how he liked things like opposite day and knock-knock jokes. I talked about how much he loved his cat and his friends Zack and Aubrey and how sensitive he was to their feelings.

I didn't mention how he sometimes came into my bedroom in the morning to snuggle under the covers and tell me about his dreams. How long would it be before we could do that again, I wondered? I selfishly didn't want anyone else to have that kind of special time with him.

"He likes school and he's very popular—with the kids *and* the teachers," I said. "He's very bright and curious, but he has some difficulty with reading. He's in a special reading group and we see a counselor once a month to help him focus on his schoolwork. He's got a lot of energy—he'd rather be out on his bike or climbing trees than studying his multiplication tables. I guess we both have a problem sitting still."

"I'll hire a tutor to work with him this summer before he starts school," Maya said. "And I think some family counseling would ease the transition to his new living situation. Why don't you give me the number of the counselor he's seeing? I'll talk to him before we leave." I tore a sheet out of my notebook and wrote down the phone number and Maya took a piece of paper from her attorney and wrote out a list of phone numbers and addresses.

I was reeling. This was not the scene I had expected. Maya interjected memories she had of Colin—how he had loved the red car she drove then. There was even some laughter about the alternating names—Colin and Luke. Then Barbara surprised me again. She squared her shoulders and explained that once Colin was settled at Maya's, I would have unlimited visitation with him at her home.

"You'll come and celebrate Thanksgiving with us," Maya said. "We're all still family, you know."

I could hardly believe what I was hearing. Barbara handed around copies of a legal agreement that had been prepared in advance of the meeting. I read every word carefully. Down in black and white were the guidelines for my unlimited visits, the invitation to spend Thanksgiving at Maya's, and the possibility of a Christmas visit. I would regain my parental rights.

Guy and Maya agreed to drop all criminal charges against me, and after a year, "if an atmosphere of trust was created," I could request unsupervised visits. On the third page was a place for our signatures—mine, and Guy's, and Maya's, and that of the presiding judge.

Maya was agreeable, almost enthusiastic, when Carla offered to drive me to North Carolina the following week to bring Colin's cat, Pearl, his mini-bike, and some of his favorite toys and pictures so his new bedroom would feel more familiar. "Remember that poster you gave him, The Banjo Lesson?" I said. "It's still one of his favorite possessions."

"Oh, yes. Bring that," Maya said.

Barbara was speaking to me. "Sharon?"

"Sorry, what?"

"If you would just sign—right there above your name." She leaned towards me and handed me a pen. I signed. "Now if you would have Colin brought over."

This was it. We could talk about the particulars all day, but my little boy was leaving me. I went to the phone on a small desk under the window. My hands were shaking and I had to dial the number twice.

"It's time," I said, when Mindy answered.

"I'll be there in five minutes." She managed to express all her sympathy in those few words. "But I think it'll be too much to go in with him. Can I just let him out at the curb?"

"That's fine. Just honk when you get here." All eyes were on me when I returned to the table. "He's on his way." Maya clapped her hands and leaned back in her chair. She tucked her hands under her chin and closed her eyes as if in prayer.

I jumped when I heard Mindy honk. A moment later, Luke strolled through the open front door with his backpack on his shoulder. He was wearing his Tulsa Oilers jersey and he walked across the living room as if he owned the place. I was on the verge of tears, but I smiled with pride at his confidence and poise. He was one terrific nine-year-old.

He tossed me a quick, "Hi, Momma." Then he scanned the room and broke out in a grin. "Hi, Grandma!" Maya rose from her chair and Luke hurried over and stood between us next to the dining table.

"Hello, my beauty," Maya said. "It's *so* good to see you." She leaned over and put her hand on his shoulder. "You certainly are a fine young man." She nodded to me in a gesture of acknowledgment.

The brim of Maya's newsboy cap almost completely shaded her eyes and Luke reached up and lifted it off of her head. Her graying hair snapped to attention. Luke laughed. "You look like that boxing guy. What's his name? Oh yeah, Don King."

Maya seemed nonplussed and patted her hair back in place as the rest of us suppressed smiles. She retrieved her cap and sat down. Unfazed, Luke continued, "Do you wanna see a magic trick, Grandma?"

"Your mother told me that you were a great magician."

"I can make a penny disappear!" He dropped his backpack on the floor and dug in his pocket for his props. He pulled out a small green box and dramatically brandished a shiny penny in the air.

"I know it may seem impossible, but watch closely," he said. "I will put this penny into this magic box." He opened a small drawer, snapped the penny into the slot, and slid the drawer closed. He waved his other hand in the air to distract his audience and smoothly flipped the box over. Then he rested the box in the palm of his hand and extended it towards Maya. "Would you please blow on the box, madam?"

She obliged with an audible puff of breath. "Thank you. Now watch closely. Abracadabra!"

He waved his hand over the box, then arched his fingers and slowly slid the drawer open. "Voila!" The round slot was empty. Everyone cheered and he bowed from the waist.

"Very good, Colin," Maya said.

"Whoa!" He looked back at me. "She called me Colin."

I wrapped my arms around him and leaned my forehead against his shoulder. "You'll get used to it," I whispered.

"Do you want to talk to your father?" Maya said. "Let's give him a call."

Maya walked to the phone and dialed, and then she fluttered her hand in our direction. "Yes, son, he's right here." Colin went to stand next to her. Maya stroked his bright copper hair and rested her hand on his head.

"Yes, I have my hand on him right now. Say hello, Colin."

He reached for the receiver. "Hi, Dad?" His voice rose as in a question. I couldn't hear Guy's side of the conversation, only the familiar rumble of his deep voice through the phone. Colin nodded and said, "Yeah. I'm doing good. I showed Grandma a magic trick."

He held up the little box as if Guy could see it. Colin was only an arm's length away, but I could feel the heavy distance growing between us. Colin looked the way he usually looked—happy, even excited. "Bye, Dad," he said. "See ya."

As soon as he dropped the receiver back into the cradle, Maya returned to the table and began gathering her things. And as if on cue, everyone followed suit, picking up papers and pens, snapping briefcases closed, shaking hands.

My vision blurred and the noise in the room became distant and muffled—as if I was under water. I stood and leaned against the edge of the table. No one met my eye. Colin shouldered his backpack. "Bye-bye, Momma." I tried to take a step, but my legs and feet were heavy—I could just barely raise my hand.

Maya tugged on Colin's arm and they walked through the front door and down the wet brick pathway to the street. A dark limo and driver waited at the curb. I watched through the open door as they moved away from me—a tall black woman in a straw cap and a small red-headed boy.

Bea Ann's voice brought me back to the darkened living room. She was holding up the agreement I had signed. "She left without signing this." Barbara looked across the table at her and made no response. Bea Ann just shook her head slightly and slipped the document inside her briefcase. I looked out in time to see the limousine drive away.

It was 2:30 when I walked out of Barbara Kazan's house and saw Mindy waiting at the curb in her Subaru. What now? I could be arrested when the police amnesty expired at 6 o'clock. I didn't want to risk it by going home. But I wanted to give Mason his apartment back.

Mindy had anticipated this. She'd packed up all our things and made a hotel reservation. I followed her and we checked into the Marriott near downtown. Mindy went to get Chinese takeout and I took the elevator up to the room, feeling like a sleepwalker. An hour later, Mindy backed into the room carrying an armful of white bags. She flipped the *Austin American Statesman* onto the gold bedspread.

Above a large picture of Maya and Colin, the headline read, *Nationwide Search Ends in Austin.* One sentence jumped out at me. "Author Maya Angelou plans to reunite the child with his father."

I had been duped. Maya's failure to sign the agreement had not been an oversight. In fact, the entire conversation with her had been a charade. There would be no visits to her home, no participating in family celebrations at Thanksgiving, no parental rights restored. The DA wasn't dropping the criminal charges. Instead, after a quick newspaper interview, Maya and Colin flew to San Francisco, where Guy walked up, with no apparent sign of paralysis, and took Colin's hand. Then Maya left on a plane headed for her home in North Carolina.

I'll never know why Maya went through such an elaborate hoax. Why the complicated deception? I'd lost my advantage the moment I walked into Barbara Kazan's house. If I had resisted producing Colin, one quick call to the police would have landed me in jail. Maya had all the power, and all the cards. She could have sat mute at our meeting or railed against me. She still would have walked out of the door with my son.

If I were to guess at her motive, I would say that Maya wanted to fan an ember of false hope, and then deliver her own eye-for-an-eye rebuke—a personal reprisal for the pain I caused her and her son. I understood the impulse. Regardless of how compelling my reasons were for running away, my own complicated deception had caused Guy and Maya four years of anguish and four irreplaceable years of Colin's childhood.

The agreement was never mentioned again.

CHAPTER THIRTEEN

BEING WITH MY SON HAD made the difficulties of life on the run bearable. Now I opened my eyes in the morning, and was flooded afresh with the knowledge that my heart was gone. I felt as if my relationship with him was lost forever. I had to force myself to get out of bed every morning and ached and felt tired all day, every day. I began to believe that one could die of anxiety and grief.

At the hearing on the fugitive warrant, the Austin judge released me on my own recognizance. When that was behind me, the Sonoma County Superior Court set August 2, 1985 for the first hearing on the three criminal charges. Margaret Anderson, my California family law attorney, would try to arrange a visit for Colin and me while I was in California for the hearing. With criminal charges hanging over me and without any parental rights, she could not predict if or for how long I would be able to see him.

As the calendar crept towards August and my first hope of seeing Colin, I went back to work at CBW. But I had lost my objectivity. I related to the clients as "fellow victims," the antithesis of CBW's feminist philosophy of female empowerment and taking responsibility for your life. Judy, usually so approving, reprimanded me for things I said in my support groups. I could appreciate the power that feminism affirmed, but I could not embody it. All I felt was grief.

Then Margaret called to tell me that she could not get in touch with Guy. When Maya gave me the list of phone numbers and addresses, I hadn't noticed that the only contact information for Guy was his office number, no home address, no home phone number. We did not have the name of the attorney who was representing Guy, and there was no response to the messages Margaret left at Guy's office or with Maya's secretary. I was terrified not knowing where Colin was and the irony of this was not lost on me.

It was not until late July that Guy's new attorney, Peggy Schmeck, made contact with Margaret and the legal wrangling began. Guy and Colin were on an extended trip on the East Coast. She wouldn't say when they would return. Guy would not agree to a visit in August even though Margaret offered to supervise a short visit in her office in Petaluma. "Guy can sit in my waiting room if he wants to," she said.

But Schmeck declined. "Guy feels more comfortable letting a judge make the decision about what's best in this situation," she said.

"These two people have to learn to talk to one another at some point," Margaret said. "These issues can be settled without a hearing. Don't you think this family has been in enough courtrooms?"

Schmeck was not moved. "Guy is the victim in this case. Sharon deprived him of his son for over four years. You can't expect him to be sympathetic to her now," she said. "It's your client who is inflaming the situation by claiming to be a victim of domestic violence. You need to get her under control. Guy will *only* allow Sharon to see Colin if she doesn't make the case a big publicity matter designed to tear down his reputation."

Margaret was angry when she told me about their conversation. "So much for the best interests of the child—protecting Guy's reputation seems to be Peggy Schmeck's top priority."

I was in a box. If I defended my actions by explaining my reasons for running away with Colin, Guy would say that I was trying to slander him. But if I didn't, I would certainly go to jail for a long time.

"Guy won't cooperate no matter what I do." I said. "He's using Colin as bait to keep me from talking about what he did. Remember, Guy knows that I'm telling the truth, and I'm not going to slink around pretending I don't know what he's doing."

Both of my attorneys agreed. We continued with our defense strategy unaltered.

I had to accept that I would not see Colin when I was in California in August, but Guy did permit a phone call once a week. I was prepared to stay on harmless subjects, knowing that Guy would be within earshot. I just wanted to hear Colin's voice and let him know I was still there. His voice sounded small and strained during our first conversation. I asked him about the trip he and Guy had taken. "I bet that was exciting," I said. "Did you go on a lot of plane rides?"

Colin told me about the cousins and friends of Guy he'd met. When they ended their trip in North Carolina, his grandmother had thrown a big party in his honor. "I didn't know anyone at the party, but people said they knew you. I got a lot of presents, new clothes, and stuff."

"That sounds great." My tone rang false and I took a breath. "I miss you, baby. I'm trying to arrange for us to have a visit."

"In Austin?" Colin said.

"No, honey, not here. I'll come to see you there—in California," I said.

"I want to go to Austin. I want to see Mindy, and Zack, 'n Aubrey."

I heard Guy's voice in the background. "Come on, son. It's time to hang up the phone."

Colin turned defiant. "I'm not done talking to my mom."

"Watch your tone, young man."

"It's okay, Colin. We'll talk again soon." But the line had gone silent.

My California criminal attorney was concerned about how the Sonoma County DA was handling my case. Because of Maya's notoriety and the length of time I was gone, my case was getting more than the usual amount of attention. Sam McKee intended to prosecute me vigorously on all three felony charges. He hoped that the severity of my punishment would be a cautionary tale for other mothers without custody who might contemplate kidnapping their kids. If McKee had his way, I'd serve ten years in the state penitentiary. He was not open to compromise.

In August, I flew to California to surrender on the criminal charges filed against me. Mindy stayed in Austin, but Judy, Ellen, and other staff members from the shelter came with me. To my relief, when Judge Guynup reviewed my letters of support and Bill introduced the CBW staff who were there and prepared to testify on my behalf, the judge released me on my own recognizance. The criminal trial would be scheduled within six months.

Now it was time to surrender on the Contempt of Court charges. In the courthouse bathroom, I changed out of my suit and into jeans and tennis shoes. I re-packed a small tote bag with books, tablets, cigarettes, and a few essentials and handed my suitcase over to Judy. My friends took off for the airport to return to Austin. I said goodbye to Bill and took the elevator upstairs to meet Margaret Anderson.

In 1981, when Guy first realized that I had disappeared with Colin, his attorney filed a motion to hold me in contempt of the custody order. When I didn't respond to the subpoena or relinquish Colin, the judge sentenced me to ten days in jail and issued a bench warrant for my arrest. That jail term had been waiting for me ever since. Today, the Court would serve that warrant and I would begin my jail sentence for violating the custody order.

Margaret entered her appearance and announced that I was prepared to surrender. After only twenty-five minutes, it was over. A deputy stepped forward and led me out of the court-room and through a labyrinth of hallways to the county jail be-hind the courthouse. Soon I was riding up the elevator to the women's unit of the Sonoma County jail with only one yellow tablet that I had grabbed when my well-stocked tote bag was confiscated.

A female officer led me silently down a hallway. She un-locked a heavy door and pointed inside. "Take a shower and stack your clothes on that chair. I'll bring you your supplies." I did what I was told. When I was finished and pulled back the thin curtain, in the spot where my clothes had been was a pink inventory slip for my personal items. All that was left was my underwear and bra, an orange jump suit, a pair of wool socks, and two thin white towels that had the texture of a Brillo pad. A brown paper sack on top of the pile contained a small, pungent bar of Cashmere Bouquet, a black comb with teeth as sharp as needles, a book of matches, a pack of Zig Zag rolling papers, and some Bugler tobacco.

Dressed in my jail clothes and in my stocking feet—for some reason, I wasn't given a pair of shoes—I followed behind the correctional officer, clutching my tablet to my chest. I spotted a pile of books on the end of a bench and snagged a thick paperback. Reading and writing would be the staples of life. Now I just needed a pen. I stood on the broken tapeline in front of the door to my cell. Women's silent faces appeared behind the small windows in the cell doors on either side. The guard walked to the end of the row, opened a metal panel on the wall, and flipped a switch. The door in front of me slid open.

I heard, "Step in." I stepped across the threshold into the narrow cell. I had been numb since arriving at the jail, but when I heard the door lock behind me, I felt my bones melting.

My cell was exactly what you would expect. It looked just like a jail cell in a movie: a cot attached to the wall, a metal toilet, and a sink with a metal plate screwed into the wall in an imitation of a mirror. The ceiling was very high, about twelve feet, with a single light bulb behind a metal grill that gave my new living accommodations a ghastly pallor. The hall lights dimmed at night, but the light in the ceiling was always on.

During inspection (around midnight that first day), I asked the guard if I could get something to write with and a pair of shoes. The guard returned a few minutes later and shoved a copy of the *Santa Rosa Press Democrat* and a pen through the slot—but no shoes. My face was on the front page under the caption, "Mother Begins Jail Term." I asked each officer passing my cell if I could get a pair of shoes, and each one said "Sure," even though they never got them for me. Of all the uncomfortable feelings I had during my time in the Sonoma County jail, having no shoes bothered me inordinately. I had felt so much for so long, it was a relief to focus all my anger on this one small indignity.

I spent my time in my narrow cell smoking perfectly rolled cigarettes and reading *August* by Judith Rossner as slowly as I could. I was grateful that the book I grabbed hadn't turned out to be some Barbara Cartland romance novel. I alternated my activities between reading my allotted pages for the day (the book had 557 pages), writing angry, maudlin diatribes on my tablet, and drawing pictures of my cell, my hand, and my feet. I dozed off and on all around the clock, but remained in a sleepy fog day after day.

On the tenth day, shortly after lunch, the toe of my white tennis shoe poked through the slot in the door and my street clothes followed. "Time to go, Murphy!" My lethargy disappeared and I was instantly full of energy. I had made it—I was being released! My one disappointment was that I would have to leave the state without seeing Colin.

A few hours later, a friend picked me up in front of the county jail and drove me to the San Francisco airport. Within minutes, I was boarding a plane heading back to Austin.

With my punishment for violating the custody order behind me, Margaret Anderson focused on re-establishing my parental and visitation rights. After traveling to California for a meeting with Guy and Mike Lentz, who was unfortunately still the mediator on our case, and then again for a hearing to receive the judge's order, I finally had the terms for visitation down in black and white. I was grateful that the process was moving in the right direction, but the conditions for my visits were far from ideal.

At Guy's convenience and with two weeks' notice, I could request a visit for no longer than two hours. But Mac Scott, a private detective and retired police officer, would have to supervise each visit. Adding to the indignity, the location of the visit would not be disclosed to me in advance. The detective charged $35 dollars per hour and $.35 per mile, which I was required to pay. After clearing the date with Guy's attorney and making the appointment with the detective, I would meet Mac at a location of his choice. The detective would then drive me to the site of the visit and Guy would drop off Colin and pick him up two hours later.

I saw Colin for the first time in late September. I met Mac at Lyon's Restaurant near the Sonoma County Administration building, the scene of some epic moments of my life had been set, including my marriage ceremony and my ten-day jail sentence. I left my rental car in the parking lot and Mac drove me to a nearby park. I sat at a picnic table waiting, scanning the park, almost holding my breath in anticipation of finally seeing Colin. Mac stood quietly behind me. Finally, Colin burst through the trees, waving both arms eagerly in the air. He exploded into my embrace. "Hi, Momma!"

I didn't recognize the blue polo shirt he was wearing or the expensive leather tennis shoes. He felt bigger in my arms and his hair smelled different. But his voice sounded beautiful to my ears, and the knot in my chest loosened. When Colin and I released each other, Mac stepped up and guided him to the other side of the table.

"Did your dad explain about Mac?" I asked.

"Yeah," he said with a surly tone. "He's afraid we'll run away again."

"Wanna make a run for it?" I laughed and pretended to jump to my feet.

Colin grinned and I saw him relax.

"You look so big," I said. "How do you like your new school?"

After some prodding to get a better answer than, "Fine," or, "Okay," Colin told me about a fight he'd had with one of the biggest kids in the class just after school started. "I'm stronger than he is, but he's taller. I knocked him down and he started crying. My dad had to go talk to the principal." Colin was picking at his cuticle and didn't look me in the eye.

"What happened then?" I asked.

"My dad said I shouldn't let anyone push me around." His eyes darted up at my face. I bit back my standard lecture about settling things with your words and not your fists. Colin had heard it before and I didn't want to contradict Guy with Mac within earshot.

"It's real different here than it is in Austin, Mom. If I don't learn to stick up for myself, these kids will never leave me alone."

"It's okay, sweetie. I know you'll do the right thing." I sounded unconvincing to myself, but what else could I say? I could see the conflict in Colin's eyes, and couldn't add more.

We couldn't do the things we would normally do in a park. We couldn't take a walk or play catch or soccer—Mac had to be near both of us and hear everything we said. When Colin had to go to the bathroom, Mac took him, disregarding his protestations that he was old enough to go by himself. Even under ordinary conditions, it's difficult to sit on opposite sides of a picnic table trying to chat with a child, and the presence of the detective checked the flow of our customary jokes and private conversation. Though I had longed to see Colin, the artificial circumstances and sentiments began to take a toll. Despite our best efforts, our conversation became stilted.

After two hours, a black SUV pulled into the parking lot beyond a stand of trees. Guy got out and leaned against his car. I could only see him in silhouette, but I felt the old foreboding and fear. "It's time," Mac said. I hugged Colin goodbye and he walked away.

The life Colin and I had together only existed in the past and quickly our visits became sessions of reminiscing. "Remember when Zack and I built that tree house?" I didn't know which was more painful, the weeks and months of being away from Colin, or watching us become unfamiliar with each other. Nevertheless, the old spark still broke through sometimes. On one visit, Colin was chuckling to himself when he ran up to me. He pulled my head down and put his mouth next to my ear. Mac took a step closer to hear. "My dad asked me if I ever saw lesbians with guns when I lived with you in Austin." Even Mac had to laugh.

Guy stopped monitoring Colin's phone calls to me and we used the time to share the details of our lives—the funny things the cat did and the good plays Colin made on the soccer field. During one call, Colin said, "My dad says he loves me, but he acts like he hates me. He says that you pampered me—that I'm soft."

"Do you think I pampered you?"

"It's not like I never got in trouble. You just never hit me."

"Some people think it's okay to hit children," I said. "But I think it's wrong."

"He thinks I'm stupid, too."

"I'm certain he does not think you're stupid. No one could ever think you're stupid."

"Dad makes fun of my reading group in Mrs. Mitchell's class." Colin pitched his voice low mimicking Guy's deep voice. "'No son of mine is going to be in a remedial reading class.' Mom, he doesn't care about me at all."

I didn't want to tell him that his feelings were wrong by defending Guy. I didn't want him to learn that someone could love you and still make you feel bad about yourself. That lesson could set him up for all sorts of problems. I'd spent my childhood searching for evidence that my mother really loved me.

"Colin, don't worry about how your father feels. Go to school. Enjoy your friends and your soccer team. Everything is still new—for your dad and for you. Things won't always feel like this. You'll see. Remember that everything changes."

Colin and I celebrated Christmas at a corner booth in the dining room of the El Rancho Hotel in Santa Rosa, with the detective reading a paperback in the next booth. We played a few rounds of Jenga and I read to him from one of his new books. Fortunately, Colin was so distracted by the stack of brightly wrapped gifts that he didn't notice the tears brimming in my eyes. I tried to make it festive. I brought a little decorated tree and a red tablecloth, but this wasn't Christmas.

In January, I paid for an additional guard and Mindy came with me for a visit with Colin. (We assumed the second guard was to prevent Mindy and me from overpowering Mac, who was over six feet tall and weighed at least three hundred pounds.)

*Mindy visits with Luke under the supervision of armed
detectives, Santa Rosa, CA 1986*

Colin and I got used to Mac's presence over time, and Mac's
loyalties shifted once he became familiar with both Guy and
me. Now he took walks with us, and Colin and I helped him
inspect the trees for hidden lesbians with guns who might be
lurking in the branches waiting to pounce. One rainy day, Mac
even brought us back to his house, where we spent a couple of
hours watching a movie and eating popcorn in his living room.
But as friendly as we might have been, I still had to pay for every minute of Mac's time.

Maya's money, reputation, and clout had always worked
in Guy's favor. If I was going to defend myself and normalize

my relationship with my son, I needed some clout of my own. Judy mailed fundraising letters to everyone on our growing mailing list. Marilyn chronicled the history of my case in an article titled "A Small Injustice." The *Lesbian News* in Los Angeles and *Off Our Backs* in Boston and other feminist and domestic violence newsletters ran regular updates on the developments in my case. I was invited to speak to Women's Studies classes at area colleges, and I was interviewed by newspaper and radio reporters. I spoke on a panel at *Women Speak Out*, a feminist conference in New York on women and custody issues.

The *Austin American Statesman* ran an article by Joe Vargo entitled "Child Kidnap Suspect Hailed Despite Life as Fugitive."

"To her friends and co-workers at the Austin Center for Battered Women, Murphy was an outstanding counselor who helped abused wives get away from husbands and start new lives. But to law officers in Texas and California, Murphy was a fugitive living under an assumed name. Staff said they knew her as a devoted mother who was never too busy to make popcorn and invite her nine-year-old son's friends over to watch movies. 'She's one of the best counselors we've ever had,' said Judy Reeves, Murphy's supervisor. 'She has compassion and empathy for the residents. She's endeared herself to all the staff and residents. Everybody here loves her.'

"The child, Colin Ashanti Murphy-Johnson, was the object of a nationwide search after Murphy lost custody after a protracted three year battle."

A Texas songwriter, Ruth Huber, heard about my story and felt compelled to help. She composed a song entitled "No More Hiding."

"For Colin and Sharon, for Luke and Anne Marie, there'll be no more hiding, no more break between who you are and who you pretend to be."

She played our song at music festivals and at gigs around the state, and then she passed the hat for donations and mailed the money to my legal fund. Donations big and small poured in. I received letters of encouragement and letters that included heartbreaking stories from other women who had struggled to hold onto their children and lost.

One woman returned our postage-paid envelope with $.65 taped to the page. She wrote her story on the bottom of our letter. She had lost her son to her attorney ex-husband. "No one cared that I had stayed home with my son for seven years while my husband got his degree. I passed up my chance to go to college. And now with all the horrible things his father told him about me, my boy doesn't want to see me at all. I hope you are luckier than I was."

I was invited to appear on *The Phil Donohue Show* on the topic of parental kidnapping. They flew me to New York and I stayed at the Drake Hotel. A limousine picked me up and drove me to the studio. While I waited in Donohue's green room with the other guests, the station's attorney came into the room in a rush. He stood so close to me that I stepped backwards into the corner, out of earshot of anyone else in the room.

With his face close to mine, he said, "You are restrained from mentioning Maya Angelou or Guy Johnson by name when you are on the air. Do you understand?" Before I had a chance to respond, Phil Donohue breezed in, greeted us, and we were whisked out before the studio audience. The producer who invited me to be on the show had promised that my appearance would be kept secret, but it must have been leaked to Maya anyway.

I was afraid to do anything else, so during the show I spoke about my case in generalities. But I did say that fear of violence had motivated me to kidnap my child. Before I finished my point, Donohue interrupted me and read from a card in his hand. "There are those not present, who want the audience to know that Ms. Murphy's allegations of domestic violence are unsubstantiated and were never proven in Court." Donohue spent the remainder of the show obstructing everything else that I attempted to say.

Maya may not have used the media to help find us, but she used it now. While many feminist presses and daily papers began following my story, Maya had her own story to tell. She was the hero of her story, of course, finding the child and saving the day. Interviews with Maya about the kidnapping and return of her grandson appeared in *Women's Day* and the *LA Times*, among others. The story in the *Times* said,

> "*After spending thousands of dollars on detectives, Maya and Guy learned that Sharon had gone underground with the help of a radical feminist group. 'All we knew about this group was that they hated men and blacks,' Maya said. 'And they had my black, male grandchild.'*"

I cannot say what effect Maya's media campaign had, but I got an overwhelming response to my articles and requests for support. Donations to the Sharon Murphy Legal Fund paid over $40,000 of my legal bills and expenses before the case was over. That amount included a $5,000 check from my mother. The help and good wishes I received still fill me with humility and gratitude.

For months, Bill Goodman had been planning a strategy for my defense. His most ambitious idea was to mount a battered woman's defense. The emotional state of victims of abuse, referred to as *learned helplessness*, had been used as a valid legal defense to keep battered women who murdered their husbands off Death Row. Why not use it as a defense for a non-violent crime?

"We could put on a real dog and pony show," Bill said eagerly. "We could hire Dr. Lenore Walker as an expert witness and have your co-workers in Texas testify and your sisters. We'll depose all the witnesses who knew how Guy treated you and Colin. I'd love to look Guy in the eye during a deposition and listen to him try to defend himself. I wonder what Maya would say in a deposition. If a jury heard both you and Guy, they'd see the truth. A trial like that could break important new legal ground. But it would be expensive—maybe over $100,000."

The possibility of setting a new legal precedent was seductive to both Bill and me. Lenore Walker was the mother of the battered women's movement. Everyone at the shelter had read her books. She had developed the theory of 'The Cycle of Violence' to explain the baffling dynamics of abusive relationships. Her theory described how abusive relationships often begin in an intense honeymoon atmosphere. The abuser is charming and makes the victim feel special, loved. Then tension builds. The abuser may get jealous or paranoid. The victim tries to mollify the abuser to maintain calm and get back to the exhilaration of the honeymoon phase. But the abuser's anger is irrational and cannot be reasonably calmed.

Eventually there is an eruption of threats, emotion, verbal or physical abuse. This releases the tension that has been building up and the relationship can return to relative calm. The abuser tries to convince the victim that it is her defects that cause him to act as he does. This manipulation locks the victim in the abusive cycle. She feels guilt and shame and the predictability of the cycle encourages her feelings of helplessness. Finally the victim comes to believe that she is powerless to improve her situation.

Bill would argue that I was intimidated and overpowered by Guy during our marriage. Having grown up with an abusive mother, I couldn't recognize his behavior as abusive until he actually beat me. After I left him, I lived in fear of what he might do to me and Colin. Guy's emotional and verbal abuse and threats to take custody of Colin were underscored by his repeated Court actions, scathing disparagement of my mothering, and occasional physical attacks.

Then when I lost custody and Guy began working to put limits on my visitation, I believed that Guy could and would eventually eliminate me from Colin's life. His mother's influence and wealth further dramatized the inequity in my situation. My inability to affect the situation led me to believe that I was completely powerless. When I saw bruises on Colin and realized that Guy was using violence and intimidation to discipline him, my feelings of helplessness and desperation led me, an otherwise a law-abiding person, to break the law. Fleeing with Colin was an attempt to protect my child and myself. Everything fit within the framework of *learned helplessness.*

While I was in a meeting with Bill in his upscale San Francisco office in North Beach, it was heady to daydream about a defense that might vindicate me, and possibly help get Colin back. That was my ultimate goal after all. And setting this kind of precedent could help other women in similar situations. But when I flew home to Austin and called Dr. Walker's office in

Colorado to ask about her expert witness fee, I came back to earth. Her review of the case and testimony at a trial could be at least $5,000 plus travel and hotel expenses. Suddenly the prospects of making legal history at an expensive trial seemed like a fantasy that only someone with money could indulge in. The poor have to make the best deal they can.

In the end, there was no trial. Instead, I entered into a plea agreement. I would plead guilty to felony child abduction and McKee would drop the two other charges of concealment and false imprisonment. The judge ordered the probation department to submit a recommendation for what my sentence should be. My attorney and Sam McKee would present their arguments at a sentencing hearing and the judge would make the final decision. Even though Sam McKee agreed to drop two of the three felonies I was charged with, he was determined that I would receive a lengthy jail sentence (maybe as long as three years) for the remaining felony of concealment of a child in violation of a custody order. A judge would not totally dismiss the arguments of his District Attorney, but with a strong defense, Bill thought I would receive only a token sentence.

Bill's investigator set about interviewing all my witnesses in Sonoma County, people who knew about my relationship with Guy. When we received his final report, it contained strong statements from Toni Novak, my Gestalt therapist, and my friend Rose who had been with Colin and me during the incident at Coddingtown. Even Mr. and Mrs. Campbell, Guy's neighbors, corroborated my condition the day I showed up at their house with Colin—bruised and bleeding, with a shredded coat and blood on Colin's clothes. With this evidence, my reputation in Austin, and my letters of support, Bill predicted that

I might receive no more than six months of jail time on the criminal charge.

In the meantime, I got news about the family case. Dr. Dorothy Huntington, a psychiatrist in San Francisco, had been appointed to make a recommendation about my request for unsupervised visitation. I flew to California twice to meet with her and she met with Guy twice and with Colin once. Dr. Huntington's report arrived in the mail on February 18th, two weeks after Colin's tenth birthday, the first time in his life that I hadn't shared the day with him.

Mindy and I sat at the kitchen table and I read the report out loud. Tears poured down my cheeks as I read. Why hadn't anyone else seen the situation as clearly as she did? Maybe different decisions would have been made.

"It would appear that for each parent, the breakup of the marriage represented a shattered dream. When she married, Sharon chose a man who had many of the same characteristics as her emotionally and physically abusive mother. Guy derided her competence, told her she was a substandard mother, and ruled the relationship via intimidation. He became insistent that Sharon must live up to his expectations—which may not have been realistic.

"Sharon and Guy were both raised without fathers and Guy created his own fantasy of what a father should be. Guy's attempts to live out his dream involved an intense anger at Sharon, which appears to have its roots in other, earlier relationships. Guy appears to be struggling with problems with women in general and mothers in particular.

"After the divorce, Sharon grew psychologically and was devastated when she lost custody of Colin. Sharon found her voice, but she felt that it was too late. Believing that she had no other way to keep her son and believing the Guy would never leave her alone, she took Colin and left. Guy admits to shoving Sharon around and grabbing Colin, but does not think scaring a child is such a bad thing, although he thinks it is untimely since the case is going to Court. Colin admits to being afraid of his father. He misses his mother and his life in Austin. Guy is less sensitive than necessary to his son's emotional needs. Guy says he wants to support Colin's relationship with his mother, but his motive is only to exonerate himself in his son's eyes.

Dr. Huntington concluded, *"I see no risk that Sharon would disappear with Colin again. Sharon should be given generous and unsupervised visitation. In addition, Guy should begin attending parenting classes and put Colin into psychotherapy."*

Now, even if I did go to jail, I would have something to look forward to when it was over. Thanks to Dr. Huntington, Colin would be in my home again—even if it was just for a visit. That would be a good first step.

On March 17, 1986, fourteen members of my family travelled from all over California to be at my sentencing hearing in Santa Rosa. Marilyn and Irene, Carol and Sally Ann, and many of my nieces and nephews filled the rows behind me in the small courtroom. My niece Susan, Colin's first babysitter, arrived with her new baby, Rahsan.

428

I sat next to Bill at the defense table and Sam McKee sat alone at a table across the aisle from us. At the brief hearing, I received a suspended sentence, which meant that if there were any interference with Guy's custody, the Court could impose a long prison sentence. I would serve five years of strict, supervised probation. The terms of my probation included six weeks in the county jail, a payment of $6,500 to Guy and Maya as restitution for the expenses they incurred searching for Colin, and 250 hours of community service with an organization trying to locate missing children.

Sam McKee slammed his notebook closed. He was obviously not happy with my punishment. I felt relieved and terrified all at once. A long prison sentence would have destroyed my relationship with Colin—who wants their child to see them in a prison visiting room? Only six weeks in jail was a sort of victory—just a token punishment considering what I had feared. But it still sounded like a long time, and the probation and other penalties seemed to extend this nightmare far into my future. Would this ever be over?

Bill smiled and squeezed my arm—he looked happy. We filed out of the courtroom and my family crowded around me. Bill put his arm around my shoulder and said in a soft voice, "The sentence could have been much, much worse. I'm pleased."

Marilyn was livid. "Sharon does not deserve to be punished. She did what any mother would do!" she said in a loud whisper.

"What I did was *a crime*, Marilyn," I said. "I could have gone to jail for a lot longer. Just think about that!"

"Guy is the one who should be going to jail," she said. "He didn't even have the courage to show up and face you."

Sally Ann leaned into the circle around me. "I'm glad he wasn't here," she said. "I may not have been able to control myself and I'd be in jail with you."

"It's over," I said flatly. "Now I can stop worrying about it and get on with my life."

My time in jail was still ahead of me, but before that happened, I was going to have my first unsupervised visit with Colin—seven wonderful days. The day after the hearing, I drove my rental car up to Guy's house in Cotati and Colin ran outside. It was a glorious feeling. I even gave Guy a small wave when I saw him looking out of the front window.

Colin and I spent the week with Carol and her boyfriend Joe at their small farm in Grass Valley, three hours east of Sonoma County. Even the car trip was festive. Colin and I played our favorite car games: counting flags and holding our breath under overpasses so we wouldn't be contaminated with the breath of the trolls who live under bridges. We sang our song at the top of our voices: *Oh, we ain't got a barrel of mooo-ney. Maybe we're ragged and fuuu-ny. But we'll travel along, sing'n a song, side by side.*

For a whole week, Colin and I had a normal life. Even better—it was life on vacation. I was so happy that I didn't even thing about my upcoming jail time. Colin helped Carol in the garden and rode her bike up and down the country roads. As an extra bonus, their dog Yuba had just given birth to six puppies—each one looked like a fuzzy little bear. Colin was in heaven.

We cooked big meals in the evening and took walks under the spring sky. I could have bought a ticket and flown away with Colin—taken him and disappeared again. But the momentum of our lives was moving forward, not backward. The worst was almost over.

On April 6, 1986, I was locked up for the final time at the Santa Rosa Woman's Honor Farm. This time, I was issued a pair of blue deck shoes, khaki pants, and a heavy blue shirt with *SRWHF* stenciled in black on the back, rather than the orange jump suit of the county jail.

Every morning after breakfast a group of us did our Jane Fonda workout in the recreation room. Then everyone did their assigned chores. My fellow inmates had all read my story in the *Santa Rosa Press Democrat* and I ended up providing some counseling to the many battered women incarcerated with me. The unit had a small library and I spent as much time as I could in that quiet room reading and writing letters. Guy agreed to let me call Colin collect once a week for an awkward ten minute conversation.

The women inmates at the Honor Farm were allowed to go outside in the yard and sit at picnic tables in the afternoon—the highlight of every day. It was spring in Sonoma County; the air was fresh, and the pale blue sky was filled with cottony clouds. If I kept my eyes averted from the fence that separated the woman's yard from the men's yard—where drugs were traded for oral sex—I could pretend that I was in the Army and not locked up in jail.

When I was released after 45 days, I met Mindy in Oklahoma and we spent a week on her parents' houseboat in a secluded cove on a lake outside of Bartlesville. Mindy gave me a lot of time to myself. I sat behind dark glasses in a deck chair, staring at my book or just watching the diamonds blinking at me from the water. I expected to be relieved to have my jail time behind me, but I was having a hard time tuning in to a new picture of my life. Without obstacles to overcome and professionals advising me, what was I supposed to do now? The life that stretched out in front of me seemed shapeless and empty. And without Colin, what was the point of my life anyway? Mindy's mantra was that we would get Colin back now, but I didn't believe it. He was gone and that was that.

After we returned to Austin, Mindy and I moved to a new house near Zilker Park. We began making plans for Colin's six week summer visit. It had been a little over a year since he had been home with us. We bought an air hockey game, a used mini-bike—we spent more than we could afford. Nevertheless, it was worth every dollar of credit card debt to see Colin playing with Pearl on the living room floor, gorging himself on foot long chili dogs at Sonic, and listening to him giggle with Zack and Aubrey while they built another tree house in our backyard.

The evening before Colin returned to California, a group of friends met us for dinner at the Lone Star Café. Colin stood on a long wooden bench and got everyone in the restaurant singing, *I'll have a chicken fried steak and a bowl of good chili, a cold Lone Star and a song by Willie. Join me and Bubba for a choice fillet. It's a mighty fine place—Lone Star Café.*

After Colin returned to California, it became obvious that Mindy and I were winding down as a couple. We had only been in the first year of our relationship when I was discovered. Since then, Mindy had been shoved into the background—a support person in my big drama.

Instead of asking how she was when friends called the house, they would say, "Hi Mindy, how's Anne Marie holding up?" Now Mindy was eager to stop thinking about fundraisers, Court dates, and jail. She missed Colin too, but she also missed romance, fun, margaritas, and dancing at Uncle Charlie's.

I tried, but it was no good. A wall had grown up around my broken heart, and I had no emotional strength left for a love affair. We held it together until Christmas when Colin came for another visit. We spent a lot of money again. On Christmas morning, Mason came over dressed like Santa and present-ed Colin with his new bike. After we packed up his bike and shipped it back to California, Mindy moved out.

I've never had a stauncher friend, and to this day I feel grati-tude and affection for her.

Austin Airport, 1986 - Colin returns to California after his Christmas visit.

During his Christmas visit, Colin confided in his friend Zack, telling him things he had not told me. Guy was on a campaign to convince him that I was lying about things he had done to me. He asserted that he had never hit me. Colin told Guy that he remembered him punching me on the front porch of their house. In response, Guy lost his temper and slapped him across the face. Colin told Zack that he and his father fought about small things and big things—once Guy broke a chair during one of their arguments. If Colin didn't answer Guy fast enough, he would grab him and shake him by the arm. Sometimes he left bruises. Zack didn't tell me these things right away—he had promised Colin to keep his secrets. But Zack was afraid for his friend and told his mother. Diane convinced him to tell me what Colin had said.

I called Margaret Anderson to ask her advice. "Huntington told Guy that Colin should be in counseling," she said. "I'll find out if that's happening." A few weeks later, Margaret confirmed that Colin was now seeing a child psychologist.

I waited a while before I contacted Dr. Allan Harrison to see if he had any questions for me. My anxiety had been somewhat lessened knowing that Colin would have someone to talk to. When I finally talked to Dr. Harrison, I was furious when I realized that he had allowed Guy to sit in the room during every one of Colin's sessions.

"Doesn't a child deserve confidentiality too?" I sputtered.

"I know it wasn't an ideal arrangement," Harrison said. "But Guy would not allow Colin to be in therapy unless he was in the room. He said he needed to hear what Colin was saying, so he could debunk the lies you had told Colin about him. I read the file and decided it was better than nothing."

"You should have called me. I wanted my son to be able to trust someone! You made the situation worse, not better."

But Guy had followed the letter of Huntington's recommendation, if not the spirit, and there was nothing more I could do.

I was distraught and filled with nightmare scenarios of Colin's life with Guy. My attitude at work continued to suffer. I was preoccupied by my own overwrought emotions. Judy gave me another official warning, and then after being my friends and my most loyal advocates, flying to California to testify and continuing my salary even when I couldn't show up for my shifts, Judy and Ellen were forced to fire me.

Colin was gone. Mindy was gone. Now the job that I loved was gone. Maybe it was time to let go of Anne Marie and Luke and return to Sharon and Colin's world.

CHAPTER FOURTEEN

IN AUGUST OF 1987, MY probation officer granted my request to return to San Francisco. My sister Carol had moved back to San Francisco and I was going to live with her and Joe and Yuba. I put my things in storage and Mindy sold me her gold Subaru. I drove from the summer heat of Texas to the cool San Francisco breezes with my new cat Emily banging her head against the door of her carrier. Our sweet cat, Pearl had died of cancer just after Colin's Christmas visit.

Carol's apartment was across the street from Alamo Square in San Francisco's Western Addition. I was less than a mile from Henry Street where Mary and I had lived with Norman, and I could almost see the Steiner Street apartment where Guy and I first lived together. Joe was a nurse at Langley Porter Psychiatric Institute where Guy had worked as a records' clerk. Carol was a librarian at the UCSF medical library, less than a block from Moffitt Hospital where Colin had his surgery and where I had been a unit secretary. I was surrounded by landmarks from the past. The road I'd travelled had been long and painful, yet it had led me right back to where my story had begun.

When Guy got a new job as a personnel analyst for the City of Oakland, he and Colin moved to Berkeley—a quick BART ride from San Francisco. From the high point in Alamo Square, I could see the picturesque San Francisco skyline and the long silver Bay Bridge reaching out towards the East Bay. I'd sit on a blanket throwing the tennis ball for Yuba and looking towards the clock tower on the UC Berkeley campus, knowing it was not far from Guy's apartment on California and McGee. But Colin still felt too far away.

I got a few shifts at an Italian restaurant in the Marina. The owner paid me under the table and I scraped by on tips and my unemployment check. I was paying off the money I owed Guy and Maya as best I could, and I tried to set aside a few dollars from every check for Colin's visits, but some weeks I didn't have much to spare. Colin often had cash in his wallet, but I wouldn't let him spend his money when we were together. If I couldn't afford to take him out for a hamburger or a movie, we'd hang out with Carol and Joe playing games or taking Yuba for long walks through Golden Gate Park or to the beach along the Great Highway. Colin didn't complain; we excelled at having cheap fun.

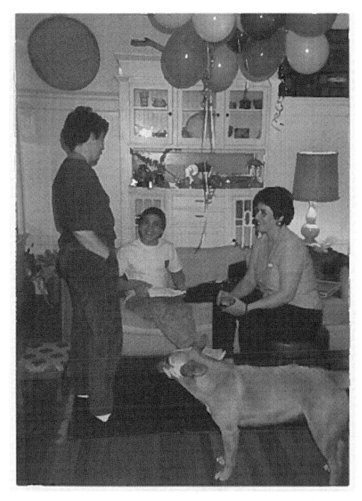

Carol, Colin, Sharon and Yuba celebrate Colin's birthday

I applied for a job at the San Mateo Women's Shelter and had two promising interviews. I hadn't settled on a satisfactory explanation about getting fired from CBW. The truth, along with everything else, was too complicated. I told the director that I left my shelter job to move back to the Bay Area to be near my son who lived with his father. I said too much about my situation at another job interview at a childcare center in Marin County. (A conviction for child stealing is not something you want to bring up if you're interviewing for a job working with small children.) But this time I said too little and the director called Ellen for a reference. She didn't mind so much that I had been fired from the shelter—Ellen had explained the circumstances—but I didn't get the job because she felt I had deceived her.

After that humiliating meeting, I drove home and sat in my car in front of Carol's apartment listening to KJAZZ on the radio. "What am I going to do? How am I going to get through this?" I looked over the tops of the trees in Golden Gate Park and out towards the Ocean Beach—totally demoralized and paralyzed.

The sun began to set and a splash of crimson brightened the pale sky behind an expanding wave of thick fog that tumbled towards me. I took a long, deep breath and for a moment, my crushing anxiety lifted. In that split second, I was flooded with a sense of wonder and awe. "How incredibly beautiful," I thought. Suddenly totally unbidden by any conscious thought, I experienced a moment of clarity so profound that it almost felt like a jolt of electricity.

In a flash, my thoughts bounced out of their rut of self-pity. I saw that the biggest obstacle in my way was my own attitude of self-hatred. If I had a different attitude about myself and my life, wouldn't everything else be easier to change? What if I laid that heavy burden down? It was a thrilling possibility. But I had many deeply engrained habits of thought and action. I needed help. I joined a feminist support group and then on June 10, 1988, almost three years to the day since Maya left Austin with Colin, I walked into my first 12-step meeting on Belcher Street in Noe Valley. Getting stoned whenever I had an uncomfortable feeling was not going to help me learn a new way of living.

One evening a week, I went to my support group and two or three times a week I showed up at various 12-step meetings. My mood perked up and I felt less overwhelmed by the task of re-engineering my life. I stopped smoking weed and drinking alcohol. Soon the compulsion to medicate my anxiety evaporated. I heard the Serenity Prayer at the close of almost every 12-step meeting and I taped a copy to my bedroom wall.

"Grant me the serenity to accept the things I cannot change, the courage to change the things I can, and the wisdom to know the difference."

I used these words like a secret formula to help me sort out problems when they threatened to overwhelm me. I pondered the idea of acceptance—seemingly a foreign concept. I was used to fighting against reality, not accepting it. Could I truly accept that my son lived with Guy? Could I accept that Guy was Colin's father? Could I accept that I would have to build a happy life without being able to alter these circumstances? Weren't those the things in my life that I could not change? I would hold my difficulties in my mind and meditate on the simple words of the Serenity Prayer. I could feel myself wanting to reorder reality—willing things to be different, better, simpler. But I never failed to get a bit of insight into how to move forward. I began to understand what acceptance and serenity really felt like.

A common experience among the newly sober is that you finally let yourself feel all the feelings that made you want to start using in the first place. After an initial "pink cloud" period, lingering shame and painful old doubts crept back into my mind. *"If you have to ask for help, you must be weak or crazy."* or *"Maybe Guy was right about you all along."* But I kept going to meetings and to my therapy group. I kept talking to people and tried to find out what was really true about me—good and bad. When I picked up my six month chip, I felt a real sense of pride. My experience of living started to transform as the est training had promised and I started to learn how to take care of myself. I didn't need to take life on the chin to prove how strong I was. There was power in admitting the truth and asking for help. I began to feel hopeful about my future for the first time in a long time—maybe ever.

I had compiled a lifetime of grievances and resentments about my mother, but in an unexpected twist, Sally Murphy became a good example for me during that hard time. She may have been short on interpersonal skills and emotional sensitivity, but my mother was very long on tenacity. No matter what happened, I never saw her lying on the couch feeling sorry for herself. I remembered once when she lost her sales job unexpectedly. She came home from work and spent the evening fuming about her boss, "Just 'cause he's got money, he thinks he's a big shot!" But the next morning, Mother was up early, in her platform heels, nails painted a fresh coat of bright red polish. With the newspaper under her arm, she was off to find a new job. "Don't ever let anyone break you," she would say. "Always keep your head up." When I started to drift into my habitual feeling of self-pity, my mother's example kept me putting one foot in front of the other, the way I had seen her do so many times, hoping to get to a place of rest somewhere on the road ahead.

Part of my emotional recovery was admitting that I needed a job with less stress—a job I could do from nine to five and forget at 5:01. I had a lot of wreckage to straighten out and I didn't have the reserves to expend energy on anyone else's struggles. Remembering all the people that Mindy helped to get jobs, I brought my resume to an employment agency in downtown San Francisco and asked, "How does my experience translate to the private sector?"

I accepted a job as the office manager at a newspaper advertising sales office in the China Basin building in San Francisco. It was a small branch office—only two women. I organized the office and drafted their letters and reports, handled the phones. After a few months, I was the go-to person for the clients. It was difficult to sacrifice the moral superiority that community activists get to lord over those who *just work for a paycheck*, but I had to admit that I liked my boring office job and was good at it. I rented an apartment and sent for my things that were in storage in Texas. It started to feel pretty good to be Sharon Murphy again.

I had a regular paycheck, but I wasn't chipping away at the amount of restitution that I owed Guy. (And I still had a full measure of resentment that made it even more difficult to write that check every month.) Failure to pay the restitution could violate my probation and a suspended sentence still hung over my head. I could still go to state prison. I whittled the amount down to $5,700, but now with my own apartment, my expenses nearly exhausted my $28,000 salary.

For years, attorneys had done the communicating for Guy and me, adding layer upon layer of ego and complication. In the spirit of trying *'to change the things I can,'* I picked up the phone and called Guy directly. My voice was shaking but I pushed forward. "Guy, I can't afford to pay you the restitution," I said. "Will you forgive the debt?"

After a small bit of wrangling and resisting, Guy finally agreed. I quickly called my probation officer with the news. Guy's verbal agreement wasn't going to be enough, though. To eliminate this debt, Guy would have to drive to Santa Rosa and appear at a hearing to revise the terms of my probation and sign off on a stipulated agreement.

Could I trust him to show up? I was frantic on the morning of the hearing. What if he changed his mind? I chanted the Serenity Prayer all the way from San Francisco to Santa Rosa—that long and familiar slog up Highway 101. When I walked into the courtroom, there he was. I didn't think it was possible to feel happy to see Guy, but I was.

When the time came, Guy stood up and told the judge that he was willing to forgive the restitution I owned him, "In the spirit of moving forward," he added with a poetic flourish.

I had to force myself, but I walked up to him after the hearing and shook his hand. "Thank you. I really appreciate this, Guy." It was the first polite moment between Guy and me for many years. It was progress, not perfection.

Colin developed a close relationship with his grandmother as he got older. Soon he was an experienced traveler, frequently flying by himself to North Carolina or New York to spend time with Maya. He accompanied her on speaking engagements and to other celebrity events. He went with her to L.A. when she was a guest on the *Arsenio Hall Show*, sharing the green room with Little Richard, who Colin reported as having the biggest head he'd ever seen on anyone. Colin was learning how to comfortably wear a suit and handle himself in formal settings. He was the only teenager I'd ever known who owned his own tuxedo.

I had a growing collection of clippings—magazine and newspaper stories of celebrity events and pictures of Colin's smiling face next to Maya and Oprah Winfrey, Coretta Scott King, and Cicely Tyson. On these excursions, Maya had Colin all to herself and he seemed proud of his favored position as "The Grand." It also seemed as if Maya was becoming Colin's confidant—someone with whom he could discuss his relationship with his father. He grew to appreciate her point of view and opinions.

On one hand, I was happy for the experiences that Colin was having. He was developing a sense that he belonged in the broader world of successful and accomplished people. On the other hand, his trips with his grandmother were usually planned on weekends or school holidays—during the time that I could have been with him. I felt that old familiar fear of being shut out of his life. I had no power to be anything but flexible. And anyway, how could I insist that Colin come over for pizza night instead of flying to Atlanta to meet Andrew Young or traveling with his grandmother to meet the dean of Morehouse College who was presenting her with an award? I wish I had felt differently but I had to admit that I was jealous of the excitement and opportunities available to Colin through his grandmother, and I struggled against feeling like the peasant woman with her nose pressed up against the castle window.

I was surprised when Guy told Colin that I was one of the funniest people he'd ever met. I hoped it was a sign that we were both trying to move past all the old hurts and resentments. But he also said things designed to drive a wedge between us. Regularly he'd resurrect the old saw about the cult of weakness, my lack of ambition, and my hippie ideas about life and child rearing. But the worst breach was when he and Colin were talking about being only children and Guy took that opportunity to tell Colin that he would have a little brother or a sister if I had not insisted on having an abortion. Colin was visibly shaken when he arrived at my apartment for the weekend and told me what Guy had told him.

"That is not something your father should have ever told you," I said. "And it is not something I am going to discuss."

Once I saw how much Colin was conflicted and hurt by the hostility between Guy and me, I made a conscious effort to tell Colin stories of Guy and me when times were different and the future looked promising. I struggled to keep my side of the street clean, but I couldn't rewrite the past. Colin created his own system to navigate between his estranged parents. He exacted a promise from each of us—Maya too—that we would not criticize each other in front of him. I was insulted that Colin demanded this promise from me—foolishly believing that it was only Guy who played the game of character assassination. But I was ignoring the obvious. If you run away with your child, change your names and hide from his father for four years, you are making an undeniable statement about your opinion of that man's character. As my mother always said, "Actions speak louder than words."

The AA Fourth Step suggests taking a searching and fearless moral inventory of yourself. This is a proposition fraught with pitfalls for a former Catholic. As a child, I was taken to confession every two weeks and made to kneel in a dark box and tell my supposed sins to a dim figure on the other side of a screen. Eternal damnation awaited those who didn't address this sin business with all due seriousness. Every two weeks, I chanted, "Bless me, father, for I have sinned. I was disrespectful and disobedient to my mother." But I always worried that I had committed other sins without knowing it and that my imperfect confession might constitute another sin. That's a lot of pressure for a little kid.

Trying to work the Fourth Step brought back all those old feelings of guilt and shame. But I was desperate to end the emotional suffering in my life. People I respected in AA assured me that this was part of the path to serenity, so I persevered. I had a general idea of what *my defects of character* looked like. But when I began to work my first Fourth Step, a disheartening awareness refused to be ignored. The Fourth Step process begins by listing your resentments and working through them to find your own role in the problem.

Of course, Guy was the chief offender—that was easy. But slowly, I began getting a glimpse of my part in our long and painful struggle. I was appalled when I began to notice some of my own arrogance. Guy was arrogant and self-righteous, not me. My sense of superiority about my parenting style, my personal values, and my approach to life was because my approach was the best approach! But didn't I defend my way of doing things as fiercely as Guy did? Maybe not with my fists, but with equal certainty that I was right—so right that I had kidnapped my son and lived underground to prove it? It was a humbling process, but I undoubtedly began to feel a sense of relief.

Colin was thirteen now and had been with his father for four years—almost as long as we had been gone. He was exploring his identity as a young man—a young black man. I could sense that he and Guy had finally bonded, and he sometimes spoke of his father with genuine affection. He admired some of the same things I had once admired about Guy: his sense of humor, his knowledge and interest in so many different things, his expansive personality. I was glad that Colin's relationship with Guy had deepened—or at least included some good aspects. I knew that Colin was still being treated harshly—occasionally even brutally.

And I still harbored my unaltered judgment that Guy disrespected women. It was hard not to interject some corrective feminism when Colin and I had conversations about the differences between men and women, as if Colin needed an antidote for the lessons he was getting from Guy. But my point of view, once supreme in his eyes, was losing some of its status and I was allowing that Colin had to make up his own mind. But Colin began to say things that upset me like, "You're white so you wouldn't understand," or, "It's different for women."

I knew the world looked different through his eyes, but Colin's developing identity felt like a rejection to me and it was a challenge for me to gracefully accept his natural pulling away. I had identified for a long time as Colin's mother—and only Colin's mother. I now faced the terrifying question of who I was on my own.

In the spring of 1989, Colin announced that he had a girlfriend named Monica, a girl who lived in Guy's neighborhood. I met her and her mother Alice when I picked up the kids to take them swimming at the Russian River. A few weeks after our outing, I received a panicked phone call from Alice. Colin was at her house. He had jumped out of his bedroom window to get away from Guy.

"Is he okay?" I asked.

"He's really shook up. It looks like Guy was punching him. He only has on a pair of shorts and he has welts and red marks on his chest and arms," Alice said.

I heard Monica's voice in the background. "Guy is at the door," she whispered.

"Don't answer it," Alice said. Their end of the line got quiet and I waited.

"Okay, he's gone," Monica said.

"Sharon, Colin asked me to call you. What should I do?" said Alice.

"Call the police or Child Protective Services," I said urgently.

"Can you come and get him?" she asked.

"I don't know if you've heard anything about our situation, but I can't pick Colin up without Guy's permission. It's complicated."

"Oh," Alice said. "I don't want to get in the middle of anything."

"Colin came to you, Alice. You have to protect him."

"But Guy is my neighbor. Colin can stay here till he's ready to go home."

"Can I talk to him?" I said.

Colin's voice was thick and low, as if he had been crying. "Hey, Mom,"

"Are you all right? What happened?"

"Dad backed me into my closet and started punching me. He went crazy, Mom. I didn't do anything. He just didn't like how I was talking to him. I shoved him and then I kicked out the screen and jumped out the window. He's gonna kill me for coming over here."

I chose my words carefully. "Colin, you were right to run. And I want you to make sure that your father knows that Alice called me. If this ever happens again, get out of the house and tell someone. The more of a secret it is, the worse it will be."

"Okay. Are you gonna come and get me?" Colin said.

From the moment I heard Alice's voice on the line, I had been furious and terrified. But now I broke down. "I can't, Colin," I choked out. "I'm on probation. If I come and take you, Guy will say that I kidnapped you again. I'm in a really bad spot, sweetie. I could go to jail again. But you can call 911. Someone was punching you—that's against the law."

Colin was silent. "Naw, I'm not gonna do that. Monica's mom made me a sandwich. I'll just hang out here for a while."

"Are you sure you're okay?"

"I'm okay."

"Call me later, sweetie."

"Sure. Bye, Mom."

I stood with the phone in my hand. My powerlessness to stop this kind of suffering for Colin burned like a knife in my gut. Over all this time, it was as sharp of an instinct as it had always been. I cried frustrated angry tears and slammed down the phone. Colin didn't call me that night, and my calls to the house were picked up by the answering machine. When I finally spoke to him later in the week, he told me that Guy had kept him out of school for three days.

"Dad apologized, Mom. He's really sorry."

"Yours are the important feelings here, Colin. Not your father's!" I said. "You have a right to be angry."

"Mom, you promised that you wouldn't criticize Dad. I can handle this."

"But..."

"Mom, it's okay."

Colin's tone broke my heart. He sounded like one of the residents at the battered women's shelter. I didn't want Colin to become his father's emotional caretaker and ignore his own feelings. That was one of the dangerous consequences of living in an abusive home.[5] Again, that same dilemma, what could I change and what was I powerless over?

My probation officer approved an organization I found where I could work off my 250 hours of community service. The project assisted the San Francisco District Attorney's office with contested custody cases. I organized files and drafted case summaries and biographical profiles. When I completed my hours, all the terms of my probation were satisfied: I'd served my jail time; my restitution had been forgiven; and now my community service hours were completed. I was released from probation early and my parental rights were finally restored.

At work, I was promoted from office manager to account executive. With my raise I was able to move to a house in Oakland. Colin could stop by for dinner during the week and have his own space when he came for the weekend. But my perfect little angel was turning into a typical sneaky teenager. The chasm between Guy and me was old news and we didn't check in with each other the way divorced parents of teenagers should. Colin used the situation to his advantage. He would leave my house to go home, but instead, he'd go hang out with his friends on Shattuck Avenue in Berkeley. His cover was blown one Sunday when he left my house at about 3 o'clock, but left his schoolbooks behind.

---

5   *Codependent No More, by Melody Beattie*

At about 7 o'clock, I noticed Colin's backpack by the front door and called Guy's house and offered to bring them over.

"I thought he was still at your house. He's not home yet," Guy said.

We pieced together Colin's little scam. After that discovery, I attempted to let go of my resentment of Guy (still a work in progress) and we tried to communicate with each other about how and what Colin was doing.

One afternoon Guy and I were on the phone, discussing arrangements to get Colin to and from his football game. Before I hung up Guy said, "You know, I see you and Colin together and I can tell how close you two are. I wish he and I had that. I'm tough on him, I'm not sorry about that. It is hard being a black man in this world and he has to be strong. But I wish I had known about nurturing when he was born. So many things might have turned out differently."

I was well-versed in 12-step lingo by that time and Guy's words sounded surprisingly like amends to me. In any event, I decided to take them as an amends. "Well..." I felt myself moving into precarious territory. "Guy, I know Colin wants to be closer to you—to know you better. You could share more about yourself, tell him how it was for you growing up; how you feel about your life—things like that. I know he would like that."

"That's good to hear. Thank you," he said.

In July of 1991, I heard a commotion on my porch and opened the front door. I was surprised to see Colin, now fifteen years old, walking up my front steps with a duffle bag weighing down his shoulder. His bright copper hair was styled in an asymmetrical flat-top and his heavy glasses hung off the tip of his pug nose, making him look a lot like his father. Over his shoulder, I could see Guy dragging bags out of the back of his black SUV. He pitched the last of Colin's suitcases onto the sidewalk and slammed the rear hatch of his Escalade.

Guy stood in the street and looked at me for a moment. "I'll call you," he said. Then he got into his car and drove away.

Colin carried the bags up onto the porch. "Hey, Momma, did you get my messages?"

"No, I just got home. What's going on?"

He flung open the screen and threw his arms around me. "I'm baa-aack!"

My mind started to race. What does this mean? Do I need a lawyer? Should I call Margaret Anderson? Will Guy fight me this time? Then I stopped myself—one step at a time, I thought. We dragged the bags into his room. "Let's talk," I said. I poured a bowlful of salsa and opened a bag of chips and we settled at the kitchen table. "What's going on?"

The spark for Colin's move out of Guy's house had been a humiliating argument in front of some of Colin's friends—some dispute with his father about plantains versus bananas, or some such mundane issue. It was hardly the worst fight they'd ever had. A few times before Colin had stormed out of Guy's house and showed up at my door angry and red-faced.

"I hate him! He treats me like I'm an idiot!" Every other time, I'd sent him home after he cooled down. I wasn't going down that road again unless I was certain that Colin wouldn't change his mind. But now it appeared that Colin had made a cool and reasoned decision, he was not just acting out of anger in the heat of the moment.

"It's better if I live here," he said. I could tell by the look on his face that this decision would stick.

And just like that, my son was home again.

Colin's high school years drifted into the kind of lovely or- dinariness that I wished Guy and I could have established when we first divorced. Colin and I once again enjoyed the kind of intimacy that you feel in the morning sitting quietly together over bowls of oatmeal or on the couch late at night having a long conversation about not much of anything.

Colin lived with me and he spent time with his father and grandmother until he left for college in 1994. Guy and I sat on different rows on the sidelines at his football games—but we were both there. We went to parent-teacher conferences and school events and sometimes we got mad at the same misbehavior. We commiserated together during Colin's MC Hammer phase and when he started flashing gang signs and walking with a hip dip.

We joined the ranks of other divorced parents who were not on particularly good terms. We kept our dramatic history to ourselves. All that time, Guy had sole physical custody of Colin, but he didn't make an issue out of that legal technicality. Guy and I were both sick of lawyers.

Maya maintained her distance from me. We never spoke again—our conversation the day she left Austin with Colin was the last conversation she and I had—even to this day. I would hear her voice on the phone when she'd call to speak with Colin. We were always polite. Occasionally I would receive a card at Christmas signed with her particular flourish. "Joy! Maya."

I interpreted Colin's decision to return and live with me as a repudiation of Guy's mistreatment, and a validation of my decision to protect him by running away. I had made a lot of progress in my recover, but in some areas I was stuck—still trying to justify my actions. I know what I did was illegal, but was it wrong? Now, from the vantage point of age, I have come to believe that Colin's decision had nothing to do with what happened before. He came back to live with me to create a more comfortable balance for himself between his two vastly different parents.

I was the nurturing parent who gave him a sense of unconditional acceptance and emotional safety. Guy was the stern, demanding father who taught Colin how to navigate in an indifferent and hostile world. Colin could relax with me, then, fortified by a feeling of safety, he could venture out into his father and his grandmother's realm, a realm that he wanted to be a part of, but where the environment was more challenging and emotionally risky. For all my feminist ideology, it was a traditional paradigm, but it worked for Colin.

No matter who our parents are, they leave us with issues to unravel. Colin is no exception. He has conflicting feelings about the story I have told here. He does not believe that Guy could have or would have kept me out of his life as I have long maintained. Colin gives Guy more credit than I think he deserves. Colin remembers our years in Austin as the happiest time of his childhood. But my decision to take him and hide caused his father and his grandmother four years of anguish. It complicates his relationship with them even to this day. He loves me and he loves them, and that creates an unresolved dilemma for him. But that is his dilemma to work out.

I have struggled to let go of the need to justify my actions as the only right thing I could have done. I understand more clearly why I made such a dramatic leap into the underground and I have compassion for the woman I was then—the young woman who felt so powerless and afraid.

I have had to accept my past decisions—they are things I cannot change. There is really no way to determine the rightness or wrongness of what I did anymore. Like a diamond dispersing white light into a spectrum of colors, human decisions contain countless angles depending on your point of view.

EPILOGUE

BY THE TIME COLIN GRADUATED from Georgia State University with a degree in business administration, he was married and the father of a son and a daughter. He and his wife, Jessica, stayed on the East Coast after graduation. I continued to live in the Bay Area and once again I returned to college and became a litigation paralegal. (Attempting to earn back some of the money I paid to lawyers over all those years.)

My collection of clippings now showed Colin with Jessica and the kids smiling next to Maya in magazine and newspaper photographs. The accompanying celebrities have gotten increasingly more famous—Archbishop Tutu, Nelson Mandela, Bill Clinton, Barak Obama. Colin has an extended family that includes world leaders, artists and famous dignitaries. He has developed a worldview that I can only imagine.

Guy and his new wife and her son travel east for holidays at Maya's home in North Carolina. Colin is no longer an only child; now he has a younger stepbrother. Maya covers the expenses for Guy and Colin and their families to come and stay with her in Winston-Salem. Jessica's family gatherings include her father, her mother, and a stepmother or two. Somehow they have figured out how to make that work, but reconciliation has eluded those of us on this side of Colin's family.

I flew to Atlanta to stay with Jessica and Colin as often as I could, and I kept Caylin and Brandon for a few days every summer and sometimes over New Years to give Colin and Jessica a holiday by themselves. I'd see Guy during the kids' visits when we'd shuttle them back and forth between our two homes in Oakland. Colin still feels like the air is being sucked out of the room when Guy and I are in close proximity. The old wounds are slow to heal. But we can have a civilized chat, even joke with each other on occasion. We share two amazing grandchildren and that bond is undeniable. I think this is as good as our relationship is ever going to be.

Sharon with Brandon and Caylin at Christmas in the
Bay Area

After Colin graduated and went to college, our relationship was nurtured during frequent, long phone conversations, emails and less frequent visits. It has been an ongoing struggle against jealousy for me. Maya can so easily bring her family together at formal and informal gatherings at her home, or at events across the country and the world. Her money makes getting together so easy.

Colin and I have both been frustrated by how difficult it has been for me to really know his children with only a few days together every year, and those awkward monosyllabic phone conversations.

"How are you, Brandon?"

"Fine."

"What have you been doing?"

"Nothing."

Occasionally Colin and I discussed my moving to be closer to him and his family, but I was very rooted in the Bay Area. As time went by, the frustration and longing became a nagging pain that I learned to live with. I thought maybe someday something would change. Luckily I didn't relocate to Atlanta when he first suggested it, because in 2004, Colin and Jessica moved to the Washington DC area.

When I finished this memoir and found myself unemployed after twelve years of being a paralegal, Colin suggested that I move in with him. He had recently become a single father. I could help him with the kids, look for a job, and put the finishing touches on my manuscript. My mother, my sister Marilyn, and my sister Carol had all died since 2000. Each loss was a terrible shock and my need to shore up ties with family became intense. I decided to go towards the love, and claim a place for myself in Colin's family. I left my beloved Bay Area and moved into Colin's townhouse in Rockville, Maryland in the spring of 2010. Colin was 35 and worked as a sales manager for a large telecommunications company.

Colin and Jessica are both the children of divorced parents, and it was sobering for them to arrive at this difficult crossroads. Gratefully, the dramatic failure of Guy and me to find a peaceful way to separate is not being repeated in Colin's life today. The children are with Colin half of the time, and he and Jessica are both in attendance at baseball games, school events. (They always sit together.) And they host birthday parties together for the kids. Their relationship is not without bumps, but I am so proud of them and how Caylin and Brandon take priority over the heartache and disappointment they both feel at the dissolution of their 11-year marriage. I am very close with Jessica and feel so lucky to still have her in my life.

Colin's face hasn't changed much since he was a child. His big brown eyes and thick lashes are still his most amazing feature. He's stocky and broad across the chest, but at 5'11, he is not as tall as everyone thought he would be. When his beautiful red hair began to thin, he finally surrendered and shaved his head. (He blames my side of the family for his receding hairline.) His smooth round head has taken the place of his distinctive hair, but his goatee is still golden red and neatly frames his playful smile.

In this memoir, I have written about my idealization of Guy and the dreamlike future I imagined for us as a feminist couple. Those of us who are the children of abusive parents can fiercely resist facing reality. Fantasy protects us from absorbing the truth that we are living with parents we are afraid of, a realization that could be too overwhelming at the time. I spun many warm fantasies as a lonely child. As a young adult, my habit of idealizing kept me from coming to terms with my own life and learning how to fend for myself. I merged my identity with Guy, who seemed so confident and invulnerable to me. I built a new dream of our life together. I reframed each bit of evidence that contradicted my fantasy so that it fit into the picture I wanted, needed. I assuaged my panic and fear at the very real signs of trouble in our relationship with the image of his strong presence at my side to love and support me through life. My own feminism notwithstanding, Guy would be the sensitive, feminist man he proclaimed himself to be and I would be the cherished wife.

Now for the first time in years, my son and I were living under the same roof. As my friends predicted, it wasn't easy. But I was shocked. We have even had big fights, with tears (mine) and anger (his.) He didn't like some of my opinions and the way I do certain things—can you imagine such a betrayal? This adult Colin was someone unrecognizable to me at times. I was devastated and couldn't understand what was happening.

During this same period of time, I was working my way back through this manuscript in the seeming endless process of editing. As I sharpened the themes in my story, I finally got it. It was shocking to accept that I hadn't stopped idealizing and fantasizing even though I have logged more than 20 years in 12-step programs and therapy. I have deepened my understanding and acceptance of myself, but damn if my fantasies aren't still seductive and can outshine reality if I let them. Why can't even one of them be true, damn it?

I had created an unconscious belief that my son was a cross between Will Smith and Mark Zuckerberg—handsome, sensitive, gregarious, an entrepreneur, successful in the world of business and finance—perfect, but in a humble, human way.

And one day Colin would probably credit all his success to the unconditional love and sacrifice of his mother. Now, don't get me wrong, Colin is a pretty terrific guy, but he has his issues just like everyone else. But I have been secretly invested in his being much better than pretty terrific—for me, not just for him. And I let red flags in our relationship go unaddressed.

In 1981, when I was considering running away with Colin, my sister Jeanne gave me good advice. Her words are worth repeating here: "Sharon, if you do this, don't expect Colin to thank you some day in the future. Be sure that you're doing it for your own reasons." I always remembered that warning and tried to heed it. Nonetheless, there was a hidden part of me that believed that Colin and I would always be aligned in the same way we were when we were two against the world. The fact that he was just a child at the time seemed to escape me. But in reality, we were not Butch Cassidy and the Sundance Kid. I secretly hoped that our traumatic years on the run would give me a pass because of what I'd done to give us those years of peace. Whereas other mothers had to surrender their adult children to their own lives and opinions, Colin and I would be forever bonded. I didn't want to see the fallacies in this construct as they were making themselves clear to me, but I truly wanted to come to terms with what seemed at the time to be the destruction of my relationship with Colin. My recovery has made reality more of a friend to me.

I didn't clearly see these patterns until I moved here and Colin and I had to deal with each other on a daily basis. Fantasy is much easier to maintain at a distance.

"You wanted me to be a free thinker," Colin said to me angrily. "But you wanted me to be free to think like you do."

I wasn't really seeing Colin as a separate, distinct person from me because my idealized picture of him and our relationship was so powerful. "Just look how perfect my relationship with my son is. All that heartache and struggle was worth it."

This fantasy provided a final justification for kidnapping my son and hiding from Guy all those years ago. I was guilty of just what I had accused Maya of doing with Guy, not seeing a clear picture of her son, of glorifying him as a way of glorifying herself. Colin doesn't come to the same conclusions about my decision to run away with him as I would have liked. I have ignored that fact for a long time. Colin knows what I was trying to do; he even accepts that some of my goals were realized, but there have been negative consequences that I couldn't have imagined and have had difficulty accepting. If Colin had written this book, it would be a different interpretation of these same events. I have had to give him room to see his own past in his own way.

I am again working in a law firm and I have my own apartment now. (...across the street from Colin in Rockville.) Living near Colin and the children has been an opportunity for us to infuse more reality into our relationship. We are working our way back to each other and enjoying our relationship again. Getting to this point has often been heartbreaking, but we are committed to each other and I predict a more authentic, loving future for Colin and me.

It may be more difficult this way, but I really do believe that the truth will set you free.

27941085R00257

Made in the USA
Lexington, KY
30 November 2013